POSEUR

POSEUR

A Memoir of
Downtown New York City
in the
'90s

MARC SPITZ

DA CAPO PRESS
A Member of the Perseus Books Group

For my friend and agent James Fitzgerald.

Author's Note: Certain names and descriptions of individuals have been altered.

Copyright © 2013 by Marc Spitz

Set in 11 point Adobe Caslon Pro by the Perseus Books Group

Library of Congress Cataloging-in-Publication Data
Spitz, Marc.
    Poseur : a Memoir of Downtown New York City in the '90s / Marc Spitz.
pages cm
    ISBN 978-0-306-82174-5 (pbk)—ISBN 978-0-306-82175-2 (e-book)
    1. Authors, American—21st century—Biography. 2. Music journalists—United States—Biography. 3. New York (N.Y.)—Biography. I. Title.
PS3619.P582Z46 2013
813'.6—dc22
[B]
                                                                                    2012042496
First Da Capo Press edition 2013

Published by Da Capo Press
A Member of the Perseus Books Group
www.dacapopress.com

Da Capo Press books are available at special discounts for bulk purchases in the U.S. by corporations, institutions, and other organizations. For more information, please contact the Special Markets Department at the Perseus Books Group, 2300 Chestnut Street, Suite 200, Philadelphia, PA 19103, or call (800) 810-4145, ext. 5000, or e-mail special.markets@perseusbooks.com.

10 9 8 7 6 5 4 3 2 1

"I need to be myself.
I can't be no one else . . ."
—Oasis, "Supersonic," 1994

CHAPTER 1

"**N**o one in the world ever gets what they want and that is beautiful. Everybody dies frustrated and sad and that is beautiful."

Upon hearing these lyrics, my father, Sidney Spitz, then forty-four, took his sneaker off the gas pedal and slowed the copper-colored Mustang abruptly. One trailing motorist honked loudly from inside her black Datsun, then sped past us. Another did the same and also gave us the finger. My father, squinting in his rearview mirror, stuck his left hand out the window to wave those still behind us around. He hit the hazards and lit up a Kent King.

"Why are we slowing down?" I asked.

I'd just turned seventeen. It was the late winter of 1987. I looked behind us. Had I missed something important in my fretting about math, girls, and whether or not the Russians loved their children too? These three things sometimes had me sleepless by day and would contribute to sleepless nights in front of reruns of *Family Ties* well into the following year. We were on the Long Island Expressway—operative word "express." Go fast. Get home in time for Sunday dinner and *60 Minutes* and an early bed. Do not reduce speed unless . . .

Punctured tire? Bloody cat? Were there cops? Sometimes there were cops. My father got into trouble. I knew his temper. I had it too.

"What did he just say?" he asked.

"Who?"

"The guy?"

"What guy, Dad?" I was pleading now.

"Your singer!"

It seemed this was an internal problem; a soundtrack predicament. I'd selected the cassette. It was the playful indie duo They Might Be Giants' self-titled debut. The song was called "Don't Let's Start." It was my property. And I'd chosen to share it as we passed time in traffic.

"I don't know."

Other cars continued to dust us as he rewound my tape, grimly.

Zeeeech. Click.

"Everybody dies frustrated and sad and . . . "

Unsatisfied, he rewound it further and more violently.

Kreeeeeeeeeeeetch. Click.

"No one in the world ever gets what they want and that is beautiful. Everybody dies frustrated and sad and that is beautiful."

The old man shook his head.

"I thought that's what he said," he muttered and ejected the tape. If there had been a button on the dash that would also eject me in my all-black uniform of baggy sweater, vintage raincoat, skinny black Stephen Sprouse trousers, and clown-shoe sized John Fluevogs, I think he'd probably have pressed that as well. The sweater was already controversial. Sid's mother, my "Grandma D," for Diane, knit it. It took her longer to make than all the other unsolicited pieces of winter-wear combined, and there'd been dozens over the years.

"Why don't you ever wear what I give you?" she once asked me before I asked her to try her hand at an all-black pullover. She'd been hurt and maybe a little angry about all the Christmas reds and ringed blue-and-tan offerings I'd politely accepted then placed in the closet forever.

"It's not personal. I only wear black, Grandma," I told her frankly.

"But why?"

"Artist."

She seemed relieved and took up the challenge, then never stopped complaining about it. Two years later, with enough Bailey's Irish Cream and pretzel nuggets in her, she'd still point a swollen finger at me accusingly and growl, "I nearly went blind making you that black sweater. Black! Black! It was all I saw!" It was as if she'd cable-knitted a death cloud and unleashed it on the world with her two pink metal needles between puffs of . . . a Kent King.

I was wearing my hair in long, draping, jet-black bangs in the spring of 1986. I'd dyed it in June for the occasion of Depeche Mode with openers Book of Love (of "Boy" and "I Touch Roses" fame) at Radio City Music Hall and placed a streak of yellow down the middle of my skull like a highway warning: Do Not Cross. But Sid still had power over me—and the brawn to stay the boss, in and out of a moving car. Normally, I found the closeness of the driver and passenger seats useful. I liked to study the old man. In the car, I could hear him breathe, watch him react, and try to figure out who he was. Those times could be tense too. I am, hopefully, a member of what will remain the last generation to be hit with fists or objects like hairbrushes (a favorite of my mother's) as discipline. Parents don't really slug anymore, and when they do, it makes the papers. When I was growing up, however, that was pretty routine. Once, when I was especially obnoxious, Sid picked me up by my legs and pushed my head into a toilet bowl. I'd mouthed off to my mother and the housekeeper, a stern Belizean woman named Olive. I never did it again. This isn't an endorsement for that kind of rough discipline, but I suspect today they'd probably send me (and Olive) to a counselor to talk about our feelings.

At seventeen, in 1987, I had my own car and a set of college applications on my desk, but I was still a minor. Sid remained entitled to these weekend custody hours, and let's face it, after someone treats your face like a plunger, you tend to defer to him when he tells you he'd like to see you on a Sunday afternoon. It was a big deal to be playing my own music for him at all. Usually dominion over the dial was his. Sid handed the They Might Be Giants cassette to me. He held the object with the edges of his fingertips, as if the toxic sentiments he believed its songs contained might somehow seep into his pores. I returned it to the case with the pink and green sleeve and placed that in my book bag with my other cassettes and notebook.

"Do you believe that?" he asked, as he turned the dial to CBS FM. Don K. Reed's *Doo-Wop Shop*. Frankie Lymon and the Teenagers was more like it, as far as he was concerned. I didn't know what to say. He asked again. "I said, Do you believe what he said? In that song?"

While I remained scared of him, on that day, my father seemed older and sadder then than I'd ever seen him look before. We'd been making these trips from Long Island into Manhattan for most of the decade, since he'd moved out for good in 1980. He was the man who introduced me to Manhattan. It took some time but I eventually realized that this was not Manhattan in full. It was only ever Sid's version of the City. We did the things he could handle. We'd emerge from the Midtown Tunnel, head downtown, park the Mustang in a garage, then eat a pair of slices at Ray's Pizza on Sixth Avenue and Eleventh Street. Ray's was a large, heavy slice, with a thicker layer of cheese than most. It was "famous," like all Ray's claimed to be, but most acknowledged that this was at least one of two or three that may actually be the "original." There were photos on the wall, after all, of the cast of the NBC sitcom *Gimme a Break!* flipping dough. Then we'd go to the Postermat on 8th Street between Fifth and Sixth Avenue. It was always the next stop. The store was deep and narrow and felt like a scene. People lingered. The clerks were hip. They played WNEW, the local rock station, loudly. Scot Muni and Dennis Elsus set up lots of Tull, Zeppelin, Neil Young, and Yes, who were my father's favorite. *"Don't surround yourself with yourself,"* he once warned me, quoting the "Your Move" suite from "I've Seen All Good People." I still don't know what he meant. The song's about chess, isn't it? My father never played chess.

On the wall behind the counter that separated the Postermat sales staff from the customers, they offered T-shirts imprinted with vintage cartoon characters like Rocky and Bullwinkle and Beanie and Cecil. Elsewhere, there were plastic bins full of wind-up walking versions of the aforementioned dinosaurs, as well as hopping sushi rolls, hopping bloody thumbs, hopping bloody penises, and the more conventional chattering teeth. Some of the teeth hopped as well but didn't bleed. One could stock up on rubber bats with suction cups affixed to their bellies if there was concern over running out. They sold rubber-gasket bracelets (the kind that Madonna had popularized in her "Lucky Star" video) and greeting cards with *Bloome County* and *The Far Side* cartoons on them. The very rear of the Postermat, however, was the only place that really interested both the old man and me. There they kept an L-shaped row of metal flip bins full of six-foot, heavy-plastic leafs, on which iconic images of movie and rock stars were mounted. Charlie Chaplin, Dennis Hopper and Peter Fonda from *Easy Rider*, Jane Fonda too (naked on a beach), and Gary Cooper in *High Noon*, Sophia Loren, David Bowie, Edward G. Robinson as Rico in *Little Ceasar*, King Kong (the original from 1933), Clint Eastwood, Bridget Bardot (naked on a bike), and the Marx Brothers. Each poster was numbered, and a customer would have to match the code from the floor copy to the shrink wrapped, rolled-up posters collected in little bins beneath them.

Sid's new house, ten minutes away from ours, out in Atlantic Beach, was covered with posters from The Postermat. His favorite was Brando as the brooding, leather-covered Johnny Strabler in *The Wild One*. Often I would spend an hour just selecting a David Bowie or Boris Karloff poster only to find that it was sold out in the bin. This store was a wonderland for a time, but at seventeen, it just didn't do it for me anymore. The difference between my father and I was becoming clearer to me. He was content to have these posters on his wall. I wanted to be one of the people on somebody's wall. I didn't care, or even really ponder, that most of those people were long dead, some of them like Monroe and Dean gone so young. I never considered the violence or the sacrifice or even the method of achieving such recognition. I only knew I wanted in. I had to make my mark somehow, find a way to let people know "I was here." There was a trick to getting in, and I suspected it had to do with size—being big, acting grander and stranger than everyone else around you.

Washington Square Park was always the next stop on the Sid-lead tours. We'd have a Coke and watch the jugglers or the stand-up comics and street performers try to hold the crowd from within the then-empty fountain in the center of the public sprawl. On lucky days, we'd catch the brilliant but doomed comedian Charlie Barnett. Some say that Charlie Barnett could have been as big as Eddie Murphy. I believe it, having been one who'd witnessed him stalk the rim of the park's big fountain in his backwards ball cap and T-shirt. You could tell when he was on by the crashing laughter that grew louder and louder as we sprinted to catch him. Nobody else was that kind of draw. Charlie Barnett owned the Park and seemed to charge the entire City with dangerous currents when he came on. Birds and squirrels crept down from the trees to listen. Tourists and strangers chanted, "Charlie! Charlie! Charlie!" Barnett didn't have a mic. He shouted his riffs in his gruff voice, improvising about the ethnic diversity of the crowd and the difference between black and white people before it became a hackneyed trope of Def Jam–style comics. He'd grab a tourist's handbag or camera and use it as a prop while they nervously looked on; their uneasiness contributing to the crackling energy of the bit. I studied Barnett. He was a window, a door, a portal, a way out of my boring suburban life and into something bigger and better. Danger, I noted, danger was necessary. Do not fear danger. Make friends with it. Like Lenny Bruce. Like Jim Morrison. Like Charlie Barnett. Everyone knew the chainsaw jugglers, who also performed in the park's ring, weren't going to lose a mitt to the blade, but it was impossible to predict what Barnett, with his elastic face and surging posture, was going to do or say next or whether that camera was ever going to be returned.

As I said, I never stopped to consider the consequences of such an approach; what happens to the ones who walk through those exits and say goodbye to polite society. Charlie Barnett was already on a path towards ruin; dead of AIDS in 1996 at just forty-one, after years as a junkie. I only knew that he'd made it to New York City (from West Virginia), and he was killing that crowd like he killed every crowd.

The back of the Postermat and the genius of Charlie Barnett were among the few things my father and I still agreed on. We didn't even meet at The Police anymore, the one band that I thought we'd always be able to share since Sting, Stuart Copeland, and Andy Summers were eccentric enough to charm the new wavers and big-rock enough to get those who came of age in the sixties (probably because, despite their spiky haircuts, they secretly had as well). My father bought me my first copy of *Ghost in the Machine*. But The Police had recently released a remake of their own hit "Don't Stand So Close to Me" as "Don't Stand So Close to Me '86." It had a drum machine beat instead of Stewart Copeland's skewed and exotic playing, and rather than sing the excellent lyric "*just like the old man in that book by Nabokov*," Sting, for some reason, now sang "*that famous book by Nabokov*," as if we were thinking of *Pale Fire* instead of *Lolita*.

Sometimes, instead of the Postermat, I'd drag the old man to Flip, the narrow vintage-clothing store directly across the street, near the 8th Street Playhouse and Electric Ladyland, the studio that Jimi Hendrix built. There, I'd buy vintage green and gold sharkskin jackets and later load up both lapels with as many of my band badges as I could. My collection was pretty vast: ranging from bands who'd already split like the Sex Pistols and the Jam and The Specials to new favorites like The Dead Milkmen and Sonic Youth. Flip had its own band-style badge, and I'd try to collect a new color each time: green, maroon, pink, black with white lettering. I'd collect them from Zoot (whose badges were green) and Unique Clothing Warehouse (black with rainbow lettering) over on Lower Broadway as well. The Flip-Zoot-Unique triumvirate of sales people didn't behave like the vendors on Central Avenue in Cedarhurst, the town that neighbored my hometown, the more residential Lawrence. Lawrence was one of the Five Towns (the other towns were Inwood, Woodmere, where I went to high school at Woodmere Academy, and Hewlett). On HBO's now-classic show business satire *Entourage*, Kevin Dillon's hapless Johnny "Drama" co-stars in a critically maligned, Ed Burns–produced prime time soap set there. Burns was from Valley Stream in real life, but *Entourage*'s writer-producer Rob Weiss was the older brother of a high school pal from the Five Towns. It was a given that in order to be or do anything remarkable, you had to get the hell out of all Five. None were safe for the ambitious, and by my teens, I was already making a mental tally of those who had done it. Jim Steinman, Meatloaf's collaborator and the composer of the mighty *Bat Out of Hell* (plus Bonnie Tyler's "Total Eclipse of the Heart" and a half dozen other immortal pop songs), attended Hewlett High. Harvey Milk, the martyred leader of the modern gay rights movement, was also from the Five Towns. Years before Sean Penn won an Oscar portraying him, I'd rented the documentary, *The Times of Harvey Milk*, and kept it out long enough to never bother returning it. The late fees outweighed the cost of the tape. Perry Farrell of Jane's Addiction planned and schemed in Woodmere, while then answering to Perry Bernstein. There was Ross Bleckner, the painter, Peggy Lipton, who played Julie on *The Mod Squad*, and Lyle Alzado, the professional football player. He was from Cedarhurst and knew my mom.

I noticed, while picking at Flip, Zoot, Unique, and Canal Jean Company, that the Manhattan sales people seemed to be in denial that they were working at all and acted instead like they were just hanging out. Years later, when I too entered the world of Lower Manhattan retail, I adopted a similar attitude toward customer service. My father found their languor offensive.

We didn't even look much like each other anymore, whereas with my full lips, long nose, and thick, brown hair, I was once his double. Now, he was thickening in middle age, and by fifteen, I'd lost all my baby fat and grown about four inches taller than him. It didn't make me less afraid of the guy. I still knew he could and might take me in a fight. And while I felt safe walking Lower Manhattan with him, I felt embarrassed too. He'd stopped dressing like a seventies velvet-and-suede-loving dandy and began showing up for our Sunday dates in oversized cotton sweatshirts (gray, sometimes white) with the names of places he'd visited on them: Miami, Chicago, Lexington—horse-racing cities with big tracks. His jeans were loose and faded, and there were sneakers where there'd once been ostrich- or snake-skin boots with hammered silver tips. After a point, some people just start dressing for comfort. I still dressed to be noticed. My tight wool Sprouse pants weren't comfortable, but nobody else in my high school had them . . . or the shoes.

It never bothered me much that my father was a degenerate gambler. I'd never known him to be anything else, and aside from throwing me a beating or two, he was as devoted as any other dad. The worst abuse he ever inflicted on me was making me listen to "Run for the Roses" by Dan Fogelberg repeatedly. It was his favorite pop song, a top-ten hit from 1982. If you've never heard it and perhaps only know Dan for his other big hits, "Leader of the Band" or the mellow gold classic "Longer Than," I will tell you that it's about a pony (a horse with no name), born in western Kentucky, that grows up to vie for Kentucky Derby glory. It's equine porn (*"The sun on your withers . . . the wind in your mane,"* the old beardo sang). I don't know if Dan's horse wins the Derby (or the Preakness and Belmont), but in the old man's fantasy, he certainly did, and my father was right there in the winner's circle, flashing a thumbs-up.

My mother, Susan, whom everyone called by her middle name, "Ricki," was a Five Towns girl who, like me, had a rebellious streak and a series of teenage exit strategies, while still depending on the comforts that an upper-middle-class enclave offered. In the mid-sixties, my father and his Brooklyn friends enthusiastically welcomed the attentions of these "classy" Jewish princesses, with their bobbed noses and blonde hair and big houses and new cars. My mother was just seventeen when she began disappearing with Sid, after being introduced by her older and better-behaved half-sister Marlene, who'd spent a few semesters with him down at the University of Miami, where he was briefly enrolled.

My mother knew that dating my father would enrage her own parents and initially found his outlaw energy and the money that he'd take home from the track and spend easily, quite the sexy thing. If you're seeing images of Ray Liotta and Lorraine Bracco in act one of *Goodfellas* (pre-Lufthansa heist), you're probably not too far off. In Scorsese's masterpiece (and in real life), Karen Hill was also from the Five Towns, and while my father was not an Italian, he dressed and acted like one and even sometimes called himself "Sonny."

"You know these Jew broads, they got a lot of money," Joe Pesci's Tommy DeVito tells Ray Liotta's Henry Hill, while trying to convince him to double date. "You might end up with a big fucking score, you motherfucker."

But my father wasn't motivated by loot. Money came and went. So did women. The only constant in his life was the post-time bugle call and the track announcement, "And they're off . . . " Life wasn't about anything but that moment; and then the next race.

My father avoided the draft into the army and 'Nam, but my mother drafted him into marriage. She'd been looking for a partner to assist in her big escape. She wanted out of the Five Towns and out of her big but lonely house where, as a child of divorce herself, she felt unwanted and ignored. Her mother, Regina, my "Grandma Reggie," had re-married a self-made successful lumber salesman named Charles Albert, my "Grandpa Charlie." Marriage two for both, they lived it up in effort to extend the romantic rush; and traveled the world together, taking cruises and treks through Asia and the Middle East. My mother, her biological brother, Peter, and her half siblings, the aforementioned Marlene and my Uncle Larry, were left at home and basically thrown in a bucket together. It didn't feel like family to her, so she began inventing her own in which she would be the wife and mother.

Fueled by the music of The Beatles and The Stones, The Kinks, Donovan, The Shangri-Las, and The Ronettes, Ricki craved her own adventures, and dramas, which my father's restless energy and dark brown eyes seemed to promise. She thought he looked like his idol Marlon Brando. He thought she looked like Bridget Bardot, with her carefully ironed bangs, the color of marshmallow chicks. She told him that she wanted children immediately, and he resisted until she explained that she needed them to somehow counterbalance the way she was raised—as if doting on me and eventually my sister would be a parenting version of carbon offsets. He felt for her, and by nineteen, she was pregnant with me. To this day, my mother and I sometimes talk like peers rather than parent and child. I've dated much younger women with much older mothers.

To his credit, my father warned her about his sickness before he proposed.

"I'm a gambler," he confessed. "I won't make you happy." It changed nothing. She didn't believe it. And so he proved it to her.

The first bet Sid ever placed was on a horse named Silver Ship, and it came in. From that moment, he was gone. The race track was a separate universe, and he no longer needed to live in the hard one, with its missile crisis and assassinations and draft numbers and riots, or even the smaller, more routine hassle of showing up to work somewhere and taking shit from some fat boss. Walking through the turnstile and buying a program was like flipping the bird to the straight world. The track had its own etiquette, and at the time some of them even had their own currency. Sid could buy a roast-beef sandwich with a make-believe gold coin, and from that point, all money seemed make-believe too.

Once they got a load of my father and his clothes and attitude, my mother finally had her parents' attention. Horrified by the notion of this Brooklyn punk marrying into the family, they did whatever they could to cancel or postpone the wedding date. As the engagement drew onward, my mother's family went from calm reasoning to begging and eventually threats to cut her off. Nothing worked. A Five Towns spoiled child, my mother couldn't even conceive of not having everything she needed. There was no frame of reference to produce any fear. Finally, they dangled intrigue.

"We know something about the Spitz family," my Grandma Reggie hinted. "The Spitzes, they have a dark secret."

"You don't scare me!" My mother replied. Every song in her record collection was rebellious and romantic: "Leader of the Pack," "You Don't Own Me," "You Really Got Me," "I'm Free."

"Trust me, you'll want to know what it is," my grandmother warned, like a storefront psychic. "And when we tell you, believe me, you'll think twice before becoming a part of their family."

The dark secret, as I would later learn, wasn't any darker than those most families hide and didn't even involve my father. It was his father, my Grandpa Jack, who was the culprit. Now, Jack was the one who made my old man the degenerate he was, and he was most likely the single battiest entry in the entire gene pool, but I adored him for his eccentricity. Jack wasn't like anybody else. He ate raw hot dogs from Grabstein's Deli in Canarsie as we barbecued in the driveway. He also let me throw one paper airplane after another onto the grill, watching them slowly burn and curl.

"They're all dying inside," he'd laugh. "You're burning 'em up."

Jack, whom I called "Poppy Doc," let me drive his cream-colored Cadillac El Dorado across the frozen ball field during the winter. I must have been twelve or thirteen, behind the wheel of a gas guzzler, playing Men at Work and the Steve Miller Band while crunching donuts over second and third base. In the spring, we'd walk Sheepshead Bay together and peer into the buckets of the fishermen as they pulled octopi and crabs from the brown drink. We went to the Kings Plaza Mall to window-shop or see a movie, but my favorite thing to do was go through his library. In their narrow house on Flatlands Avenue, I'd sit with his *Gray's Anatomy* books and marvel at the human body with all the veins and muscles and things I knew I had in me, even if at the time, I felt like a giant brain connected to a dick. Jack kept medical books on freaks and the severely afflicted as well, and these were not off-limits. I fixated on patients with massive goiters, Siamese twins, or men with their arms chewed away by leprosy. I'd take it all in as my grandma sipped at her Bailey's or saw to a customer in the basement where she ran a small yarn and knitting-supply business. The office, just off the laundry room, was always chilly, but the soft balls of tightly rolled and binned yarn, while poor natural insulation, gave it the illusion of warmth, and there was a big dish of butterscotch candy that I had a taste for, so I found myself down there a lot, listening to Frank Sinatra and Tony Bennett on the radio and "helping out," mostly by keeping her company.

There were Sunday brunches that lasted three hours. Every offering had its own plate: ham, cheese, butter, bagels, smoked whitefish, pungent, onion-y kasha varnishkas, and dense, nutty, sickly sweet halva candies. For dinner we'd go to Tomasso's, where the waiters and waitresses took turns singing "What I Did for Love" and other impossibly loud show tunes at the piano. Sometimes we'd eat in the darkly lit Joy Teang, with it's red-and-gold dragon banners, where the host would always grandly remove our coats, and the bus boys filled the heavy-bottomed porcelain cups with strong black tea. Before supper ever came, I'd munch on the dry Chinese noodles they served, dipping one into the duck sauce and always avoiding the hot mustard since Poppy Doc warned me that it would burn a hole clean through the lining of my stomach. This was my first "dangerous substance," and I immediately became obsessed with it; taking little bits onto the tip of my finger and flicking my tongue at the veneer like a skink. Did hot mustard lead to hard drugs down the road? Probably not, but it lead me to see the world differently. It was there for pleasure, but it could hurt you, like the cigarettes and the liquor, and something about that was sexy already.

"Why would they serve it if it does that to people?" I wondered, but I didn't dwell on it. I liked "Poppy Doc" when he was being mischievous but less so when he was morose. The subject of sex seemed to combine these elements of his personality. At the newsstand he bought me *Playboy* magazines where the women seemed so clean and literally shined under the gloss of the printed pages, but he also told me stories about having sex with hookers when he was in school at the University of Alabama. One of them had stabbed him in the leg.

Jack traveled to Edinburgh in the thirties to get his degree because it was easier for Jews to do so at the time. My favorite photo of him depicts a handsome, almost smug, young medical student, standing over a flayed cadaver. He gave it to me one afternoon without warning me that it might be disturbing. "Wasn't I handsome?" he laughed. All I could see were the flaps of skin hanging off the dead guy's ribcage.

When I knew him, he wasn't as debonair. Jack weighed three hundred pounds, maybe more, and resembled William Conrad, who played Cannon and later Nero Wolfe on TV, but I was loyal.

He'd also saved my life. Maybe.

Poppy Doc claimed to have rushed into the delivery room when I was born blue. The umbilical cord, he maintained, was wrapped tightly around my throat, and nobody knew what to do.

Removing it apparently did not occur to the doctor who delivered me or to any of nurses. As he told it, Jack shoved everyone back, scrubbed up, and quickly untangled me. I then began to breathe and go pink. When I asked my mother if this was true, she shrugged. "I don't know, I was out."

"Do you think it's true?"

"I don't know, Marc."

I don't suppose there's a way to find out, so I prefer to identify his claim as the moment I learned by example how to bullshit excellently; an essential tool for any writer. So in a way, he *did* give me life, whether it was in the ER or not.

My mother and father knew a different Jack Spitz. She knew the man who swallowed handfuls of painkillers and kept a loaded .38 in his black leather doctor's bag . . . sometimes. Other times he had it in his hand and would wave it at motorists who'd cut him off on Rockaway Parkway.

"Hey! What? You wanna fuck with me?" my grandfather would ask. "I didn't think so."

It was this Jack Spitz whom my mother's parents had the scandalous poop on. Long before the engagement, when my father was still at the University of Miami, my grandfather went down to visit him and do some gambling over at the Gulfstream course. One night he found himself in the same bar as my mother's stepsister, and after consuming too many cocktails, he'd simply made a pass at her. Did he know it was my mother's sister? Yeah. Was it a flirtation or a proposition? Who knows. Marlene kept it to herself until the engagement. Then she told her parents, and they threatened to share with mom what they hoped was this deal breaker. It's funny to me now to think that was the "dark secret." The Alberts didn't know the half of what these two men were capable of . . . how their values were just different and how deeply the scumbag ran through the blood line. It's certainly there in mine and will likely be there in my kid's, if I ever have one. These weren't men at all, the Spitzes. They were space creatures, only visiting this planet and due back on planet Belmont or planet Aqueduct shortly. "Farewell, Earth Woman and boy. It's post time." And he's off.

Still, my mother got her way. My parents got married on October 2, 1966, at Temple Emanu-El on East Sixty-sixth Street in Manhattan, had their wedding night in the Plaza Hotel (they were promised a view of the park but could only see it through the window in the bathroom). They moved to a small apartment in Far Rockaway Queens, where I was born on their third wedding anniversary in 1969. Once the vows were said, my grandfather Charlie figured he'd better make the best of it and offered the old man a job in one of his two lumber yards, where everyone in the family worked. What was done was done. Sid was family now. And there were children. So, as was common in Jewish families then, he was generously given a title and a salary in the family business. It was implicit that the gambling and the lifestyle would have to stop. But they didn't. *"A gambling fiend that does not bet,"* the Sugarhill Gang would later rap, was as rare as *"Dracula without his fangs"* or *"the boogie to the boogie without the boogie bang"* for that matter.

And with the mid-seventies and the invention of coke culture, we were soon in the second act of *Goodfellas* (jail, blow, "Monkey Man," and Carbone in the meat truck).

I don't recall my mother and father speaking more than a half-dozen times after the divorce. They'd communicate through me, as my sister, Nicole, born in 1972, was too young to really know what was going on. My father would get drunk and imply that my mother had been unfaithful. I'd ask her about it, and she'd tell me the opposite was true: he was the one who'd strayed. After divorcing my father, she buried the creative and rebellious side of her personality for years. I don't know if she gave away all those great, old 45s, but I never heard her play and enjoy rock-and-roll music again. She only played Jane Olivor and Barbara Streisand in the car. Even a fleeting infatuation with Charles Aznavour was deemed ultimately unwise. It was like she went to bed one night as Kevin Bacon in *Footloose* and woke up the next morning as John Lithgow in *Footloose*.

After all the drama, my mother's parents got their way. She ended up marrying a well-heeled and clean-cut Five Towns boy after all; a socially acceptable, tan, and handsome jock named Al Josephberg. He drove a Stingray and wore his Lacoste polo shirts with the collars turned up; the kind of Five Towner whose nasal bone Ray Liotta pulverizes with a gun handle. He came from a solid family, kept fit swimming in the Atlantic Ocean, and, most importantly, made it clear that he would not force her to share him with anyone or anything. He was going to be all about her.

Freed from even the superficial responsibility of wife and kids, my father started doing a lot more coke as the eighties progressed. I remember sitting in his car outside a house in Woodmere as he picked up his blow. Sometimes he'd come out in ten minutes. Other times, he'd lose track of the time, and I'd wait for an hour, listening to Casey Kasem count down the country's Top 40 and send out his long-distance dedications. When he was too strung out, my grandfather would shoot him up with B-12 and iron in the middle of the living room out in Canarsie, as my grandmother pruned the yellow rose bushes out in the small square of backyard and my sister played with her Barbies. I watched it all go on with the same sick fascination I had for the lepers and the dude with parasitic elephantitis. My father would pull his shirt off and slap his belly, then the meat of his right arm, and Grandpa Jack would eliminate the pains of the previous evening's carousing. He could have used Grandma D's help with his own gardening. He was living in a small house with an overgrown lawn by the beach just about fifteen minutes from my Lawrence house. He shared it with a few other middle-aged divorcees and a young, new wave shoe salesman named Billy Burdon. Billy Burdon would later run a footwear empire bearing his name. He'd encounter some legal problems in the early-twenty-first century but emerge stronger and more successful then ever by mid-decade. In the mid-eighties, Billy was a wild-eyed Long Island boy with a trove of Clash, Joan Jett, and Missing Persons albums that I coveted. I worshipped him because he worked in the city, subscribed to *Rolling Stone*, wore men's ballet shoes, and unlike my old man, always had food (cold cuts and sodas). When Billy was away at work and I was off from school, I'd hang out in his room and wish I were him. He seemed bigger than everyone else in the room, destined, like Charlie Barnett, for great things. You could tell. In the classified section of one of Billy Burdon's old *Stones*, among the ads for "I Heart Pac Man" stickers and E.T. fan club membership offerings, I once saw an ad for custom T-shirts emblazoned with the faces of writers—Kerouac, Camus, Hegel, Kierkegaard, Eliot, Tolkien, Sartre, Poe—along with silk-screened T-shirts with portraits of James Dean, Elvis, and John Coltrane, writers mixed in with rebel rockers. This was a revelation to me. "More Great Faces!" the ad announced. Writers could be like James Dean? Writers could have "Great Faces" too?

My father was clearly jealous of Billy Burdon's youth and bravado, and my treating the guy like Fonzie didn't help matters. Sid tortured him. One night while Billy Burdon was racing, most likely on the same speedy drug that my father was still racing on, he begged the old man for some "downs" so he could sleep and get to work in the morning.

"Yeah, yeah. I was out on the beach, and a few fell out of my pocket. They're right out there," my father promised, then snickered as he watched Billy Burdon take off up the road toward the edge of the sand, fully intent on combing through it until he found himself a dropped Tuinal.

That was 1983 or so, when my old man was still in his late thirties. By 1987, the time of our They Might Be Giants–blighted Sunday outing, the blow had long taken a toll. I guess if you have a kid (which I don't), once the drugs and the life begin to make you feel tired and the hangovers grow harder and harder to recover from, you begin looking to that kid to revive your dying dreams, the ones your own parents invested you with. On these last few drives, my father would sometimes park his Mustang in someone else's driveway; a rich family in the "Back of Lawrence," where great lawns, not just white fences, separated the houses. "Look at that," he'd say as we idled and trespassed. "You could have one of those some day. If you work hard enough. Anything you want will come to you. You understand. If you want it, you can get it." I always nodded but I didn't buy it. His values weren't mine. They weren't even his, but they were very much the dreams he needed in place to keep from disappearing into that shadow-world of the track, and the choking failure of middle age. My dreams weren't born in the fifties and sixties. I didn't care about having a house or a car. And I didn't think everything was going to be alright, and Utopia was graspable, or life was fair and the good willed out. I would not be my father's second chance to experience any kind of triumph beyond the race track, nor was I content to function as his courier or tether to the straight world. This was the late eighties, and I was full of indie rock, loneliness, fear, and rage. If I had a dream at all, it was that the coming decade I would finally be permitted to explode.

When I first told my father that year that I wanted to be a famous writer, he replied, "Like Anne Frank." We were both teens, both Jews, and both wrote diaries, but I was thinking about Lenny Bruce, and Lester Bangs, who'd been name checked in R.E.M.'s "It's The End of the World As We Know It (And I Feel Fine)." Thanks to bands like R.E.M., U2, and The Smiths, I'd started to respect pop music as serious stuff and suspected I'd somehow come to use it in my writing. At least two dozen songs had already changed the way I saw the world forever; ones I can remember first hearing and then thinking, "Well, what could be the same now?" I won't give you the full list, but here's a partial one: "Fish Heads" by Barnes and Barnes, "Money" by the Flying Lizards, "Warm Leatherette" by The Normal, "Buffalo Gals" by Malcolm McLaren, "White Horse" by Laid Back, "Ghost Town" by The Specials, "Pull Up to the Bumper" by Grace Jones, "Da Da Da" by Trio, "Go" by Tones On Tail, "A New England" by Billy Bragg, "World Destruction" by Time Zone, "Controversy" by Prince (pretty much everything by Prince), "Thieves Like Us" by New Order, and "Din Daa Daa" by George Kranz. "Don't Let's Start," by the two buttoned down Johns of They Might Be Giants was not on this list. The first time that I heard it I loved it, but I can't say it changed anything. I never would have imagined that it would be this particular song that would, in a matter of second, finally set me on my own road; away from my father's path, his past, his habits (but not his vices) and most importantly, his Manhattan.

"I asked you a question," the old man repeated a second time as we drew closer and closer to my mother's house in Lawrence.

"Believe what?"

"That everybody dies frustrated and sad? And it's—good?"

We were on Rockaway Turnpike now, near the Sherwood Diner, a chrome spaceship trimmed with neon and full of firemen, cops, coaches, and Jewish American Princes and Princesses dragging steak fries through gravy or sip-ping tall Cokes with lemon. I'd be home in less than five minutes. I had to give an answer. We passed over the tracks by the graveyard that peered onto my first public grade school (who builds a public school next to a boneyard, anyway?). My father never pulled into the driveway of his old house anymore. There was another car there now, permanently. There was another man in his old bed. He lingered on the street like a taxi. We stared up at the house. The lights were on in the kitchen. Supper was probably warm. My mother was peering through the window, waiting to make sure I was okay, that he wasn't returning me to her with a gambling problem or a social disease.

"I don't know," I finally said.

He was relieved that I didn't seem determined to act on this mode of thinking but I was only forswearing. I believed it completely. He patted my shoulder, then put another Kent King in his mouth and punched the lighter. He reached into his pocket and handed me a $20 bill. This wasn't a reward so much as another part of the ritual. Sure as I always took an overcoat (even in the summer), I walked up that drive with twenty bucks for lunch or gas or sometimes to go right back into the city on Monday afternoon when I should be in "Introduction to Philosophy" class. Manhattan *was* philosophy instruction, and art history, and physical education.

I grabbed a cigarette too, as I sometimes did. I liked the taste of the paper-covered filters, and they reminded me of him when he sometimes disappeared into the South or the Midwest. We'd never have another one of these post-divorce Sundays. This would be the last of them.

The lighter popped out. *Phuttttt.*

He handed it to me with a look that seemed to say, "Smoke if you're gonna smoke. Don't just play with the thing." The metal was hot, and I could feel my cigarette end crackle and a dazzle of blue smoke fill my mouth. I exhaled and handed the lighter to him. It was still glowing orange. I nodded a thank-you and took another drag then spoke.

"But I think it's a really good lyric."

He frowned as I blew my smoke out over the lawn and pulled my book bag, full of about a dozen cassettes (XTC's *Skylarking*, Robyn Hitchcock and the Egyptian's *Globe of Frogs*, The Dead Milkmen's *Big Lizard in My Backyard*), tightly into my ribs. This was the first time that an opinion I had about a rock-and-roll song had any consequence at all. I didn't know it at the time, and it would be another decade before anyone paid me to be one, but from that moment on, I was a writer. Like Anne Frank, and Kafka and Kerouac, Sartre and Camus, Lenny and Lester, and Charlie Barnett, like anybody but myself. *That* would take even *more* time.

CHAPTER 2

attended Woodmere Academy, a sixty-five-year-old private school, but "attended" is probably strong. This was my high school. Some weekdays I was in class, other weekdays, I was in the City. On days when I'd cut class, I could be in Manhattan by ten a.m.

Especially during the morning rush, the Long Island Railroad, like little else in my life since puberty and my parents' divorce, was dependable: forty-five minutes there, forty-five minutes back. There are ten stops between Lawrence and Penn Station. I can run them down in my head like a Buddhist chant: Cedarhurst, Woodmere, Hewlett, Gibson, Valley Stream, Rosedale, Laurelton, Locust Manor, and Jamaica.

At Jamaica passengers had to switch trains and catch the Manhattan-bound train when it arrived on a nearby track. "Change at Jamaica," the ticket taker would instruct flatly. And I did—from a nobody into a somebody. From there it was Kew Gardens, also in Queens, then Woodside, and then "New York, Penn Station," as the conductor always announced with some increased excitement in his voice. "New York, Penn Station" just sounded different coming out of the dude's mouth than "Locust Manor" did. The wait for the Manhattanbound train at Jamaica Station could be long, but it was a good time to blast my eardrums with noise that put me in the Manhattan mind-set, an opportunity to get into character. Music helped. I was in a post–Jim Jarmusch affair with Bebop. Listening to "Salt Peanuts" or "Moose the Mooch" through my Walkman headphones made me feel like John Lurie, his gangly, frowning star. My Uncle Ed (not a blood relative but the husband of my mother's best friend, Jane) was a jazz buff and let me tape his entire collection one afternoon. I sat on the floor with his LPs and a box of tapes from lunch until sundown, staring at all those hot sleeves. Blue Note had the best. I was tiring of my new wave heroes. Billie Holiday, Dizzy Gillespie, Stan Getz, Charlie Parker, Dave Brubeck, Chet Baker, Thelonious Monk, Lester Young, and Anita O'Day provided a much-needed break from my black-clad, gloomy, Gothy familiars. Bebop and swing sounded like streetwalking felt. It was a better fit for a faster kid, and I was speeding up.

Once the train rolled in, finding a window seat was optimum. I could then witness that moment when the blurring trees and stores, backyard swing sets, water towers, and sedans literally zipped into black like a pirate's knife sliding into a sheath. This phenomenon occurred about ten minutes after the train departed Woodside and never failed to thrill, the car shaking left and right as it bulleted into place under the terminal lights. I heard nothing but the wheels rumbling over the tracks; felt nothing but electricity. I hadn't had sex yet, but I imagined it was a lot like speeding into Penn Station from Woodside. "Please exercise caution," the disembodied voice would warn over the PA system, but I wasn't about to. I was there to exercise danger.

Then it was up the old stairs, grabbing the brass railings, and out onto the concourse with its ice-cream parlors, pizza places, newsstands the size of bookstores, and hundreds of people with attitude. The concourse is two stories below Seventh Avenue, "Fashion Avenue," and I could never get to the street fast enough. The first smell of smoking skewer meat and pretzels meant I was home—my true home. I crushed out on Manhattan, and not just on its street people but on the streets themselves. A gasoline-puddle rainbow was enough to take my breath away. I'd inevitably be carrying a copy of the *Village Voice*. The pages inside were circled with red pen. Things to see. Things to learn. A better kind of person to become: an artist, whatever that meant.

I couldn't sing. All my drawings and paintings were a little off. I did clown portraits mostly, but they never looked quite as good as Arthur Sarnoff's or even John Wayne Gacy's clowns. I only knew one dance, the pogo, which Sid Vicious invented. Clay was too messy. My appreciation of the culinary arts consisted of determining which Manhattan diner had the best grilled cheese sandwiches and chicken noodle soup, the Veselka or the Kiev. But I could write. That is to say, I was beginning to express myself confidently with written words in a way that I could not with spoken words. My book reports, for example, had none of the predictable and clunky phrases that many of my peers' papers had. I wrote like people spoke and read enough to know that the good writers did the same. My fellow students wrote like beauty pageant contestants spoke, using "be it" instead of "whether it's" and "for" instead of "because," fearing that they weren't going to be considered intelligent by our teachers otherwise.

Sometimes I'd type my short stories (initially nearly all of them were about Major Tom–esque astronauts, mad scientists, or Jacques Cousteau–like undersea explorers) carefully and bind them like an actual book, drawing a cover image and writing the title and author line as professionally as I could. Then I'd have an object, something I could hand to someone—my mother, my stepfather, maybe even a girl. Of course, I was too shy and never did. I'd simply re-read them once or twice, then file them away and begin another. It was not unlike jacking off—a passive act that required one burst of focus, then left me feeling instantly relieved but eventually empty until I began the process again. There were no star writers at my school. There were star football players and baseball players, golfers and basketball players. There were popular cheerleaders and beloved coaches. The magnetism of the athletes and the power of jock culture were so palpable and the adulation the lettering heroes received so institutionalized that the notion of being applauded for anything else was foreign, even to me. I went out for the teams because it was aggressively encouraged (with an eye towards the well-rounded college application), but more so because the promise of being noticed and worshipped was irresistible. Like most, I always got picked, never got to play. That's how they keep you in line. You can never say you were rejected. You get the jersey . . . and the bench. Until I discovered I could write, this was all that was available to me. As a writer, I was the equivalent of a short stop. I won all the awards and citations they offered. Of course, unlike with athletics, there were no perks other than a growing sense of self (no small thing but no blow job either). It was clear that I was going to spend the next four years without being kissed or touched or even looked at for more than a quick moment in the hall. And yet, in my stories, I could have all that and more. I could be anyone and get whomever I wanted to do whatever I wanted. I guess a lot of the young people who take to writing this way begin with fantasy stories of monsters and outer space or submarine travel because the notion of even holding hands with a pretty girl or boy or getting anywhere beyond your shitty little town might as well be science fiction. I know I did.

I had a few real friends, and we were all bent in our own way. Ricky Sherman was a grade ahead of me. He knew and could perform two dozen magic tricks, but there were never any parties to attend where he might have shown them off. Erik Robinson played guitar like Peter Buck and drove one of those vintage cars, a Plymouth, but he spoke in an affected robot voice and didn't seem to even notice the girls who haunted me. He was a year older as well. Ricky was from Rosedale; Erik lived in Valley Stream. Only Adam David was from the Five Towns, like me. All four of us gravitated toward anything preceded by the word "cult." My favorite book was called *Cult Movies* by Danny Peary, in which I read about *Beyond the Valley of the Dolls*, *El Topo*, *Eraserhead*, and *The Honeymoon Killers* (which took place in Valley Stream) before ever seeing the films. I'd look them up in my *Movies Unlimited* catalog and, when I had the money, order the tapes. Occasionally USA's *Nite Flight* broadcast would contain a cult film like *Breaking Glass* or the Clash's *Rude Boy*, and I'd record and memorize them. By my early teens, there were already three dozen books, movies, magazines, and TV shows that spoke directly to me and my friends and that almost nobody else at school could either understand or muster a shared interest in John Waters's *Female Trouble* and *Desperate Living*, Paul Bartel's *Eating Raoul, Times Square, The Uncle Floyd Show, The National Lampoon, Mad, The Truth about De-Evolution, Blade Runner, The Dr. Demento Show*, Kenneth Anger's *Hollywood Babylon, Rock 'n' Roll High School, The Forbidden Zone, Ladies and Gentlemen, the Fabulous Stains.*

My first contributions to Woodmere Academy's monthly newspaper, *The Echo*, were initially reviews of these "cult movies" like *After Hours* and *Blue Velvet*, both of which I saw, ironically, while playing hooky in Manhattan. Eventually I had my own column, *Flicks with Spitz*. I enjoyed attending meetings of the paper after school. It was a skeleton crew of writer kids headed by a girl named Nisha, who was tall and Indian and seemed Ivy League bound. Driving home from an editorial session, I felt a little more useful in the world and was a little less inclined to play hooky. Putting out *The Echo*, I had a reason to stay on "Wrong Island," as I sometimes called it (Manhattan Island being all right). I cut class less and worked harder than I ever had before. I eventually began submitting personal essays like the one I wrote about dressing up like a clown and giving pony rides for the annual homecoming. I sold helium balloons to benefit the PTA, and when my day was over, I kept the suit on. I got into my little Toyota in clown drag, went to the bank, the convenience store, and the Blockbuster, recording the reaction as I strolled in and out of each place. Some people didn't do anything at all. A few children pointed and cried.

By my junior year, I noticed a few teachers who seemed to appreciate what I was doing. The math teachers still treated me like a fool because I could barely add (I still can't balance a checkbook or count backwards to figure out how old someone is when I see their birth date listed). Arnold Friedman, a cheerful, gnomish man, who taught me how to use a computer and begin to literally "process" the words that gave me confidence, was one of the few who seemed to show me patience and care. Sadly, in the winter of 1987, Friedman was being investigated on child-molestation charges. Years later, after he pleaded guilty, he and his family would become the subject of the now classic documentary on small-town xenophobia *Capturing the Friedmans*. It seemed like one day he was there, an easy-going, middle-aged nerd with glasses and a head full of jargon like "garbage in and garbage out," then he was gone after that, he was a black mark on the entire Island; a boogie man. And maybe he was. I'm just saying I preferred him to my Trig and Algebra teachers. *The Echo* staff were tacitly discouraged from exploring what had happened ourselves. It was typical, suburban-think: you just remove the "monsters," and things will go right back to normal. Garbage out. In some of the coverage of the scandal, the press had revealed that Friedman had once led a mambo band.

"We should run a huge exposé on that," I told my traumatized fellow *Echo* reporters, frustrated with the gag we'd been given on the matter. "Never mention the child thing once. Just a huge banner—ARNOLD FRIEDMAN: MAMBO BAND LEADER!—with a photo of him holding a baton." Few were amused, but how else are you going to cope with such a horror show at seventeen besides black comedy?

Mr. Schwartz, my English professor, was my favorite teacher and the only one to make me feel as a writer how the Woodmere Wolverine's baseball coach must have made the starting pitcher feel. Schwartz wore tortoiseshell glasses and cotton crewneck sweaters. If he wore a oxford shirt underneath, he'd fold the sleeves over the sweater, then push the whole thing up his hairy forearm. One night in the early winter of 1987, I took the train into the city to see William S. Burroughs, John Waters, and John Giorno read at an AIDS Treatment Project benefit at the Beacon Theater called "Where the Rubber Meets the Road."

"You like William S. Burroughs?" Schwartz asked me, and I nodded. I'd never read any Burroughs, but I owned a black-and-red mass-market paperback of *Naked Lunch*, which I brought in the next day to show him, hoping he wouldn't quiz me on any of it. Sometimes it's almost enough just to hold an important book. "Debbie Harry sang too. And Laurie Anderson," I bragged, trying to steer the conversation toward things I actually knew about. I could quote Blondie lyrics verbatim.

"Pretty cool," Schwartz said.

We were more like friends than teacher and student. I never asked him about his life. I didn't know if he had a wife or kids or was happy or frustrated with where he'd ended up in life, but none of my actual friends, the ones who were teenagers like me, ever spoke about those things either. Ricky, Adam, Erik—all their fathers, like mine, were gone, so we talked about whether *Evil Dead 2* merited a second viewing, or about old episodes of *Dr. Who* or *Monty Python*, or whether *Pleased to Meet Me* was as good as *Tim*.

And while I considered Schwartz "one of us," there were times when I simply couldn't make it to class the day after an evening in the city, seeing a rock show at the Ritz down on Eleventh Street or a weird play like Lydia Lunch's and Emilio Cubiero's *South of Your Border* at the New Theatre, which climaxes with Lydia naked, crucified, and urinating on the stage (in the lobby afterwards I saw my all-time-favorite MTV VJ Kevin Seal and bought a T-shirt that read, "Fuck the World—Feed Lydia Lunch."). When I got a B on my report card, I waited after class and confronted Schwartz about it. Every one of my reports had drawn an A– at the lowest. I was one of the only people who spoke up about the books we were assigned—probably one of the few who actually read them. I'd aced my fucking *Canterbury Tales*, which basically amounted to the painstaking memorization of the original Old English. I could have traveled back to the 1300s and ordered a pint. I didn't even question why a seventeen-year-old kid from Long Island needed to memorize Chaucer, what with AIDS and mutually assured nuclear destruction out there.

"If you're going to get an A, which is still possible, you're going to have to stop missing so many classes," he warned me. I wanted that A in English. I didn't care about Chemistry or Algebra or Trig, but I couldn't very well consider myself a real writer if I didn't ace AP English. I didn't know what being a "real writer" even entailed, but I knew more than ever that it was what I wanted to be and figured I'd know it once I got there. The late eighties had kicked off a new age of literary glamour not seen since the Lost Generation in the twenties or the new journalists in the sixties. An aspiring kid didn't need to look much further than the author's photo for Tama Janowitz's *Slaves of New York* to realize that these new writers were flamboyant, confident, and sexy as any rock-and-roll star. On nearly a full page, Janowitz lays herself out in red satin pajamas, her hair ratted up like she's just had really great sex, and she's half smiling as if to say, Yeah, I'm in pajamas. What are you going to do about it? What I was going to do about it was jack off. It seemed to be the default answer to any question between 1982 and 1988, when I first started having actual sex with other people. Brett Easton Ellis, Jay McInerney, Susan Minot—every month there seemed to be a younger, better-looking literary star sitting in the Odeon or on a banquette at Nell's, both places I'd never been. My banquette was still at the Sherwood Diner, where I'd sit with a vanilla milkshake and read about these supernovas in the pages of the *Village Voice, Interview, Paper,* and *Details.* The latter at the time was not the men's mag it is today but a downtown, club-centric magazine that even had a column featuring the sets of various "star" DJs. This was valuable when you are too young and too broke to actually go clubbing. I'd never been to Danceteria, but I knew they were spinning there ("Dominatrix Sleeps Tonight" by the Dominatrix and "All Night Passion" by Alisha). There was even a DJ who only spun tunes with "white" in the title: "White Punks on Dope," "White Horse," "White Rabbit," "White Wedding," "White Lines," "White Christmas," and The Beatles' entire "White Album."

After a point, the only books I read that weren't on Schwartz's reading list were written by Charles Bukowski. Following the death of Andy Warhol in

February 1987 and the breakup of The Smiths that summer, Bukowski filled the void in my hero worship. Morrissey (a militant vegetarian) would have detested the Los Angeles–based writer (a poet, novelist, and columnist) just for titling a book *Ham on Rye*, but by 1987, The Smiths, like my father, had let me down, and Bukowski, already a cult hero for two full decades, was having what would today be called "a moment."

Before I ever read a word of his writing, I came across an interview with him in *Film Threat*, one of my can't-miss-an-issue, favorite magazines. *Film Threat* ran features on Nick Zedd, Richard Kern, and that whole "Cinema of Transgression" underground Super 8 film scene, but also it functioned as a sort of thinking man's *Fangoria*, with articles on highbrow splatter films of the early David Cronenberg oeuvre. It had a glossy cover but newsprint-style pages and often ran its features in the cut-and-paste/Xerox style of the decade-old punk rock fanzines. The Bukowski interview (done by mail) was published that way. The editor, Chris Gore, asked the writer, "If these four jockeys were in a horse race, Charles Manson, Jesus Christ, Ronald Reagan, and Allen Ginsberg, who would you bet on?" I've been a journalist now for fifteen years, and that's still the best question I've ever heard any fellow journo ask a subject. Bukowski replied, "Christ, Ginsberg, Manson, and Reagan in that order."

Adam David already had several of Bukowski's books. Adam had dark hair and olive skin, deep brown eyes and a short, muscular body. He seemed like a young but fully grown man, whereas I still felt and looked like a gawky child. He always had the new issue of *Playboy* or *High Society* laying around. He played guitar, which was cool, even if it was more from the node-shredding Steve Vai school and less from the elegantly jangly style of R.E.M. and Guadalcanal Diary, which I much preferred. But the coolest thing about Adam was that he was way ahead of me when it came to "Buk."

Adam had an older friend who worked in the garment center in Manhattan, who'd turned him on to *Women* by reading aloud the passage where the narrator Hank's new girlfriend Lydia explains why she chose to be with him, despite his antisocial disposition: "Another thing I liked about your place was that it was filthy. . . . Dirty dishes, and a shit-ring in your toilet, and the crud in your bathtub. All those rusty razorblades laying around the bathroom sink. I knew that you would eat pussy." Adam found a copy of *Women* at Gotham Book Mart in midtown Manhattan on one of his own extracurricular sorties into the city and read it in a single day. Then he read it again. Then he let me read it.

Bukowski's books were published by Black Sparrow, a small press out of Santa Barbara, California, and each one was like a fetish object, with its pre-faded color scheme of blues, creams, and beiges, high-quality textured-paper covers, and carefully reproduced drawing by the author on the jacket. The first page of each edition encouraged collectors. The guy was prolific and produced about a book a year between 1960 and late 1987, when I discovered him. He really had a way with titles too, which seemed to make them all the more covetable: *Shakespeare Never Did This, You Get So Alone at Times that It Just Makes Sense, Mockingbird Wish Me Luck, South of No North*, and best of all, *Play the Piano Drunk/Like a Percussion Instrument/Until the Fingers Begin to Bleed a Bit*.

Bukowski tended to divide our little group of nerds who ate lunch in the art-supply room and wore Team Banzai pins and all-year-round overcoats. Ricky, for example, read to feed his imagination. He favored Harlan Ellison and Phillip K. Dick or Richard Miller's wild, cosmic alternate history *Snail*. Books were a different kind of companion for me. I read to "feel" writers and figure out how to be one myself. Bukowski, in the author's photo for his novel *Women*, looks like he's actually been with a few. This isn't to say that I shunned all of Ricky's books. When he recommended *Snail* to me, I loved it. I read Stephen King as well. *Christine* kept me up for three nights. But I wanted to fight and drink and fuck and be a man ... whatever that was.

Gotham Book Mart quickly became our main Bukowski supply post too, but sometimes we'd have to troll deep and often returned to the Island by train with nothing new to inspire. Later, when I started working in bookstores, we always kept the Bukowskis behind the register because they were the most frequently stolen. I understood why. There were many times I stole, or attempted to steal, them myself. They weren't cheap, and I didn't receive an allowance. Once my mother agreed to divorce my father and return to the Albert fold, her parents promised to provide my little sister and me with all our basic needs until and through college: food, shelter, school books. Everything else, from a pack of gum to a ticket on the Long Island Railroad to a copy of *Love Is a Dog from Hell*, I had to work for ... or find and gank. But it was worth the risk or brown bagging it for a week.

Bukowski swiftly put my father into practical context the way my rock-and-roll heroes just did not. Bukowski too was both appalled and strangely fascinated by his very macho pop (his novel *Ham on Rye* is dedicated to "all the fathers"). Suddenly, what seemed like a permanent and heavy resentment of my old man turned into secret and lasting gratitude: Thank you for being a fucked-up, absentee parent. You are excellent material. You are ... *material*. You're raw. I will use you from now on. You will fuel me. You ... are a gift.

Bukowski even made all those wasted hours I'd spent with the old man at the track whenever he'd managed to drag me there seem retroactively glamorous. The writer's alter ego, Henry Chinaski, was always winning and losing at the windows and processing the vicissitudes philosophically. I quickly began bragging to Adam about the hundreds of hours I'd spent walking around the concourse with my father, taking his cash and making bets for him at the window, eating greasy food, getting my boots shined, and pondering some particularly gruesome looking rail bird: dog-mauling victims, cancer patients still smoking, rat-faced children, men with enormous tits, and women with shrunken heads and waists that seemed to begin at the chin.

Browning's *Freaks*? Fellini's *Satyricon*. Woody's *Stardust Memories*. Forget about it. None of the images of human oddity from any of those films could beat any tri-state-area track back in the eighties. And yet, I began to appreciate the elegance too. Shoe-shine booths were disappearing. Smoke-free environments were expanding. The track was an old, vanishing world as the rest of the population bent lazily toward the casual. I even saw Cab Calloway there once, dressed in a three-piece suit and playing a hunch. For much of my adolescence, these degenerate gamblers had made me scared, confused, even angry, but now, post-Bukowski, I realized I'd amassed a lot of material and not a little cool too and hadn't even realized it. I didn't tell Adam about all the bitching and moaning I did there or how I'd sometimes face the opposite direction as the horses took off and made my father's fellow degenerate friends think I was a walking *mal de ojo* and cross themselves as I passed lest I fuck up every one of their tickets.

My mother and stepfather didn't really understand my fidelity to all things Bukowski.

At the very point in the mid-seventies when my parents moved from their small apartment in Far Rockaway, Queens (where I was born), to a big house in Lawrence, modular Formica furniture became very fashionable and almost immediately turned kitsch. During this short window, my mother seemed to buy all of her furniture. My bed, for example, resembled a large Lego piece, and the desk and tables had edges so sharp you could brain yourself in a William Holden–like fall. She was horrified when I launched a mission to swap out all the vestiges of this design proclivity and replace it with furniture purchased at the warehouse-sized Council Thrift on Central Avenue in Cedarhurst.

The thrift stores were amazing. I couldn't believe nobody wanted these old leather jackets, stiff like beef jerky and smelling like shellac and cologne, or the fraying, sun-bleached LPs that smelled like summer mold and sold for twenty-five cents each. I bought my own coffee mugs of thick porcelain, like old steakhouse sinks and toilets, and insisted on drinking out of them. I found wingtip shoes made out of plastic and ostrich and snake and wore those to school, where all the other kids, even Adam, wore K-Swiss sneakers or penny loafers. I pulled hand-knit, loose-loomed scarves in pale greens and blues from rolling canvas bins. I scoured the bookshelves and found mostly crap of the Harlequin romance and outmoded self-help variety, like *Games People Play*, but every once in a while unearthed a real discovery: a first edition of *Edie* or a perfectly preserved old *Peterson Guide* with its elegant illustrations of wood ducks and purple martins.

My mother came home from lunch with her girlfriends one afternoon to find the tacky, white wood folding chairs, the desk, and even the bed in the trash.

"What are you going to sleep on?" she asked.

I pointed to the mattress on the floor.

"No, no. Not in my house."

"Fine, then I'll get a futon." The *Village Voice* ran ads for futons. They were very chic at the time.

"What's a futon?"

"It's a Japanese bed."

"We're not buying you a Japanese bed."

"It folds up."

"I don't care what it does."

Bukowski called volumes of poetry "chapbooks," and so did I. He talked of "the novel" and I did as well. I sought out writers he endorsed and found some in the local Peninsula Public Library and others at St. Mark's Bookshop on trips into the city. Catullus, Hemingway, Li Po, de Maupassant, Pound, Tolstoy—he talked about them as if he knew them, even though they were long dead, and so did I. I did know them, anyway, as much as I knew myself. I started learning what writers drank. Faulkner drank mint juleps. William S. Burroughs drank vodka and Cokes. If there was a movie or a sitcom on TV about a writer, I was interested; even *Murder She Wrote*'s Jessica Fletcher held some mystique. I knew about their women. Every real writer had a muse, or a specter: June to Henry, Joan to Burroughs, Zelda to F. Scott. I had muse envy. I'd never had a girlfriend; not even when I was a kid and just holding someone's hands or sharing a couples-only skate would qualify. I was only ever alone and felt convinced that in order to be a real writer, I would soon have to lose not only my virginity but every trace of it. I'd have to fuck soon and make up for lost time with the same rapidity with which I could type. It was another reason why I suffered over those college essays. They were like flares shot up for my sexual rescue. "*Don't bother with the local girls,*" Graham Parker sang, and I didn't. They didn't bother with me either. I didn't even go to my senior prom. And yet, women meant everything. Once when Adam was over for dinner, we all started talking about our upcoming senior year at the academy and beyond: what we were going to do with our high school diplomas, where we were going to go to college, what kind of contribution would we make to the workforce and society in general.

"Marc doesn't know what he wants to be," my mother told Adam ruefully after he informed her that he was thinking about going into business for himself—making a lot of money fast and then figuring it all out at his leisure.

"Yes, I do," I corrected her. "I know exactly what I want to be."

"What?" she inquired hopefully.

"A womanizer."

Bukowski made us organize as far as our horniness went. We couldn't very well be disciples of his without plenty of naked women around. One afternoon Adam and I took the train in together and, once in the city, walked up from Penn Station to Times Square in a fit of horny exuberance. Times Square felt edgy at the time. You couldn't walk unmolested past the Port Authority. Nobody cleaned the streets. We could smell the rotting, acrid rubbish as soon we came out of the subway. It was hard to move an inch with any speed. Someone got in your way and forced you to sputter polite "No, no, that's okays" as you pushed your way free. Two teenaged boys, clearly off the train, were certainly conspicuous. We might as well have been carrying hot pretzels and counting the bills in our wallets. But we had nothing to hustle away. The crackheads weren't interested in our Charles Bukowski books, and the junkies couldn't even get up. We were too homely to be pimped out. Too restless to linger like marks in the arcades anyway. Too uncoordinated to break-dance. We were not interested in buying pot or coke or "what you need." Whatever money we had was reserved for the peep show. This was where the naked ladies were. Our destination was the neon-lit strip of theaters that catered at the time to horny teenagers, tourists, and lonely old men. I worried that someone I knew would catch me entering the Three Treats Theater, my aunt and uncle or cousins—but once inside I felt safe. It was dark and oddly quiet—like a library. Adam and I split up and each entered a glossy, black wood booth.

"What are the three treats?" I wondered.

"Think about it," he said.

I did.

"If you drop anything on the floor, don't pick it up," he warned me before I entered.

"Why? Oh. Okay."

I pushed four quarters into a brass slot, and the monolithic shade rose, revealing a zaftig black woman in a glossy red, wallpapered booth. She had on a complicated array of satin bows and leather buckles, which seemed odd considering her giant breasts and expansive ass were already fully exposed.

"You wanna feel me, baby?" she asked. There was a weariness in her voice that I initially found shocking but soon thought made perfect sense. How could you do this all day and not lose your joie de vivre. I'd never felt a naked breast before. I'd seen so many of them on cable TV and in the movies or in *Playboy*. I could identify Bo Derek's breasts from a breast police lineup. Barbi Benton's, Barbara Bach's, Barbara Carrera's too. All the *B* girls. Barbara Crampton stood high above all the other *B*'s. She appeared naked in a brief cameo in Brian DePalma's *Body Double*, and I preferred it to Frankie Goes to Hollywood's own cameo, even though I was a huge Frankie fan (I owned the "War: Hide Yourself" T-shirt). She's strapped to a table in Stuart Gordon's *Re-Animator* while a mad scientist's severed head (held in the hand's of her character's own zombified father) attempts to eat her pussy. Gordon's follow-up, *From Beyond*, was based, like *Re-Animator*, on an H. P. Lovecraft story (not that I read any Lovecraft either). In this one, Barbara falls under a mysterious sex spell that compels her to dress in bondage gear and straddle a sleeping, mutated Jeffrey Combs (who'd played Dr. Herbert West in the superior *Re-Animator*).

The thing that made Barbara Crampton special to us was that she seemed like she could actually act and got the joke. She appeared, for example, in a pictorial in the December 1986 issue of *Playboy*. I tried to ignore the extras in cheap werewolf and zombie costumes as I spent time with the edition, but in a way the monsters were part of the appeal. This was a nerd's goddess feeding the fan boys. The issue quotes Pauline Kael on Crampton's now legendary turn in *Re-Animator*: "Barbara Crampton, who's creamy pink all over, is at her loveliest when she's being defiled." I had no idea who Pauline Kael was at the time and had barely even heard of the *New Yorker*, but you couldn't convince me at seventeen that my nerd posse and I didn't have an intimate relationship with Barbara Crampton (whom Ricky simply called "Cramps," as if we all lunched together in the art room eating chicken nuggets and blasting *Candy Apple Grey* and *Hate Your Friends*). And yet, as familiar as Barbara Crampton seemed, as real as the emotions she stirred felt to me, I couldn't write about her. I needed to know what a woman felt like, smelled like, tasted like, and this desire lead me to a sticky booth in midtown, my fingertips stroking a pay-to-cum tit, my brain recording it all. As a writer, I'd be able to put that tit anywhere, I reasoned, even on the divine chest of "Cramps."

Only later, on the train home, did Adam explain that real breasts felt nothing like that.

"They weren't real?"

"No."

"Serious?"

Barbara Crampton's breasts were bona fide. She seemed even further away, and so did some sense of authenticity and achievement.

"Real tits feel like a bag of mice," he explained, sliding an Enrico Caruso pizza slice into his stubbly lips. What I lacked in tit connoisseurship I made up for in pizza expertise. Enrico Caruso was a favorite. It sold impossibly large and bland slices. It's like the whale shark of pizza—docile to the taste buds but massive.

"Mice?"

"Not mice. Newts."

"Newts." I made a mental note. "Bag of newts." It seemed implausible.

"Not newts."

I needed words. I needed accuracy. I needed tit help. A real woman who would stay, occasionally get naked, show me things, and help me write like a man.

"They're unwieldy? You're saying."

"Yes, exactly . . . unwieldy," Adam agreed. "Unwieldy. You have to really grab and hold them. And wield them. Didn't you feel how hard those fucking titties were?"

"Yeah."

"That's because they're plastic."

"Well then why'd we pay her?"

"I paid to see the pussy. You didn't?"

We'd already rented a kind of shitty film version of the Bukowski oeuvre called *Tales of Ordinary Madness*, starring Ben Gazzara as a less-than-convincing Buk. It's hard to fuck up Buk, and it's harder to fuck up Ben Gazzara (perfect as Cosmo Vitelli, the hero of John Cassavettes's *The Killing of a Chinese Bookie* and, decades later, the swaggering Jackie Treehorn in *The Big Lebowski*), but this one managed to do both. We didn't have high hopes for *Barfly*. Still, the fact that Bukowski himself was involved in this production and Mickey Rourke, the "pope" himself, was cast in the lead helped us lift them. When we finally saw the film at the Lynbrook theater in the late fall of 1987, it was better than either of us ever imagined it could be. Having never been to Los Angeles (or anywhere else), I just assumed it was balmy and swampy all the time, like Florida usually was when my mother, stepfather, sister, and I visited in the summers, but the blue-lit LA of *Barfly* was a revelation. In one scene Rourke gets up in the middle of the night and rubs his body to shake off the cold. He's wearing his boxers, dirty socks, and a thin white T-shirt. He sits down at the coffee table and starts scribbling out a poem with a worn-down yellow pencil. I'd never expected grace to look like this, but I finally understood that this is exactly what it is, and all it ever is: quiet moments of reflection and truth and holy rebellion.

Midway through the film, Rourke's Chinaski hooks up with Faye Dunaway's Wanda, a "distressed goddess." I made a mental note in the dark: required, one distressed goddess. Nobody else will go near Wanda, not even Buk himself (who appears in a cameo in this scene). The bartender tells Chinaski that it's because she's crazy, which only makes him want her more. When they do get together, after picking ears of green corn then fleeing the cops, she warns him, "I don't want to fall in love," and he replies, "Don't worry, nobody's ever loved me yet." In that moment, my template for the kind of relationships I would seek was formed. Each time we went back to see *Barfly*, we seemed to be the only pair in the aisles. Why couldn't everyone see how this movie was just so . . . correct? Why were they all abuzz about the glossy, big-budget *Fatal Attraction*?

"Wrong Island is so lame," I explained it away. I had no idea how "Wrong Island" I still was until I met Sara Vega.

I figured I had all the right clothes and books, records and shoes, but once I started interviewing for college, I quickly realized I only had the right look for a Long Island virgin kid with city hours. I was far from sophisticated, more like Bette Davis's frumpy, un-plucked Charlotte Vale in *Now, Voyager*. If I had my own version of Claude Rains's Dr. Jaquith, it was Sara Vega, who worked in the admissions department at Bennington College, founded in 1932 as a liberal arts school for girls. Carol Channing, the ageless stage star of *Hello, Dolly!* fame, was one of those first creatively inclined ladies. In a documentary made about her life nearly seventy years later, she claimed that it had appealed to her because it was only "two hours from Broadway," and it was true. It was surrounded by the Green Mountains of southern Vermont but somehow cosmopolitan. You could still smell the City somehow through all that wood smoke and cold, clean air. Bennington went coed in 1969, the year of my birth, and by 1988, it was notorious for a half dozen reasons, none of which frightened me. In *Now, Voyager*, as I noted after a recent screening, Dr. Jaquith is even stationed in Vermont as well, and once he liberates Charlotte from her domineering mother, she quickly becomes a chic and charming force. "People walk along the road," the suave Jaquith explains to the initially nervous girl. "They come to a fork in the road. They're confused. They don't know which way to take it. I just put up a signpost. 'Not that way. This way!'" Bennington was my "Not that way. This way," and I never looked back.

We met in a suite at Le Parker Meridien in Midtown. Her hair was straight and black. Her eyes seemed black as well, and they looked me over in a way that frightened and excited me. She spoke calmly and slowly.

"What do you hope to get out of Bennington?" she asked, and the wool that covered her crossed her legs seemed to fall elegantly from her tan skin, revealing a bare ankle. Her suit seemed cut for a slim man, and she wore no socks under her black, oil-treated Dr. Martens shoes. I shifted, one hand buried under a butt cheek.

"Well . . . I'd like to learn about poetry? And meet people?"

Every statement came out in question form, and I wished I hadn't shaved that morning. Sometimes I didn't, when I was hoping to affect a gruff, Bukowskian poet pose.

"I don't currently know any other poets? On Long Island? It'd be good to be able to talk to someone, more than one person maybe? About poetry?"

"What do your friends talk about now?"

"Oh, I don't have any." It wasn't true, but at least it was a declaration.

I smiled, and so did she, both of us relieved that I'd found a new conversational dimension to explore.

"I have a lot of friends. I'm just sick of them."

Ricky was already at NYU film school. He'd made it. He lived in the Village. At the time, that was success in and of itself—having a place in the city. He didn't need to make a film at all as far as I was concerned. He could have just walked around Bleecker Street with a tripod, and I would have held him way above me, convinced he was going to be the next Spike Lee or Jim Jarmusch. Adam had been accepted to Vassar. I was girding myself against losing the only friends I actually had and ending up entirely alone and, worse, stuck on the Island with my mother and stepfather, who watched the feisty local anchors Jack Cafferty and Sue Simmons on the nightly news while they ate dinner in lieu of having a conversation. I removed my hand from under my rump and fiddled with my book bag.

"What are you reading?" she asked.

I reached into my bag and pulled out a copy of *Ask the Dust* by John Fante. She didn't seem impressed.

"Do you know Fante?" She nodded as if to say, "He's been processed and rejected."

"I just finished Celine?" I was back on the bad punctuation.

"*Death on the Installment Plan*," she said, as if I was waving a lottery ticket and insisting I had lucky numbers. "Of course you did."

Still, I thought the interview went pretty well. I even detected some kind of physical attraction between us but reminded myself that this could not have possibly been the case at that time. Girls didn't like me. I liked girls. Girls responded with indifference. This was intractable, wasn't it?

"Here, why don't you try this instead?" she asked and handed me a paperback on my way out. I wanted to ask, "When will I return it to you?" but luckily could not form the words and absorb the image on the cover of the book at the same time. The cover was black and white, and there was a photo of a kind of fetish on it: a creepy plaster statue of a man with scraped away skin, like those structures Christopher Lee built in *The Wicker Man.*

"Your 'black' essay made me think of it. You can give it to me the next time I see you."

As part of my application, I'd also submitted an essay about why I wear "black on the outside," a reference to the oft-quoted lyric in The Smiths song "Unloveable" (*"because black is how I feel on the inside,"* being the answer). I had no idea if I was ever going to see this person again, but clearly she had plans for me.

The book was titled *Les Chants de Maldoror* by Comte de Lautreamont. Lautreamont had all the qualifications that it usually took to become one of my best friends: He was a writer; he was dead. Instead, he became the first to whom I refused admittance to the private fraternity of ghosts and icons I kept in my bedroom. Maybe it was because she'd forced him on me and I wasn't allowed to discover him myself. Everybody wants to discover their heroes, not have them handed down by an older brother or, in this case, a sexy twenty-three-year-old woman in black.

I was a prude, and the audacious acts described in the book worried me, even if they were clearly allegorical and not (I hoped) instructional. "One should let one's fingernails grow for fifteen days," he writes. "O, how sweet it is to snatch some child brutally from his bed." This child, a baby with "wide eyes" and a bare "upper lip," is mutilated in one scene. Is that what they do up there in Bennington? Are they a bunch of baby-snatching vampires? And if so, is that . . . like . . . a thing to be? I interviewed with a few other schools similar in style to Bennington—Sarah Lawrence, Bard, Hampshire, all the big New England liberal arts colleges—but I kept thinking about Sara Vega, daydreaming through math class about her scary, black eyes. My math teachers treated me like a subnormal. The headmaster punished me for my dress-code violations. My parents reacted with alarm and selfish concern. Sara treated me like an artist. About a week later, I followed up our initial meeting with a phone call to arrange a tour of the Bennington campus.

While she would soon come to regret it, at the time, my mother was excited by the notion of my attending an art college. I could tell by the way she'd eagerly drive me to the art store for canvases and oil paint that she missed that element in her life. Now here was her chance to absorb some of that energy once again. We drove up to Bennington together in her white Mercedes. It was the day after the pop singer Andy Gibb died. Divine died that same week in Los Angeles, which made me much more sad. John Waters's Dreamland Studios crew out of Baltimore were just one short rung under the Warhol Factory crew as far as the icons of my early teens went. I loved both Waters's books, his memoir, *Shock Value*, and his collected essays, *Crackpot*. One was pink, the other green, and I scarfed them like candy.

Sara Vega met us at the end of College Drive by the security check-in booth and instructed my mother about where to park. As she dealt with the car, I followed Sara into her small, book-lined office. There was a steaming cup of black tea on her desk, and everything was arranged fastidiously. There were faded, sepia-tone photos in gold frames. Rosaries hung on hooks, purple and pink glass beads reflecting the sun that streamed in through the windowpane. It smelled like books and records, if that was possible, that year-round summer smell of mold and dust . . . the way thrift stores smell. Things had happened here. Great thoughts and ideas had been shared. History had gone on, and traces of it remained.

"How did you like *Maldoror*?"

I shrugged and searched the back of my mouth for words, but nothing came out except, "Cool."

I reached into my bag and handed the book back to her. She placed it on the desk next to the tea, picked up the cup, took a sip, and rested the base of the mug on top of the book. She reached up to the shelf and pulled down another book, a slimmer volume. There was a photo of a big, brown eyeball on the jacket sleeve.

The Story of the Eye, she said.

"Bataille?" I was hoping I'd pronounced his name correctly.

"Yes. Bataille."

Whew, I thought. At least this book was thin. I wondered if she was going to hand me a book every time I saw her, like an alternative curriculum. Maybe I didn't need to go to college after all; I could just continue to visit Sara Vega and flirt and read.

"Take a look," she said, pulling a black shawl across her bony shoulders. "You can read it on the drive back. But you might not want to in front of your mother. Or while eating eggs."

"Why? Is it dirty?" I wondered hopefully. She was definitely flirting with me now. It wasn't that I was any more confident than I'd been when we first met; she had simply stopped trying to hide it. *The Story of the Eye* turned out to be sufficiently dirty. "Milk is for the pussy. . . . Do you dare me to sit in the saucer?"

I wondered what the old man would think if he caught me reading it. Once again, I sort of hated a book she'd given me. And once again, I was thrilled to have it.

Before I left to find my mother and our tour guide, Sara pulled me closer and casually let me know that I'd been formally accepted to Bennington College. I could smell the tea herbs on her tongue, alive with natural medicine. I bit my lower lip so that I wouldn't start giggling and did my best to play it cool as she opened her desk drawer and handed me a letter on college stationary that stated as much. It was dated that same day, March 11, 1988.

Dear Marc
I am pleased to offer you a place in the Bennington College class of 1992. Congratulations.

It was from the Director of the Admissions Department, Sara's boss.

The admissions committee enjoyed reading your application. As you said in your interview, you have an unusual way of looking at things. Just as Kafka let his readers into his "world," we hope that you will do the same. We are confident that you will find Bennington's environment conducive to your needs and look forward to seeing the world that unfolds in your writing.

I looked up at Sara. Was this it?

"Don't tell your mother yet. Have a look around. See if it's really for you."

She picked up her teacup, tapped the *Maldoror* paperback, and winked at me. This wasn't how I thought it would be at all. And it wasn't how my college advisor said it would go either.

"You're supposed to get a letter in the goddamn mail!" I wanted to complain. I was a little disappointed. Suspense was a huge part of the whole getting-into-college pageant. Every day the halls would be abuzz with gossip about who got in where? Who was rejected where else? Who made the Ivy League? who made State? This is why they prepped us a year in advance: the stacks of applications, the essay, the huddles with advisors, the meet-and-greets in the city. You were supposed to have a good think and decide which place was for you. But Sara Vega's will was stronger than mine, and I felt I could resist or refuse her power of sexual suggestion and intellectual direction. Those papers were orders. I got the sense that if I chose a different school, nobody would ever hand me another dirty book again.

My student tour guide was clean-cut enough to put my mother at ease until he started barking. She'd been marveling at the charming New England feel of the place, the gray sky, full of chimneys and trees and no airplanes, only Gothic trees, centuries old, shedding dry burnt orange and deep green and warm yellow leaves, the looming Green Mountains out past the "End of the World," where the long, wide Commons Lawn finally bowed and a pile of rocks suggested a steep cliff beyond. There was no cliff, but there sure was a leap and I was ready to make it.

"Arf! Grumph! Grrrr! Helen Frankenthaler. Romph!"

"Are you alright?" my mother asked the guide.

He explained, very sweetly, that he did not have Tourette's but rather had just seen the Swedish film *My Life as a Dog* on video and couldn't stop imitating Ingemar, its sullen, cow-licked boy lead.

"Arf. Grarph! Milford Graves. Wowrf!"

"Did you like the film?" my mother asked politely.

"Ramph! Arrrrrf! Rowrrrrr! Martha Graham. Ruff!"

"I haven't seen it yet."

"Definitely rent it."

I promised I would. I loved that everyone here had a book or a film to share.

"If you took five hundred students from the five hundred different schools throughout the country, throughout the world, the Bennington student would emerge as the most creative, most interesting, and most fun member of each new student body. So imagine the concentration of all those people on one campus," the tour guide said. The speech sounded prepared and, under the circumstances, superfluous. I was already in. I just needed the okay from my mother and grandparents, who would be footing the bill, per the details of the divorce pact.

"Oh, and don't worry about Brett Ellis," the guide said in a whisper. He was off script now. "That's a total fiction."

"Who's Brett Ellis?" my mother asked.

Brett Easton Ellis, one of the new breed of writers I spoke of earlier, the ones who made fiction feel glamorous again, had graduated from Bennington two years earlier. Ellis had recently published *The Rules of Attraction*, which was the follow-up to his debut novel *Less Than Zero*, written while he was still a student. Ellis probably should have loomed much larger in my life than he did at the time. I'd certainly read and enjoyed *Less Than Zero*, around the same time I'd read *Bright Lights, Big City* and *Slaves of New York* but didn't let it into my heart as I did so many other works because it was recommended to me by my stepfather, whom I detested at the time. I used to pray that he'd be taken by a shark when he swam in the Atlantic every week, a small flotation device strapped to his ankle. That wasn't Sara Vega handing over a paperback;

that was, to me, the Antichrist saying, "Hey, man, have a look at this." I've come, over the years, to love the guy and consider him as much of a father, if not more, as my biological dad, but in the mid-eighties, he was just the guy who'd moved in and started fucking my mom, walking around naked, and bossing me around. He was a high school teacher over in Seaford, Long Island, and I guess someone out there had mentioned the book. As a way of "relating" to me, and perhaps getting me to stop keying his silver Corvette Stingray with the T-top roof, he'd purchased me a copy.

Had it come from anyone else, and perhaps after I discovered Bukowski and later Fante, Nathanael West, Didion, and all the other great Pacific Coast voices, I may have been too intimidated even to attend Bennington, where Ellis had studied and written and from which he'd launched himself into the culture.

By early September 1988, I'd packed up my books, notebooks, typewriter, music (cassettes in a case on the floor of the passenger side, CDs in a box in the hatchback), black sweaters, and suits and left home. I drove up in my little red Toyota, and by the time I crossed the state line into Vermont, the local rock station came in clean and static-free. Michelle Shocked was singing about being *"anchored down in Anchorage."* After that, Bruce Cockburn declared that if he had a rocket launcher, he would make somebody pay. I never liked either song, but both never sounded better. I was open to anything.

Still, there were strange bits to work myself through. For example, I'd never lived with anyone before. Now I had to share a room with a total stranger. All my books and cassettes and videotapes were stacked neatly next to someone else's stuff. My clothes were hung up in the closet next to someone else's fashion statements. And this person, named Dan Lehman, for some reason felt the need to put the one sheet of the movie version of *Less Than Zero* on the wall, so now it spoke for me too. I'd managed to see the film in the fall of 1987 between repeat *Barfly* viewings and left the theater strangely unmoved. Anyone entering our new room would think I had loved the book. I reminded myself that the soundtrack was excellent, especially Public Enemy's "Bring the Noise" and LL Cool J's "Going Back to Cali." It made being culturally grafted to an utter stranger a little more bearable.

Every freshman, I would soon discover, brought some kind of poster up there for the wall as a sort of nametag or orientation banner: Hello, I am ... "My Robert Doisneau 'kiss' poster says I would like to fall in love."

"My Ansel Adams oak tree says I am in touch with the Earth and have weed. Or I would like some weed, please."

"My *Dali Atomicus* says you will never, ever truly figure me out."

I had no posters. Franklin, where Dan and I lived, was a "quiet house." There were quiet houses, semi-quiet houses, loud houses, and party houses on campus. The quiet houses weren't exactly like libraries or churches, but it was where the serious students were placed, the ones who read and wrote a lot. Booth House was the notorious party house, full of equally intense, creative types but also proto-Klebold/Harris potential psychos who wore real combat boots (not Doc Martens) and made their own Dungeon and Dragons weapons out of rebar. They listened to Ministry, and not the early disco Ministry either. *The Land of Rape and Honey* had just come out and seemed to throb out of Booth's windows all night long, when *Master of Puppets* by Metallica wasn't. Dan was just thrilled that Franklin was mentioned in *The Rules of Attraction*. While the school in Ellis's book is called Camden, probably for legal reasons, all the student housing is the same, as are some of the class buildings and even the recurring parties and off-campus stops like the supermarket Price Chopper. If you were so inclined, you could actually imagine yourself entering the book and living as a character in it. This was no different from how I treated my Bukowski books, but I didn't behave like a surly drunken poet in actual Los Angeles flophouses, and there's the difference. Dan had made a pilgrimage to "Camden."

Dan, with his long, handsome, slightly horsey face, long but clean hair, and pronounced Adam's apple, was from Indiana. He wore Ralph Lauren head to toe. He'd worked for years in the Polo outlet in Indianapolis, and his relationship with Ralph was similar to my relationship with the Warhol and Waters stars I'd idolized, as well as with Morrissey or Bukowski. Ralph was his North Star.

"When does the sex start?" Dan asked as he watched me unpack and waited for me to accompany him to the bonfire that was scheduled to take place at the "End of the World" after sundown. Dan didn't mean sex with me, although for a second, I'd worried just that. I probably knew a dozen homosexuals already, but didn't *know* I knew them. Nobody came out in high school, not to me anyway. But within the first week at Bennington, it seemed to happen hourly.

"Marc, I have to tell you something, and it's really hard."

"Okay . . ."

"I'm gay."

"Okay . . ."

"You're the first person I'm telling." This was almost never true. "Please don't tell anyone."

"Yeah. Don't worry. So . . . what . . . do I do now?"

Were we supposed to kiss? Dance? Hug? Shake hands? It was always an anticlimax. I was jealous. I wished I was gay, the same way that I wished I was Irish Catholic. Gay kids were just braver somehow, especially the ones from the Midwest and the South who had fought their way out. Maybe I'd have had more respect for some of my high school peers on the equally provincial Island if I'd known they were in the closet too, but I was pretty much in the dark with the gay-dar. I thought John Waters was straight.

Dan meant sex in the "when does it get like the book" sense? I had no clue. The sex had never started for me, and the gun had gone off years earlier. Was it supposed to start now? Was I even dressed for it? My hair was clean and blown up into a quiff. I wore wire-rimmed glasses, a maroon wool turtleneck, and a vintage gray flannel suit. Not too sexy. Pretty clean-cut. I figured this was the way a college student dressed. I was unsure just how or when a college student undressed. I'd brought a box of condoms with me, along with all the cold-weather sweaters, but I'd had them literally since my bar mitzvah. Were they even any good?

Once the "sex started," the question of condom durability, as the Reverend Jesse Jackson said when he hosted *Saturday Night Live* four years previously, "was moot." I'm sure that there were many responsible Bennington students who practiced safe sex. They just didn't practice much of it with me. Or rather, I didn't with them, and very few ever suggested I start. If I have any defense, it's that I simply had no idea what I was doing in that area. The sex started fast and never stopped. At Bennington, the writer was the short stop who did get blown. Discounting some lawn Frisbee or the smashing of teed-up Rolling Rock bottles, sports didn't count for shit. Going from the Five Towns to Bennington, sexually speaking, was like not knowing how to swim and being instructed by getting thrown over the side of an ocean liner at night rather than led by a lifeguard into the shallow end of a chlorinated pool in your water wings. Superstition played into it as well. Even after the tenth or eleventh fellow freshman I fucked that fall, I hesitated to stop the proceedings in order to put one on, lest all the sexual attention be proven a fluke and I suddenly woke up in my old bed at my mother's house a virgin. Guilty, I collected "Jimmy hats" from the health services office in the Commons building. I kept them in my wallet. I kept them under the mattress. I kept them in my toiletry kit. I kept them in cool, dry places. But there they remained. It was as if the AIDS crisis weren't going on, and people weren't dying from the big disease with the little name. I treated the crisis like President Reagan initially treated the crisis: denial, denial, denial. I knew it was out there. And if you contracted it, you got sores, and you got pneumonia and fever, and you most likely died young and in agony. And this discouraged almost nobody I knew. There were Bennington students at the time who were members of ACT UP. It's not like the risks were not apparent to me. Maybe many of us just felt invulnerable, secluded by all those Green Mountains, Aurora Borealis overhead, *The Dark Side of the Moon* booming out of some Marshall guitar amp that had been pushed to the open living room window of one of the loud houses, all the animals in the woods singing along.

"Us . . . and them . . ."

I tried to convince myself that bad things like AIDS happened to "them." It seemed about right after someone handed me a joint of strong hippie weed and put on a copy of *A Love Supreme*, an album I'd never heard, one my uncle Ed hadn't supplied me with. The Coltrane, the smell of burning leaves in the air, the chill, the constellations, maybe a few beers, a hit of mellow gel acid or a line of cocaine, and take off the Coltrane and put on *Rattle and Hum*. That long fade-out on "All I Want Is You." It suggested angels watching overhead. Sure, there were a few reminders that all was not well out there in the real world. I woke up one morning after one clinch with a purple blotch on my neck. I didn't know where it could have come from, and stepping into the bathroom and catching it in the mirror was like touching a live wire.

"Oh my god, is that . . ." I didn't even dare say the word "lesion" or "sarcoma." I couldn't. It turned out, of course, to be nothing more than a hickey brought on by some sloppy necking in a toilet stall with a dance major, but I didn't deduce as much immediately because of the hangover and the guilt over getting out of Long Island, of making it here and getting to live here, surrounded by artists and misfits just like me. The other shoe was going to drop, wasn't it? In the form of plague? I mean, I wasn't even really studying hard. I deserved what I got. I can't count how many last wills and testaments I wrote out, as if there were anything to leave behind.

> *To my mother, I leave my poetry. To my sister Nicole, I bequeath my copy of* Shooting Rubberbands at the Stars.

But wasn't this school? The point was to learn how to be an idiot and perhaps how to be a better idiot along the way if not less of one. I already knew my rock and roll, but sex? It was a process. Drugs too. I made a point to try every drug once in order to figure out what I liked and what I didn't. I'd never done anything, so I was a tabula rasa as far as my nervous system went.

Pot was perfect.

Acid? Depends. There were the aforementioned mellow gels that the Zappa-heads in the more modern houses beyond the Commons lawn sold while deconstructing *Over-nite Sensations* and *Apostrophe*. Then there was the strychnine-soaked, hell-trip kind that led to the formation of temporary cults and six-in-the-morning screenings of *Faces of Death*, or a videotape of disgraced Pennsylvania politician R. Budd Dwyer, shooting himself in the mouth on live TV over and over again, and the pondering of how you were ever going to get through the next sixty years on this violent planet and eternity after that.

Speed: see bad acid above. Plus, we couldn't get speed on the East Coast.

Cocaine: I liked the numb, ready-for-action feeling that took over immediately. The first time I snorted coke was with a fellow student named Charles Harbin. We assumed a position that I would later make twenty-five thousand times over the next twenty years: huddled around a mirror in an enclosed space, chattering like gibbons. When Charles tried to hang the mirror up again, he couldn't find the hook, and it fell on my skull. I didn't feel a thing. I liked coke. Years later, I heard that Charles was hit by a car while crossing the street in Atlanta, where he was a teacher. I couldn't imagine him dead, but then I couldn't imagine him forty and teaching either. When I knew him, he was a white Rasta kid in a knit red, yellow, and green beret. His greatest hero was Eazy E.

Heroin: This was still the eighties. Nobody spoke of it; nobody had it. *Yet.*

Day in and out, whiskey and beer were more than enough to enable me to nourish my long-in-the-works writer identity. The constant altering of the senses literally changed my face. Not only would I pose in the cafeteria or at parties; I posed when I was alone. I'd developed a mirror tick, which I still have. I'd stand for an extended period, high, in front of the mirror and squint my eyes until I could see just the raw outline of my facial features and the crown of hair on my head, like a punk rock cartoon. That person was the one I had to become. That was Marc Spitz . . . real writer. If I opened my eyes wide, I'd get a good look at myself, and a voice in my head would almost surely ask, "Really?" The trick was to achieve permanent squint. Shades helped. I started wearing them everywhere—big, black "you can't reach me" specs. "You can't tell me I ain't who I'm pretending to be here."

Nobody showered much either. It was cool to be dirty. There were children of bank presidents who dressed like Mike Watt (both the young men and women). A good Long Island boy underneath, I always changed my socks and underwear and T-shirt, but my hair, which I had shampooed every day before, grew long and greasy. Wearing the same clothes every day allowed us to focus our energies on art. It was like that scene in the Cronenberg remake of *The Fly* where Jeff Goldblum's Seth Brundle shows Geena Davis his closet full of five identical sets of clothing. "I learned it from Einstein," he says. "This way I don't have to expend any thought about what I'm going to wear. I just grab the next one on the rack." I wonder if Einstein changed his T-shirts, socks, and underwear.

CHAPTER 3

"I might look like Robert *Frost*, but I feel just like Jesse James," I muttered as I threw my cigarette on the hard grass and pushed the flame out with my new pointy, black Cuban boots, purchased from the Salvation Army in Bennington and a half size too small, but I didn't care. They'd break for me. I'd mold them, and everything else, to my vision. It was of course—and, at nineteen, could only ever be—a flawed vision. For instance, I didn't know that the actual Bob Dylan lyric named Robert Ford, another outlaw who shot James in the back like a coward. I'd misheard the lyric and assumed Dylan was saying that he looked sensitive and bookish—how I imagined Frost, the lauded poet—but inside he was a bad mother not to be fucked with. Frost is buried at Bennington, and some students visited his grave to pay their respects and stare in awe. I visited it to piss on it. By the end of my first semester, I'd also worked a few bloody-minded beliefs into my brain, all of which I was willing to defend with my fists. I could not be told differently. The one that had brought me to Robert Frost's grave was that a real artist had to hate all art.

Let me say that again for proper stupidity-emphasis: I began to believe that a real artist had to hate nearly all other artists. And all art. There were exceptions, I wasn't going to chuck out Dylan or Bukowski just yet. If anything the otherwise blanket dismissal of most other writers (great writers, singer, painters) made the ones I kept that much more precious. Bukowski himself did this and as I started to assemble a galaxy of my own, with a taxonomy that made sense for my new life (person suddenly getting laid a lot and actually being taken seriously by a few teachers and peers), a lot of great writers had to go. Frost was one of them. Wallace Stevens was another. William Carlos Williams. All the poets born before Allen Ginsberg and Gregory Corso. When I was in high school out in the culturally fallow Five Towns, anyone remotely arty, even a dude with an earring or a That Petrol Emotion record, was an instant fellow traveler. Now he or she was a nuisance at best and a threat at worst.

Most of these new, foggy notions came to me when I was high on hash. When waiting for the lump of hash to glow orange on the pin and fill the stolen cafeteria glass with smoke, it was useful to pretend that I was a sickly, opiate-consuming poet, almost feminine in my pale beauty. I wore thrift-picked velvet coats with moths in the pockets and faded elbows and missing buttons. I grew stubble and allowed my finger nails to get dirty with charcoal and liked the looks of them smeared with ink. Sometimes I smeared the ink on my face. I was a poet. High. In nature.

One day, I wrote, "'All writing is pigshit.' —A. Artaud," on my notebook and made sure it was well within the vision field of my fellow students as I took my seat in poetry workshop. Not that this statement really fazed anyone. It was a student body that dealt in absolutes; there were literally hundreds of similarly crackpot, bloody-minded opinions about art and culture at work all around me. Even the teachers would not be moved. Alvin Feinman, my poetry instructor, who smoked in class and had giant choppers the size and shade of foam-rubber earplugs, was lecturing us one afternoon and said, "And here in this stanza he is talking about the most beautiful music in history. Now what is the most beautiful music in history? Anyone?"

Nobody volunteered an answer. We all sensed this was a trap. I thought, well, "Waterloo Sunset" by The Kinks if you ask me. "Walk Away Renée," perhaps. He *was* asking me. But I knew I had the wrong answer and kept quiet.

"Well, it's Mozart," Feinman, the old tortoise, wheezed, answering his own question for us and stubbing out his cigarette. He got up to open the large barn window. Some students wrote "Mozart" in their books. I stared out at the trees as the sound of farm equipment motors buzzed in the distance—paths cut, fields plowed for future harvests. It felt good that I was dealing with abso-lutes and that I was collecting my own. My poems had titles like "Blues from a Gargoyle," "Weasel," "Blight," "Kiosk," and "Northern Sleepy Blues."

"*How cruel to dream you are in love/And wake to find your mate unborn.*" It's basically the theme of "I Had Too Much to Dream Last Night" by The Elec-tric Prunes without the style or, if you prefer, "Undercover Angel" by Alan O'Day without the panache. They should have taken me somewhere and caned me.

"All writing is pigshit." At the time, mine certainly was. Still, the look of poems on a page excited me. And I was improving. One had to in such a competitive microcosm where talent was sexual and social currency. Feinman taught me where the commas went and what they meant, which gave me a little more confidence. I even wrote a poem about Artaud. I liked that he was handsome and ended up in the madhouse. If you're going to go mad, you should really be good-looking. I never read a single line of Antonin Artaud's other writing. I don't even know where the "All writing is pigshit" line appears in context. I just liked the cut of Antonin Artaud's suit, his hair, his scowl, his jawline, his loco stare, and his name. I liked that Bauhaus wrote a song about him. As I suspected with Mr. Schwartz back in high school, when I'd implied that I'd read *Naked Lunch*, I realized that even at the college level (the Bennington College level anyway) reading might not be necessary, even if a paper was due. I once got a stellar comment on Andre Bely's *Petersberg* without ever cracking it. I wrote about how I imagined *Petersberg* to be, given a picture I found of Bely smoking a cigarette in a tweed coat. I know today that a real writer must read, and read daily. It's sunk in, but as I was figuring out my pose, I felt that in order to have my own voice, I couldn't read a thing that anybody else had put out there, lest any of their style should bleed in—this, of course, while trying to act and dress as much like my favorite writers as possible. At the time, the prince of this lot was the orange-haired, lanky poet, diarist, and bandleader Jim Carroll. Carroll's *Catholic Boy* album was never too far from the CD player. I'd found a used copy at the "cool" record store in town, as opposed to the corporate one on Main Street, where the clerk would play R.E.M.'s new *Green* nonstop. Actually that guy was pretty cool too, and at least he was playing R.E.M. and not Britny Fox. I still have a soft spot for *Green*, even though some consider it the line in the sand between the classic "old" band and what would soon become a distressing stadium attraction. I started talking in a drawl even when I wasn't high, slowing my phrasing to match what I gathered to be Carroll's arresting, narcotized, New York–down meter.

"Yeah, heyyyy, let me try some of that there . . . whazzat, tem-payyyyy? Coool. And I'll take, lemme take a potatowwwww. Yeah. Alright. Potatoes!"

Catholic Boy was already about a decade old but obscure enough to have a sort of permanent newness, to be one of those "What do you mean you haven't heard . . ." icebreaker albums). The immortal "People Who Died" and "It's Too Late" (*"to fall in love with Sharon Tate"*) were the best-known tracks (Carroll's band performed the latter in the James Spader movie *Tuff Turf*). My favorite track was "Crow," which was about Patti Smith, whom Carroll had briefly dated (she is rumored to be the woman who brings him chocolate ice and soothes his junkie pains in the first bit of Carroll's collection *Forced Entries*, which had become one of my favorite books). The lyrics described two young, skinny, glowing poets living together in the Chelsea Hotel just before they made it as famous artists. I played it over and over. The Chelsea Hotel, the Gothic structure on West Twenty-third Street, was at the time already one hundred years old. I'd passed it a few times but never dared go in, even though there wasn't a doorman or any real security by day. I just didn't feel ready. Now, with a semester's worth of studying poetry, a head full of things real women had said to me while naked, and a totally new wardrobe that included no maroon turtlenecks, it was go time. Wintertime was coming, and so was Bennington's sleeper semester, the nonresidential, two-month period known as Field Work Term. February and March are too cold to fuck, make art, and drink from kegs apparently, so they clear out the student body not working on a thesis project and send us out into the cities to get jobs in our chosen field. We actually got graded on these ventures, but then all Bennington grades came in the form of paragraphs, not numbers or letters. Field Work Term, what a racket. Still, knowing I had no choice, there was only one place in the universe that was going to keep whatever this was that I was becoming warm until spring. *"You cover me with blankets in the Chelsea Hotel lobby,"* Carroll sang. But if I had my way, the whole Chelsea Hotel would be my blanket.

For my first field work experience, I'd applied for a job as the assistant to the curator of The Kitchen, which was also in Chelsea, just off the river. I was a little ahead of the game as I already knew what The Kitchen was about, thanks to the *Village Voice,* which covered many of the future art, theater, and culture stars who had emerged from the collective at one point or another since it was founded in the early seventies: Eric Bogosian, Laurie Anderson, Cindy Sherman, Spalding Gray, Diamanda Galas, and Arto Lindsay of the great No Wave band DNA. The Kitchen was a raw space, a venue where you could show off, only I'd be presenting nothing. I'd spend two cold winter months assisting other artists as they expressed themselves—already famous fucks too. What a drag at nineteen when you are about ready to burst with ambition. Suddenly you have to get out of the way of Karen Finley while she screams up all the attention in the room? At least there was the Chelsea Hotel. Just living there, I reasoned, would put me closer to being one of the people who got ushered into The Kitchen by gushing employees. I didn't get off Long Island to be one of the gushers.

My mother's parents, who were, as promised, paying for my Bennington education, weren't entirely sold on my becoming a professional writer to begin with, much less one living in Bohemian squalor in the Chelsea Hotel. Writing wasn't "work" to them. Lifting things was work. Selling things was work. Getting out of the shtetl and onto the steamship, landing on the Lower East Side, peddling dry goods, getting a piece of New York with the Italians and the Irish and the Chinese and the African Americans—that was work. They'd been through the Great Depression. "Work" wasn't writing bad poems about

Boho women and graveyards and hoping some quarterly would publish one for $5 to be spent on Strawberry Hill wine and Marlboros and maybe a chicken-flavored Cup O' Noodles with the little dead peas and carrot chips that came to life when you heated them up. Convincing my generous but thrifty grandparents that a winter stay at the Chelsea would technically qualify as the education they'd promised to provide was a feat.

After a few beers for courage, I shut the door of the phone booth in the hall outside my room and called my grandmother, Reggie. She was by then in her mid-sixties in Fort Lauderdale (where she and my grandfather lived by the eighteenth hole of the Woodlands Country Club golf course). After a catching up and assuring her that my "grades" were excellent and I'd never been happier and "Thank you so much for this opportunity, Grandma," I explained that I would need a little extra money toward my tuition, and I would need that money in cash once a week, please. There was silence on the other end. Dan passed by the thick glass window quickly, and I grabbed at his gold wool scarf.

"Beer," I mouthed. "And pot."

"Why do you need more money?"

"It's still for school, Grandma."

"So you go back and forth from Vermont every day? How long does that take?"

"You don't go back. You stay. Until March."

"You're out of school until March?"

"It is school. It's just not at school. It's in New York."

"We're paying for the whole year."

"I know. This is part of the whole year. It's called the Field Work Term. You get a job in your field of study. It helps you become a real artist."

"Artist?"

"That's what I want to be. An artist."

"Like a painter?"

"No, a writer. A poet."

"So you're getting paid?"

"A stipend. Not enough to live on. I'm kind of a volunteer."

"In a kitchen? Like a soup kitchen?"

"Not a kitchen. *The* Kitchen. It's a nonprofit."

"Well someone's profiting, I know that. Why do you have to live in a hotel?"

My grandmother heard the word and saw gilded palaces, like The Plaza and the St. Regis.

"It's not a luxury hotel. It's a hotel for great artists. It's famous."

"I've never heard of it."

"Listen, let me see if I can't get them to lower the weekly rent. Sometimes the manager gives you a lower rate. If he likes you. He likes artists."

Stanley Bard, who'd been in charge since the late fifties, had supposedly let Arthur Miller live there rent-free while he was completing *Death of a Salesman*. If he sensed you had value and were the real thing, he'd do what he could to make sure you succeeded under his roof.

"Well, you better talk to this Mr. Bard because we're not paying $200 a week for you to stay in a hotel when you should be at school studying. I can't believe what I'm hearing."

I knew this would be coming, and I was dreading it, even up at Bennington as I devised my winter plans. In order to move into the Chelsea and avoid a winter of traveling back and forth to my job at The Kitchen, then home to my mother's on the Long Island Rail Road, I had to convince Stanley Bard that I was a real artist and receive the possibly mythical discount that would keep the rent from being financially prohibitive.

Just before Christmas 1989, I took the train from my mother's house, with my blue suitcase occupying the other seat. I stepped onto the platform at Jamaica Station and sat on my baggage as I waited for the train to emerge from the yard. I pulled up the collar of my tweed overcoat, with its ripped, tangled, black silk lining, and sank my head down until it was buried in the musty, rough material. I was afraid that people would notice the huge grin on my face, so I hid it. But even as I stepped onto the warm train car and looked at the conductor, I was beaming. I wasn't going back to sleep in Lawrence that night or ever again. Even if Stanley Bard rejected me, I had enough money to stay at the Chelsea for a few nights, enough time to figure something else out. There was just no way I was not going to move in.

Mr. Bard was all-powerful and strode the marble floors of the Chelsea lobby, with its hanging sculptures and mounted paintings, like a benevolent monarch in his court. His office entrance, across from the fireplace, was situated behind a thick wood door, the kind you'd find in the entrances of museums and cathedrals and Ivy League study halls. In person, Bard was a slim, elegant man with neatly combed, dark hair. He seemed soft spoken and thoughtful but still somehow, thanks to reputation, carried a sort of bronzed aura. The office itself, once you passed through the august gateway, was tiny and cluttered. A takeaway coffee cup sat on the edge of his desk, drained to reveal a wrinkled Lipton tea bag—another human touch that somehow comforted me. I stood until he asked me to sit, wondering whether a real artist would just fall backwards into it and belch. I wasn't wearing sunglasses. I'd shaved the night before, showered, and changed my sweater. I got accepted to

Bennington almost instantly. I was given The Kitchen gig with a well-worded cover letter. But this? This seemed to be the real interview, the first true challenge of my adult life.

Bard, in his coat and tie, seemed pleasant but scattered as he took his seat. I gazed around at all the art, the sculptures, photos, raw, chunky canvases on the walls. I'd heard that he sometimes took art in exchange for rent, but I doubted I'd get far offering up my small leather folder full of poems, many of them still in the process of being perfected and revised. He asked what I did, and the tire-kicking ritual began. It was happening—a tête-à-tête, a negotiation, really an initiation. It wasn't a rumor or a myth; it was true. Stanley Bard really did this with potential residents. If I could prove my worth, it would be like getting paid to write.

"What are you?" he asked.

"A poet?"

This flew, even though answered in the form of a question. He didn't roll his eyes. He didn't ask, "No. What do you really do?" That didn't happen here. Poets were real here. Dylan Thomas real.

And I didn't tell him I was a full-time college student who would be leaving at the end of February, no matter what, to resume his freshman year at the most expensive school in the country. I only said that I was working a few blocks away at The Kitchen and would be finishing my first collection in the Chelsea. I figured he'd love that. Together, we could imagine a dedication ceremony fifty years in the future, the unveiling of a bronze plaque that read in part,

> *Marc Spitz b. 1969. The poet laureate of the United States, winner of multiple prizes, and seducer of women who look like Emmanuelle Béart lived and labored here, even though his grandparents suspected he was grifting them like his no-good, deadbeat old man did. Thank God that motherfucker's out of the picture, right? Also, free Mumia!*

"What kind of poetry?"

"Modern?" I knew I had to stop answering with questions, but I couldn't seem to correct myself.

"Who are your favorite poets."

"Bukowski?"

"He stayed here. Brendan Behan lived here too," Bard said, proudly revisiting a rap he'd been giving for decades, as if I'd missed the bronze plaques out front and never read a book or listened to a record before. For a minute, I debated how far a wide-eyed gaze and a "No fuckin' way! Behan?" would get me. But then it occurred to me that I might profit from calmly letting him know that yes, I was aware of the place's massive legacy, and that my book collection and my record collection, once full of Gothic new wave, were now fortified by not only jazz but also vintage Cohen, Dylan, Ochs, and Waits, plus Nick Drake and Tims Buckley and Hardin. Cool shit–wise, I was approaching watertight. And once in the office, I realized that I wasn't just looking for a place to warm my bones for the winter. I really was after the big prize.

"Jean-Paul Sartre, Simone de Beauvoir," he continued.

I nodded.

"Of course. I mean . . . they're always together." They lived together in my head. I'd never read either but kept them close.

"The way you were dressed, I thought you were maybe a musician? We've had a lot of important musicians living here as well. Chopin. Piaf. Bob Dylan," he added. Was Bard selling me, or was I selling him? I couldn't work it out. He knew I was poor, right? Or could I not hide my childhood of relative privilege?

Check the dirty fingernails, guy, I thought. I'm real.

"Virgil Thompson."

Virgil Thompson? Who the fuck was Virgil Thompson? This was going wrong. I was failing. Virgil Thompson had lived and labored here. He was "important." I was convinced that if Mr. Bard would simply take a chance on me, I could be important too. But it was quickly looking like another cold winter of desperate commuting. Then Mr. Bard said, "I don't know. I think I'd like to read your poetry."

"What?"

"Okay." He got up and held out his hand.

"Do you mean? I mean. When?"

I weakly pumped his fist and worried that my palms were soaked. Turns out Bard didn't even know that moving in was not an option for me unless he gave me the rate. This was merely a routine "welcome new long-term resident," meeting. He liked to know who was moving in, especially if they seemed creative. He probably didn't even know he had a reputation for cutting artists a break. He liked to think of it more as a special relationship with the artistic. In the end, the rate wasn't even that much cheaper, maybe $40, but that was something to bring back to my grandparents, who could not resist a bargain. Maybe he couldn't even remember the last time he offered the legendary discount.

"I will make copies for you," I promised.

"I'd like that," he said and offered his hand again as if to say, "Let's try this one more time."

When I walked to my room on that first night, I ran my hand along the cold, glossy walls as I padded down the stone hallway. There was a calming amber hue in this tunnel, set so deep in the guts of the Gothic structure that I could easily imagine it was 1919 or 1959, and an insistent buzzing of deeply buried electronic circuitry, like something off the *Eraserhead* soundtrack, wires and fuses that will never been seen again, man made things that have become some kind of urban dust or mechanical moss. I found my room on the eighth floor and let myself in with the key. My key! Not just a room key or a door key, but the key to something more exciting and dangerous and, yes, important. I believed it, like all I had to do was check in, unpack, and lay on the single bed (which was too short and narrow to accommodate my lanky frame) with its rough, brown, flowered bedspread (that looked flammable), close my eyes, and when I woke up, I'd be Bob Dylan. I'm not sure what I expected to happen. I unpacked my typewriter, with its nearly worn-through ribbon. I removed the spools and examined them. They seemed to remind me, You still have to write something, you jackass . . . and it has to be good. No black-clad elves were going to do this for me while I slumbered. And as the sun began to set and the TV I called and requested was still being located among the depraved, and maybe even the deceased, locked away in similarly tiny rooms, it occurred to me that I'd just moved into a severely haunted house. I realized, to my utter shame, that I was scared.

When Patti Smith, the muse of "Crow," recalled her very first night at the Chelsea Hotel in the late sixties, she wrote that "it felt like coming home." My own emotional response was slightly different. It wasn't an instant sense of belonging or a sensation of returning to some cosmic origin point. I felt more at home on Long Island, not that I would ever admit that. Bennington had become a home as well. The Chelsea was the home I wanted, but it was also a place where people suffered and sometimes died: Charles Jackson, who wrote *The Lost Weekend*, and, most famously, poor, strung out Nancy Spungen, with her broken nose and bad, fake British accent. Yes, nearly every building in New York is a place where, technically speaking, somebody, perhaps many people, died. We tend to think we're the first tenants, even when we move into prewar tenements, but the Chelsea actually suggested death, the natural flipside to the raging, intense life it also seemed to bleed. It was a place where you could hear people shouting, sometimes howling at night. The building was full of strangers, and I had to somehow make them all family.

"Hey, you out there," I said to myself as I pulled up the sandpaper covers and tried to find sleep in full Bohemian dress. "Listen. Nobody try to rob or kill me for twelve hours, okay? Because I don't want to be a Jewish American Prince anymore. I would really like to be a ragged poet. Thank you!"

I don't know if I was afraid of someone literally breaking down the door and stabbing, ravaging, or strangling me, or if I was wary of actual spirits and what they would show me, afraid of the challenge coming and not really being ready for Manhattan. It was why I didn't go straight to the city from high school. I had so much to learn. But I was so impatient.

"Kerouac, Warhol, Ondine and Mary Woronov, De Kooning, Tennessee Williams . . . even my best friend, Charles Bukowski—they all had to find sleep in this very place too," I told myself as I shifted.

If I stayed up all night, I felt, all would be lost. If I could only enter natural sleep, it would mean I had a chance of being one of them—a natural Chelsea boy. Janis, Leonard, Edie—they weren't mythical figures like the griffin, with the body of a lion and the head of an eagle. They were real people, and they had lived here. They took shits in the communal bathrooms. They had head-aches and cravings for pretzels and chocolate. They had bad sex in addition to the good sex they sang about. They worried about the coming bills. I couldn't force that truth into my brain. I tried to make myself believe it, but it didn't take.

"Herbert Huncke and Corso are still here! I saw Huncke in the lobby, with his hunched shoulders and skull like a little boy's, welded to an old man's body. If I could follow them all to the sleep they found, then I could also fol-low them out, and into the infinite. This is how it's done. You get here . . . and the rest . . . just . . . happens . . . doesn't it?"

I made it through that first night, bolstered and comforted by the tapes I played: Dylan singing about these very heat pipes coughing in "Visions of Johanna," Tim Buckley singing his song to the siren, and, of course, Joni Mitchell trilling about her bowl of oranges. I woke up, and it was a Chelsea morning, and I was still alive. That very fact made me bold. I might have only slept an hour and a half. I sensed it was still early, but I believed that it was the most important hour and a half in my life. That ninety minutes embold-ened me to take my clothes off, shower and shave, and dress again in the same clothes (with fresh socks and drawers). If I was visited by ghosts, they didn't do much, but I did notice the hot and cold taps in the sink were both run-ning. Did I get up and turn them on in the middle of the night? Did I pee in the sink? Was it the plumbing? Or was it Nico, the imperious chanteuse of the early Velvet Underground. I cherished her *Chelsea Girl* album and still do. It's a gentle and glorious thing, easily as good as any of the three classic Nick Drake albums. Inside the Chelsea, I'd linger outside the rooms she sang about on the album's title track, 546 and 115, but Nico and I would not be meeting on this plane. She had recently perished on a roadside in Ibiza. She was dressed all in black. It was suggested that she might have refused to adapt to the July heat, which made hers the ultimate Goth rocker death (that's not crucifixion). She sang a eulogy for Lenny Bruce at the end of *Chelsea Girl*, and I wrote one for her in my black-and-white composition book. It was less accomplished but equally heartfelt. That's what artists did for one another when they passed over. We wrote about each other. Patti Smith was the queen of this, with poems or songs memorializing Hendrix, Morrison, Edie Sedgwick, Brian Jones. She's still writing eulogies for dead stars: Kurt Cobain, Amy Winehouse. She must prep them in advance like the *Times*. You know she's got one for Pete Doherty on file somewhere.

In 1989, the elevators in the Chelsea lobby were twin chairlifts of evil that seemed to scale the shaft of the structure like drunken chameleons, stopping and starting and hanging and swaying and hissing in the stolid, windless black. Other times the lifts just jammed, leaving one in there, panicked and doomed like Maurice Ronet in *Elevator to the Gallows* (minus the nerve-cooling Miles Davis score). I took the stairs whenever I could. I had only just started smoking, so I was good to go both up and down with good lung power.

Everything in my new rented room was set up to look like a black-and-white postcard, the kind I'd buy off the spinning racks in the back of bookstores and bring home to the Island in my tweed pockets. There was no toilet, just a slim bed, more like a cot, made up with heavy, white sheets. These were army- or hospital-style sheets, with faint red chalk lines on the seams. A gold foil ashtray sat atop a small dresser, the kind with drawers lined with orange floral wallpaper. Someone had left a navy-blue Bible inside for me, but I had my own bibles, and I laid them all out on the windowsill.

I'd taped my sketches of insane cats with Mickey Mouse ears or grinning and deformed children (also with Mickey Mouse ears on their pointed skulls) to the wall, along with some of the poems I was proudest of. While in my poetry professor Alvin Feinman's workshop, I might have others believe that everything that fell out of my mouth was gold, I could secretly tell which poems were real and which were still searching, and I kept them separate, as if the weaker ones would infect the clean and tight writing. I had so many superstitions. Writing was something I could do naturally, and I was proud of that, but almost from the start, it came with such a voodoo. The closet had a flimsy bar and three complimentary wire hangers. I'd placed my boom box on the windowsill too and my pale blue Smith Corona suitcase typewriter on the long desk. The wood was scored on top and cut with doodles, like a school desk, which seemed appropriate. As the theaters, record stores, bookstores, and bars of Lower Manhattan had been in high school, the Chelsea was a school of sorts as well. My actual suitcase, also pale blue with white trim, would double as a chair.

My mother would rarely see me in the Chelsea, even though I was technically "home" from school and available for family visits. I assumed that she feared it, and that made me proud, even if I secretly feared the whole neighborhood too. Twenty-third Street in the winter of 1989 was a lot seedier than it is now. Hustlers and junkies still poured in and out of the YMCA. There were longhaired stoners at the guitar shop and intense old men with judgmental stares in the aisles of Midnight Records, the low-ceilinged indie record store directly across the street, where I found a copy of the Crispin Glover record *The Big Problem Does Not Equal the Solution, the Solution Equals Let It Be.* There's a cover of "The Daring Young Man on the Flying Trapeze" on that album, and that's exactly how I saw myself . . . as a daring, young man.

On the first day of 1989, I put on my black wool watch cap and took a taxi down to attend the annual New Year's Day Poetry Marathon at Poetry Project in the old St. Mark's Church in the Bowery. It was an all-day reading that had become, after fifteen years, the place for a young writer to be. I thought about bringing something to read, but I was still too shy and unsure of my work. There was a writer up at school named Patrick Murray whom I'd befriended and secretly kept as my watermark. Until I could reach his height, I risked drowning out there as a poet. Patrick Murray, who lived in the card room downstairs in Franklin House, was an intense, black kid, tall, stoic, with wild hair and a perma-stoned squint. He was a cross between Ted Hughes and H. R. from Bad Brains. Into a half dozen stuffy wine-and-cheese poetry-reading affairs in the candlelit living rooms of the lawn houses, Patrick brought the dynamite, and I'd witnessed every detonation. He'd read his own work, but his showpiece was Dylan Thomas's "Do Not Go Gentle into that Good Night." Each time he'd read the line "Rage, rage against the dying of the light," his intonation would grow louder until the final stanza, when he'd be screaming "Raaaaaaaaaaaaaaaaaage!" with the urgency of a man being devoured by a hellhound.

"And you, my father, there on that sad height," he'd soften, rocking his hunched body back and forth. "Curse, bless, me now with your fierce tears, I pray. Do not go gentle into that good night. Rage, raaaaaaaaage against the dying . . . of the light!"

It was painful and beautiful. He sounded like he was stripping muscle off his larynx, like John Lennon on "Twist and Shout." The first time I saw it myself, I thought, "Yeah, I'm not ready yet." I couldn't do what Patrick could do. I knew I had to become his friend and study him. I brought him smoke. I brought him food. I sat at his feet. I studied his cassettes: Ornette Coleman,

Art Blakey, Willie Nelson's *Stardust*. I figured just being around other writers, some of them famous, most of them unknown, would be like spending a whole day with Patrick Murray and inspire me to write, and perhaps next year, I'd have something I could swing from the podium too? I went gentle into the fifteenth annual poetry marathon. Others brought the good shit. Poetry, in the late eighties, was having something of a resurgence, thanks to the rise of stars like Max Blagg and Maggie Estep and Marc Smith's slam movement out of Chicago. The notion of a poet actually making some bank at it was not as abstract as it had been just a few years before. There were now poets in Gap ads. Poets on MTV. Poets in the cupboard. Poets under the stairs.

After about an hour in the St. Mark's Church, I picked up on a change in the electrical current in the room; it was as if all our sweaters had suddenly touched, and a crack of static stopped our hearts at once for a millisecond. I turned and saw an older gent, gray bearded and balding in a well-made tweed coat and complex patterned "Cosby" sweater, the kind my Grandma D would have loved to knit me, heading right for my chair. Was he delivering me a message? Did something happen to my mother? Or my sister? Had someone pushed the button? Were there nukes in the air? Who was this guy, and why couldn't he just leave me be? I had a great seat? I wanted to meet some real poets.

He stood over me, and I quickly determined that it wasn't me he wanted at all but my prize chair. Who the fuck did he think he was? What, just because he's old, I need to let him sit? He smiled at me, and for a moment I resented the fact that he assumed this would be enough to charm me into giving up my seat. I had the sense that everyone was glaring at me now. I was suddenly the disrespectful punk? There was a part of my brain that identified him before I could do anything practical about it . . . like rise and offer my seat. I knew who this was. I processed it, but now I was frozen in awe. And while I was frozen in awe, the LL Bean–clad urban-hippy type who'd been sitting right next to me rose and gallantly offered his own seat to Allen Ginsberg. *The* Allen Ginsberg.

"Please, it's an honor," he said, and Ginsberg nodded gratefully and took a seat next to me. The room seemed to calm down as the poet and songwriter Todd Snider began to read. I had two choices, as I saw it: I could construct a brick wall between us, or I could acknowledge that I knew who he was and let him know, somehow, that I was going to be cool about that and not lose my head or ask him a million questions. I turned to him and just said, "Hey, sorry about that."

He raised his eyebrow and smiled faintly at me with serene expression, as though he was preoccupied by the depths alone, and I couldn't begin to rattle him. I noticed his skin; it was tan and seemed to glow. His ears were enormous, as if he could pick up signals from the cosmos. I was tempted to look over at Ginsberg, to check what he made of each poet who performed, among them his longtime love Peter Orlovsky (who rambled more or less incoherently). Tuli Kupferberg of the Fugs was the hands-down highlight of the chunk of marathon that I witnessed. He performed a song-poem called "Beloved Enemy," which borrowed the chorus from Bobby McFerrin's number one hit "Don't Worry, Be Happy" and addressed the warming Cold War, the notorious Willie Horton ad that got Bush I elected president, and the persecution of homosexuals at the height of the AIDS crisis. What would happen to the power structure if all the "boogie men" were gone. It was the specter of these boogie men that those in power manipulated to stay in power after all. "We need an enemy, we need an enemy!" Kupferberg sang, before shrugging, "Don't worry, be *nappy*" (and later "Don't worry . . . eat curry"). The crowd adored it, and even as I did too, I was jealous. How does one get up there and not only entertain but deliver a good idea? Make people think? And smile. That was the key. So many poets up at school whined and didn't care about their audience. Kupferberg was giving a lecture, but it didn't feel like one. How does a poet bring down the house? Patrick knew. Ginsberg, at my side, knew. Patti Smith knew. This very stage, after all, was where Smith first recited poetry while Lenny Kaye played his guitar. But once again, I had no idea what to do while I was there. I had nothing good enough to read—not here. Up at school, in a classroom full of rich kids and pretty European girls, sure, but not here. Ginsberg was about my age, nineteen, when he realized that he wanted to be a great poet. He'd figured it out. As I gathered up my coat and hat, I felt proud of myself for not asking him how (or rubbing his bald head or belly for luck).

The Kitchen staff was really exulting in that adrenaline-rush feeling of being under siege in the winter that I interned there. The first shots of the culture wars had been fired two years earlier with the PMRC succeeding in getting stickers placed on the covers of all my favorite hip-hop and heavy metal CDs. But those artists were already rich and famous. Madonna wasn't going to suffer much if Pepsi pulled her ad campaign, but now thought police were going after the struggling artist. The American Family Association was on the rise, powered by actual or put-on outrage over NEA-funded pieces like Andres Serrano's "Piss Christ" photo and Robert Mapplethorpe's "The Perfect Moment." Karen Finley and David Wojnarowicz, both New York–based artists, would become targets of Republican senator Jesse Helms of North Carolina and his proposed amendment to rescind funding of art deemed obscene by, well, Congress, I suppose. I was already drunk and full on that delicious "us-versus-them" vibe after a full semester at Bennington, but once I got back down to Manhattan, I realized there were stakes involved. Not just parties. Declaring yourself an artist was simple and fun, but there was responsibility and sometimes real persecution.

The Kitchen's staff's emotions were permanently flared, and when I'd frequently find my boss, "the Curator," an elegant and slim woman in her early thirties, deep in conversation about censorship and totalitarianism, I'd nod my head in sympathy even though it was the much smaller and more immediately practical matters that vexed me. I just wanted to have enough money to buy a bologna-and-cheese sandwich, some Kit Kat bars, and warm cans of Pepsi.

In addition to being a performance space, The Kitchen was also an archive—or, I should say, had the potential to be an archive. You can't really be an archive until your collection is actually fucking archived by someone working for a small stipend and living on Boar's Head products. They'd recently relocated to Chelsea after nearly two decades in SoHo on Broome and Wooster. It was there that all the legendary performances had taken place: your John Cage and Philip Glass and Meredith Monk and Bill T. Jones events. Even though I found the Curator to be full of beans, I was in awe of the place's mission and legacy, but the actual day-to-day operations were really no different from working at, say, Blockbuster. In fact, the Curator grabbed my hand on week two of my internship and led me into a room where literally two thousand video cassettes were stored, many still unpacked from the move, which had happened over three years earlier. There were tapes on the shelves, on the floor, in bags—hundreds of them. It would be my job to isolate, identify, label, and file them in some kind of new, working order. Tapes, and tapes, and tapes, and more tapes. Many of them were unmarked, which meant I had to locate a rolling TV and VCR cart—which the Curator knew they had "somewhere"—pop the tape in, and determine what exactly it was. "If you have a question about something, bring it to me, and I'll ID it, but it should be self-explanatory." She assumed that because I went to Bennington, I could tell Charles Atlas from Vito Acconci, but I was just a new wave hick. I was still learning all this shit. I only knew Laurie Anderson, whose U.S. piece had premiered there, because "O Superman" was sometimes played on my local new wave station, W-LIR. Some days I'd uncover a real treasure, like The Residents video for their cover of James Brown's "It's a Man's, Man's, Man's World." When I was twelve, this video used to really terrify me whenever it came on MTV. The Residents wore top hats and tails and had giant eyeballs for heads. A demented-looking man, painted green and wearing a black hood, lip-synchs the lyrics, but he's out of time and doesn't seem to mind. There are tentacles squirming in a corona around his hood. It wasn't Wham! I decided that I needed to watch it again to gauge just how much Bennington and the Chelsea had toughened me up. I closed the storage closet door, shut off the lights, and pushed in the tape.

Whenever a performance was scheduled, I swiftly shifted roles to chief operating backstage gopher. One afternoon, the performance artists The Kipper Kids came in to rehearse for their upcoming event. They were only my third-ever famous artist encounters—if you want to consider Mickey Mantle, whom I'd met at a baseball card convention once, an artist. Between "The Mick," Ginsberg, and Harry and Harry Kipper, I have to say I saved my greatest gushing for the latter as they had appeared in my then all-time favorite film, 1982's *The Forbidden Zone*, alongside Susan Tyrell, Viva, and one of the funniest and most underrated (outside of Los Angeles anyway) new wave bands, Oingo Boingo (then still known as The Mystic Knights of the Oingo Boingo). Other than as a semi-animated, musical tribute to Fleischer brothers cartoons, *The Forbidden Zone* is difficult to describe accurately. It's easily the most anarchic and politically incorrect (and hilarious) film I've ever seen. Viva was actually living in the Chelsea at the time, and I would soon encounter her. A real, live Warhol superstar, she was the last Chelsea Girl to vacate. Viva was a bit older but really hadn't lost any of her high-strung appeal or unconventional beauty. At the time, she had a child living there, a daughter who would grow up to be the successful actress Gaby Hoffmann. I'd sometimes see her playing with her pet rabbit in the hall outside my door. I'd come out of my room, smile at her and her bunny, then head for the stairs or the terrifying elevator and try to pretend that I didn't have a culture crush on her mother.

The Kipper Kids, who dressed in bathing caps, boxing gloves, diapers, and little else, were infamous among the punk performance art community for covering themselves in jellied cranberries. It was one of their signature bits, so it was a thrill to spy a crate of canned cranberry sauce in their gear when I helped load them in. I actually stole one and put it in my book bag, then lugged it back to the Chelsea after work, placing it triumphantly on the windowsill. I still have it, and I don't suppose I'll ever open it, even when the earthquake hits and the seas turn to fire and I need an emergency nosh. It felt cool to be a small part of their performance, to watch it with my coworkers from a privileged view at the side of the stage. I liked that view. I wanted to look out at an audience and not be just another guy sitting in one. It was something to know what they were going to do beforehand, having seen them rehearse, and then to see how it went over live.

I wrote a lot of poetry in the Chelsea Hotel, but much of it was piffle and probably written just so I could preface the reciting of each one for all time with, "Oh, I wrote this in the Chelsea Hotel." Late at night, after coming in from The Kitchen or a Bennington party, I would pull my chair up to the desk, play my Al Green's *Greatest Hits* or John Lennon's *Plastic Ono Band* tape, and type out my days. Some of the poems were promising. They were the words of someone just beginning to know things but determined to be world-weary. I knew drugs, so I doubled down. I wrote about heroin before I ever did heroin. It seemed like a shortcut to depth. That's depth, not death.

When my mother finally came in to Manhattan to visit, she predictably fretted aloud about the state of my room, the missing toilet, and all of these strange people coming and going.

"Who lives here?"

"*I* live here, Mom."

"I mean what kind of people live here?"

"My kind of people."

"It's such a little room."

"I don't need a lot. I have my typewriter."

She wouldn't sit on the bed. She didn't want to touch anything.

"Alright, I've seen it," she said with a laugh. "I've seen where you live."

"What's wrong with it?"

"Nothing. It's just . . . that sink . . . it's so close to the bed. And it's filthy."

"No it's not."

"Okay . . . " She didn't have the words so she laughed again.

"Why is it funny? It's not funny. Don't do that," I told her. "It's rude, you know? I live here."

"I know. You're right. I'm sorry. I just can't imagine."

Her first visit was really the beginning of that strange—and for me, belated—city-kid state where a good friend or two (if not the city itself) becomes your real family. I wasn't so outraged that I didn't let her take me for meatloaf and mashed potatoes at the nearby Chelsea Square all-night diner and buy me some groceries and much-needed toiletries and art supplies. It must have seemed to her like I was camping. Maybe it looked that way to anyone who observed me, but by the second month, I was not only sleeping in my sweats, I was treating the staff like family—that is to say, hitting them up for cash.

When I was broke, which was all the time, I'd call my mother or father from the phone booths in the lobby, and if that came up cold, Jerry the desk clerk would front me money out of the till and charge it to my bill, which my grandparents, pleased with my ability to bargain the weekly rate down, indeed agreed to pay each week. Jerry was an old, bald, bespectacled, and avuncular Jewish man who, I suppose, took pity on me. I'm sure I was one of dozens and dozens of pet starving artists.

"Mr. Spitz," he would greet me after I emerged from the elevator. "Good morning."

"Hey. So, dig. I need to do some shopping today. Pick up some supplies?"

"That'll be an adventure."

"Problem is, I'm waiting on a money transfer. It hasn't come over the wire yet."

"That *is* a problem, Mr. Spitz."

He would hand me a chit, I'd sign it, and he'd produce a $20 bill from the register. I had this cordial relationship only with Jerry. We just felt each other out. He decided to trust me, and I decided not to fuck him over. None of the other clerks would even look up when I said, "Excuse me . . . " I was a no-count. On days when I was hungry and broke and confident that good ol' Jerry would hook me up, sometimes I'd emerge from the stair corridor only to find that he was not there. I would fill with that terrible, hungry, empty-belly panic; the minutes on the clock would seem to slow instantly, and I'd taste phantom bologna and cheese in my mouth. "How am I going to make it through?" I'd sit in my room trying to work and read Kerouac's long descriptions of food in *Visions of Cody* (one of my bibles on the sill) just to torture myself—"egg salads big enough for a giant decorated and sprigged out on a pan in great, sensuous shapes."

I knew that the Five Towns, my mother's egg salad, her chicken, and her baked ziti were only an hour-long train trip away. There'd be a climate-controlled bed, cable TV (the Chelsea only had network at the time), and a sparkling tub, but I was too proud to go back. I didn't live there anymore. My address was the Chelsea Hotel. I would pool change or go down to the phone booth and call up a Bennington friend to see what he or she had in the cupboard. I would shoplift if I had to. I would make it.

For all its increasing familiarity, the Chelsea could still remind you that it had an unpredictable and dangerous side too, that it had housed Valerie Solanis and Sid Vicious. Violence hanging in the air was payback for getting to see Dee Dee Ramone on your way to the bodega for morning coffee, I guess. Between the eighth floor and the lobby, my entire day could change for the worse too. One afternoon, Ricky, who was in his third year at NYU film school, came over to see me. Ricky was now old enough to buy liquor, and I'd just discovered Jägermeister, the superstrong German liqueur. Up at Bennington we devoted a theme party to it. We weren't allowed to call it the Jägermeister party without getting campus security riled, so we called it the "Master of the Hunt" party instead, and it became a perennial. If you drank enough of it, you could pretend that you were nodding on smack. It seemed like the perfect elixir for a night in the Chelsea. We were going to get high and smoke cigarettes, and I'd proudly show off my notebooks and onionskin sheets of poetry to Ricky.

We were riding down in the elevator with a grizzled actor named Paul Wilmot, who was supposedly some kind of stage genius. Each time I saw him, however, he seemed very drunk and angry. I never liked sharing the lift with him, but I was late for work, and the Curator would fix me with her frosty glare if I didn't make it over to The Kitchen in good time. Wilmot was muttering to himself about Vaclav Havel, and I made the mistake of asking who Vaclav Havel was. That's it—an innocent question, by way of entering into a conversation, comes out of your mouth before you think it through. No red flag intended.

"Hey! Who's Vaclav Havel."

I even mispronounced it, using a hard *c*: "Vak-lov."

Wilmot ratcheted up his anger from crotchety to furious and pushed me against the wall of the elevator as it chugged toward the ground floor. Ricky flinched and backed himself into the corner, not because he was especially craven. Wilmot looked like he could be rabid.

"You don't know Vaclav Havel? You should open a fucking newspaper once in a while! Vaclav Havel! What the fuck is wrong with you?"

I didn't push back. I remember thinking, If I resist, this man will bite me. I was also weakened by a palpable shame. I had a witness there, my old friend, and I was supposed to be cool now, like he'd become. Up in Vermont in the late eighties, news was harder to come by. Current events were never really "current." None of us had TVs in our rooms, and in order to get the *New York Times*, you had to drive, and often walk, into North Bennington and hope there was one left at the general store. After the Wilmot elevator incident, I made a point to buy and read the *New York Times* every day. Back up at school, while art and sex and indie rock rained down all around me, I'd sacrifice at least an hour and enough beer money to read about the Exxon oil spill and the human rights protests in China. I hated feeling ignorant and, worse, having Manhattan-ites consider me ignorant. I was prepared to inform Wilmot the next time I saw him that I was changing my ways current events–wise, but when this finally happened, he simply smiled at me and seemed to have no memory of assaulting or educating me. He was one of those blackout drunks, I suppose. I knew a few already. Over the years I would see him on television in small parts, playing a piano teacher or a small-town mayor, and I'd point at the screen and shout, "Vaclav Havel!" Correct pronunciation.

When Havel died in December 2011, I thought of Wilmot too. Anyone can be a teacher in Manhattan, even violent drunks.

For some days after the encounter, I was a little shaken and left my room with less and less frequency. At night, I'd pee in the sink rather than venture across the hall in the dark, lest Wilmot suddenly materialize in his threadbare Sherpa coat, graying hair all wild, and lecture me on glasnost and the opening of the Soviet Union while kicking me in the balls with his cruddy hunting boots. Meeting some of my other new neighbors and being invited into their much larger rooms—homes, really—made me feel once again like a real resident of the Chelsea Hotel. There were sisters, Emily and Mindy, designers of clothes and jewelry, and one afternoon, they invited me in for coffee and a chat. I noticed they had a better view and a lot more light than I did as well. Their place seemed more like an actual Manhattan apartment than a hotel room. It was homey and warm, with yellow walls, easels and sketches set up, and little picture frames and potted cactuses on the mantle over an actual fireplace. They even had a cat. Candles burned on the coffee table as I sat and smoked and told them what I was doing there.

"Working on a book of poems. Volunteering over at The Kitchen too."

"Oh, The Kitchen," Mindy nodded. "Sure."

Everyone loved The Kitchen. In truth, I'd already "resigned" my post there and was working on Greenwich Avenue in the Village at a tiny video store called New Video. I simply needed to eat and couldn't afford trailing the Curator around for free anymore. When anyone asked, however, even my fellow students in the city, I told them I was still at The Kitchen and kept up appearances, praying none of them had membership cards at New Video.

An elderly woman emerged from their kitchen and sat on the couch next to me, squinting in the bright sun and dunking a Lipton tea bag in a chipped, cream-colored mug. She had an elegant face, with suspicious, dark eyes and high cheekbones. Her long silver hair was tied in a kerchief, and she wore a pink wool shawl with flowers sewn into the knitting.

"Hi," I said, trying to keep my shyness in check. I thought this was merely a cool-looking, frail, artsy-fartsy old duck here; maybe one time she had sat for a painter or frolicked in some play down at La Mama. The sisters giggled, and I braced for another scolding.

"You don't know who that is do you?" Mindy asked finally. I considered bullshitting them, but I was outnumbered and, unlike my encounter with Mr. Bard, these were yes or no questions. This old lady was most definitely a somebody. But who?

"No, sorry," I confessed. She didn't for a moment seem offended. She actually smiled, as if this evidence of some obscurity validated her outsider status.

"That's Shirley Clarke," Emily said.

"Wait, who?"

"Shirley Clarke. She lives above us."

I actually knew of Shirley Clarke. And I'd seen her filmed version of Jack Gelber's play *The Connection*. It was, along with the works of Jim Carroll and Jane's Addiction's new *Nothing's Shocking* (my favorite album of that year, which is saying a lot since 1988 also saw the release of *Daydream Nation*, *Straight Outta Compton*, *It Takes a Nation of Millions to Hold Us Back*, and *Surfer Rosa*) one of those works that made me fascinated by heroin and junkie culture. Her film had been on my junkie-studies reading list: Smack 101. A faux documentary, before that had become a modern trope, it features actors from the Living Theater and is shot in grainy black and white, with the full, loud, bitchy, and brutal immediacy of a staged theater event juxtaposed with moments of lulling, modern, "cool" jazz, all in real time. The only plot concerns a few sick junkies waiting around for their "connection," named Cowboy, to return with a fix. One of them even has a boil that's about to pop. I didn't care. I devoured cautionary tales as if they were motivational speeches; I only digested the glamour and shat out the warnings.

Shirley Clarke? I thought. *The Connection*! I love that movie. I've seen it like ten times. I know you. Of course I know you.

Clarke had also made a film called *The Cool World*, which I'd heard of but hadn't seen. She'd recently made a film about Ornette Coleman and won an Oscar for a documentary about my pal Robert Frost. She seemed much more concerned with the strength of her tea than these twitty sisters reciting her CV to me. She had nothing to prove anymore. Nearly seventy, she'd already been invited to teach everywhere there was a film studies class and started receiving lifetime-achievement awards.

"We're going to the movies tonight," Mindy said. "And dinner. You should join us."

"Okay. Thank you."

That night Shirley, the sisters, and I walked next door to the cinema and bought tickets to see Tom Cruise in the new film *Born on the Fourth of July*. Shirley grabbed my arm tightly as we walked through the lobby. I didn't know what it was at the time, but she seemed drawn to me in a very relaxed and natural fashion. It felt good walking through the Chelsea Hotel lobby with Shirley, like I belonged there again after the Havel fracas.

Years later, this spiritual clicking would be easily explained. Not only did we have similar backgrounds (Eastern European immigrant lineages, overbearing fathers, rebellious streaks, and a desire to flee our privileged upbringing in extremis), we also shared the same birthday, October 2. She'd even attended fucking Bennington, back when it was an all-girls school. I'm no lover of the cosmic. I don't buy my Tarot readings, but I have moments when coincidence can seem spooky and shut me up.

The Stone/Cruise film was very Hollywood, full of voice-overs, flash-backs, and other tropes that made her tsk loudly and gasp, "Oh, my God," as it unspooled. I thought she was hysterical. At the point when Cruise, who plays the solider and future activist Ron Kovic, is shot and spits up blood, she tugged on my coat sleeve and giggled like it was high camp. As Kovic (who was from Long Island too) went on his journey of self-discovery through acts two and three, Shirley Clarke slept peacefully against my side, occasionally snoring loudly. Some in the audience grumbled, but they clearly didn't realize they were grumbling at Shirley Clarke. If they had, they would have shut the fuck up and paid respect. She'd earned the right to behave that way as far as I was concerned . . . even if I secretly got into the movie as she sawed her wood.

Afterwards, as we headed toward El Quijote, the dimly lit, cavernous, old Spanish restaurant that used to be the hotel's cafeteria, for some wine-soaked chorizo and grilled shrimp. The place smelled like garlic and fish and cologne and fruity wine. I loved that smell, but I never had money for the bill of fare. I'd only eaten an entrée there once, when my father had won some money at the track and sent me a few bills to share the wealth as he was one to do. I ordered the house special steak, which came wrapped in bacon and covered with cheese. It was so good that I felt existential dread as it began to disap-pear from my plate. Sometimes I'd splurge on a black bean soup with crusty white bread and cold butter at the bar. I'd sup quickly like a prisoner, leave whatever tip I could, and split with a handful of matches and mints. Real art-ists dined, I supposed. Leonard Cohen, Ginsberg, Dylan—they probably sat at tables, like Shirley Clarke, and never looked at the prices on the menu. They ordered what they wanted: the lobster in brandy sauce, the whole red snapper, and *arroz con pollo*.

I asked Shirley what she thought of *Born on the Fourth of July*, knowing well what her verdict would be.

"Why would anybody make that?" she muttered. "Really, why would any-body make that movie?"

"Money," Mindy suggested. Shirley looked at her as if that was the most ludicrous thing she ever heard. She had come from money. She must have. She lived in the fucking penthouse. She'd even attended Bennington when it was a posh all-girls school. I didn't let on that I was attending it now. I didn't want her to think I was just a student, a poser, slumming here. Not when I had a seat at the table, when walking the lobby with her made me feel safe from the Paul Wilmots.

"They wouldn't even let Shirley release her films back then," Mindy told me. "They tried to ban them."

Shirley looked proud as she picked at her fish. Back in the sixties, and more so these days, it was fairly routine for underground filmmakers to take their own personal journeys and end up with careers as major directors with mainstream or semi-mainstream followings and big budgets, but Shirley refused this path. She still lived in the Chelsea Hotel. She'd won the Oscar early for the Frost film and lived and continued to work on her own terms despite offers from Hollywood. Yes, it's easier if you're rich, I guess, and a lot of the least compromising artists are, aren't they? Or they had patrons.

There's a scene in *The Connection* in which some of the jazz cats hold down Leach (played by an actor named Warren Finnerty, who looks a lot like Steve Buscemi) and pop his boil. "This cat is corroded!" one of them gags. The explosion of an infected junkie abscess marks the end of Carroll's *Forced Entries* as well. But as the nineties began, I felt corroded for not being sick enough. Junkies eventually become victims, but most drug tales overlook the fact that most of us start out with "become heroin addict" on our to-do list. We don't begin under the thumb of the drug. And it's beyond a choice, really. It's more like an ambition. I decided, by the time I walked out of 222 West Twenty-third for the last time that winter, that I would need to get serious. I would need to become hardcore too. I would have to get dirty. Jägermeister wasn't going to cut it. It was time to get good. Time to get pure.

CHAPTER 4

The first time I ever remember being intrigued by heroin was when I heard The Nails' song "Things You Left Behind." Most people know The Nails as the band that sang "88 Lines About 44 Women," but they have another great "list song," with densely packed lyrics that seem like stream of consciousness but are actually intricately crafted. The premise of the song is an ex going through the belongings of an estranged lover.

"A bottle of Chanel No. 5, a postcard of a band called Dead or Alive . . . a dozen contraceptive sponges, anyone here got a rhyme for sponges?"

Like "88 Lines," it's tough and funny up until the very end, when the singer finds a glassine bag of smack among the personal effects.

"Heroin? Oh, shit, not heroin . . . "

The dude in The Nails had an unflappable drawl, and this little discovery seemed to blow his urban cool to bits. I was impressed.

I have no idea why my generation so embraced heroin. One sample of the scraping nausea that follows a good, long nod should really be enough to discourage even the most curious and erase all memory of that light, float-y goodwill which the drug seems to conjure as it lightens everything in your life-weary body and brain (except the lungs, which somehow seem to fill with a heavy, glittering dust). I only know what motivated me to do it was a desire for simplification and, as antithetical as it may seem, a real need for trust. Not that my life was exactly complicated at the time. I had a bed and a card that I kept in my wallet and showed to a lady at the top of a staircase, thrice daily, which permitted me to eat nutritious food. There were well-meaning professors trying to enrich my intellect. There were three parties a week, on Thursday, Friday, and Saturday, each in a different house and funded by a collection taken up in the cafeteria. Some of them had themes, like the aforementioned "Master of the Hunt" and "Viva Gillette!," which seemed to celebrate the cosmetics giant testing its products on animals in a punk rock fashion but was really just an excuse to spray walls with shaving cream; Sucking in the 70s (self-explanatory as far as the mixed tape); and Dressed to Get Laid, immortalized in *The Rules of Attraction*. At any of these parties, despite the fact that I had zits and was wearing what was technically a woman's paisley blouse under my velvet coat, I could easily hook up with three different women. I was just nineteen; I didn't get hangovers that put me down for a full day, as I would later. Life was good . . . and untrustworthy.

If you isolate a few junkie icons, I bet you will find a lot of suspicious children with separated or divorced parents: Keith Richards, Sid Vicious, Kurt Cobain. When things are too good, we are tempted to wreck it all to make us feel safer. Like Svetlana Kirilenko, the one-legged Russian nurse tells Tony in the "Whitecaps" episode of *The Sopranos* after he tells her that he and Carmela are splitting: "Divorce is very hard for kids. After this, they don't trust."

We were a generation with better knowledge of the behavioral mores of the previous generation's famous artists than any generation before us, and this applied not only to the way we dressed and created but to how we polluted ourselves. Whereas I sometimes think I started smoking Camel filters instead of the Marlboros everyone else seemed to smoke, because that was the cigarette pack on the cover of Eno's *Here Come the Warm Jets* album, and that was just the legal drug. Upon returning to the Commons green after my stay at the Chelsea, I fell in with a group of writers who also seemed to know every move their heroes made and were retracing them too in a way that seemed celebratory and correct.

We were the "Lit Fucks." We referred to each other as such, and the only thing missing from our ritual was smack. This was still crack time. Heroin was in the wings. It was hard to find. Every few weeks there'd be a rumor that someone had some on campus, but once we sorted out the truth, it was just the same old hash or shit weed.

My best friend among the Lit Fuck crew was Ron Shavers, a stylish black dude from the South Side of Chicago, who wore berets, had a goatee scruff and stylish, tortoise shell spectacles. He spoke fluent French and read Perec, but his biggest hero was the Philadelphia MC Schooly D. Ron (who sometimes spelled his name "Rone"). He worshipped "Schooly School" much in the same way I had sworn my heart to Morrissey as a teen.

"You want to play me some real hip-hop, you play me some Schooly D," he maintained. *"Pussy ain't nothin' but meat on a bone. You fuck it, you suck it, you leave it alone!"*

Why would you leave it alone? I wondered.

Ron would later dread his hair, but at the time, he combed his hair up as high as it would go, then tamped it down with a bandana. He had thick glasses and a goatee but wasn't remotely nerdy. Like most of the other Lit Fucks, he was gifted but aloof, probably due to some family trauma or loss. I never asked. You could get close to people like us but not demonstrably so . . . unless we were high. Then we hugged. Then it came out. But in the morning, it was never spoken of, the confessions or the details; it was a given that any good, strong emotions would go into the writing where they were truly needed. Why waste them on a Lit Fuck buddy when they could be the key ingredient in the next *Drunken Boat* or *The Happy Birthday of Death*. The fact that Ron was black and from the city and I was Jewish and from the suburbs didn't seem to matter, not even in the year of *Do the Right Thing* and *Fear of a Black Planet*. Bennington was a meritocracy. Nobody cared how much money your parents had, whether you were "full tuition" or not (yes, some people did qualify themselves this way, as if to remind you that Bennington was at the time the most expensive college in the country). There were other subdivisions among the student body, and students either self-identified or felt flattered when we did it for them. There were the "Jazz Cats" (in porkpie hats) and the "VAPA Rats" (the painters in overalls and sculptors in combat boots, named for the visual arts facility, VAPA). We had no clever name for the photography majors because for some reason they were mostly gorgeous women like Anna Gaskell and Jenny Gage and tied our tongues. The "Drama Fucks" had the best food at their parties, and discounting a few scruffs like Ian Bell and Peter Dinklage, they seemed to have the cleanest clothes too, oxford shirts and chinos. Brooks Ashmanskas, later a celebrated Broadway actor, was among them too.

Our Lit Fuck posse couldn't be contained by the Green Mountains. We drew our energy from New York City. It had taken about seven years since my first solo trip from the Island on the railroad, but I finally had a crew to travel Manhattan with for the first time in my life. Amazingly, I was the tour guide. This Five Towns jackoff was suddenly down by law like Grandmaster Melle Mell. I knew my way around the streets. I knew where the good record stores and bookstores were. I knew the bars that didn't card and the cafés where you could linger over just one cup of coffee and a cheap almond cookie. How did that happen? I was always the weekender or the hooky player, logging an hour or two here or there between high school and homework. I guess it made sense. Ron was from the Midwest; Herve, one of our other Lit Fuck mates (from a French family and given to vintage cardigans and one beloved Lunachicks T-shirt), was from rural France or somewhere like that; Jin Soo was a sweet but precocious Korean kid from West LA, who played an array of expensive electric guitars and always seemed to be stifling some great amusement like he on the verge of a pulled prank.

New music came before anything else. The record stores were always hit first. Nothing else happened without fresh sound, and our old tunes needed constant refreshing then, which meant new cassettes and CDs. It was a gamble. Sometimes you'd buy something that did nothing for the mood at all, and you'd sell it back a week or two later for half the original price.

I was doing about sixty-five on the Henry Hudson when the instantly recognizable bass line from Lou Reed's "Walk on the Wild Side" came on. I nearly pulled off the road. It was our latest discovery—the debut cassette by A Tribe Called Quest, *People's Instinctive Travels and the Paths of Rhythm*. When Q-Tip rapped, "*Mr. Dinkins would you please be my mayor? You'd be doing us a really big favor*," Ron whooped "Yeah!"

It was just so current and right and smart, and the samples they used kept you on your toes. We stayed on our toes most of the time. There was always something coming, especially in music; it felt like a golden age. "Event records," we called them, the release date being the event. *Goo* was an event record because everyone adored Sonic Youth's previous album, *Daydream Nation*, so when someone scored the first on-campus copy of it, word spread fast, and soon we were all gathered around a boom box in someone's room in a random house like Swan House, listening to the opening detuned chords of "Dirty Boots" like it was a presidential address. Similarly, Public Enemy's *Fear of a Black Planet* was an event record because of *Nation of Millions*, and that was like nothing I'd ever heard either, when Ron showed up one day and said, "I've got it," and I insisted he put it on right there before anyone else came over. *De La Soul Is Dead* was yet another. There was Ice Cube's *Amerikkka's Most Wanted* (his first solo album, made with Public Enemy's producers, The Bomb Squad); *Green Mind* by Dinosaur Jr. was one more, after the agreed-upon *You're Living All over Me*. We were investing in these bands, investing in our own sensibilities. They were growing and getting better, and we were growing with them. An event record didn't even have to be new. We discovered Sly Stone's *There's a Riot Goin' On* together, and Funkadelic's *Maggot Brain*, and made them honorary indie rock records. The biggest event record of them all in 1990 was *Bossanova* by the Pixies, the follow-up to their masterpiece of the previous year, *Doolittle*.

The Pixies were always right, our most agreed-upon music. They were the band—flawless. Everything from their Vaughan Oliver–designed sleeves to the between-song noise and chatter ("there were rumors he was into field hockey players") seemed to induce a smile and a gasp simultaneously. We were writing and eating and fucking and dressing the way *Surfa Rosa* and *Doolittle* sounded to us. We really had to get it all right. A lot was at stake. We weren't quite sure what; we just knew it was big. The Lit Fucks would linger in the St. Mark's Bookshop, then walk a few blocks east to drink at the round tables in the Holiday Cocktail Lounge where the old bartender, Stephen, liked us and didn't card. Nobody carded then. I remember stopping into the Holiday to pee while shopping in the East Village when I was in high school!

Illuminated by warm Christmas lights, which glowed all year round, we'd fill the gold tin ashtrays with butts and gulp our drinks in cups so short and narrow it only took about a minute to down one. The Holiday had low ceilings, like a suburban rec room, and it was painted a shit brown. It was nearly always empty except for a few drunks at the semi-circle bar out front. There was an old-fashioned phone booth with a sliding door and a jukebox full of vinyl 45s. Stephen sometimes drowned out the rock and roll and sang old German love songs in broken English: "It's yoooo! I love yooo! Troooo!"

He could also switch from pie-eyed gooeyness to a hard, withering stare that would chill your blood by ten degrees instantly; there were rumors he had fought for the other side during World War II. He was an honorary, off-campus Bennington student in those days in that he was always drunk and never seemed to change his clothes: burgundy velour top and black plants. A customer at the Holiday circa 1990 could wait literally twenty minutes for a vodka and grapefruit juice, which is what I'd started drinking then: Greyhounds. If you rubbed salt on the rim they became "salty dogs." It just seemed like a cool thing to request: "Yeah, lemme get another Greyhound." Like the bus that would take you away from whatever troubled you. Hop on the Greyhound, mix it around with the skinny, red, plastic straw and get gone.

The Holiday had real barflies too—men and women who showed up at noon, read the paper, did some business in the phone booth, and got slowly lit until they staggered home once happy hour was over. I was so enamored of its authentic Bukowskian air that I made out with one of them outside under the bar awning and against the neighboring wall. She was a dog groomer with bite marks all over her orange, leathery arms. She tasted like Malibu and smelled like hairspray, and I never got her name, but I thought of her every time I passed the cement lion with its elements-burnished face that kept guard in front of the bar entrance.

Sometimes we'd catch a movie that wouldn't be playing up north: *King of New York*, with Christopher Walken, Wesley Snipes, and Larry Fishburne, was one of Ron's favorites since it's scored with Schooly D songs. "Schooly School" is virtually the Greek chorus.

We'd get loaded and quote it all night ("I never killed anybody . . . who didn't deserve it!" "You know what I'd like to do with you? I'd like to take you on the subway"), drawing it into our arsenal of inside jokes and forming a real communal sensibility that was exciting and gave us the confidence to write and to read those pieces "short and loud." Once a homeless person stumbled up to us and asked for money so he could get "cool mellow drunk." That became another catch phrase. Who didn't want to get "cool mellow drunk?"

Our trips down to Manhattan always included frustrating sojourns to various bus stations and launderettes and the back of some kitchen in Chinatown where heroin was rumored to be sold.

"Yeah, man, this is where G. G. Allin gets his dope. It's the spot-spot."

"Alright. Cool. Good lookin' out."

It never was. Some dude who smeared his naked torso with poop was hipper than we were.

Those of us who didn't want it, didn't care and would rather have done something touristy or taken in an art film. Those of us who believed that heroin was something to explore, and perhaps even a pathway to authenticity, would always get cranky when none of the spots yielded any drugs.

Back on campus, we'd compete for the attention of our professors by lobbying to drink with them off-campus, discussing that winter's fatwa on *The Satanic Verses* author Salman Rushdie with grave concern. We were an ambitious group, but sometimes I worried that I was the only one worrying about carrying it over beyond Bennington. We all bought copies of the book as a gesture of support, but as they lamented Rushdie's circumstance, I secretly thought, At least he's published. How could my supertight Lit Fucks help each other get published? When did we go from being at school to being a school?

"You go to Naropa, man. You go to Yaddo. Naropa. And Yaddo," someone once told me, to which I responded with a dismissive eye roll.

"Yaddo?"

"Yaddo, bro."

I didn't even like saying it. I wanted the answers, but not the clean, easy ones. I wanted the hardier, rockier path, but couldn't even find a map to the treacherous way to glory. Even with a Camel dangling from my lips, I still felt like a suburban goof inside. Heroin would burn the rest of him away. It had to. Yaddo? Naropa, they didn't seem like experiences, or methods. They just seemed like more school. More fraternity and I went to Bennington because there were no frats or sororities. It was anarchy. New York City on a mountain. Every time it felt like "college," I grumbled.

And I didn't want to get along by social climbing or sucking up to teachers or professors anywhere. I wanted to be discovered, like Henry Chinaski. I submitted ten of my poems to the Academy of American Poet's contest. I remembered all those Bukowski books and that scene in *Barfly*. That's what you do. You print your stuff out in the lab (yes, then it was a "lab"), you lick stamps, you go to the mail room, you light a fucking candle, and you hope something comes back. Part of what motivated me was the $100 prize. Money was always an issue, even if food and rent weren't (yet). I had no cash that I didn't get from my old man in the mail after a good week at the track or from some girl I was dating. I remember being hungry at all the wrong times. I'd cook a can of Campbell's soup on the radiator and drink my hobo wine: Boone's Farm Strawberry Hill, which tasted like poisoned Jonestown Kool-Aid. I'd thumb through the pages of my favorite Berenice Abbott book of portraits and wonder if the artists in Paris in the twenties and thirties felt this knot in their bellies too? Joyce, Gide, Cocteau? A photography student named Jennifer Pliego took a series of black-and-white photos of me sitting on an old Salvation Army suitcase, cigarette dangling from my lip, New Orleans porkpie hat on my head. I looked hungry and rangy, like I was waiting for my train to come in, and I was.

When the smack finally came, it came from, of all places, the Midwest, courtesy of a Lit Fuck named Hazy Jane. Hazy Jane was a study in curious contrasts. She owned a handgun and a German shepherd and spoke with a tough, streetwise rasp, but she'd develop these deep, girly crushes on Lit Fuck boys (who never wanted to fuck other Lit Fucks and usually chased after dance majors or Drama Fucks, who threw the nicer parties with lots of good wine and much fancier cheese, maybe even a country pâté). She brooded over these boys, and I guess the smack comes in handy when you're put out in matters of the heart . . . or all other matters. I had a crush on her too. She wore her thick red hair in careful curls but tomboy-ish (or homeboy-ish) clothes and no make up on her pale skin. She always smelled good, like the Egyptian musk oil they sold on the corner of Third Avenue and St. Marks Place, and who wouldn't want to kiss a girl that smelled like such a magical corner? Jane, of course, isn't her real name, but I didn't change it because she's now a semi-public figure with a good writing career and a notable husband (she is, I hear) or because I blame her for sticking a needle in my arm, for being my first. I would have done it myself if I'd known how. And if she refused or gave me the "Just Say No" rap spontaneously, I would have been pissed to the point of . . . well, what could I do? Gun and guard dog. My point is, I was obsessed, compelled, not to be stopped. I was going to become a junkie. It wasn't my only ambition, but I'd decided it was the key component there. There was simply no other way I was ever going to become a real writer.

We were in her apartment off-campus watching *Drugstore Cowboy* on video, which was probably an utter cliché, but it seemed like the perfect first course at the time, geared directly toward the smack fascinated (complete with a William S. Burroughs cameo). When Matt Dillon talks about why people start using "dope," how it keeps people from having to face the mundane things in life, part of me wanted to put it on pause and shoot up right then and there. "Nobody can talk a junkie out of using. You can talk to 'em for years, but sooner or later they're gonna get a hold of something," Dillon says. "Maybe it's not dope. Maybe it's booze, maybe it's glue, maybe it's gasoline. Maybe it's a gunshot to the head. But something. Something to relieve the pressures of their everyday life, like having to tie their shoes." If I were a junkie, I rationalized, I wouldn't worry about winter and summer jobs or small press–rejection letters or reading and understanding Stendhal and Thackeray. I certainly wouldn't care about any pretty girl who snubbed me. I would only care about heroin. Singular. Oddly practical. It's a declaration in a way; you say, "I'm not normal, and I will never be normal again," like the people who get tattoos on their faces or have their lips pierced. Who is going to give them a job? Boil down everything, the pressure of creating and being in love, to just one thing, and then nothing can hurt you or fuck with you. That's was the fancy idea anyway. The baseline idea was that I wanted to nod. But in a subtler way, I wanted to reverse the order of things: I wanted to make the hard things (figuring out the meaning of life) easy and the easy things (not nodding off into your pancakes at the Pink Teacup soul-food café . . . or vomiting on your fellow New Yorkers and Vermonters) hard.

Jane got up and put on a record. The dog and I both watched her as she walked. Lenny Kravitz's new one, *Mama Said*, began to play "Fields of Joy." She then returned to the couch with the drugs and a syringe, and I could smell the oil on her warm skin.

"I'll do myself first; then I'll do you."

The dog and I watched her prepare her fix. He didn't appear worried or to sense that Jane could overdose and die. I took my cue from the pit. She drew the heroin up from a piece of wet cotton, slapping her strong arm casually and smoothly guiding the needle in. Her eyes fluttered, and she smiled a big, toothy grin.

"Okay, do me. Do me," I said, holding my arm out and shutting my eyelids tightly, waiting for the pain and then . . . whatever heroin did.

She didn't want to work anymore. She was enjoying herself too much. She patted the dog's head.

"Please!" I was whining now. "You promised." I lit a cigarette and sulked. "Thanks a lot!"

She looked at me and giggled.

"I'm just kidding." She was fine. Coherent. She could handle it.

"Calm down, okay." She carefully unwrapped another syringe.

"Hold that," she said. I put down my cigarette and held the syringe up to the light. She wrapped the belt around my arm and picked up the spoon.

"Give it back," she said, and I handed her the needle. When she fixed me, the muscles in my neck turned into melted ice cream, and a warm floating feeling spread throughout my body, total amniotic well-being, and a pleasure that wasn't sexual but just as intense as an orgasm. It didn't make you horny; it made you love everything.

Jane and I started making out, and the dog was barking at us, and the handgun was sitting on the coffee table, and Lenny Kravitz was singing, *"It ain't over till it's over,"* and it was over. *Mama Said* is a highly underrated album, front to back. Years later, I would tell Lenny Kravitz himself as much. But in that moment, with real smack running through my veins and a real woman's head nodding into my armpit, it was the wrong music, the wrong album, the wrong vibe . . . but it didn't matter anymore.

We finally had the secret wink we wanted, our Lit Fuck junkie unit, and somehow just tasting it seemed to illuminate all those hidden dealer spots down in Manhattan. That first shot was the helicopter over the city with the searchlight. G. G. Allin's guy, every guy, we were wise to them now. We smoked them out of their nooks and alleys. All we needed was the taste, and the motivation came. At first, anyway, junk is a real motivator. The pushers, they were there all along; we just weren't looking hard enough, didn't want it as badly as we thought. Overnight, as that all changed, the Lit Fucks seemed to divide into those who did the junk and those who didn't (all the Jazz Cats seemed to do it, so they didn't have to address the same issues). Once we started bringing it up ourselves, most of the consumption would take place in one room, with a bunch of kids in a great dog pile, as an agreed-upon song (preferably a long one like The Stone Roses' "Fool's Gold") played. We huddled around a CD jewel box the way most other students huddled around a pizza. Hazy Jane's junk was brown and needed cooking up and needles. The New York City dope of the era was a superstrong China white powder that you could snort like coke. It came in paper bags, stamped with brand names like "Tango and Cash" or "Eyewitness News," which appealed to our sense of "found art" eclecticism. Once the bags were licked clean (the taste usually stayed at the back of your throat and in your nostrils for a day and a half), they were usually saved and sometimes turned into collage art. Occasionally a straight kid, a good student, a square, would crash the nod-party and try to yank one of us to safety. I once saw a straight girl plead with another who was on the shit, "Please come with me. You don't know what this stuff has done to my hometown!"

She was from Seattle.

Rock and roll, dance music, and hip-hop seemed to be moving us ahead as a species in the early nineties: Jane's Addiction, Sonic Youth, Deee-Lite, Soul II Soul, N.W.A., De La Soul, The Stone Roses, Happy Mondays, Nick Cave and the Bad Seeds, Red Hot Chili Peppers, Metallica, Massive Attack. I'd never really experienced that before. I was too young for The Beatles and Stones and, later, the first wave of American and British punk rock. This was my time to see it and be a part of it all somehow and make the feeling of riding a revolution last forever. That's the junkie's dilemma, isn't it? How do I make this rapture go on? That brings me to possibly the worst consequence of my self-designed heroin addiction, which unfolded shortly after the Jane's Addiction show. I didn't steal a TV set or stab an old lady as a result of my habit. I didn't hijack a dirty needle and start an outbreak of hepatitis C.

I started . . . a band.

That is something I never, ever would have done if I hadn't been on drugs and very skinny. I think the only reason my college band existed was so I could take my shirt off and expose my new heroin-thin Stiv Bators–like physique. I would have taken my pants off too if we ever ended up playing anywhere but the rehearsal space over the campus café. We rehearsed a lot. When you were high, it was easier to sing than study. I would go to the snack bar in the Commons building, order a large chamomile tea, and with a big flourish, ask for a dollop of honey "for my voice." My band was a four piece: two Jazz Cats, a stoner on drums, and me, a deluded and jaundiced Lit Fuck on lead vocals (and tambourine), as we covered The Stones ("Monkey Man") and AC/DC ("Back in Black"). I was mostly screaming over the volume, so it mattered little that I'm about as on key as Mitt Romney. It felt good to scream and flash looks of camaraderie at the guitarist and the drummer—the kind a lead singer does before shouting, "Let's rock!" or "Guitar!" Did heroin make me less shy? Probably. More talented? I was betting big it would.

I named the band Fruitslaw. Maybe someone else named it, but I heartily endorsed the name for being wonderfully obscure. It was from a decade-old (at the time) *Saturday Night Live* skit starring John Belushi and guest host Sissy Spacek as "The Newlyweds." Belushi, with a beer-gut-stretched white T-shirt, sits at the kitchen table and berates his white-trash wife. "You always ignorin' me when I ask you to buy fruitslaw," Belushi rages. "You didn't explain it!" she pleads. "It's fruitslaw! You buy it in the dairy case. It comes in a plastic thing. It's like coleslaw, only it's made of fruit! It's fruitslaw!" That was our band and our life: something obscure you could still explain to the squares with extreme frustration.

Our ruckus drew a freshman girl with blonde- and black-streaked hair named Lillian, whom I started hanging out with. She wasn't into smack, despite her Jane's Addiction–worthy nose ring; she was just really into indie rock, a music major seeking out like-minded rock 'n' rollers. She actually liked our band, which shocked everyone else. Actual musicians knew we were terrible. I welcomed the adoration. I thought we were hot.

One afternoon, rusty foliage swirling in the cold wind, Lillian and I piled into her car and embarked on a routine liquor run to Williamstown, which had less strict laws about buying booze. Lillian was driving and put in a mixed tape of standard fare: Mazzy Star, Fishbone, R.E.M., Natalie Merchant. Then a song came on that I hadn't heard before. The bass line and drums were jazzy and melancholy on the verse. The singer was sad and conversational. Then it all exploded on the chorus when he screamed, *"I like it I'm not gonna crack! I miss you, I'm not gonna crack, I love you I'm not gonna crack! I killed you I'm not gonna crack!"* At first I thought, Wow, what boo-hoo lyrics these are. Like teenage diary entries, but by the second verse, it had got me. I felt like I knew the song already, like it had always been there. It had snuck up on me and moved me. I'd figured I'd made that impossible with all the smack and the forced cool, but this band, whoever they were, got around the goalie.

"What is this one?" I asked.

"Isn't it good? Nirvana."

My default mode when emotionally affected is to deny it, but I made her rewind the song and play it again.

"Is it an old record?"

"It just came out."

"Is it worth buying? Or should I just get the single?"

"This isn't the single."

"Really?"

"Do you want to hear the single?"

She ejected the mixed tape, then reached into the glove box and rummaged through some cassettes, finally freeing a jewel box with a blue album cover, the color of a chlorinated swimming pool. That was all I could see. She placed the box in her mouth as she drove, then took one hand off the wheel, pulled the cassette out, and pushed it into the console.

"This . . . is the single."

Hearing Nirvana shamed me into breaking up Fruitslaw. Jane's Addiction was great, but there was no point in dicking around when a band like Nirvana existed. It was like, Oh, right . . . talent. I didn't want to pursue anything that I couldn't be great at in the first place, and Nirvana was so good that it seemed somehow disrespectful to be a rock-and-roll dick, which is probably why Kurt Cobain lost his sense of humor so quickly. It's the last thing to go once you start doing smack, and the drug will always take it sooner or later if you don't quit. Once that happens, you're doomed.

CHAPTER 5

"What's your novel about?" Phillip Lopate asked me when I met him in his small, clean office in The Barn, which housed the literary department as well as the administrative offices and the student bookstore. I'd already been through one thesis tutor, the writer James Lasdun, whose creative-writing workshop I'd taken and been especially obnoxious in. While my eye rolling and snickering as the other students read their prose in earnest should have been enough for the polite Englishman to tell me to take my novel in progress, and while I was at it, the phallic Bennington war memorial monument, and shove them both where the moon doesn't glow, nothing as scandalous as that transpired. It was more of a scheduling glitch that sent me looking for other takers.

"It's a celebration of decay," I said.

"Can you take those off?" he asked, pointing to my sunglasses. I removed them. He had an unchecked Brooklyn accent that reminded me of my grandparents and put me at ease.

"Now, what's it really about?"

"I don't know. The basic story is there. I've been sketching it out for nearly a year. And I'm happy with the writing, but there's something missing. It's about a guy, and he loves this girl, but he loses her to drugs."

"Have you lost a girl to drugs?"

"Um . . . not really. No."

I reached into my folder and handed Lopate a dog-eared copy of the introductory chapter, which he read aloud: "Let's see. 'I fumbled with a comb then drew up my trousers, soaked in cum and bugs and urine. The Siren laughed cruelly. Somewhere in Tibet, Stella spared herself the humming of her clitoris with an hour of mediation. I wanted to disappear.' Who's Stella?"

"The one who got away. She was doing drugs with him, then got clean and left him alone . . . with the drugs and their drug characters and his friend Rank, who's black. Black, yeah. They make their money doing sex stuff for this rich perv named Rana Diablo. That means 'Devil Frog.' In Spanish."

"And the Siren? It's Homer obviously."

"Yeah, I'm gonna change that one. Maybe I'll make it a talking cat or something. A Siamese cat. It's just a vision that comes to him. Like . . . a hallucination?"

Lopate, with his balding pate and clean corduroy sport coat, didn't look much like a connoisseur of hallucinations. I gathered he was really hungry, like I was keeping him from some pasta salad and an ice tea. But a sparkle in his eye suggested that not only did my attempts to be shocking and bold not shock him or make him think I was bold, but he also found me amusing—funny even. And if you're teaching a few dozen students who are writing, almost to a man, about nothing but themselves, and how mommy did this and daddy did that, and about that party when they were six where they didn't get the car, maybe it would be entertaining, at the very least, to take on a camp, wanna-be Burroughs or Ballard (who had no idea how camp he was).

"I want you to know that I think this is interesting," he assured me. "I do, but it's going to be a lot of work."

"I know."

I shifted in my chair. Did he think I was high right now? Had Lasdun trash-talked me? There was no way. He was too nice, too classy, but who knew what these professors kibbitzed about when the students weren't around. How could I show him that for all my affectations, I was serious about this. I would stay clean to finish this. I just wanted it to be good—good like *Less Than Zero*. Good enough to be published. I figured Lopate was already a made enough guy to make that happen.

Will you help me? I wanted to ask. Yeah, maybe this is a stretch, but I know that I have something in me that could be good. Tell me how to get it out. Instead, I put my shades back on and stared out the window as my fellow students hurried toward the cafeteria. The lunch-hour window was dwindling; soon there'd only be the salad bar, no hot food. He stood up and shook my hand and nodded.

"Smile," he said.

"Okay."

I smiled. It was a real smile and felt like a release. It felt good. Who knows when I'd last let that happen. Us Lit Fucks walked around with such put-on pusses.

"Why are you so sullen?" he asked me. "Look around. It's a beautiful day."

As it was with Shirley Clarke, a real artists thinks about . . . lunch, or replacing the paper towels on the roll. They don't fear preoccupation with the mundane. They work, and they live, and some of their projects are more successful than others, but the most successful of them all is the artist himself or herself who has nothing to prove and everything and anything to express beautifully and truthfully. But even if I got that intellectually at twenty-one (and there were moments of rare sobriety when I certainly did), I still couldn't allow myself to believe it. The voices in my head, and now the confident, even-toned voice that heroin added to the caucus, insisted that there had to be weight, suffering, heartbreak. Fights. Jail. Venereal disease. War time experience (during Desert Storm, I briefly considered enlisting just so I would have something on my Lit Fuck friends, a Mailer or Hemingway or Salingeresque combat experience). Lopate walked ahead toward the door, and even though I was headed the same way, I took a detour to give him some space and not further detain him from his pasta salad and iced tea, or whatever it was that was torturing him at the moment.

"The rules of attrition," my ex-roommate Dan Lehman would always say about the fact that every semester a whole army of good friends seemed to leave Bennington. Those determined to go all four years without a break were truly rare. Garbage in, garbage out, as Arnold Friedman used to say before his downfall. One scene gets cut down, and a new rotation moves in. I was more than well used to it all by senior year, determined to form only the loosest of attachments before storming Manhattan with my debut novel in hand. And yet, I was already searching for Zoe Poledouris before I even met her. I was walking with my lunch one afternoon in November 1992 when a freshman girl stepped out of the salad bar. I nearly dropped the tray. She had a bleached-blonde explosion of hair, thick and unwieldy. She wore heavy black eye makeup, a black leather biker jacket, fishnet tights, a pale denim skirt, and platform boots, which added about six inches to her height. Her eyes were big and brown. Her lips were big and frowning. Her face was cherubic but somehow sleek and Arab or Mediterranean looking, like a cross between Isabelle Adjani and Nancy Spungen. To me, at the time, she was just . . . Stella, my novel's heroine and the face and feeling that I was waiting for. I had the clothes, I had the drugs, I had the City-cred. Zoe was the missing piece in my novel and my life, which meant basically the same thing in autumn of '92. I finally had a real live heartbreaker in my sights.

Zoe was a Valley girl from Encino who had gone to Harvard-Westlake. Her father, Basil, was a famous composer of film soundtracks for movies like *Conan the Barbarian*, *The Blue Lagoon*, and *Robo Cop*. He won an Emmy for his score to the miniseries *Lonesome Dove*. And she had a serious boyfriend.

That didn't bother me. I'd taken girls away from their boyfriends before. I was like the Jewish Positive K.

"What's your man got to do with me? I'm not tryin' to hear that, see?"

When we finally spoke, it was clear that she not only knew she'd been checked out but wasn't especially bothered by it. She seemed to be intrigued by me as well, which set me to shy again, my default state. When Gary Oldman pulls Winona Ryder down in a darkened picture show in *Bram Stoker's Dracula*, she heaves, "God, who are you? I know you." And he says, "I've crossed oceans of time to find you." It's a great pickup line. I needed something like that to break our nearly weeklong silence. I came up with "You have really nice feet." One night I walked into my friend U-Floria's room (her real name was not U-Floria, but this is not a pseudonym I'm making up; it's what she called herself then). Zoe was there, sitting on the bed, barefoot. I sat down on the floor and began to play with her toes. Flora clearly had crossed oceans of time to find Zoe as well.

"You have really nice feet," I said.

"Leave her alone," U-Floria groaned, shaking her head. "'Feet.' Jesus."

Flora grabbed her pot pipe and fired it up, then handed it to Zoe, who took a hit and handed it to me. Flora put on *Aladin Sane*. It was her favorite Bowie record. We'd bonded over Bowie and pot and often raided the basement apartments of the "new" houses at the far edge of the woods, blaring a Bowie album on her portable boom box and demanding pot . . . and food.

"Your ankles are so muscular."

"I skate."

"What, like Roller Derby?"

"I'm a figure skater."

I crossed oceans of time to find a figure skater?

"Serious?"

She nodded.

"Competitively?"

She nodded again.

"You have trophies?"

"And ribbons."

"Do you want to hang out?" I asked her.

"When?" Her voice was deep and sandy, slurred with weed.

"Whenever. Tonight? Do you have any plans?"

"Well, actually, I have this thing . . ."

The thing was purportedly a tab of acid. Whether it was actual psychedelics or just some cut up, beat postage stamp full of a hodge-podge of chemicals or just speed, it was a rite of passage I'd long ago completed. Acid was what freshmen did at Bennington, not seniors.

If you'd asked me at twenty-two, "Hey, what's the last thing you want to do at 11 p.m. with a thesis to finish and a nice buzz already going," I'd have put eating acid close to the top of the list, next to driving to the bus station and screaming, "All townies are fags, man!"

Here we go, I thought. You are going to relive every shit ritual for this girl. You are going to go backwards for this girl. Is she worth that? I stared at her feet, her competitive feet, her blue-ribbon feet, and that mass of blonde hair. I smelled her like an animal. Yes. Yes, she is.

"Do you have any for me?"

"We can split it."

That was a relief. U-Floria grunted and walked out to the bathroom. I held out my hand, and Zoe took it. I pulled her up.

That night we shared a hit of acid and sat on her bed in McCullough, that "quiet house." The acid was speedy, and as it surged through us, we drew closer, finding links in our limbs that seemed carved to fit. She put on a Cocteau Twins album. *Heaven or Las Vegas*. "Iceblink Luck."

"Is that what you want to be? A skater? I wasn't aware that Bennington had a program for that."

"I paint."

She said our connection had something to do with her being a Virgo and me being a Libra ("They just get along, I don't know why"). I think it had more to do with the Lit Fuck–VAPA Rat fit. Lit Fucks usually didn't fit well in romance with other Lit Fucks: too much competition. But the Lit Fuck–VAPA Rat pairing usually worked well. For the high-strung thinker, watching someone paint slowly zoned you out and brought peace. It wasn't like dating a dance major (too kinetic and usually stronger than I was); it was like dating a tropical fish tank. Drama Fucks were too prissy. Jazz Kitties, you couldn't write while they practiced. It was too noisy and intense. Plus they drank and drugged even harder than I did. But the writer-painter combo was near perfect. And both required a serious measure of delusion that you might find financial success writing or painting since most of them labored in obscurity: life in the Van Gogh bag. Zoe had the same lack of realism as I did: upper-middle-class family, indulgent parents, shy fellow students who took their hats off to her for being flamboyant. We were already famous in our heads and become famous in every scene that we moved through, two natural leaders. It was just up to the rest of the world to catch up.

"Sometimes I think Elizabeth Fraser is speaking to me. Like I know what she's singing without reading the lyrics. When I figure out what she's really saying, it's usually exactly what I imagined."

We listened to the record in the candlelit room. I had no idea what the fuck either of them was saying, Zoe or Elizabeth Fraser of the Cocteau Twins, but it didn't matter. When her roommate popped her head in, Zoe warned her to stay away for the night.

"You're the match of Jericho that will burn this whole madhouse down," Zoe recited. To me it sounded like, "You and I are chilly so we'll burn this whole madhouse down," which felt then like some pact and seemed a more practical agenda.

"I have to tell you something," she said. "I can't sleep with you."

"Okay."

"I'm with someone."

"I kind of am too." I'd been seeing a music major named Kim, who was in my class and would not be happy at the notion of me chasing some freshman around. "Plus, I don't know if you heard, but I'm sort of a junkie."

"I know."

"You asked about me?"

"People say."

"I haven't done any in a few weeks. I don't need to do it every day."

"Good."

We kissed that night, but as promised, that was as far as it went . . . for about a day.

We parted before class in the morning but made plans to drive together to New York to see the Pixies who were playing at "the new Ritz," with Pere Ubu that November 23. The club, where I'd seen so many new wave and punk shows in high school, had moved from its East Eleventh Street home (now Webster Hall, although technically it's always been Webster Hall) into the old Studio 54.

Zoe's boyfriend had moved from LA to be with her and lived over in Troy, which is probably why it was already closing in on the end of my penultimate semester by the time we hooked up. Things were already heading south with them, which is why she was on campus more frequently. George was some kind of musician and a tweaker. He wore pink tutus as part of his stage gear. Everything pink. His favorite song was "Think Pink" by the Fabulous Poodles (which, to be fair, is a pretty wonderful tune). Apparently someone let him on a stage. Maybe in LA you could sell tuneless industrial pop while dressed like Cheech Marin in his "Alice Bowie" drag. I gathered, hoped anyway, that

George was responsible for her semi-alarming taste in music and that I could somehow reverse it, or at least get her into the new PJ Harvey album, *Dry*, which was my current favorite at the time. I could abide Siouxsie and the Cocteaus but drew the line at Alien Sex Fiend, Clan of Xymox, Skinny Puppy, Front 242, and Nitzer Ebb.

Zoe drove a white Saab turbo at illegal velocity. We made it to the city on the night of the Pixies show in under an hour. As soon as I got to New York, I started playing up the heroin-withdrawal-symptoms thing for attention, even though I hadn't done it in a few months on account of my thesis duties. There was no way I was withdrawing, not even psychosomatically. I just liked that she was concerned.

"Don't worry," she said. "I will make sure you stay clean. I'll stay with you."

"Cool," I nodded, conjuring up my best memory of a withdrawal shiver and a junkie victim's fever frown. "Thank you."

The Pixies (really just Pixies, but even later, when I met them on their 2004 reunion tour, I always said "the Pixies") would be no more inside a year. They'd notoriously break up by fax after an unhappy support slot on U2's Zoo TV tour and be replaced among my Lit Fuck crew by Pavement. That night, however, you'd never know there was any discord among the quartet. I guess they already hated each other, but we loved them so much, we overlooked any tension there. They could have been twice as shambolic, and we would have sweated and pogo-ed and sung along to "Broken Face," "Planet of Sound," and "Caribou" just as maniacally. The band was sputtering, but the songs would always feel aflame and alive, and as the crowd pushed Zoe and me around, we'd literally bump into someone else from school who we hadn't known was heading down. And they'd have a great smile just like ours. It felt more like a community gathering, or church on a Sunday, and seemed to bring Zoe and me closer; all that unhinged love in the room, it opened us up somehow. We drove back from the city late that night after the show, and as Herve and Ron slept in the backseat of her car, we held hands. There was nothing behind us but black, nothing ahead of us but cold black, illuminated by the Saab's halogen heads. We were the only two people in the universe. Just us, the deer, the cold air, and the traffic cops on the snooze. We made it up to Bennington, again in a blink, parked the car, and walked across the lawn, hand in hand. We spent the next two days in bed, with people occasionally knocking at the door to make sure we were alive and us ignoring them. When it was time to clean up, we bathed together. I passed her the soap. When we were hungry, we ordered in pizza and fucked over and over again, as Tex Avery cartoons or a Blondie video album ran on my little TV (they were the only two cassettes I owned). I'd never been that close with anyone before—never let anyone in.

Zoe broke up with George a few days later. She realized, as I did, that we were deeply in love, but she felt guilty and maybe a little scared. He seemed to have some kind of mind control over her, like James Woods has over Sharon Stone in *Casino*. Already more openhearted than I'd ever allowed myself to be, I fretted about it all ending but played it cool. Even if she dumped me, it would let me finally authenticate the novel that I'd all but written. The plot was already there. I get her, then I lose her. It was just waiting for some kind of emotional jump start. This would certainly be it. But I really didn't want to lose her so quickly. If it had been any other girl, I would have gone and found some dope or a spite fuck, but something about Zoe made me check that shit. I tried to have faith in love. I'd waited forever for it.

For two days I didn't see her and prepared for the worst news. He'd talked her out of it. We wouldn't be spending the winter together. We were done. I would have to finish my book without being able to look at her face whenever I wanted to. Maybe I should ask her for a picture. I was sitting in the lunchroom when she finally emerged. She seemed shaken but forced a smile. She reached into her pocket and handed me a copy of Nirvana's *Nevermind*.

"I already have one," I said.

"I know. But now you'll have one for your car."

From that point on, we never left each other's side. "Soul mates," our friend Luke wrote on the wall, with little sketches of our heads together. Luke was one of the first Bennington students I ever met; he was singing "Goodnight Irene" at the orientation bonfire back in 1988. One of the well-behaved Lit Fucks, he could play guitar like Keith Richards but adopted none of his behaviors. Luke was equally obsessed with Christy Turlington and James Joyce. He had a Kilroy-style logo that he'd tag all over campus. You'd walk into a classroom, and it'd be drawn on the blackboard. He modified it to resemble my head touching Zoe's, as if we shared one mind, and for that winter, we did.

I cleaned up significantly during the winter of 1991–1992. Zoe and I spent the freeze in a tiny apartment we'd rented off campus in North Bennington at the top of College Drive, past a waterfall and across from a small country store. We had more space than my little room on campus, but we kept our nest sparse and airy. Zoe set up an aisle in the bedroom where the sun came in the strongest, and I placed a writing desk in the far corner where it was dark and shadowy. She'd paint, and I'd work on a second draft of the novel. It was a process of tightening and polishing and not nearly as stressful as constructing the initial pages. I had moments when I worried that the whole piece had no center. It was all attitude, flashy but brittle. I hadn't really earned the world-weariness that my characters possessed. I was projecting, but I kept my doubts to myself. At night, we'd cook supper, then head up the road to Herve's. He was also writing his thesis in a rented house and nesting with his girlfriend, Janet, a wry brunette visual artist who was painting one canvas after another in a Jean Dubuffet style. If Zoe was indebted to anyone, it was Hasbro, makers of *My Little Pony*. Her canvases were pink and glittery, with unicorns, rainbows, and seahorses, but somehow not ironic. One night we got drunk and gathered around Herve's TV to watch Nirvana make their debut on *Saturday Night Live*. While driving back from the grocery store one day in the white Saab, Zoe and I saw a sign for kittens to adopt, so we drove out to a little farmhouse and took one home. "Just Like Heaven" by The Cure came on while we were driving home, so we decided to call her Heaven. We were an inviolate union: soul mates, dressed in each other's clothes and sleeping entwined with a yellow eyed, bible black pussycat at our feet.

When you finish a book, it doesn't matter if it never gets published; it doesn't matter if it even gets read by another human being not obligated to read it, like a girlfriend or a thesis tutor. You change. You are not the same. Whether or not the book is any good doesn't matter. You are better. I picked it up and felt the weight of all the pages. I smelled them. I flipped them to make that card-shuffling sound. I opened to one page and read a line, and it was good. I did it again, and that line was good too. I held one eye shut, opened to a random page, and read the first word I saw. It was a good word. I'd done something here. I truly believed that it was good enough to publish. I really did. Elizabeth Fraser of the Cocteau Twins was signaling that it was good enough to be published. Ron, Herve, and some of my other professors responded in kind. Only Lopate provided a dose of reality.

"There are some terrific things in here," he told me, and later, while formally reviewing the work, wrote, "Even as I resist going once more around the park with a junkie's tale, I think you are definitely going to be a writer."

"*Going* to be?" I raged later to Herve and Ron, who shook their heads and laughed, as they usually did at my hubris and unchecked ambition (which more often than not manifested itself as fitful impatience). "*Going* to be?" What the fuck did that mean?

In six months, I would be in the real world. No more meal plan, no more weekend parties and heroin dealers on every corner, and no Zoe's face to remind me of the beauty and luck of just being alive: just closed doors in New York, or worse, open doors on Long Island. I could not afford a work in progress. *Loose* was supposed to be a finished statement, a debut, like that of Brett Easton Ellis.

"*Going* to be a writer? Come on, man," I repeated. "Fuck that guy."

"That's kind of cold," Ron said and returned his gaze to one of Herve's old issues of *Raw*. "He helped you a lot, man."

"You just gotta get yourself minted, man," Herve said with a smirk, as he got up and changed the CD from Pavement's full-length debut *Slanted and Enchanted* to a cassette dub of their *Perfect Sound Forever* EP. "That's all that's wrong with you. Nobody's minted you. Gotta get that stamp. The stamp of approval. From an agent. A publisher. Someone with power, down in the city, yo."

"Maybe he is," Steve Malkmus sang in his adenoidal, laconic voice on the track "Debris Slide." *"Maybe he's not . . . "*

Years later, in a *New Yorker* piece someone would refer to Pavement as "Frat rock for the Bennington/Sarah Lawrence set," and it's basically true. A lyric like that might as well have been "Fight for Your Right to Party" to us.

Being with Zoe gave me hope, but it also brought fear. Her mother, Bobbie, always a handsome, cautious, and nurturing presence, stuck with her slightly wilder and brooding father Basil for years before he'd made it. She supported and encouraged him, and his success became their success. This was the Jackson Pollock/Lee Krasner model, I suppose; common to any number of artists and their spouses over the long slog from obscurity to earning a living at this shit-ness. If I didn't find a home for my novel, I knew that I would eventually lose Zoe, either to another boy or to the sadness of her own disappointment, like Betty Blue. Or worse, she would become the Pollock and I'd be demoted to the Krasner. As '92 approached, it was clear that neither of us were equipped to live in a world where I was not going to get published and famous. Someone might lose an eye. And Zoe hated losing anything. It was the skater in her.

I saw this firsthand in the late winter of 1992, just before the start of my final semester. Zoe and I drove to Lake Placid, where she was entered into a figure skating competition. It would turn out to be the last of her professional career. We checked into one of those quaint faux-snow-lodge-style hotels, strung with Christmas lights, just like our room on campus. We sipped hot chocolate on the back porch and slept together in a big, clean bed. The next morning, we drove to the event, which was full of girls who seemed much younger than Zoe. She'd choreographed a number to "Lady Grinning Soul," which is the final track on Bowie's *Aladin Sane*, the album that was playing on the night we first spoke. It really seemed to freak out the Lake Placid judges, who were used to competitors skating to classical gas. I got the feeling that Zoe had won a lot more of these when she was younger and art was less a part of her life. She had put on the same spandex getup that all the other little girls wore, and she just crushed them all. And at one point she had made a choice to make it harder. She expressed more and more of herself: her record collection, her drugs, her nutty boyfriend and his tutus. She lost a lot of friends. She chose to be an artist. It was one of the reasons why I loved her, one of two women I had ever really loved in my life.

"The teacher used to put on the Blondie song 'Rip Her to Shreds' and lecture the class about how they treated me," she once told me. Can you imagine? And she fought back by becoming pretty and smarter and fierce. Only like me, she didn't know what to do when this failed her. When she won, it was a validation for all weirdos. But when she lost . . .

"Goddamn it, Marc!"

She was stomping and cursing at the motel.

I grabbed her and said, "Fuck them! You're beyond all this. Look around. This is stupid. Everything's covered with snow, but these people still buy clothes with pictures of snowflakes on them. What's that about?" I knew what Zoe wanted. She was a suburban kid like me. She wanted both. She wanted what every artist wanted. She wanted to be weird and still win.

In the late eighties and the nineties (but for some reason, not so much in the twenty-first century), there seemed to be a newly invented drug every few months. When I first arrived at school, of course, Ecstasy, or MDMA, was the "must-try," and toward the end of my matriculation, it was Special K. It went, if you will, from the euphoric to the catatonic, from the highest, head-in-the-stars, unable-to-say-anything-but-wow! high to the deepest and stickiest of black holes. Still, most of us welcomed the advent and influx of new drugs as good omens. We were moving into a future. The drugs usually hit Manhattan first and took at least a full season to work their way into our water supply, but by the spring of 1992, K had found us. It had its origins in a monkey or horse tranquilizer, and I, as ever brave in my consumptions and confident beyond deservedness, volunteered to be the monkey or the horse. It was the middle of the day, between morning and afternoon classes, when I greedily snorted the new chemistry, and within a few minutes I was trying to walk down the hall, but both my legs seemed to have melted out from under me like hot candle wax, and I was clawing the paint off the walls, trying to stand up. Those monkeys must shit for days afterwards because I spent the next twelve hours in the can. I was doing my business when Zoe said I had a phone call. It was an agent from New York, and at first I thought she was kidding and was a little mad that she was fucking with a subject so sensitive, but she insisted that she was serious. An actual agent was responding to my unsolicited manuscript and wanted to meet me.

"Which one?" I called as I hastily prepped myself. As with my acceptance to Bennington three and a half years earlier, this wasn't how I'd imagined it would happen.

The agent's name was James Boorman, and he ran a small company called The Literarium out of his apartment on Hudson Street in the West Village. At the time, it was a strange neighborhood. I'd become much more familiar with the East Village and Lower East Side. Boorman told me that he found the book funny and exciting and very fresh and that he would love to meet me in the city at my earliest convenience. I should bring Zoe, and we would all get lunch and talk about the future. "Now that's how it's supposed to happen," I told myself as I hung up the phone.

"I'm so proud of you," she said. "I knew this would happen! I knew it. Do you think we should do something special to your hair?"

I'd dyed my hair jet-black, but it ended up looking too much like Vince Taylor's or Jerry Lewis's coif so I shaved it all off and bleached out the stubble, burning the top part of my scalp in the process. I now had a scabby, platinum blonde buzz cut like Lou Reed at the height of his speedy dissolution, and she had dyed her hair "fuschia shock," a manic-panic color, kind of like a pinker version of the color Kurt Cobain had on the cover of the April 1992 issue of our favorite magazine, *Sassy*. It was the famous one where he is posing next to Courtney Love, and she's pushing her thick, red lips against his cheekbone in profile. They were about to get married and buy a "Victorian house in Seattle" together. Maybe have a baby too. The headline on the cover read, "Ain't Love Grand?" Inside? "Kurt and Courtney Sitting in a Tree . . ." Reading the article by Christina Kelly twenty years later, it's heartbreaking to think that Kurt would blow his head off in the guest room of the house where Courtney confesses, "My favorite thing to think about when we're doing record company meetings and stuff is what color we're going to paint the walls." Nirvana was the biggest new band in the country, and Hole (described as "foxcore") was being offered millions by major labels, but they seemed so protected. They were nesting. They had each other. Drugs were not mentioned once in the piece. Yes, they showed up "late" and, during a photo session, appeared "very Sid and Nancy," but that was about it. If they were getting high, it was part of the cleaving together, wasn't it? It was for Zoe and me, spooning as tightly as we could in our single bed as the cat lolled at our feet. Who could hurt us? And as far as we knew, I was about to be famous too. And she, like Courtney, would be next. The unhinged duo Ween, by the way, was the featured band in the magazine's monthly "Cute Band Alert" . . . an omen if there ever was one.

Boorman, the literary agent, was middle-aged, clean-cut, and vaguely effeminate, not swishy, more affected, like Vincent Price. He had a calming air, which I suspect he'd cultivated while dealing with insane writers. He wore black spectacles on a pair of Croakies, and his office looked like the real thing, full of manuscripts and equipment and supplies. I was a little taken aback by a large, green stuffed macaw hanging from the ceiling on a wooden perch, but maybe it was a gift from one of his best-selling clients. I didn't even ask whom else he represented or kick his tires in any way. I just wanted an agent. Just wanted to get published. Just wanted not to have to get a job. Just wanted to write. If he wasn't a Republican or a Grateful Dead follower, then he was my guy.

Over lunch I assured him, as I had assured Lopate before him, that the drug thing was a phase and the book was a form of healing, and I think he believed me. It was sort of true. I hadn't done any since Zoe and I began living together. I'd stayed away from heroin for the winter after all, and I wasn't about to get hooked on monkey tranquilizer.

"Do you know Will Self?" I asked him.

"Sure," Boorman said.

"I see this as a kind of Jewish American *Cock and Bull*."

Will Self was Jewish too, but this didn't seem to matter. Nothing did. I was twenty-one and meeting with a real agent.

Three or four days later, I received a letter from Boorman, along with a contract, which I signed without reading.

April 7, 1992
Dear Mark,
I was good to meet you (and Zoe) today glad you were able to come down and join me for lunch. All ready a senior editor at Harcourt Brace Jovanovich is reading Loose. I called her and walked it over to her shortly after you and Zoe left. Let's hope she feels as strongly about it as I do.

I tried to ignore the fact that he spelled my name and the word "already" wrong and that he wrote "I was good" instead of "it was good." Maybe he meant "I was good." As far as I was concerned, he was good to agree to represent me. Ron and Herve had no agent. None of our Lit Fuck crew did.

Zoe was in her painting studio in VAPA listening to Daisy Chainsaw's *LoveSick Pleasure* EP. She was obsessed with that band and sometimes conversed in full-on squeaky, bratty Katie Jane Gardside speak the way some stand-up comics mock the way Björk communicates with the people of Earth. I was hovering. It had not been more than two weeks since our meeting with Boorman, but every day felt like torture, especially without the distraction of writing or drugs.

"I'm not going to have a get a real job, right?" I paced the length of the wing. "I'm not gonna have to be normal?"

"You're distracting like eight different people," she said, pulling the shower curtain that covered her little painter's nook closed. "In or out?"

I knew that, at least in part, my lack of rest on the subject had a lot to do with the predicament of wishes coming true and the superstitions they breed. It's like when you're getting dressed and pulling on a sweater, and your eyes are closed, and you're brain is saying, "It's the wrong way around," so you twist it, and that's the wrong way around, and you were right the first time. You can fuck yourself up with doubt. There was no doubt when you were sitting there writing.

Perhaps in part to drown me out with loud guitars and feedback, but most likely as the next stage in her growing Courtney Love fixation, Zoe had formed a band called Table Grade that May with four other female students. Early on it was apparent that all four members wanted it to be a different band. Rachel, the tomboy indie rock bassist, wanted it to be CCR. Emily, the drummer, wanted to be Max Roach. Zoe wanted to be Hole, of course (with a measure of Daisy Chainsaw). Vanessa, the strange, quiet guitarist, was a Stooges gal. They all agreed, as everyone usually does, on The Breeders, Kim Deal's new Pixies side project, and quickly learned to play and harmonize on "Fortunately Gone" from their debut *Pod*. The name Table Grade came from a Bennington professor, Richard Tristman. Supposedly it was dirty. Zoe had T-shirts printed up and booked the band to play various keggers on campus. Table grade. Ready to eat. I had nothing to do but bite my nails and wait to become the Jewish American Will Self, so I wrote them lyrics like *"Let's go down to St. Mark's Place. Punch somebody in the face."*

I helped out lyrically with some of their other "hits," like "Egghead" (about a girl dating a guy who wants to study all the time instead of fuck) and "Mangez Moi" (self-explanatory). After a set at some raucous kegger, Zoe could pretend that she was a rock star, a real one, bound for Lollapalooza and a guest-hosting slot on *120 Minutes*, and I could already smell the lime in the gin and tonics at the major-league Lit Fuck cocktail parties I'd be making the rounds of after graduation. It was a daydream Bohemia, but reality kept crashing in. We were scarfing french fries in the Commons together one day when footage from Los Angeles came over the mounted TV. There were riots, beatings, people being dragged out of cars, burning, and looting. Zoe went to the pay phones to call her parents.

This is the real world I am about to enter . . . with no book contract, I thought as I watched the fire and the looting and the beating. I am so . . . fucked.

CHAPTER 6

If you visit Thirteenth Street between Avenues A and B in 2012, it's really the only street in the area that doesn't seem fully gentrified. In fact, it looks much like it did in 1992, when I moved into my first real Manhattan apartment. The old Roberto Clemente community center remains, as does the Dias y Flores garden, with its upended, buried green-glass bottles in the earth; the old Stuyvesant Town red-brick buildings are still in the distance on Fourteenth Street; there's the same dusty bodega to the east, smelling of incense and cat piss, a thin layer of gray dust or dried, sticky mystery syrup on most of the canned goods, and the same Chinese laundry to the west. There's the little whitewashed Church of the Bible Crusades nestled among the scattering of prewar walk-up tenements. Yes, the price of renting these tenements has tripled, if not quintupled. When I moved to East Thirteenth between A and B, I felt like a carpetbagger, with absolutely no ties to this particular community and, given my drug-crazed state, very few ties to the planet. I guess it would have inevitably seemed like I was being watched by the neighbors as I walked with difficulty toward my door, a twenty-two-year-old kid, moving like a sixty-year-old man, strung out again. There was an unspoken but steamy, seething air of unfriendliness coming my way with no delay from the Puerto Rican and Dominican families who shared the block with me at the time. Yes, it was probably nothing more than a by-product of my drug paranoia or simply a result of my looking like I had worms; I'm not saying I didn't deserve this uneasiness.

In 1992, East Thirteenth was known to some as a "crack block." Apparently one crack spot ruined the entire block's reputation. When I told some of my friends where I'd found a semi-affordable apartment, a few Benningtoners patted my shoulder and said things like, "Good luck, man. That's a crack block." What did that mean exactly: a "crack block"? There were no crack vials on the pavement. Crack was an eighties thing. This was a new decade. Was it a slyly racist way of saying that I could do better than Thirteenth between A and B? Did they mean that I was low-rent? Proud and determined to become a published writer, I vowed not only to make a home and work space there but to single-handledly turn East Thirteenth into a "smack block."

Despite my dope habit, Zoe, was also holding out her Betty Blue hopes that I would soon be an author to brag about. She helped me set up that home, organizing my books and records with me and prepping a nice little writer's nook in the corner of my living room. My desk faced a wall, not a window. The living room had none, but I put up photos and postcards of my heroes, as I'd done in the Chelsea Hotel. We bought candles with paintings of saints on them from the bodega and stuck them in every available corner for warmth, color, and protection. My mother donated some white Naugahyde furniture that had become unfashionable over time out on Long Island, but transport it through the Tunnel (in one of the trucks borrowed from the family lumberyard) and place it in the East Village, and suddenly you had some very enviable "retro" décor. The little bedroom had the best light. We slept in a futon on the floor and managed to jam an alarm clock and a little boom box into the corner. Nothing else would fit. Heaven, our *gato negro*, padded around, picking out her favorite spots. In the morning, we could hear the bells from the Russian Orthodox church over on Tenth Street . . . and the chirping sparrows. With a naked Zoe next to me, it was thrilling—the sound of New York City coming to life. Once I'd moved in, Ron, Herve, and a bunch of our other Bennington friends came over for a housewarming, and I used my new kitchen to cook up a big pot of *arroz con frijoles*. It was honest, inexpensive, good food that a hungry writer waiting on his book deal could survive on and stretch. Goya's fine line of products would keep me energized.

We went to the Wigstock Festival in Tompkins Square Park where Lady Bunny presided and a half dozen drag queens reminded me that I'd better work. Zoe was obsessed with drag culture and borrowed mightily from its aesthetic for her basic, day-to-day ensembles. She considered herself the first female drag queen. We got drunk and danced to TLC, Deee-Lite, and Right Said Fred, but I knew that she was going to leave me, and I couldn't enjoy any real abandon. The day she returned to Bennington to start her sophomore year in September 1992, I of course had a panic attack. The past year had been about our book, our paintings, our plans for success. Now, I was alone and could not seem to remember how to breathe. Even the birds and the bells seemed to disappear; she took them with her somehow, or maybe I just slept through them, no longer in a hurry to get up and take Manhattan (then Paris . . . then Berlin . . . then Tel Aviv). With Zoe in Vermont studying, I'd wake around noon and check the fridge to see if there was any rice and beans left. It's all I can remember consuming at this time: red beans, sofrito, yellow rice, maybe some hamburger meat if I could afford it, and a few onions. One could eat for a week for ten bucks. I'd start a pot on a Monday, slow-cooking a half dozen fine Goya products all day. When the pot was down to its burnt, shellac dregs, I'd scour it and start another pot. After eating, I'd make some Café Bustelo coffee and smoke four cigarettes in a row. I'd shave with a disposable razor and shower in the little pink-tiled toilet where I'd hung my Bennington diploma, then clean and fully awake . . . do nothing at all. I'd sit and stare at the dozing cat or MTV and wait for a call from my agent. It never came. I was back on smack in less than two weeks. I didn't make a big show out of the heroin this time, since there was nobody to impress, no pose worth striking. A snort of dope was just a mother's little helper now, something to get me through the day and eat up some time until Boorman, the agent, rang with the news: someone, anyone had accepted *Loose*.

By October, as I turned twenty-two, I was fully strung out again, using every day, and soon it was fuck the rice and beans, fuck making the coffee, fuck changing the cat box and shaving with the disposable razor. I'd wake up, figure out whether the darkness was dawn or dusk, and either way, do a few lines, then walk downstairs and buy a sugary "regular coffee" (this means different things in different New York bodegas as far as the lightness or darkness goes; mostly it's on the dark side, but it's always the small size and always has at least three scoops of white sugar in it). I'd pick up the *Post*, and if it was a Wednesday, the *Free Press* too. The *Press* had a lot of pull at the time; many of its writers were even better than the *Voice*'s. And it was obviously cheaper as the *Voice* cost a dollar. Best of all, it featured Kaz's *Underworld* strip, which had become a favorite among most of my not scattered Lit Fuck crew.

Herve was living over on Eleventh Street between B and C in similar desperation, working on his own novel and growing his black hair out. He didn't even have an agent yet. He was hoping to land a job in an art gallery, maybe the Whitney or the Guggenheim, because we'd read that's how the members of Pavement supported themselves before they made it. We went to the former in October to see Jean-Michel Basquiat's exhibit. Neither of us had enough money to buy a catalog, even though we really wanted one, even if it was a little ridiculous to put out a glossy coffee table book full of art that I'd passed on the Manhattan Streets at twelve and thirteen without caring. It was all just graf then; now it was some kind of lifestyle statement. Still, we coveted it, and when Herve's girlfriend purchased one for herself, we spent hours losing ourselves in all the sly, subtle details and street-smart text. Basquiat was soothing for writers. If he'd gone to Bennington, he'd have been a VAPA Rat. We claimed him, as we did with all beautiful and worthy artists, as one of our own.

"What were Pavement? Docents?"

"Guards, man. Guards."

I don't know. Those dudes didn't seem too tough. If I was hanging a Van Gogh, I think I'd rather have Glenn Danzig or at least someone beefy like Greg Dulli to guard my Basquiats.

I'd sit on a bench in Tompkins Square Park with my free weekly and flip over to *Underworld*, hungry for an anti-aphorism or at least a chuckle. Kaz's universe featured a bevy of strung out, nihilistic characters: muggers, drunks, junkies, the Grim Reaper, and my favorite, the Smoking Cat ("Alright!!! So I'm a cat smoking a cigarette, OK? Will you leave me alone already?"). I knew which book and magazine stores had a loose policy when it came to standing and reading. Most of the locally run smoke shops shooed you out the door unless you bought a pack of gum or a lottery ticket, but you could linger in See Hear on Seventh Street or Tompkins Square Books pretty easily. A few singles got you a cup of good chicken-noodle soup and eggy yellow challah, maybe even another coffee, at Kiev or Veselka, the two Ukranian diners along Second Avenue. Then it would be time to call Boorman without seeming desperate. If I placed my daily call at ten, as he was opening up shop, I'd seem pathetic. But at two or three, I'd be pathetic but seem cavalier. I'd smack my cheeks with my palms and shout, "Raaaaah!" so as not to sound high. I'd wake up my system. Then I'd ring, knowing quite well that if there were any news, he'd be the first to ring me.

"You know, if I were you, I'd just say fuck it and start another book," Herve said as I sat on his bed and thumbed through an article on the David Wojnarowicz, who'd just died of AIDS. He clipped a black-and-white image of the artist smoking a cigarette from the paper and carefully taped it to the wall. "*On the Road* was Kerouac's second book. Nobody cared about his first until after that one got published. *Loose* exists, man. They could publish it five years from now. They could publish it after we're all dead. You won't even know."

"But I *want* to know." I fretted and aimlessly ran my finger across the keys of his typewriter as *Loveless* by My Bloody Valentine, our favorite album during that period, played. My Bloody Valentine sounded like dope felt, droning and drowning. Our long, eventless afternoons together could sometimes resemble the "Space Madness" episode of *Ren and Stimpy*, a turgid, six-year mission to the Crab Nebula. We got on each other's nerves, and hunger of all varieties just exacerbated it.

"They say you should put your first novel in a drawer anyway. The second one is really the first. In that light, you haven't even written a novel yet. You should start one. Just start typing. Right now."

"Whatever."

I wrote nothing. I was a stronger person when I began *Loose* that winter. I had nutrition. I'd gone off the dope. I got to see my Zoe every day. The notion of beginning another novel in this state? I'd rather push the History Eraser Button. Herve got up and took the MBV out.

"Leave it," I begged.

"I'm getting sick of it. It's all we listen to anymore."

He popped in a cassette. Some Ethyl Meatplow song came on his boom box. It was a mixed tape his girl had given him, and I guess it had sentimental value, and much as I loved him and was grateful for his proximity, I just found it predictably grating. Years later, the band would morph into the rootsier Geraldine Fibbers, whom I found much more charming but still never listened to. Herve was probably the smartest Lit Fuck at school, a more natural writer than I was anyway and much less self-destructive but he had a tendency to be taken in more easily by the charlatans of the new alt. culture, whether it was spending his money on every Pavement-inferior band that also happened to be signed to Matador Records or investing in what then seemed to be utterly wiggy ideas like a form of literary hypertext that would self-update on a computer screen or auto-edit every few seconds; rendering any concrete narrative impossible, and I suppose, impossibly dated. I was more of a romantic; a classicist about it all. I still used a typewriter when I could. Maybe it was because he didn't grow up anywhere near Manhattan. He lacked our suspicion-chip.

One night on his way home after hanging out with me at the Holiday, Herve was mugged in his vestibule at knifepoint, like a Kaz character, only the mugger and the knife were dead real. He was shaken but unharmed, largely because he had no cash to spare, and the assailant had taken pity on him, felt sorry for him even. He'd spend that week broke until the next care package from home or his own good news call from the Whitney came over the wire. At least he wasn't in the morgue. I snorted some smack to numb myself, but at that point it was barely enough. I could no longer afford the amount I needed to really do the trick. And even if I had the money, I was afraid now to go anywhere on my own. I knew that it was just a matter of time before it happened to me too—a mugging, a murder—and the feeling made me sick. I never saw cops anywhere in my neighborhood then. I don't think I saw one cop between the fall of 1992 and winter of 1993.

To kill time between getting published or stabbed, Herve suggested that we collaborate on a play. I agreed, figuring maybe it would jump-start the old Bennington workshop–born creative competition and get me writing my own stuff again. I'd wake up, do my rituals, then walk over to his apartment. We'd put on *Selected Ambient Works* by Aphex Twin, U2's *Achtung Baby*, or Sonic Youth's *Dirty*, sit on his bed, and throw ideas at each other.

"I have an idea for the title," he'd say. "Welschmerz!"

"What's that?"

He picked up the Oxford English Dictionary, opened it, and read: "Mental depression or apathy caused by comparison of the actual stare of the world with an ideal state."

"That's a good word," I said. "That's like . . . *our* word."

We didn't really have that collaborative chemistry. Our personalities were too strong and stubborn, and *Welschmerz* (later retitled *Welschmerz 2000*) never really got anywhere.

"It doesn't matter," Herve shrugged. "There's not going to be any text in the future anyway. Not like this. It's all going to be hypertext. What we just wrote, that will change in a blip and become something else. Or someone a thousand miles away will change it and make it her own play." I never followed his train as he basically foresaw the coming Internet culture. Ink, paper, maybe a cloth jacket, that's all I cared about.

"You wanna go check out DJ Spooky later?" he asked.

"What's the cover?" I couldn't remember the last time I paid to go anywhere or do anything. DJ Spooky was another one. Herve got him. I didn't, although I admired him for being able to hustle a lot of people into believing in his vision. I didn't even have a vision.

Sometimes we'd have no money for dope and have to throw ourselves on the mercy of a scattering of wealthy, vaguely Euro-trash friends who'd been satellites at school—non-Bennington students who came up to party and date Bennington girls. They all lived in Manhattan in luxury, attended private schools, and spent part of the year in Italy or South America. They always had money for dope. And food. We dug them because they were a blast to hang out with, naturally decadent as they were, but we all secretly resented them too. They were already rich, first of all, so there was no real camaraderie as far as a sense of struggle went. Second, they'd never really be "one of us." You had to live up there, year-round. Take the classes. Breathe the air. Eat the tempeh. The best of this crowd was a kid named Tony. He was Brazilian, with a high forehead, curly black hair, big white teeth, a dark sense of humor, and a formidable charisma—enough to make him a sort of honorary Bennington kid. Tony lived in a two-story loft across the street from where Jean-Michel Basquiat lived and worked and died on Great Jones Street. His stepmother lived on one floor, and he lived on another. His father was dead. Anthony's real mother wasn't around, but there were rumors that she was cut out of the family fortune and kept on to cook and clean. That had to have put the whammy on his kinky head because Tony did more heroin than anyone I knew and had no qualms about copping dope himself, even though he could easily afford a courier. He had a minifridge full of methadone as well for days when he decided to come off the junk. When I was at a loss and tapped out, Tony was always good for an evening of posh danger. He was Sanity Claus, in the sleigh overhead, loaded with goodies; the eye in the sky with the highest tech security cameras scanning our pinned retinas. As I tried not to appear too sick and hungry in the lobby, security cameras scanned me while Tony sat in his throne chair upstairs, playing some computer game about medieval warfare and deciding whether to let me in immediately or make me shake for his amusement. Just the sound of the click when the electronic locks released made my nose run.

The place was cavernous and climate controlled. Long, black leather couches and rococo pillars lined the glossy hardwood floors. A giant Botero oil hung on the back wall. We would always have to ask for a line, and Tony would ruminate on whether to be generous. He'd roll out a scroll and stare at it.

"This is a Picasso," he'd say, and I'd have to admire and discuss it, when I was really only interested in the smudge of white flakes that smeared his *Bizarre Ride to the Pharcyde* CD jewel box. We had a thing: we'd only snort drugs off albums we loved. All part of the movie. You'd never catch me snorting dope off a Cop Shoot Cop CD.

"He could really draw some bitches down," he'd sniff.

"Picasso. Word." I'd agree. I would have agreed with anything.

Tony would always share eventually if he had it to spare. He was just amusing himself, killing time with dangerous distraction, as we all were. At heart, he was a brother, even if he just didn't get the Bohemian urchin style. It wasn't his fault. Too much money. Tony dressed in new, expensive clothes and sunglasses. He'd never think to incorporate a vintage coat or shoes. We didn't get his aesthetic either. It was complicated, expensive, and cold. Even Tony seemed alienated by it sometimes. A Nam June Paik video installation flickered in the bedroom on the wall behind the couch, but he couldn't be bothered half the time to plug it in and would often prefer watching the same John Woo film (*The Killer*) while chopping out more lines. I knew *The Killer* back to front by that point. He'd amp the volume and smile his big toothy grin.

"Watch this coming up . . . watch . . . you watching? You tell me who ends up standing after this gunfight, and I'll give you some."

"It's the guy in the brown suit. He's the undercover cop."

"We'll see."

Tony would always forget that he'd screened *The Killer* again and again. He's cut out a line and hand the CD box over to me.

"Easy to pick up," Tony would say, quoting a line of dialogue in the film that references a gun, not a line of dope. "Hard to put down." He was a funny kid, sweet and generous in his way, and I'm sure that we would have been friends if we'd been into baseball and shot-gunning beers, but who can say? Junk was how we rolled.

When we'd all get restless or happy enough to go out and float, we'd take a short walk over to Second Avenue and shoot some pool or play the jukebox at Nightbirds, a dive with none of the eccentric character or Old World soul of the Holiday. Robert, the bartender, had ass-length hair like Anthony Kiedis and was clearly wise to the fact that we were all high. But we bought drinks and only threw up on the floor a handful of times, so he let us be. Tony and his friend Mags bought drinks anyway and commanded the pool table, while Herve and I voluntarily took our billiard beatings and cadged him for cash for drinks and cigarettes and the jukebox. Sometimes, a little buzzed, I'd place a collect call to Zoe from the pay phone by the toilets, but she was never in her house, and usually the charges were rejected.

Occasionally the old man would wire me a portion of his racetrack winnings, which I would pick up at the Western Union in Times Square. It was always worth the trip to the main hub because it never closed. One of the worst things in the world was to trek all the way to a Western Union office in a grocery store or pharmacy or check-cashing place only to be told that the machine was broken or they were only sending and not receiving money.

"You don't deserve to put that yellow-and-black sign in the window!" I'd slur. "That sign is a fucking covenant!" Then I'd slink off back to *Underworld* to suffer. I only panhandled once. My shyness saved me from a life of begging, I suppose. In order to ask people for spare change, you had to actually make eye contact and speak with them.

"Please help me out." I just couldn't do it. Public speaking and all.

Whenever I did have a little loot, I'd go over to the Angelika movie theater on Houston Street. This was especially good as the weather started getting warm. I'd disappear off the street into the blue-lit lobby and ride the slow elevator down into the air-conditioned asylum with "Human Fly" by the Cramps, "The Selecter" by The Selecter, or any number of "this sounds like heroin feels" tracks, like all of *Loveless*, playing low in my headphones. The rumble of the subway through the theater walls was the only intrusion of reality—people going places, to work, home to their families, or out of town. I was going nowhere at all.

Yes . . .

Of course, I knew that a hot meal, laundry, and a good night's sleep on clean sheets were always, always an option. The Five Towns were forty-five minutes away, as they'd always, always been. An hour counting the trip to Penn Station. I could be hungry on the corner at 1 p.m. and fed and clean at 3. Twice a day. I still had a key. I still kept the train schedule in my pocket.

"Just go home," I'd sometimes tell myself when I'd wake up early and get that sickening feeling, like single days were now three full years long. I didn't want my mother and stepfather and sister to see how bad I looked, how sallow and thin I'd become. I was ashamed of how stringy and greasy my hair was, how bad my skin had gotten. Besides, it was their home now, not mine. I would just be an unwanted guest. What's worse than being somewhere you know you're no longer wanted? Especially if you've talked big about leaving it behind.

I'd gone full circle from wanting attention to wanting to disappear. When I'd call Zoe, I'd sense a distance. She must have heard I was on dope. Ron had stayed away, finishing up his senior year.

"It's a bad scene down there," he'd tell those who asked after us.

"She's not sleeping around," Herve assured me. "She wouldn't. Why would she? You two are in love."

"I don't know." Because it was college? Because that's what you do in college?

"Would you if you were her?" Yes. Absolutely—which is why I knew she was having her fun. We'd become the same person, grafted together after all those nights sleeping in our spoon formation in that tiny, tiny bed. We saw the world the same way; we were ambitious and opportunistic and spoiled and impatient, and losers would not be suffered. I was losing. Herve grabbed the *Post* out of my hand and began pouring over it with scissors. He cut out a photo of an NYPD officer and hung it on the wall next to a postcard I'd stolen from a stationary store on Bleecker Street. It showed a brick wall. Someone had spray-painted, "Come in my house. I want to hurt you!" on it. They still sell those postcards, and every time I see them, I feel a tightness in my stomach and some bile in my throat. I smell dope. I eat worms. It was and remains the perfect junkie totem—down and out in the East Village in the early nineties personified. Two disinterested pigeons hung out in the foreground.

"Come in my house. I want to hurt you!"

Not every Bennington friend stayed away. When Jack Madagascar, a smart, hip sophomore rolled down from New England, he always made a point of stopping in and making sure we were alive . . . or at least only half dead. Jack was Bronx born, gay, and typically fearless, as most of the gay dudes I knew back then were and perhaps had to be. He was wired all wrong and tended to rock back and forth whenever he sat in his chair. I don't even think he realized he was doing it, and after a point, it didn't seem strange. The rhythm was actually kind of soothing, like one of those desktop metronomes filled with colored oil and water. When down from school to visit, he not only refrained from passing judgment but used either my apartment or Herve's as a sort of weigh station, a place to rest, piss, play Pavement, or get high. Whenever he got high, for some reason Jack started cleaning. He was short and boyishly handsome, with a dyed auburn fringe in which he sometimes clipped baby barrettes in ice-cream yellow, pink, and blue. Up at school, when we were still classmates, we bonded over The Smiths (of course) . . . and junk (inevitably). Zoe loved him too. He was one of our favorite people; he had a camp sensibility, a really dark, black, nothing-is-sacred sense of humor.

One night, while I was hanging out with Herve, Jack brought over a pair of strangers, a teenage boy and girl who initially made us nervous. They looked very clean-cut and bewildered.

"It's okay, they're not cops; look at them!" he said as he dusted Herve's stack of CDs.

"Who are they?"

"They're giving me a ride back up."

"How is it up there?"

"I'm not spying on Zoe for you, girl."

Jack called me "girl." It wasn't an insult; it was a term of endearment and maybe a little bit of a warning, like, "Stop acting like such a fucking girl."

The two kids looked at me like they knew who I was. Herve offered them a beer, and they nursed it while we all shared another bag of dope. I guess we were showing off for them because we were snorting it up with even more disregard for safety than had become the norm: "just enough to get happy but functional." We'd overdone it for the captive audience of fresh-scrubbed straights.

"I'm high," I smiled.

"Alpine." Herve deadpanned. Jack didn't say anything. We looked over at him, and it became obvious really quickly that something was wrong. Jack was bloodless and blue. His mouth was distorted into a stiff, dead-guy rictus. Herve and I pounced on him and tried to slap him awake, but he fought to stay wherever he was. It was nicer there than in Herve's bedraggled apartment with its collaged walls and roaches.

"Fuck, fuck, fuck, fuck, fuck!" I shouted.

"What's happening?" the clean-cut boy whined.

"Shut the fuck up," I ordered. "Jack! Come on, man."

"We have to get him to the hospital," Herve said.

"Where's your car?" I asked the girl.

"It's parked downstairs."

"Alright, come on. Let's get him up."

All of us tried to pick Jack up, but he was dead weight. We dropped him and decided we'd have to drag him. We grabbed his feet and pulled him into the hall as Herve grabbed his keys. We tried to protect Jack's head as we slid him down the stairs, but the back of his skull hit three steps on the way down. He did not react to the impact.

He's gone, I thought. You don't come back from that. Nobody comes back from that. I tried to determine, as if I'd had years of legal training, just what crime, if any, I'd committed. I didn't cop the smack. It was Herve's. Or was it? Maybe it was mine. Fuck. And who knew how much he'd taken or drunk earlier. Was it our fault? Did we need to flee as soon as we dropped him off? Were we all going to jail? And would that help me get published? Was there a way to spin this in my favor—no publicity being bad publicity and all?

"Boorman? Spitz. Guess what, man? I'm at Rikers! I know it's dangerous, but it sure beats Thirteenth Street. So, publicity-wise, does that get us any-where with *Loose*?"

We drove across Ninth Street to St. Vincent's even though we were on the far East Side. It was the only hospital I knew, and I only knew it because Dylan Thomas died there after drinking at the White Horse Tavern, then staggering home to the Chelsea Hotel. At least Jack would die in good, liter-ary company. I knew that Herve was devising the same thing. He had an agenda, just like I did. He wanted to be a badass writer, but only just. We both wanted careers, not criminal records.

"What do we do?" Herve asked. The kids up front were shaking, and Jack was drooling, draped across our legs.

"We roll up, throw him out, and drive off," I say.

"Word." Herve said.

They pulled into the driveway of the emergency room, and I opened the door.

"Okay, push him out?" I asked.

"No. We'll walk him in," Herve said.

There were no cops in the lobby, and once I saw the light and the nurses, I felt like we could risk it. With our luck, nobody would see him in the drive-way anyway, and he'd be run over by a couple of paramedics. We picked Jack up, one shoulder each, and dragged him through the glass door and offered him up to the gods.

"Help!" I said. "We found this guy, and he's messed up. He's overdosed. We just . . . found him. Okay?"

Two orderlies materialized and grabbed him, and I remember feeling bet-ter noticing the absolute lack of panic or surprise in their expressions. They'd seen this a hundred times already that year, maybe even that month. They routinely took him off our hands and disappeared with him into the hallways of the great Gothic building. Herve and I looked at each other and shrugged, then quickly beat it out the door and hopped into the backseat of the Bennington kids' car.

"Can we get a ride?" Herve asked. The kids, now thoroughly freaked out, obliged us, probably out of fear or reflex. We made a request, and they mechanically fulfilled it to avoid dwelling on the fact that they'd probably just seen a fellow student pass away.

"So," I said, lighting a cigarette without bothering to ask if it was okay. I was convinced that I'd lived up to the bad reputation they'd undoubtedly heard about and was now absolutely determined to exult in it since I'd probably be in prison soon enough. "What's your major?"

Once we got back to Herve's apartment and the Bennington kids had made their escape, Herve paced, and I did a bit more dope to try to calm down.

"He's dead."

"He's not dead."

"He wasn't breathing. He was blue."

We chain-smoked and didn't say much. After about an hour, there was a buzz at the door.

"Cops?" I asked. We looked at the pile of dope. Neither of us wanted to flush it. Herve answered the intercom.

"Yeah?"

We waited for the baritone of an NYPD officer and instead heard the irritated, high-pitched whine of Jack Madagascar, back from the dead.

"Why did you bitches leave?"

We buzzed him up. Jack looked annoyed but pink and full of life. He was drinking a can of root beer from a straw and had a hospital bracelet on his right hand. He sat down and lit a cigarette.

"What happened to my ride?"

"They split."

"Shit. How am I going to get back to school?"

"What'd they do to you?" I asked, gesturing to his bracelet.

"Do you like it? I think it's faboo." He wrist-modeled the hospital bracelet. "I'mna work it."

A few weeks later, Boorman and I had reached our endgame. I met him at his office, and we decided to get a "business lunch." It seemed like a normal thing for an agent and his client to do, and it made me feel like I too had been revived after some glimpse into the abyss.

"If I'm honest, I'm not sure why you're upset." Boorman was eyeing me over his heavy-based ceramic coffee cup like a disappointed parent.

"How can you ask that? It's been a fucking year, man."

"Sometimes it takes five years to find the right editor who truly shares your vision."

"Are you fucking with me?"

In five years, I'd be twenty-seven. I wasn't going to live past twenty-seven. None of the good ones did. I wanted to be published in my lifetime. Meet Jim Carroll. At least get my cable turned back on. I'd ordered a burger with no money to pay for it. I assumed he'd pick up the check. That's what an agent was supposed to do—what a surrogate parent was obliged to do. We were in a little tavern in the West Village for a strategy meeting, but it was more like a tragedy meeting, a wake for my painfully short and abortive writing career.

"What about St. Martin's?"

"Passed."

"Goddamn those cocksuckers! Sons of bitches."

"Are you upset because you believe in *Loose*?"

"Yes, that's why I'm upset! God!" It wasn't why I was upset. Not even close.

I'd long stopped believing in my book. It was the kind of thing a college kid writes to make himself seem tough to other college kids, and I knew it now. One week actually living and not autodirecting stray, cinematic moments in Manhattan, and I knew it. The book had no guts. It was a tourist account. A "real" New Yorker could see through it before chapter two, even one in an Oxford shirt or a nice blouse, an editor living in a doorman building in the West Seventies. First Long Island. Then Bennington. I was still frontin'. Still posing like I knew what was up. And with every morning I woke up and instantly counted out the few bills in my black leather wallet, with every time I managed to feed myself and to not get jumped and to get what I needed from a day on my "crack block," I knew I was getting closer to authentic. The time to write something with truth and soul was now. A book? A play? A letter to Zoe? A sign to take on the subway when asking for change? A suicide note. Whatever it was, it would be better than my first novel, *Loose*. Brett Ellis got published out of college because he was smart enough to write about a world that he knew inside and out before expanding on his style. I was not as smart as Brett Ellis. I was still writing about a world that I wanted to know. And then I lived it, after it had already become played out. It was as ass-backwards as it gets.

"Can I just talk to someone? If you set up a meeting for me, I'm sure I could get St. Martin's to reconsider. Please, man."

"I warned you about getting a reputation."

"I don't have a reputation. I want a reputation!"

"Even if someone agreed to meet with you for lunch or a coffee, I don't feel comfortable sending you in there. I have a reputation."

"What's wrong with me?"

"You're like Sean Young."

"What?"

"Sean Young. She was one of the biggest actresses in Hollywood, but she didn't play by the rules. She acted like a crazy person, and now she has to do a nude scene in every movie."

"Is this what you're doing instead of selling my novel? Watching Sean Young movies?"

"It's an example. It's a cautionary tale. You should learn from Sean Young."

It didn't even strike me as strange that a New York literary agent was using Sean Young and not, say, Anne Sexton or Frank O'Hara or Hart Crane as a cautionary tale. I didn't stop to analyze much of anything for too long then. All I did was want. I wanted money. I wanted Zoe. I wanted an identity. I wanted out.

CHAPTER 7

"**P**erot." This was among my grandfather's final words. Charlie, the alpha male of the family, was the guy who'd kept everyone, myself included, fed and sheltered. He'd sent me to Bennington. He'd paid for my stay at the Chelsea Hotel. He'd made my uncles wealthy men and would have done the same for my father if he'd stuck around. The company he built from nothing, Bay Ridge Lumber, is in shambles today, but at the time it was big business. Charlie got sick in late 1992 and passed away shortly before the presidential election, after his prostate cancer spread to his bones. He had a TV in his private hospital room and, in one of his last moments, pointed at the screen while watching the nightly news.

"Perot," he muttered and pointed weakly.

Charlie was a lifelong Republican. He got Christmas cards signed by the Reagans. I assume he would have voted for the incumbent George H. W. Bush, but maybe, had he lived, he would have cast his ballot for the eccentric billionaire spoiler, H. Ross Perot. He certainly wouldn't have been pleased to see Bill Clinton defeat them both. We had a bond. Charlie took me to see my first R-rated movie (*Apocalypse Now*) when I was just ten, and whenever they visited from Florida, I would sometimes find him doing calisthenics in my room so as not to wake my grandmother Reggie. I guess he assumed I'd understand, and the familiar slapping sound of his aging, sagging muscles being flexed was weirdly soothing. He was the protector, but I'd gotten so far down that I didn't think anyone could save me anymore.

Turns out I was wrong as usual. Even in death, Charlie would take care of me.

The family gathered down in Florida for the funeral. My grandmother was in a fog and needed round-the-clock care, and there were affairs to put in order . . . tributes to be paid.

There was no way I could avoid showing up, even though I didn't want anybody in the family to see how decrepit I'd let myself become. I sat in my shower the night before the funeral, hoping to steam all the poisons from my pores with the shower spray.

It was hopeless. Maybe if we were Catholic, like I wanted us to be, and there were a weeklong wake . . . Jews bury their dead so quickly. As it stood, there was not enough time between now and the ceremony for me to make myself look remotely healthy. I gave up and decided to own it.

When I showed up at the airport, it was balmy, but I was wrapped in a heavy, black-leather jacket that I'd purchased at Cheap Jacks vintage shop on Broadway just off Union Square when I was still a senior up at school. I kissed my mother and shook my stepfather's hand. My sister was back at the house on the eighteenth hole, holding our grandmother's shaking hand with the big gold rings on every finger. Nobody said anything as they drove me from the airport in Florida out to my grandmother and grandfather's house in Fort Lauderdale. Nobody said anything at the funeral. I put on a tie and a shark-skin sport jacket with black jeans and combat boots. I wore aviator glasses and smoked my Camels. Nobody said anything back at the house as I dove into the swimming pool, with its unskimmed surface full of dead bugs and leaves, and did laps in my black underwear. Nobody said anything as I picked low-hanging, overripe tangerines from the trees in the yard, punctured them with my dirty fingers, and brought the juice up to my mouth like I was Ratso Rizzo and needed to be healed by sun and citrus. I laid out in the sun in my jeans, boots, and Circle Jerks T-shirt, listening to the local station on the transistor radio I'd borrowed from the housekeeper who worked for my grandparents. Classic rock. "Let My Love Open the Door," "More Than a Feeling," "Roadhouse Blues," "Killer Queen," "Roll with the Changes," "Too Much Time on My Hands," Paul Rodgers warning, like my father once warned my mother, that he was "bad company," till the day he died. Radio hadn't switched whole hog to the alternative format yet, and it was oddly comforting to hear the songs of my preteen years, when I didn't even know what darkness was. It was good to get out of the city, with the drugs and the business and the no business. I knew where my next meal was coming from. There were cookies and cable TV and air conditioning.

As we were going to fly back to New York, my mother and stepfather confronted me in the yellow and white, air-conditioned kitchen.

"Marc, we have something for you," my mother said and produced a rust-colored leather folder with a rusty-looking zipper and thick, baseball-mitt-sized stitching.

"This belonged to your grandfather. I'm sure he would feel good knowing that you were keeping your poetry in here."

"Mom, I don't write poetry anymore. I'm a novelist. I have an agent."

"I know."

"There's something else," my stepfather said gravely.

"What is it?" It couldn't be good news. I braced myself.

"Grandpa left something for you. It's just a little bit of money. He was very proud of you. You know that right?"

The blow never came. This was something different. I tried not to grin, perhaps a little too hard. I looked depressed, which made them more concerned.

"Yeah?"

"We talked about it, and we decided that we're not going to give it to you. Not right away. We're going to hold onto it. For you."

"How much?"

"A little money, that's all," my stepfather repeated. "It doesn't matter."

"It's for your future," my mother said.

Ten dollars would have been "fuck you" money at that point. I couldn't afford the flight down to Florida myself. I had to fly a day behind everyone else because I couldn't purchase my own ticket. I had no clothes that didn't smell like cigarettes and junk sweat. All my toiletries were travel sized since that was all that I could afford at one time: tiny shaving creams, half tubes of toothpaste, miniature bottles of baby shampoo.

"We know you've been using drugs," my stepfather said. He didn't have the blood connection to me and kept no real sentimentality. Even later, when we made amends, he maintained the ability to disconnect when things got hairy. It was his killswitch, typical of step parents.

"We're not going to hand you a rope to hang yourself with," he said.

He sounded just like my agent.

"I'm not doing drugs."

"You might not be doing drugs this minute, but you don't look so good. We want you to see a doctor, and we want you to go away for a while. Somewhere you can get clean."

"I'm not going to rehab."

"What's rehab?"

"Rehab? You want me to go to rehab, and you don't know what rehab is? Rehab. That's where drug addicts go. If I were a drug addict, which I'm not, that's where I'd go."

"If you're not doing drugs, how come you know about rehab?"

"Everyone knows about rehab. Come on." Kitty Dukakis, who could have been the First Lady four years earlier, had recently published her memoir, in which she confessed to drinking rubbing alcohol when she couldn't get any booze. The culture of addiction and recovery hadn't peaked yet, but it was hardly in the shadows, as it had been when my mother was married to a coke-head in the sixties and seventies.

"I don't know anything about this," she protested. "I don't even know what drugs you're doing."

"We don't care," my stepfather said. "It's not important. Whatever it was, it's over now."

"I know. You're right. I'm fine. I experimented. It's over."

"What did you experiment with?" my mother asked. Maybe she'd heard I was living on a crack block.

"Nothing. I didn't experiment. Stop this . . . trickery!" They were playing hardball, good cop, bad cop, using hoodoo and witchcraft on me. Running smoke screens. Kicking sand. I was too weak to defend myself. And the waterworks hadn't even begun yet. They were coming. The subject had been put on the table.

"Then what's wrong with you?" my mother cried. "Why are you so skinny? And dirty?"

"I'm despondent!"

My little sister walked into the room in a red bathing suit with a pink-and-white towel draped over her shoulder.

"Are you wearing sunscreen?" my stepfather asked her. She rolled her eyes as if to say, "I'm not the one you need to worry about." She patted my shoulder as she passed and continued to the pool.

"Good luck," she said. I watched her go and heard the splash as she dove in. I felt grateful that someone was willing to use the pool after I'd done my laps. Maybe I didn't have as many cooties as I thought. I lit a cigarette.

"Not in the house," my mother said.

I walked to the sliding glass door and opened it slightly. The radio was still on. I'd just abandoned it under the tree. It was playing Elton John. He was singing, *"Get back, honky cat . . . living in the city ain't where it's at."*

"What legal rights do I have? I mean is it in my name, this money? I wanna see the papers. Where are the papers? Show me the papers! The legal papers!"

"He's lost his mind," my stepfather whispered. "You can't reason with someone who's out of his mind, babe."

"We weren't going to tell you about it at all, but . . . then we saw you," my mother said.

"How much did you get? Where's your money? How much did Nicki get?"

"See," my stepfather said to her. "Here we go. Did I tell you this is how it would go?"

"It's none of your business," my mother said.

"She got the same."

"And she gets to just have it?"

"She's not on drugs!"

"I'm not on drugs! I've been rejected! By publishers! I'm *despondent!*"

They held firm. My mother was made the executor of the will and could have easily given me nothing. She probably should have, but eventually I cracked and agreed to see a drug counselor so long as I didn't have to be shipped away somewhere and institutionalized with round-the-clock room checks and peeing in beakers. I would ride it out for as long as I needed to put on a good show, and then I'd have my "fuck you" money, and I'd party with style and go out in a blaze of glory. When the money ran out, I'd walk a few blocks and jump in the East River. Everyone—Boorman, Zoe, St. Martin's Press, the muggers, Mayor Dinkins—could kiss my junkie ass. It would be a glorious flameout, the stuff of legends. Someone would publish my novel posthumously, and I'd be a Lit Fuck star like John Kennedy Toole. It was . . . a plan.

It didn't go quite that way. Instead of jumping into the East River, I crossed it. Back in New York, I kept up the ritual of getting high, then frantically purging my pores with shower steam. I guess the humidity this ritual produced slowly corroded the bathroom ceiling. Or perhaps there was a dead body in the tub in the apartment above me. In that building someone could have been Jim Morrison–ing it for weeks, dead-body bathwater dripping onto the floor, and nobody would have broken the door down. This was where they filed away fuckups after all. Better dead in the bath than out on the street, fouling up the view. All I know is, one morning around three o'clock I awoke to a violent crack, like someone had driven a wrecking ball into the sidewall of my apartment. The cat was missing, hiding somewhere in panic. I got up, walked to the bath, and stared naked up into my neighbor's apartment. I covered my cock with a towel and surveyed the damage. My Bennington diploma had been hanging on the green wall of the john. Now there was just a hole in the wall. The frame had been shattered, and the paper was quickly becoming an inky paste. Even though Zoe and I were estranged, I called her mother. I don't know why it didn't occur to me to call my own mother. In those instances, I felt like Bobbie Poledouris just liked me better than my own parents. Bobbie was well connected. She knew realtors. She knew lawyers. She thought that I was talented, if perhaps not the best influence on her daughter. She was just more maternal than my own mother.

"I need to get out of here," I said. "Please, help me!"

"What's wrong?"

"My bathroom exploded."

Bobbie put me in touch with a realtor who told me that the incident was grounds to break the lease and get the hell off my "crack block." The cat appeared the following evening and gave me a look that put my mother's glare of disappointment and pain to shame.

"What the fuck is wrong with you?" Heaven seemed to ask. "Seriously. I'd be better off on the goddamned street."

I couldn't make plans anymore. I just didn't have the strength. Routine questions landed like punches. I couldn't even decide what to eat for lunch when I had money. Fortunately the options were static, the menu unchanged for almost two full years: coffee, chocolate donuts, cigarettes, and junk.

"It's the new Bohemia," Herve announced one day as we sat in my room in the Chelsea. I was running out of whatever money I'd been given by my parents down in Florida after the funeral. I had a bill with Jerry at the desk that would have to be paid. I knew there was only one way to settle it. Rehab.

"Like Paris in the twenties."

"Brooklyn."

"Brooklyn!" he cheered. "Come on! Brooklyn! It's perfect. You can start another book. I can finish mine. The rent is so cheap, we can take as much time as we need!"

"Brooklyn."

"Brooklyn!"

"Well, you know, technically I'm fourth-generation Brooklyn," I bragged as I dragged from my cigarette. "On both sides too. Great-grandparents on down. I'm Brooklyn down."

"Perfect."

"But, I don't know. Brooklyn."

"Come on. At least see this place."

I didn't want a roommate and was concerned that another writer under the same roof would muddy my focus. Of course, there was nothing to focus on, but if I did get clean once again—as I'd been back when I was finishing *Loose*, and the air was cold and clean, and Nirvana's *Nevermind* pushed Michael Jackson's *Dangerous* out of the number one spot on the Billboard charts, and it felt like anything could and would happen to smart former losers in love—then I would need to man up and write something new. And if I began such a project—a novel or a tuna recipe—in such a depleted state, would Herve's intensity and creative energy box me out? He was an excellent writer, probably the best of our Lit Fuck crew, and had an enviable conflict going for him. His family was old-European, and he had already written some incredibly sophisticated passages in short stories all about being torn between the old world values and fears and his desire for American culture and girls and indie rock. I knew my upbringing was as strange to him as his was to me, and if he wasn't worried about being boxed out by my writer mojo, then maybe it was silly for me to worry about it. A sense of competition can be really valuable anyway, especially sometimes among good friends. Seeing Herve write would certainly fire me up to work hard.

And yet, in early 1993, moving out to Brooklyn from Manhattan just seemed like backsliding. Why on earth would I want to move to the land of my unhip ancestors, human stuffed cabbages who looked plump and frightened in the old yellow photos from the New World. Growing up, I'd seen dozens of these shots in frames and family albums. Wasn't it a triumph for at least one of their offspring to truck it across the bridge to makin' money Manhattan and not look back? It took us hundreds of years to get across the Atlantic and only fifty years to get across that East River. Now I had to ride the motherfucking L train backwards in time?

"Brooklyn."

"Brooklyn!"

Brooklyn. I'd learned to drive on her abandoned baseball diamonds in my grandfather's Caddy. I'd strolled her fishy, dirty docksides. I knew her delis and party stores, red sauce joints, newsstands, stray dogs, and dark secrets.

"If you're an artist, you can make art anywhere. Notebook's portable," Ron pointed out when we brought him into the argument during a visit down to the city. We went to the Holiday for cocktails and discussed the move. "Ain't like you're playing the piano, kid."

"Easy for you to say."

I hated him then for being able to see Zoe whenever he wanted, and I hated myself for being too proud to ask after her. She'd cut me off and was dating someone else, a student named Tom Fox. He was handsome, like a young Jeremy Irons. British. Rich. His father was a famous writer. I know that can be a problem in itself for the children of the celebrated, but Martin Amis turned out okay. If my father had been an achiever in the arts somehow, I bet that I would have had the confidence to live anywhere: Staten Island, Astoria . . . Siberia. I wouldn't have suffered so long over settling the new Bohemia.

But settle it we did, planting our Lit Fuck flag in a place that had seen no footsteps like ours before. The Williamsburg of winter 1992 and early 1993 was dead quiet. No food trucks, no cheese shops, no boutiques or big banks and drug store chains, and no Times Square–style tourist traffic on weekends. No nothing. On the north side, by the Bedford Avenue L station, there were Polish families and bars like the Green Point Tavern. There was a Salvation Army too, but the further you walked south from the Bedford Avenue station, the more desolate it became. At night, you could hear the clop-clop of your own gait as you shivered and sped up, imagining ghosts on your foot-path—I imagined Polish ghosts, Lithuanian and Russian ghosts, welcoming my family back to the second borough. If a mugger suddenly appeared, no-body would hear me scream; nobody would help. It was a dead, frozen strip. On Grand Street, where the loft Herve and I had found was located, one got the sense that if there were a fire in an old building, nobody would come put it out; it would simply burn at its own speed, straight down to the pavement. And after nine in the evening, the only food you had a chance of scrounging would come from the tiny Chinese takeout place on the corner, where they stir-fried behind bulletproof glass.

Our friends Peter Dinklage and Ian Bell, the scruffy Drama Fucks from Bennington, were even further south, endeavoring to open a theater space in a place where even the drug dealers were too smart to set up shop—the no-where of nowhere. They were sleeping in their overcoats. It made our loft seem posh. I went to see Pete's terrible band Whizzy play some bar along the tourist trap strip of Bleecker Street. There was a scattering of old Bennington people there, showing support and smiling politely as Pete played the trum-pet, rapped, and chanted while a bunch of beardos made a racket behind him.

"Do you know how much space we have?" he raved, sweaty, as we had a couple of beers after the show. "It's an industrial space."

"Yeah, I know." I was used to comparing square footage at this point with Bennington-ers. Bard kids too. A few Sarah Lawrence grads. A little café called The L had opened up, and some Bennington students ran it and waited tables there. It felt familiar and hopeful to stop in on the way back to the city for a café au lait and listen to good, new British soul like Lisa Stansfield or the kind of indie rock that made me feel at home—*It's a Shame about Ray* by The Lemonheads or *Peng!*, the first Stereolab album, two of my favorites at the time—while thumbing through the *Press* or the *Voice* as they made you a bagel with cream cheese, sprouts, red onion, and tomato.

But doesn't that mean we have to be, you know, industrious? I thought. Or are we all falling into that inevitable New York City trap of real estate dick-size comparison?

I wasn't feeling very productive.

"We're going to do *Balm in Gilead*," Pete promised.

"Cool."

You'd have an easier time getting someone to travel up to the Cloisters for an all-coyote production of *Balm in Gilead* or *True West*, but he seemed evan-gelical, as if the sacrifices he and Ian were making were meaningful. I wished I felt the same way. I just felt like a loser. At least I wasn't in a band.

Slowly, the giant loft became a home. We furnished it with finds from the Salvation Army (as ever). We moved a long, yellow, flowered couch into the center of the room and filled the wide kitchen with a number of chipped diner plates and bottle-green glasses. The air smelled of spices, curry and burning sugar, and chemical smoke, but we got used to it. It started to smell like home too. Herve's mother sent him care packages of highly spiced chicken and lamb packed in dry ice. We ate so much of it, we could no longer feel our tongues, but it was delicious and free. The super, Harry, a scraggly sculptor, lived downstairs and operated a virtual high school woodshop. We could see through the floor as he busied around sawing wood and accruing giant piles of sawdust. He was always good for a quick repair or help carting in a table or chair, sometimes found on the curb, abandoned by someone else and soon to be carried upstairs and cherished by us.

The back of the loft was a panel of floor-to-ceiling windows, smudged and gated, only hinting at a view, but it didn't feel stifling. One could play a game of full court b-ball in there without stepping on the cat. A medieval-looking sliding wooden door bisected the space and made it habitable for two very strong-willed, naturally competitive, struggling-writer types. It was thick enough to stop a charging herd and instantly soundproofed both sides of the loft. The door was so heavy you needed two hands to slide it closed.

We painted the walls pale orange and blue, and Herve tacked up some of his collages or the pastel drawings that his girlfriend had made for him. By day, we wrote. Herve situated himself at the big blonde-wood table in the living room that the previous tenant had left behind. I took a little dinette table in the kitchen. He usually chose the music. He had the better boom box and prided himself on his selector abilities, so I deferred. Plus, he'd found the place—essentially rescued me. I was so familiar with his record collection, it was like my own anyway. We'd blast Dr. Dre's *The Chronic* and The Beastie Boys' *Check Your Head* most of the time; sometimes he'd slip on a Nusrat Fateh Ali Khan CD, which was romantic and entrancing but always a challenge to write by since I'd find myself daydreaming rather quickly. Nusrat didn't do background music. He demanded your ears. When we needed a break, we'd throw a pink handball against the wall, smoke, pace, or call the Revs/Cost hotline. Herve was smitten with the graffiti artists and their wheat-pasted flyers, which had been sniped up all over downtown with cryptic messages like "Cost Fucked Madonna" and "Zookeeper Revs." Like Kaz's *Underworld*, Revs and Cost seemed to speak directly to our worries and make them seem clever and sexy. The Revs/Cost hotline played messages from "The Infamous Grandma of Graf," an old lady with a tough, streetwise, adenoidal voice that Herve would imitate. It had the same cryptic appeal as the

Pavement album covers and triggered something in him that I eventually mustered some affection for. It was tough, funny, in the pocket with our own sensibility, and clearly a product of the New York street culture, which we considered ourselves a part of.

Living in Brooklyn was actually not like moving back to the Island, as I'd feared. It still very much felt like New York City, but there was one ritual that reminded me of my teenage railroad-riding experiences. One still had to pack up supplies for a trip into Manhattan. This usually meant a CD folder for your Discman, a book, and a journal. New Bohemians were never without a heavy bag. The people who could just go home, then pop back out, had it easy. Our shoulders always ached. I was also quite used to the weird Zen state of waiting for trains. I'd been waiting for trains for over a decade, so when the L was sporadic, sometimes just dormant for upwards of an hour, I used my time well. I read Luc Sante's *Low Life*, which was, along with Mark Leyner's *Et Tu Babe*, the book to be seen reading on the L at the time (the former reminded the reader that no matter how bad New York seemed now, it was always, at one point in the past, much, much more oppressive). I'd purchased an old Polaroid Land Camera and traveled with it over my shoulder as I road to and from Manhattan. If I saw a cool, postcardy subject, like the partially burned-out neon Chow Mein sign on Second Avenue and Twelfth Street, I'd make Herve or a visiting Ron or Jack pose under it. I'd put on some healthy weight, having stayed off drugs for a few months, and some of the old lust for art and creativity had finally returned.

I dyed my long hair red like Jim Carroll's and slicked it back with Murray's viscous pomade, which has a picture of a smiling, happy black man and woman on its orange tin cover. I liked old-looking cosmetics and grooming products like Murray's or Lucky Tiger, which I used only because Tom Waits sang about it on the title track of *Swordfishtrombones*.

By February I was enrolled in a parent-approved rehab program and began drawing an allowance off the fund my grandfather had left for me. I lucked out with my specialist, Petunia Cox, whom my mother found. Primarily, nobody made an issue of my drinking. Usually it's the first thing that's addressed when you get into a program: What else are you using besides the drug of choice? What food? What relationships? What bad habits? They all go in the bag, and the bag goes down the chute toward the cleansing fire. But Petunia didn't piss-test me and didn't seem to care too much that most nights, I could still be found slurping Greyhounds and playing the jukebox in the Holiday Cocktail Lounge. She wore caftans and conducted our sessions in her Central Park apartment, barefoot. She'd hang my coat in the kitchen and offer me an ice water. I'd take the coach, and she'd take a lotus position in a comfortable purple chair in front of the mantle and begin to iron me out. My mother would send her a check. My mother would send me a check. And somehow I stayed off the heroin. I suppose it was ideal for a spoiled Jewish American Prince—retail therapy. Nothing, after all, fills the body with goodwill and optimism like shopping. Petunia spent my money freely. She played with me, my insobriety, and my tentative steps toward wellness. And it was actually easier for me just to listen to her. I would have followed anyone at that point; I was vulnerable to cults.

"Your posture is terrible," Petunia'd say. "Your chiropractic needs attention. I want you to take this number and make an appointment." She'd whip off a piece of pad and hand it to me. It was easier that way.

"You look pale and anemic. I want you to take this number and go down to Chinatown. This man is a genius. He will restore your energy." And she'd whip the page from the pad and hand it to me, and a few days later I'd find myself naked in the back of a storefront on Elizabeth Street with an old man rubbing my ribs with magnets.

"The best way to build up your immune system? Two words. Chicken. Soup. Have you ever made a chicken soup, Marc?"

"Make it? No. I eat it."

"I want you to make it. It'll be good for you. Chop the vegetables. Boil the chicken. And wait as it becomes soup. You have to start somewhere."

I thought maybe I'd start with a letter? To Zoe? Her family? My family. That's what most addicts do when they start to make amends, yes? The eighth step, I think. And if we weren't going to go there, then maybe we could focus on getting me writing something else? A short story, perhaps? A vignette. What's with the soup?

"Here, here's the recipe."

"I really have to make a soup?"

"Making this soup is the single best thing you can do for yourself now. As an artist. As a man. Make sure you have enough lentils. And barley. And dill. Dill is very important. Get fresh dill weed."

"Dill weed?"

"Smell it. Smell everything as you prepare it. Slowly. Take it in."

There was nowhere to get fresh vegetables of the kind that Petunia insisted on along our little strip. Few people had heard the term organic. If you managed to find a fresh carrot in the bodegas in Williamsburg, it was peeled and shrink-wrapped along with some rubbery celery and sold for $5 on a bed of Styrofoam. I had to drag everything home on the L after buying it at an organic market on Second Avenue in the East Village. Herve and Heaven the cat would watch with amazement as I covered all the available surfaces in our kitchen with parsnip and celery and real carrots with bushy green tops, pulled whole from the earth. I filled a huge steel pot with organic chicken and vegetables and barley, smelling each sliced onion and sprig as I added it to the cauldron.

"Who is the man with the master plan?" Dre and his posse would ask. *"A nigga with a motherfuckin' gun!"*

The stereo would blast as I chopped the dill and parsley, then peeled the raw potatoes and parsnips, and the big back room filled up with a salty, homey, stocky steam.

"What the hell happened to you?" Herve laughed. "You're scary, dude."

"Nothing can kill me!" I'd shout, waving a weedy green carrot top at him. "I'm a Catholic! I'm blessed!" It's a line Harvey Keitel says, shortly before getting shot dead in front of Penn Station in *Bad Lieutenant*.

Petunia would feel my shoulders as she hung my coat up in that little kitchen and poured the ice water slowly into a pale blue plastic mug.

"You're still knotted. Stiff. Tight."

"Sorry."

"What color is your apartment, Marc?"

"It's sort of . . . peeling. Is that a color? It's more like a texture."

"You've got tension in your muscles that you don't even know about. You've got tension in there from your childhood. From your parents' divorce."

"I do?"

"I want you to take this and make an appointment. This guy is an artist. He will knead your parents right out of those quadriceps."

I don't know if Petunia got a commission, but she was a veritable home-shopping network of self-help.

"And go over to Pearl. I want you to paint your room a nice, soothing blue. Blue is calming. Blue."

"Blue."

"Cornflower. Or maybe Iris. Yes, definitely Iris."

She prided herself on being well connected.

"And don't worry about getting published," she pooh-poohed on another day. "You have bigger problems than that. Your liver is swollen. Your aura is yellow. When the time is right, I will help you. I know someone at *Lingua Franca*. Do you know *Lingua Franca*?"

"Sure." I didn't know *Lingua Franca*. I just knew it was good for me to get above Fourteenth Street every week for our sessions. Living downtown you can sometimes forget how long and diverse Manhattan Island is. We have museums and zoos, not just bars and record stores and shadowy places to cop dope. Wandering Central Park after our sessions or browsing in shops on

Columbus Circle, staring at the lights and fountain in front of Lincoln Center, I imagined myself older, respectable, married to Zoe, both of us over our punk rock phases. We'd giggle about what bastards we'd been, to each other and to others, how depraved we'd been in our youth.

"What were we thinking?" I'd ask as I lifted my tea mug and pulled one of my dozen books from the shelf. Heaven, our cat, would have grown plump and lazy with age. We'd be able to pick her up without waking her and place her on the rug by the fire on cold New England nights. New England? Would that be where we'd end up? Where we met? Where we were happiest. Maybe I'd be a professor like Alvin Feinman or Phillip Lopate. Zoe and Marc. Gray and content, dignified and old together, like the Modern Lovers once sang.

Petunia was serious about getting me published. She wanted me to know that she was connected. It seemed too easy, but then I was never much of a networker, even up at school. Everyone lobbied to become friendly with the hottest professors, maybe smoke a joint with one at an off-campus party. I wanted them all to come to me.

"I will bring some of my stuff next time. For your friend." I shrugged.

"Good."

I hadn't even looked at my old writing since signing with the agent. Maybe there was something true in there whose time had finally come? Or maybe I'd just write something new. I had so much energy. It felt like I could bang out another novel in a week. There were a lot of vitamins and minerals in all that goddamned Brooklyn soup.

Another Bennington writer had swung with a novel and hit a home run. The hottest literary property of the moment was Donna Tart's murder mystery *The Secret History*. Like Ellis, Tart had graduated a couple of years before Herve and me. And her novel took place, like *The Rules of Attraction*, at a Bennington-like college (called Hampden instead of Camden). It gave Herve and me hope that we were cut from the same cloth somehow, but neither of us knew a way in. We wrote in obscurity; we may as well have been hobbyists. We were living in industrial lofts, but the industry didn't know we were alive.

I was sitting in the Holiday one night and met this sleek-looking woman at the bar. She was blonde and athletic, with a rubbery grin that seemed to signal constant amusement. I introduced myself, loose with a few Greyhounds.

"What do you do?" I asked.

"I'm a cool hunter."

"What the fuck is a cool hunter?" I slurred, a few Greyhounds deep into my evening drunk.

"I spot trends and write about them."

"For whom?"

"*Spin.*"

Suddenly, my confident rap dried up. *Spin* magazine was, in the late eighties and early nineties, a glorious thing. Running into a real *Spin* writer was akin to brushing up against a senator or congressmen. These were people with real power, and the Nirvana-led "alternative revolution" had only increased this. *Spin* writers had cool handles like Bonz Malone, Legs McNeil, and John Leland. Glenn O'Brien wrote for Spin. He was friends with Debbie Harry and Keith Haring and Jean-Michel Basquiat. I'd been collecting every issue since the first, back in 1985, with the young Madonna on the cover. As a weird teen, I felt like I knew these writers in a way that I didn't know those who filed for *Rolling Stone* or even *Creem.* Spin writers were the cool nerds of the larger rock press, and because of them, I felt like I knew about Fela, Kuti Eugene Chadbourne, Emo Phillips, The Mentors, *The Indestructible Beat of Soweto*, Tackhead, and Jandek, even though I've never heard any of their music and could never find most of it on the Island. I couldn't believe I was talking to one of them face to face.

"No shit. Really? I read it every month. What's your name?"

"Julia Chaplin."

I'd known Julia's byline before I even knew it was called a byline. She wrote a lot for *Spin.* I was never in one place long enough to subscribe to any magazine, but I always made a point to buy *Sassy* and *Spin* whenever I could find or afford them. As familiar with the writers and the content as I was, I had no idea how either magazine got produced every month, how it was fashioned together. It simply appeared at Tobacco Road, or on the Bennington College bookstore magazine rack, or at Gem Spa. I had no idea how people did whatever it was that Julia did, where they did it, or who made it appear on the newsstand, where I picked it up religiously or stole it if I couldn't afford the cover price. I was clueless, so I did what I usually did when I felt stupid; I acted arrogantly. Julia was lanky and unpretentious, clearly intelligent and cute in an athletic and chic way. She wasn't the art school type. I doubted she read Kathy Acker. She seemed somehow cleaner. Sophisticated. Like she should be writing for *Vogue* or the *New York Times Magazine.* She was cool to the point of being utterly inscrutable. At the time, I felt like that was probably the optimum state for a human being, certainly a good New Yorker.

"Anyway, that's cool. Cool hunting. My mom's a bargain hunter." I put another cigarette in my mouth and felt around for my matches. "Coupons."

"What are you into?" she asked, and I could tell this was a person who was always on duty in New York City. You never knew when the gophers of cool would pop up and show their furry faces.

"I used to be into heroin, but it's over."

"Yeah, heroin was very '91, '92. It's all about health now. Do you surf?"

"Sure. You know what's really cool? Soup."

Jack joined us at the table. He was down from school and taking advantage of our loft space. It was so big he could have lived there for a week before we even noticed we had company.

"Hey, Jack, this is Julia Chaplin."

"From *Spin*!" Jack said. "Wow. Who's on the next cover? L7?"

He read it every month too.

"Are you into soup too?" she asked Jack.

"I'm sorry, what?"

She was no dummy. She knew we were taking the piss, but affectionately so.

We continued drinking and talking, and I finally worked up the courage to ask her what it took to get to write for a magazine like *Spin*.

"Ideas," she said without hesitation. "It's all about ideas."

Jack and I followed Julia back to her place off Union Square, right next to Coffee Shop.

"Have you been to Coffee Shop yet?" she asked as we followed her like culture-hungry strays. Julia's apartment seemed subterranean, like a drained swimming pool, with thick, round glass windows. While Julia used the bathroom, Jack and I looked through her roommate's CDs out of habit. Jack pocketed the second Sugarcubes album, *Here Today, Tomorrow Next Week!* I shook my head, and he put it back.

"*Eesh not even ash good ash zhe firsh one,*" he said in a near-perfect Björk. Jack did a good Björk. It was hot like soup. He could have taken it on the road: *Jack Madagascar in They're Schmoking See-Gars! A Tribute to Björk Goumunsdottir.* He had her down. Years later, he would marry a famous music writer and actually befriend Björk and Radiohead and a half dozen other highbrow modern rock geniuses. I always wondered if he ever did his Björk for her.

I found some photos on the desk. They were all of Julia surfing. She came out of the bathroom and walked to the kitchen to grab some beer.

"Do you surf for fun, or is it something for work?" I asked.

"Why can't it be both?" she asked. Something clicked in my brain when she said that. That's the key, I realized, to turn something that you already have enthusiasm for into a subject. We were about the same age, but she seemed so much farther along when it came to understanding her powers as a writer and, more importantly, a manipulator of the subject. She was surfing through life. I was skidding.

On the way home, most nights, instead of copping, I'd stop at Kim's video store on the end of St. Mark's Place and pick up a movie. Quiet nights in were becoming more and more acceptable the healthier I felt. I really wanted Zoe to know how well I was doing. It seemed illegitimate somehow unless she knew about it. Sometimes I'd watch the cat chase an invisible fly across the floor of the loft. I'd call her and say, "You don't know what you're missing watching this," and I could tell that she was able to detect the life in my voice. I would buy those glassine-bagged vitamin packets at the bodega with my cigarettes and my morning coffee. I had no idea what was in them; maybe they were placebos, all algae green and bright orange, or capsules full of yellow oil. Sometimes Zoe'd be drunk at a party and call me, and all I could hear in the background was the familiar buzz of my past.

"I miss you," she'd confess. "Are you okay? I had a dream that you died."

"What was I wearing?"

"Marc-clothes. Black jeans and a T-shirt that said, 'More Rats Than People."

"It's true. There are."

I owned a T-shirt cribbed from a *Post* or *Daily News* headline warning that the rats could take us if they only had a charismatic leader and some thumbs.

"How are you, Marc Bird?" She sometimes called me Marc Bird, and I called her Zoe Bird. It's gross, I know, but that was her nickname before we met, and I sort of absorbed it, the way some people begin calling cigarettes "fags" or potato chips "crisps" after they've been in London a while.

"I'm really good. I'm getting published."

"No! Where?"

"This journal. It's no big deal. But it's really prestigious. *Lingua Franca*?"

"I want to see you. You sound good. Really good. I miss the cat."

"Come out. There's plenty of room."

That's all we had was room. A little food, a lot of music, but most of all, we had space—cheap space. The more the merrier way out here in new fucking Bohemia.

Petunia hit the ceiling.

"No. No. No. Bad. No, no, no. Dangerous." My unorthodox, barefoot therapist did stick to one of the classic Twelve Stepper rules. "People, places, and things, Marc. People, places, and things." She insisted that I couldn't fall back into a relationship with Zoe. I showed her a cartoon drawing that Zoe had sent me. It depicted her as a bird leaving the nest—our nest, I guess—cluttered with CDs and thrift store junk, clothes and shoes . . . and then her returning to the nest, where I suppose, I was waiting. Eating worms.

"Oh, brother," Petunia groaned. "She's really working you. This girl will have you back on your knees in record time. No time. You can't get back together with her."

"But we're in love."

"You don't understand. This girl will always find you the minute you're on your feet. I've seen this before. She will always come back to ruin you when you've pulled yourself together. And she will leave you on your knees all over again."

"She's not like that. She's not cruel."

"She can't help it. She's angry with you. For abandoning her."

"I never left her. She left me."

"You left her for drugs. Before she ever even considered leaving you. Run. Quickly. In the opposite direction. Please. Trust me. And run."

I didn't listen. In February 1993, Zoe came back to town for a week before heading back up to school after her field work term, and it was as if we'd just hooked up. I couldn't imagine anything bad ever happening again; it was how the saved must feel, the grateful, the paroled. I would follow the sun from that point on, walk the line. And hopefully we would last. I decided to mark the occasion of our reunion with a tattoo. I'd found a drawing of a siren in an old dictionary that my mother had purchased and displayed on an antique metal stand. I figured if the Siren was on my flesh, my forearm, I could never be tempted again. I would be able to keep my eye on the bitch.

At the time, tattoo parlors were illegal in Manhattan, but out on Long Island, you could still find one here and there. One day we decided to take the train to the suburbs. We sat in the bulkhead seat, holding hands, drinking coffee, and staring out the window en route to Valley Stream station.

"This is the train line you took when you were in school?"

"As often as possible," I said.

"I like it. It's cute."

The train car never seemed particularly cute to me, but it was safe, almost womb-like. Nothing could penetrate the capsule and vex me. Time froze, especially when the train passed through the tunnels and everything went pitch black. Outside the buildings, cars, trees, and stores went by much too fast to figure. When we passed Valley Stream, I pointed out the window at the Green Acres Mall.

"I used to work there," I told her.

"You worked in the mall. I can't picture it."

"I was a square," I confessed.

Once I was inked, we got back on the train, and once we changed at Jamaica Station in Queens, we began to notice people getting on and off the car covered in dust and soot and looking dazed. At first I thought it was Ash Wednesday or something. I still never got used to seeing people walk down the street with the black cross on their forehead, so the fight-or-flight part of my brain just went right to that deduction. But none of the ash bits were in the shape of the cross. And some people had ripped clothes. Others were crying. The ticket taker approached us. He was a tall, ruddy giant, the tip of his cap nearly scraping against the fluorescent tube lights at the top of the car.

"What happened?" I asked him.

"Bomb."

"Where?"

"Wall Street. Some idiot just thought he could blow up the World Trade Center," he said and shook his head. He punched our tickets and moved on down the aisle.

I didn't see it as an omen at the time, but still, this simply did not make sense. When I was on the train, I figured I was safe, especially on the way back to Lawrence. No matter what kind of adventure I'd had in the city, I could count on a slow, steady, chugging ride back to suburbia. People behaved themselves on the train, even the commuters nursing beers purchased at the deli or cocktails bought from the porters. There was an etiquette. I wasn't living in the city anymore when I heard the news about Colin Ferguson's rampage in early December 1993, but it really shook me up. On any given day, I could have been one of his victims. Ferguson got his ticket just like I or anybody else would at the window at Penn Station. He got on the east-bound train. He waited. And then he stood up, pulled out a 9mm pistol, walked down the aisles, and shot random strangers, killing six and wounding nineteen. I couldn't believe it then, and I still can't. This wasn't supposed to happen on the LIRR; it was a safe zone. The whole Island was. People were shot while reading their papers or drinking the cups of beer they had bought at a rail-side minibar, as they transformed from their city selves back into to their suburban selves. That shift was sacred. If I wasn't certain that it was inviolate, then like my father, when I played him that They Might Be Giants cassette a half decade earlier, my tether back to the shore was surely vulnerable to fraying. What was happening to the city? Blowing up buildings? Shooting commuters? Could we get any sicker? It was time to make a change. To head out to Hollywood where people were decent, trustworthy, and moderate.

CHAPTER 8

Zoe had only become a bigger fish in the tiny art pond that was Bennington College in the early nineties. The students Herve and I had left behind had no idea how nowhere we were. They only knew we were living in New York City, and for most that meant we'd made it. Zoe's proximity to me and my Lit Fuck friends gave her an edge over any other flamboyant Bennington kid interested in vying for queenly stature. The respect and compliments fired her dream of genuine rock stardom; how easy it was to swap out a crowd of moshing, smiling kids in some lawn house living room with a crowd of moshing, smiling kids at the Pyramid Club in New York or the Whiskey out in LA, especially under those stars, with that safety and the drugs and the scarcity of any practical or financial worry. You could literally dream all day up there and make plans. And so, when another of her breaks came up, she decided that she would spend it with the full band in her father's studio out in Encino, recording the first Table Grade demo. From there, I suppose, the record companies, the opening slots on national tours, and eventually the cover of *Spin* . . . and *Sassy*. In a post-Nirvana industry, they were handing out huge record deals to quirky and hard modern rock bands left and right. Helmet, a solid but unremarkable heavy alternative rock act, signed to the fairly new Interscope Records for what was rumored, among the rock-snob community, to be over $1 million. It seemed too easy. I knew the symptoms of her disease pretty well at that point. I was a deluded would-be artist, just starting to suspect that making it would be a little harder than I initially though. I couldn't share this misgiving, of course, and even if I did, she wouldn't be able to process it. And if she could process it, she wouldn't want to know from it. She would just tell herself that she was more talented than I was. And it would make sense. Instead, I agreed to follow her west and be the supportive boyfriend, hoping that we would get it right the second time around. Instead of printing up a resume at the copy shop and trying to get a humble gig somewhere and start a new novel, I decided that I would become a Hollywood screenwriter. The conversations I had with Bobbie and Basil Poledouris made that seem slightly more tangible than, say, becoming a rodeo cowboy or an astronaut.

"Sure, become a millionaire screenwriter. Win an Oscar. Why didn't I think of that sooner?"

Bobbie and Basil knew movie people who might read my stuff and were typically generous with their connections. They sent a copy of *Loose* to the director Randall Kleiser, who'd directed *Grease* (the first film I ever saw by myself at the Central Theater in Cedarhurst) and made *The Blue Lagoon*, which Basil scored. He sent over a nice note, saying that I was talented. One night, while I was visiting LA for Easter, Basil introduced me to John Millius, the bearded, neck-less he-man he'd with worked on *Conan the Barbarian*. Millius wrote pieces of *Jaws* and *Apocalypse Now*. He was a legend, and the Cuban cigar he gave me as he recounted stories of old Hollywood by the pool might as well have been laced with pixie dust. The West Coast is always going to frighten and intrigue a natural-born Easterner. It is wild to us, the Gold Rush, the horrible, brutal desert where we pump in water and say "fuck you" to Mother Nature and to God too. Basil was debating whether to do John Waters's film *Serial Mom*, which would star Kathleen Turner as a suburban mother who is secretly a serial killer.

"Look at it this way, it's a part of history. Like scoring a Fellini or Godard movie. John Waters's body of work will be considered in the same way one day, and you will be a part of it."

"That's a good point," he said and lit up another of his Marlboros. Basil smoked and drank like a rock-and-roll pirate—reds and rum—but he was sensitive and contemplative, like most composers I met in later years.

"Always give money to musicians," he told Zoe when she was a kid, referring to sax players or guitarists in the subways and bus stations with the open cases full of singles and nickels. It's a hard life, he'd meant to say, and the guy never seemed 100 percent comfortable to me with the success he'd finally achieved after a few years of struggle. I think he might have been happier just composing for himself, like Steve Reich or John Cage or Philip Glass, instead of trying to figure out the strings to put under an onscreen image of a young boy hugging a killer whale, as he was then tasked and handsomely paid to do as composer of the upcoming film *Free Willy*. Something about Hollywood struck him as vulgar, and I got that. Maybe that's why we got along. I adored him, and he seemed to consider me a fellow artist, even though I'd done nothing but corrupt his daughter, eat his food, drink his rum, bum his smokes, and pass out on the rim of his swimming pool. He never judged me, and so I spoke freely, but respectfully, around him too. I don't think anyone in my life has ever been as generous or patient with me as that family was—surely more so than my own. Once the band and the boyfriend moved in and the cozy living room with the low ceiling and the fireplace began to fill with suitcases, cords, and amps, Bobbie essentially became a mother to all of us, making sure the band and the writer boy had whatever food and equipment and gas we needed.

Leaving Williamsburg was easier than I thought it would be. Essentially Herve and I shook hands and went our separate ways. I owed him some back rent, which I couldn't pay but promised to square up at some point. I still don't remember if I ever did. Probably not. We were squatters. Our status as new Bohemian pioneers was only ever going to be short-lived. Eviction threats came down after only a few months. The owner of the building let us know one afternoon that he considered us illegals. Our arrangement with Harry, our sculptor subleter, made no difference to him or his lawyers. He wanted the two of us and all our art, cats, and attitude back on the street. He saw the future: 1 million college kids where once there were maybe a hundred. A full hipster theme park was coming, like the killer bees they warned us about in the seventies.

I still had my little Toyota out on the Island and spent $1,000 of what was becoming a smaller and smaller personal fortune to have it shipped west on the back of a trailer. Once it arrived, a few weeks after I did, it would cost me another $500 to make it inspection worthy. They're serious out there about things that made absolutely no sense to me: movies, smog. And yet, I read their concerns as frilly and petty. I'd recently seen the Mike Leigh film *Naked* and was obsessed with the character of Johnny, the venomous, damaged, violent protagonist (played by lanky David Thewlis), who has come down to London from Manchester (rather than Hollywood from Brooklyn). While obviously a terrible person, Johnny wields his intelligence over the self-absorbed and fashionable in the capital with such a lack of regard for politesse that it's oddly charming. He is regarded as lost but also as a genius, and it gives him an air of grace. Johnny became my hero. I would be him in Los Angeles, channel his pain, his unappreciated beauty, and his cruel, wounded wit. Johnny would be the outfit I'd wear to the beach. Johnny would help me stay a freak. When the Toyota arrived on the truck, it was full of mail and other effects from the Five Towns. Among the letters was an invitation to my five-year high school reunion. High school reunion? How did that happen? Five years? Had it really been so long? I had nothing to report to my class. Some of my ex-classmates were married. They were businessmen and cops and teachers. They had been students, and now they were teachers. What was I? A freak. Could I report that? I decided I would wait till my ten-year anniversary. Surely by then I'd be famous.

How could I not feel superior in a booth at the Formosa Café on Santa Monica Boulevard, surrounded by actors and actresses in discussion about auditions and their skin and weight, as actors are want to be.

"Rubbish," I'd remark in my best Thewlis. And they'd smile, as if they could appreciate a fellow role player. The dirtiest, most insulting commentary that I slurred was never, ever viewed as malicious. I was acting too.

Clientele aside, I adored the Formosa as a haunted house full of old Hollywood romance and alcoholism. The site of the red-and-white candy-striped awning alone was enough to make me happy, coming up Santa Monica Boulevard. Nobody ate much. Wontons, if you were adventurous. The soup was watery, the chow mein gummy, but the crackling history more than made up for it. Humphrey Bogart drank there. So did James Dean, Judy Garland, Clark Gable, Liz Taylor, and Marilyn. Like at the Chelsea Hotel, you couldn't pee in the old-style toilet without wondering who else had peed there. Sinatra, probably, after too many glasses full of Jack Daniel's while trying to drown the memory of Ava Gardner. The cocktails were expensive, but you got to drink them in front of walls literally covered, inch to inch, with framed, autographed portraits of movie and television stars, both iconic and kitschy. The best table was all the way in the back under the photo of Sorrell Booke, who played Boss Hogg on *The Dukes of Hazard*, and my new Los Angeles crew—rich kids, poor-but-pretty actor kids who were fast becoming rich kids, and middle-class kids like me with crazy ambition—and I held court there every night.

The Formosa set was revolving but often consisted of Zoe and me, the band, and another Bennington student named Nicole, who grew up in Beverly Hills with a TV producer father. Nicole introduced us all to her new friend Michelle Burke, an up-and-coming actress. Michelle had already shot a part in Richard Linklater's *Dazed and Confused*; she was cast as Connie Conehead, a part originated on *Saturday Night Live* by Laraine Newman, in the feature adaptation of the classic TV skit. Dan Ackroyd and Jane Curtin would play her parents, Beldar and Primak. The film was expected to be a big hit. I guess nobody had actually sat and watched the thing yet. On paper, it probably looked good.

Michelle's boyfriend, Scott, fronted the hot local band of the moment. LA seems to have had one every few months since the days of love and the Doors. In 1993, this band was Annapurna. They were an alternative, postgrunge combo but more romantic and dramatic than Nirvana or Screaming Trees. Annapurna couldn't be ironic or depressive like the grunge bands. They were from Hollywood. There was a dark glamour and intrigue to their look and sound—the whole "package." These weren't hicks who'd hit the lottery. These were sexy LA dudes. Ten years earlier they would have been sprayed and glammed, but now their clothes were correct. Hot actresses came to the shows: Alyssa Milano, Drew Barrymore. I studied Scott when he wasn't looking and wondered, What does it feel like to know that you're going to be a millionaire? You're going to travel the world. You're going to be a famous rock star? An artist? Like Michelle, Scott never really made it, but if you asked anyone at the time who was next in the queue to be a superstar, both of them would certainly have come quickly to mind.

My father, if he'd been around, probably could have told me that there's no such thing as a "lock." Even when it seemed like a done deal, it never was.

Table Grade had huge advantages, as well as good looks. While they weren't as talented as The Breeders, they weren't The Shaggs either. They had easily as much potential as Babes in Toyland or Lunachicks or any of the all-female groups Zoe idolized. They also had free, unlimited studio time, free gas, no bills, and all the time in the world to write songs and self-manage. Thanks to the Poledouris family, they were already living like rock stars in every way but the fame. They booked a few small club shows as the summer dragged on, playing twenty-minute sets in shit holes like the Alligator Lounge. While Zoe's mother, father, and little sister Alexis and I all showed up and clapped, these gigs didn't feel like an Annapurna show, like an event about which you could one day say, "I was there." They felt like children's birthday parties. Alexis was heavily into No Doubt, another soon-to-make-it LA band, probably the biggest cult act on the scene at the time. She was a smart little kid, a student at the progressive Crossroads School. Surely she knew the difference too. I watched her watch her sister and wondered what it must have been like growing up in Zoe's shadow. Probably the same as it was for my own little sister Nicki growing up in mine. Zoe and I were so much alike, we even infuriated our siblings identically. For them, you were never the freak, so it was certainly an easier ride, but you couldn't rebel even if you wanted to because the parents had just about had it with that jive. You were deprived of even the option to act out because your older sib has acted out enough for a dozen lifetimes in just twenty odd years. We'd ruined misbehavior for them.

As the band wrote, skinny-dipped in the pool, drank up the beer, and ate all the food, I went out for supplies, both comestible and musical. I'd roll up and down Ventura Boulevard in the thick desert heat, blasting KROQ and hitting Gelsens for food and Zima (Zoe's beverage of choice at that time). I charged it all to the family's card. I'd hit the newsstand for the latest *LA Weekly* and issues of *Spin* and *Rolling Stone*, then head to Tower Records out in Sherman Oaks to pick up whatever was required to inspire. Because this was Zoe, that usually meant albums by bands fronted by women: it got her tough, competitive, blue-ribbon figure skater side fired up. And so I'd come in with the cigarettes, the vegetables, more beer, soft drinks, and the new Breeders album, *The Last Splash*, or *Become What You Are* by Juliana Hatfield one day and Luscious Jackson's debut *In Search of Manny* or *Palomine* by Bettie Serveert the next. Zoe's favorite album was still *Pretty on the Inside* by Hole, and she was now styling herself even more aggressively as a prettier, vaguely more Goth, younger Courtney Love. She striped her bleached blonde hair with jet black, so she looked like a skunk. She pulled it off. There was very little she couldn't sell. I'd taken to wearing a wool ski cap, like the Beastie Boys favored, no matter what the temperature. It was a New York touchstone, my nod to a place where the climate is cold and the people are real. I guess it was a security-blanket kind of thing. The headgear equivalent of whining, "Hey, guys, remember my plan? I was supposed to be a millionaire screenwriter. Guys?" There was no furthering my career (or finding it) and Zoe's at the same time—not on my own, anyway. I was the boy groupie, Table Grade's Yoko Ono. One day I wrote in Sharpie marker, "I'm fucking the lead singer, and all I got was this lousy T-shirt," on one of their silk-screened merch items. And I wasn't joking.

Toward the end of the summer, as we were all waiting for the release of Nirvana's follow-up to *Nevermind*, Zoe's friend Justin Dixon came out to visit. She'd promised him a rent-free stay as well. Justin was old Bennington, like me. I remembered him from writing workshop . . . and I didn't like him. He didn't ascribe to the "short-and-loud" credo that my Lit Fuck posse lived by when we did our poetry readings in the Bennington café with our bebop and our cheap wine and our Vermont cheddar. That was our golden rule. Fucking short. Fucking loud. This wasn't a therapy session. It was show! Make show!

"Oh, blah, blah, my dad," I said one day by way of constructive criticism after Justin shared one of his new pieces in class. "So, what? You think you're the only one with a fucked-up family? Please."

Justin had good posture, good hair, and a brand-new, black Mazda MX-6. In LA you were only as good as your car, and it put my rusty, dented Toyota to shame. I was standoffish at first because of, well, the hair, but once you leave Bennington, with all those intense factions and poses, it's easier to just talk to someone. Maybe it was because we were the only two boys and the only two people not in a punk rock quartet, but we very quickly found ourselves together a lot once he arrived. Justin made me laugh. That never happened up at school. And I guess I showed him a side of me that wasn't affected. We became fast friends, mostly because we needed each other. Neither of us had a clear idea of what we would do once the summer was over, and it was quickly winding away. Justin was kicking around a screenplay idea or two and thought maybe he would get an agent and see if he had any luck selling it.

"We should write a screenplay together," I quickly suggested.

"What would we write about?" Justin asked, intrigued when I suggested we collaborate.

"What we know," I instantly replied, having learned a valuable lesson from my failure to sell my reaching fantasy of a novel and the success of *The Rules of Attraction* and *The Secret History*. "It's the easiest way to go."

"School?"

"Yes, we will write about Bennington. Something about Bennington."

"I don't know. Really?" Justin had just graduated too. He wanted to get on with his life. Bennington was in the rearview.

"Trust me."

"Marc, do you even remember what a dick you were to me at Bennington?"

"So, we'll write about that. I was a dick to you. That's like . . . the leap off. What else happened?"

I worked him. I roped him in and sold it, just like Herve had sold me on Brooklyn. When summer was over, I would not go back east. I would stay in Hollywood. Zoe would always return here after school, after all. It was like a guarantee that I would inevitably get to see her face, which I still loved looking at, even as things grew tense between us. I resented all the time she was putting into the band, and she wished I would be less passive and more of the cocksure figure I'd been up at college.

Shortly before we were fully moved out of the Encino house and Zoe was packed for her return to Bennington, we lost Heaven, our cat.

"I think maybe the coyotes got her," Bobbie said, comforting me with typical motherly concern.

"Coyotes?"

"They're up the cliff there." She pointed up to the vertical slab of rock that rose up from the pool area, tangled with sagebrush and nettles. Heaven had been playing on that rock only a minute ago, it seemed, chasing a black-and-orange butterfly. Now she was dead? Forever? Taken by a coyote? I thought of our "conversation" back in my apartment on Thirteenth Street: "I'd be safer on the street!"

Maybe Heaven saw an opportunity to free herself from Zoe and me forever and just took it. She was probably very much in love with a handsome tabby, and they were running a car wash in Tarzana. Or maybe she got really wise, went back to Bennington, and was auditing art history classes. Coyotes? Maybe LA was going to be harder to take down than I thought. I had assumed that a pale person was simply smarter than a tanning-booth orange person, but the orange fuckers knew enough to keep their cats indoors, didn't they? "Nobody knows anything?" Hardly.

Justin and his boyfriend, Elvin, a handsome, wavy-haired Jazz Cat from Georgia who played the upright bass and spoke with a thick Southern accent, which he'd gradually trained himself to dilute, found a two-story, white house at 2015 North Beachwood Drive, just off Franklin Avenue, about fifteen minutes on foot from Scott and Michelle's place one way and five from a strip that at the time included the Bourgeois Pig café, the Daily Planet kiosk, a chicken joint called Birds, and a deep, dusty used book and record store called Counterpoint. There was the Tamarind Theater, where ex–*Happy Days* players directed Neil Simon comedies, and the old Hollywood coffee shop Victor's just around the corner on Bronson. It had been there since the twenties, which I found comforting. As Zoe's demo circulated and she waited up in the Green Mountains for the call that told her she was going to get to be a rock star (a call that never came for me), Justin and I ate our eggs there in the morning, read the *LA Times*, and plotted out our script and our future. We always walked there and back to the house. It was like a little pedestrian village amid the Hollywood car culture, not unlike gentrifying Brooklyn or the Lower East Side. Franklin Village. The Scientology Celebrity Center was kitty-corner to the Bourgeois Pig and the Daily Planet newsstand and maintained its own security force. Say what you want about Scientology, but a part of me will always be grateful to them. They kept the hood pretty safe at the time.

Above us rose the Hollywood Hills and straight up the drive, at a dead end, the Hollywood sign loomed over everything. As with all new homes, it seemed clean and full of promise. By day, the entire living room and kitchen filled with lemony sunlight, and the bird-of-paradise plants that lined the drive swayed in the wind. We even had a winding staircase that led up to a pair of bedrooms and a large, tiled bath. It was a real house for about the price of a one-bedroom apartment in Lower Manhattan. Plus, they gave you a hose.

"What do we do with a hose?" I asked.

"Wash the cars? Water the grass?" Justin said, shaking his head. I don't think I'd ever washed my car once. I just waited for it to rain.

We threw a somewhat humble housewarming party that September, shortly after Zoe flew back to school: a handle of vodka from the Mayfair in the freezer, some red plastic cups, pretzels and potato chips, a boom box, and a mix I'd made that I figured wouldn't be too abrasive to our mutual writer friends, like Matt Selman (non-Bennington, that is to say, much less fucked-up but more awkward and with a capacity for sweetness). Matt, who would contribute to our generation's penchant for ironic humor, would go on to write and produce *The Simpsons*. I felt ashamed doing drugs in front of him. And there'd be no *Wu Tang Clan*, my favorite album of the moment. No anger. No "hard." Just the new De La Soul, some Jamiroquai, and a little softer modern rock, Cracker and The The, whose new album *Dusk* (featuring Johnny Marr on guitar) was pretty much a masterpiece.

It was there, at our open house kegger, that I first met the actress Julie Bowen, another beautiful actress friend of Nicole from Beverly Hills. In the autumn of 1993, Julie looked like Tuesday Weld on the cover of Matthew Sweet's *Girlfriend* album. She'd recently moved into a room in a one-story, two-bedroom house up in the Hollywood Hills, just above us down in the flats. Our Bennington friend Lisa, now working in an art gallery downtown, was her new roommate, but Julie wasn't Bennington, which is probably what drew me to her. She was from an East Coast family and had the crispness of an Ivy Leaguer, which matched her classic, blonde beauty. She didn't smoke, barely drank, exercised regularly, and always smelled clean, whereas there was always something pretty laid-back and funky about art school girls. Most of the actors from the Formosa scene had nothing but their bodies and faces to travel on. Julie was smart enough to do anything she wanted. Why she chose to settle in Hollywood and pursue a career in acting, I have no idea. Probably the same reason I felt like I could be a top screenwriter. When you are from the East, with a degree, the movie business initially seems so easy, so plunder-able. At the time, she was shooting some dinky television pilot about crime-fighting rock climbers or some other silly shit. Nicole's father was pro-ducing it. None of us had made it or given up yet, and among our little crew, the odds were even money. There was no real way of handicapping what was going to take off. If anything, I wouldn't have been surprised if Julie had be-come fed up with the auditions and the superficiality. She actually read books. She romanticized writers as much as I did. It was the only thing that made me think I stood a shred of a chance with her, and yes, I was quickly calculat-ing those odds too—the minute I met her. Even if Zoe and I hadn't formal-ized our second breakup just yet, I knew it was coming. I was waiting for the long-distance call from Vermont.

There was really no chance of my not falling instantly in love with Julie Bowen. The first night we met, she bet me that while not pregnant, she was currently able to lactate. I took that bet fast, since it would require the re-moval of her flimsy, silky T-shirt to win. As a small crowd gathered around the couch, Julie pulled up her shirt, grabbed her little, pink nipple, and squeezed it. Sure enough, a convex spray of watery breast milk arced over the space between us. To me, it looked like a rainbow after a long, soaking storm. She pulled her shirt back down, smiled proudly, and collected her winnings.

At that moment I started making her a mixed tape in my head. Idiot rock boys like me always start our courtships with a mixed tape, and while the songs and sequences of this rite of passage vary, the lead track on mine was always the same. Without fail, I began such tributes with what I considered the ultimate indie boy crush song, the one that says, "I am really impressed by you, girl. Please love me, but hurting me is okay too, because I will eventually hurt you too." It's the song that best signals to a young woman, "I am fucked-up and will ultimately disappoint, but nobody will ever romanticize your beauty and grace the way I can . . . from afar, but it would be cool if you know, it wasn't always from afar." I'm talking about "Perfect Skin" by Lloyd Cole and the Commotion, their debut single from 1984. It's available on *Rattlesnakes* and their flawless best-of, should you want to make a tape of your own.

"At the age of ten she looked like Greta Garbo," Lloyd hiccups like a raincoat-wearing Buddy Holly over a jangling guitar. *"And I loved her then, but how was she to know that?"*

I still give copies of *Rattlesnakes* to young men out of college girding themselves for life in cities, especially if they're single or heartbroken. "This will make you poetic." Or at least it will telegraph to girls that your raggedy, black clothes and the bags under your eyes and the chain smoking aren't real, it's just you acting like Johnny from *Naked* and beg of them, "Please see through it and remove your top again." I knew that Zoe was probably making out with some freshman as I passed out, face first, on my sheetless mattress that night, but fuck it. Zoe could have Bennington from now on, I decided. She could have her punk rock band. She could wait for the record deal. I was never going back to my old school. I wasn't going anywhere this new, amazing, lactating woman wasn't. If Julie was going to be a part of this Hollywood thing, then Justin and I had better get to work so we could stay too.

And so we breakfasted at Victor's, then took our slow strolls back to the house on Franklin as cars sped past toward Silverlake and the beach. We typed up a second draft of our script in the dining room where Justin had set up a desk against the wall. By the time that was finished, Justin had landed a job at Castle Rock, which was one of the most successful production companies in town thanks to *Seinfeld*, which, after a couple of seasons building, was now the biggest hit on television. He rose early, worked during the day, then came home, at which point I'd just be getting dressed and pouring my first vodka cocktail. Usually I woke and took a long walk for coffee and to get the blood flowing. Sometimes I'd find myself as far as Melrose Avenue or Canter's on Fairfax. It felt good, walking in LA, like I was unique somehow. The only other people on foot were the dudes selling oranges in front of the free-way entrances. I'd come home, take a long, hot bath, soaking the edges of whatever book I was reading, and hope the afternoon would pass quickly and it'd be time to drink soon. Justin would get home, and we'd walk over to La Poubelle, the dark, candlelit Italian restaurant up the street, for some of its locally famous penne *arrabiata*, red wine, and cigarettes. *Arrabiata* means, I believe, "angry," but at the time, the place was anything but: warm, candlelit, and funky, with a piano against the wall and a bunch of pretty drunks at the bar. James Duval was one of the waiters. James would soon star in Greg Ara-ki's *The Doom Generation* alongside a pale, snappish, brunette Rose Mc-Gowan, owner of what I consider the quintessential nineties face; her natural expression seemed perfectly unimpressed but needy. James would later appear in the megahit *Independence Day*, but at the time he was struggling and dreaming like all of us were. La Poubelle, like Victor's and the Bourgeois Pig, seemed like an extension of our pad, an anterior clubhouse full of like-minded young artists, all of us just burning to succeed, screaming inside for the good-news phone call that would deliver "Hollywood" and everything that went with it.

Elvin was the odd man out, the tagalong by circumstance, not for lack of charisma or intelligence. He and Justin were only romantic partners. Justin and I were writing partners. It was a much deeper bond, with higher stakes and, as it would soon prove, a lot harder to shake off. Elvin was sweeter than we were, and it made his genuine talent seem somehow fraudulent. He lacked the pitch-black sense of humor that bonded Justin and me and kept us writing sometimes just to crack each other up. If I could make Justin laugh at a line, I could visualize smart movie audiences laughing too, perhaps down in the Angelika.

Everything seemed to happen quickly once he slipped a copy of the screenplay, which we called *Terminal Gossip*, to his bosses at Castle Rock. Our script was all about how the social structure and the kibbitzing damage the lives of students on a tiny, hyper-fashion-conscious college campus—how pursuing an identity for the sake of having an identity can be dangerous. A Jazz Cat named Shaky wants to be down, so he gets strung out, and, well, it ends badly. It was part *Heathers*, part *Stoned* (the after-school special starring Scott Baio), and 100 percent Bennington, as much as *The Rules of Attraction* had been, if not more so. I resolved to go to the meetings with a bit more of a gleam; still, it was hard to look clean-cut when standing next to Justin, who seemed to awake every morning perfectly coiffed like a Republican candidate for high office. By October or so, we had an agent and were taking meetings at every major studio in town: Paramount, Sony, Warner Brothers. I was 100 percent convinced that we would be attending the premiere of our first film by Christmas. I had absolutely no idea how slow the process was—the amount of money and micromanagement involved in making even a low-budget independent film. It only took us a few weeks to write the script. The fact that it could take five years, sometimes even longer, to make a film was crazy to me.

"But so many of them are terrible. They go right to video tape." Why even bother? *Terminal Gossip* could still be in development for all I know, twenty years on.

"You don't know how rare this is," Justin told me, after the first few meetings didn't end with the presentation of two enormous Publisher's Clearing House–sized checks. "This almost never happens so fast, getting the agent, taking the meetings."

"But what are they for?" It seemed like people took meetings just to take meetings, to say they'd been active, to move their lips and breathe in and out. They didn't produce anything but noise, then long, horrible stretches of silence.

"If they like the script, why won't they make it?"

"It doesn't work that way, Marc."

Nobody could tell me exactly how it did work, not Justin, not our young, ambitious agent, Jessica Swirnoff. The actors and actresses at the Formosa seemed to know. Basil Poledouris was attuned to the rhythm, even if it sometimes made him spit. I felt like there was a beat I simply could not hear, the pounding, pounding, pounding of the Pacific against the shoreline. I was lost out there. I didn't even like to drive my little Toyota because I always got lost and was quickly tiring of the metaphor.

"If you really want to help this process along, please, for the love of shit, do not wear that fucking sweater to the next meeting," Justin said.

Zoe had given me a wool agnès b. sweater for my birthday. The sleeves didn't end at the cuffs but formed a sort of half glove that went around the thumbs. Like my crocheted, brown and yellow Beastie Boys–style beanie, it was more of a security blanket than a fashion statement, and I simply could not imagine attending a meeting with a suited studio executive without it.

"I hate it. I would hide it if you ever took it off. It smells. You smell. Are you high?"

"No. What do you mean? On heroin? No. No. Just pot." I'd added the pot to the booze after Zoe left to combat the codependent thing without resorting to the white, which out in LA wasn't even white. It was brown—Mexican tar that the dealers over on Bonnie Brae kept in their mouths in little red balloons. You had to smoke it off foil, or cook it up in a pan, then chop the hardened resin into a powder and snort it, or find a clean needle (one hoped) and a vein.

"Stop smoking pot before these things," Justin warned. "Also . . . that's my pot."

"Come on. It went fine. They said they loved us."

"They say that to everyone. You really don't understand how this works, do you?"

I really didn't.

"When we win our Oscar, you can wear whatever you want to accept it. Until then, please just . . . shave." It's true. Look at what some famous people wear today. Whoopi Goldberg. Mickey Rourke. You can be sure they didn't dress like that when they were young and hungry and auditioning. The funky agnès b. sweater, the weed, the BO, and the stubble, all that needed to go into storage until the contracts and the checks and the productions started rolling in and out. I had it in me. I'd used restraint in my housewarming mix. Intellectually it made sense. Nobody rebels when they first get meetings. They rebel only once they can. The writing was good too. It deserved more sincerity than I was giving it. I would have to discard poor Johnny from *Naked* if we were ever going to get anywhere. I would have to truly become one of the crew I so snobbishly held myself above because I'd read better books (or at least bought better books) and had better records and lived in the Chelsea . . . once.

Justin always drove to the pitch meetings. We'd play Nirvana's *In Utero*, and Justin would sing along to the most abrasive tracks in the sweetest voice, like he was singing along to John Denver or Kenny Loggins. *"I wish I could eat your cancer, when you turn black,"* he'd croon as if it were a love song, and I suppose it is. Sometimes, if I was glum, he'd cheer me up by singing certain KROQ hits in the voice of our fellow Bennington alumna Carol Channing. You haven't heard "The Wrong Way" by Sublime until you've heard Carol (or Justin as Carol) render it: *"Nee-yo bah-deee ever chtold her itch the wrong way, Dah-lly!"*

The meetings went on and on and on and on.

Everybody loved us. Nobody gave us money. Nobody gave us plans. We never knew what was next. We had the "Screenwriter's Blues," like Soul Coughing. Men built Paramount Studios and Columbia Studios, and men in booths at those studios gave us tickets and directions, and we tried not to get lost, but really we were lost when we rolled the fuck up.

Jessica, our agent, would ring us after each meeting and give us the low-down, but it never seemed to include anything concrete. Each meeting only ever led to more meetings, dozens of them—so many that Justin was given a leave from Castle Rock. Forget that he was the only one of us who was employed. Like Scott and his band Annapurna and Julie and her pilots, we all felt like if we could just hold out a few moments longer, the rewards would be great. It was worth eating forty-nine cent burritos from the Mayfair, standing in line with two of them while the carts before and behind you were loaded with organic groceries. Sometimes I'd steal a pint of liquor or a copy of *Rolling Stone*. Here I was, on the list for entry at every studio lot in town, resorting to petty theft to get a little buzz or to read about the new Jon Spencer Blues Explosion album.

"*Terminal Gossip* huh? Great title. Did you see *Terminal Velocity*?"

"This is different."

"Good movie."

"Ours is good too. Buy it."

As with *Loose*, my first, still unpublished novel, all of my self-worth was tied up in how my writing was received; that acceptance was love to me. I was a nothing unless I made people raise their eyebrows and respond to the quality of whatever thoughts and ideas I was selling . . . or trying to sell. I had to blow people's heads off with what was coming out of me, or I could see no reason not to stick needles full of cooked black Mexican tar into my right arm. In a way, it would have been more honest if I'd just kept a rolled-up dish towel full of needles and charred spoons in full view. Instead, I hit the bottle like a sixties housewife. I carried a half pint of vodka in my back pocket with my cigarettes and two-key chain. One for the house. One for the car, which had no gas in the tank.

Tipsy, I'd make passes at Julie, and sometimes she'd drag me into the bathroom of her clean, airy house, and we'd make out against the wall, but I knew that I didn't have what it took to close the deal (that being . . . a deal). She was dating another screenwriter named Scott Silver, who would go on to write Eminem's *8 Mile* and be nominated for an Oscar for *The Fighter*. That guy knew how to work the town, work his own talent, and work Julie. A mixed tape with a few sad Grant Lee Buffalo, Tindersticks, and Morphine tracks wasn't going to get me ahead of him in any race for her love. Without the green light from the studio, I was just a sad, scared Long Island boy with a badly self-cut head of greasy hair, holes in my cowboy boots, some zits, and a bad case of a-long-way-from-homesickness. I wasn't Mike Leigh's Johnny. I was just playing tough, and soon it would begin to show. Julie's attraction to me, which I believe was real, would dry up as soon as she realized I wasn't really a bad boy, so I kept pretending to be in a lot more pain than I was, when really it was just your basic worry. And it worked well enough for a while, but

I suspect deep down, she knew something was off. In the middle of fooling around, Julie would push me away and ask, "God, what am I doing?" her face flushed red. "You are bad for me." Sometimes I believed her and felt, well, bad, meaning good, as Run DMC once sang. Other times, I wondered if she could sense my fear, being so close to me, tongue down my throat, arms around my shoulders. She'd usually grab me and kiss me one more time before returning to the cocktail party, but maybe that was charity. She was a sweet girl, the kind who'd lend you her car and never bitch if you returned it with an empty tank. One night, we slow-danced to Neil Diamond's "Girl, You'll Be a Woman Soon" on the juke in the Frolic Room, a dark, dive bar on Hollywood Boulevard, next to the old Pantages Theater, in full view of Justin, Elvin, and our other friends, but that was just a dance. Most of our clinches occurred in secret places reserved for cook snorting and reading the *LA Times* Calendar Section on the throne.

Urge Overkill was about to have a big hit with that Neil Young song. *Pulp Fiction* was coming out, and everyone in town knew it. It was like the winter of 1964 when you first heard The Beatles were headed over. Justin got a copy of the unedited script, and once he was finished, I got to read it, which I did with a flashlight in my bedroom. I still didn't own a lamp, just a radio and a mattress. The script read like a novel, and I knew it would change everything. I couldn't eat or shit or drink or even think about Julie while I was in it, and it pulled me right in, so much so that when I saw the movie, I felt like I'd already seen it. We were writing indie film scripts at a time when indie film scripts were becoming less and less distinguishable from big studio films—if not in budget, then in attention, and attention was all I cared about. David O'Russell had released *Spanking the Monkey*. Paul Thomas Anderson's *Cigarettes and Coffee* was circulating as a much-bootlegged videocassette. Todd Haynes's second feature *Safe* was getting made. The aforementioned Greg Araki was hooked up. So was *Party Girl*, which would break Parker Posey through, and Todd Solondz's *Welcome to the Dollhouse*. Kevin Smith was making *Chasing Amy*, his best film, hands down (although *Dogma* is a close second in my opinion). Killer Films, Good Machine: these were some of the companies that our agent began talking about with regard to getting *Gossip* made. It seemed entirely plausible that we could enter this world too, Justin and I, if we only had a little bit of luck and the right people behind us. Greg Araki's scripts were just as camp and crude as ours. And an even bigger wave was coming, one that would switch nearly every yellow-lit, talky, indie film project to green. After Cannes that spring, the floodgates opened, and nobody didn't know it, but Justin and I were aware way before that, that *Pulp Fiction* was going to be the biggest indie film ever made. I'd stayed up all night reading the *Pulp Fiction* script in the dark, illuminating the pages with a flashlight. It was long, full of scenes that didn't make the film, and read more like a novel than a screenplay. We would almost certainly get our deals once it hit. Every smart nerd would. This was the Beatles in 1964 or Nirvana in 1991, and Justin and I were not too proud to be Gerry and the Pacemakers or Seven Mary Three.

Even with a breakthrough feeling inevitable, I found a way to bitch. I was the less patient of the two of us. As the meetings piled up and the frustrations mounted, Justin remained smart and patient. His self-worth was tied up in his family and maybe his car, definitely his hair. He liked himself. He didn't need praise. He was satisfied. Like Julie, he could have done anything. He chose to be in Hollywood. He liked the weather. He liked the trees. He liked the men. I only liked the promise of attention. And Julie. And maybe . . . Canter's. Canter's was good.

The more I hated these studio executives we were still meeting weekly, the more I wanted them to love my writing. Even when these executives placed their feet on the coffee table, right on our script, and made us stare at the heels of their shoes, Justin kept a smile on his face. And who does that, with the shoes anyway? Was it some kind of feral signal of dominance? Because it happened with more frequency than you would suspect. "Welcome. I am the boss of you. Smell my feet." Then the meeting would end, and you would exit with your parking validation and your unopened bottle of Poland Spring wondering what had happened, which you would not know until you called your agent later in the day, and she'd say, "Oh they loved you. They loved the script." And you'd never hear from them again. Not only did it make me dizzy; it made me ashamed that I once believed I would have the muscle to swim in such a current. Justin could tell that I was already divesting, pining for New York. Pining for the fjords.

"Do you have any other ideas?" one executive asked me as we were about to leave yet another fruitless sit-down.

"Yeah, I have an idea," I finally said.

Justin looked at me. We hadn't discussed any new ideas, any second acts or follow-ups. For a moment, his eyes pleaded, "Please don't . . . Whatever it is . . . please . . . do not."

"It's about a poor family that adopts a cat that shits money."

Julie and Lisa had people over on Halloween night, and we were all considering meeting some of the Formosa clique at the Viper Room. Some went, but Julie didn't, so I decided to stay and get drunk at her place. I ended up walking down to the flats alone at the end of the night, shivering every time I heard the click and claw of insects scurrying through the brush. I never liked nature. It was unnatural. The walk down was better than the walk up. In the morning I came downstairs, and Justin was sitting in the kitchen.

"River Phoenix died last night," he said.

"How?" I asked, but I already knew the answer.

"Heroin," he said and looked at me with a vague hostility, as if I'd been somehow responsible. Like I'd given it to him. My culture had killed River Phoenix.

Ron had moved out to Venice after graduating from Bennington that June. He was still wary of settling in New York, as the stink of heroin was still thick in the air. He'd gotten a job at a food co-op and moved in with an electric piano player named Jeremy, who would later play with Macy Gray and Fitz and the Tantrums (fronted by a mutual friend, Michael Fitzpatrick, the younger brother of Lisa's then boyfriend Joel, another former Bennington student). Whenever Hollywood and the meetings and the pressure got to be too much, I'd take the bus out to the beach and hang out on the boardwalk with him. Ron was doing even worse than I was. At least I had an agent and a plan, albeit one that required a kind of faith that I just didn't possess. For someone working for a food co-op, he was slowly going hungry out there. Ron was living on rice. No beans, no meat, just rice and cigarettes, which he was smoking twice, once for pleasure and a second time for whatever nicotine was left. If he scored a block of cheese, it was a good day. I had barely enough cash to see a movie with popcorn. We'd walk around the Santa Monica promenade and watch people eat and shop. Sometimes we'd sing "A Deeper Shade of Soul," that terrible Dutch rap hit by Urban Dance Squad, at the top of our lungs, altering the lyrics to "a deeper shade of po'." We were crazy and free in our suffering. It brought to mind that description of slum denizens in Orwell's *Down and Out in Paris and London*: "*Poverty frees them from ordinary standards of behavior.*" We would stare and point at diners as they ate their poached eggs at outdoor cafés until a hostess or host shooed us away. We'd sometimes sit in this café, ironically named The Novel, that offered free refills. He'd drink the first cup, then I'd take it up to get a refill and drink the second.

Back in Hollywood, our agent, Jessica, had ways to neutralize my impatience and keep Justin and me focused. She floated several "helpful" tasks our way, tasks designed, more than anything else, to kill even more time. I didn't buy it but agreed to carry on with the charade. So we went to the Pig and made our wish list of directors who would "get" the script.

"Let's see, Todd Haynes, Cameron Crowe, Alex Cox, Pedro Almodóvar."

"Almodóvar?"

"Why not? It's a wish list."

"Actresses who would be good for Mary? Ashley Judd, Juliette Lewis, Winona Ryder, Ione Skye, Mary Stuart Masterson, Michelle Burke."

Michelle was the only one we actually knew. I could have added Frances Farmer. It was a wish list.

Yeah, let's get Michelle, I thought to myself. And Fassbender can direct her as soon as he finishes being a dead German genius. Or Orson Welles. Or . . . Pasolini . . . or Herzog, with Kinski in the lead. And we'll all buy property in Malibu and date Margot Kidder and mix our Bloody Marys with actual blood.

I was walking home from the Bourgeois Pig one day when I ran into him—one of those handsome, kinky-haired runaways from the Midwest, another raw, good-looking rube, learning social skills and figuring out if he had any real talent. Sometimes those folks turn into multimillionaires with homes in Italy and on the moon. We'd bummed smokes from each other on the street before, and I knew he was a user, the way some gay dudes know other dudes are gay.

"I've seen you around."

"So."

"So you wanna come for a ride?" he asked one afternoon. I'd actually reached into my pocket because reflexively I figured he needed a smoke or a light. This was different—a confirmation sure, but also a dare. Maybe he could tell the same thing about me.

"You have a car?"

He nodded.

"Where to?"

I already knew the answer. I'd been so good all summer, all fall. I'd even thrown away my agnès b. sweater to please Justin, who was paying all the bills. Justin had the gift of faith.

Chris pointed to a paint-stripped, beat-up Chevy van parked on the corner. It looked like the kind of car kidnappers cruise around in looking for people to abduct, or the kind that secretly contains FBI agents and bugging equipment. Nothing good could ever come from getting into that van.

"Do you even have a license?" I asked as we pulled onto the freeway, and he threw the engine into high gear. I punched in the cassette that was jutting out of the deck, and the Violent Femmes' first album came on.

"When I'm out walking I strut my stuff and I'm so strung out."

"Because I can't drive this thing. It's a stick," I warned.

"Can't drive stick?" He shook his head. "Not much of a man, are you?" He said it in an Australian accent, even though he wasn't Australian. Maybe he was working on some sides for an upcoming audition. He was pretty good. The

familiarity of the old Violent Femmes music calmed me down. I actually felt
good, careening toward certain chemical doom. It was the calm just before the
explosion—a perfect sense of control. It had been months since I felt in charge
of anything. Zoe had been the boss. She had all the money. She had Bennington. She was younger. Nobody had forced her to throw any ballast over the side.
And once she went back to school, Justin, and later Justin and Jessica, our agent,
had the power. He was paying the bills; she was setting up the studio meetings.

Chris circled the block until we found a dealer, a Mexican kid in a gray
hoodie, baggy jeans, and sneakers. We rolled up and handed him the money;
he reached into his mouth, pulled out a half dozen red balloons, handed them
over, and we sped off. The rubber balloons felt warm as Chris placed them in
my palm. The spit had dried as soon as it hit the air, but the heat and sticki-
ness remained. We drove back to the Franklin strip, and I braced myself for
what was coming next. Chris was crashing with some girl in the Villa Carlotta, an enormous, Spanish deco apartment complex between our corner and
the Pig—all vintage sconces and clamshell arches, cold stone, and thick, dark
wood. Like the Formosa and Victor's, the Villa Carlotta was old Hollywood,
almost too beautiful for the depravity that went on inside. It seemed to be
bathed in a shady, golden-orange hue no matter how high the sun or viscous
the smog. The lobby was dark and filled with deep, shabby couches and potted plants and bookshelves, like some opium-eating scholar's study. The street
and every boring new car outside, as well as all the plans I'd made, seemed to
vanish as we passed through the door.

"We can fix at Mary Beth's," Chris said. "One of those is for her anyway."

Mary Beth, a skinny, witchy, blonde model and actress, was waiting for us.
She had a dozen candles lit and Nick Drake on her stereo. She also had needles. She led us into the bathroom, and we watched as she cleaned them with
bleach.

"You don't have any clean ones?"

"These are clean," she said. "The bleach cleans them. It's *bleach*." She
looked at me like I was a total novice.

"I can't stick myself," I said, remembering my slightly embarrassing whining back in Bennington with Jane (again, not her real name).

"I didn't think so," she sneered. "It's okay, I'll do you."

As the candles melted, and Nick Drake sang, *"I never held emotion in the
palm of my hand,"* she fixed herself, then me. Chris sorted himself out. He
drove a stick. He could shoot up on his own. He was much of a man. The
three of us fell onto her bed, which was covered with antique tapestries, as
were the walls. It was like nodding inside a change purse. I could feel the
drugs flower in my belly and spread goodwill toward man throughout my

extremities. I loved Zoe. I loved my mom. I loved Justin. I loved our agent. I loved Quentin Tarantino. I even loved Roger Avary. Mary Beth grabbed my sweaty hand and played with it.

"You have girl hands," she said.

"What the fuck does that mean?" I laughed. "They're huge. Look how much bigger they are than yours." We compared, and then Chris offered his hand, and I dwarfed his fingers as well.

"You're out of your mind."

"I'm not talking about size. I'm talking about essence."

"The essence of my hands is female?"

"Yes."

What was she implying? Was this why I hadn't been published? Because my fingers, typing all those lines, all those pages, were sexually compromised somehow? How was I ever going to make it as a real writer . . . with girl hands? The idea nearly ruined an otherwise perfect high.

By the holidays and the start of 1994, I'd given up on any studio taking *Gossip,* and we adjusted our plans and tried to attach it to a major star who would help us get it made on the back of his power in town.

"Brad Pitt. Johnny Depp. Leonardo DiCaprio. Christian Slater, maybe?"

"He's good," I shrugged.

"Why are you scratching yourself?"

"I'm not."

"You have scratches all over your arms, Marc."

"Mosquito."

Justin shook his head. He knew I was getting high again, but nobody wanted to be the one to say it out loud. That would make it real, and we would almost be obligated to fight.

Instead of Johnny Depp and our own table at the Viper Room, we got Josh Miller.

Joshua Miller was already a veteran stage and screen actor by age nineteen. You may remember Josh as Keanu Reeves's demonic little brother in the 1986 film *River's Edge,* in which he pulls off the seemingly impossible feat of being creepier than his costars, Crispin Glover and Dennis Hopper. Compact, feral, but cherubic, with a dangling earring, he is probably the most unsettling juvenile delinquent I've ever seen on screen. He plays a similar demon child in Katherine Bigelow's *Near Dark.* The vampire Homer is part of a gang of white-trash new wave bloodsuckers that also includes Bill Paxton, Lance Henrickson, and the eighties' most spectacularly sexy actress, Jenny Wright. Forever on the edge of puberty thanks to his undeadness, he's a hostile kid, and this results in some of the film's best lines ("Do you have any idea what

it's like to be a big man on the inside and have a small body on the outside?").
These, he delivers in a toothy, campy lisp.

Josh fell in love with our script and saw himself in the key supporting role
of Shaky, the tragic Jazz Cat who overdoses. Unlike Homer, Josh had grown
up since his child-star days and was eager to show other directors and cast-
ing agents that he could play a young adult. Young actresses do this by showing their breasts. Actors play doomed junkies. It was just the way the town
operated.

Josh could easily part with a few thousand dollars to develop the project and
get some of his friends and associates to support us as well. Although Justin
knew that many good scripts go to the desks of mercurial actors to die, and
everybody has a story about a sitcom star or short-film director driving a
Guild-less and unprotected screenwriter to dementia with months'—sometimes years'—worth of "notes" on a script that he or she has ponied up a few
grand for, I absolutely insisted we give Josh the rights because I needed cash for
heroin. I'd already sold my poor, die-hard red 1987 Toyota to our ex-Bennington friend Lisa for about $500, and I'd blown through that after about a week.

Josh, in his way, was charming. Even Justin had to admit that his pedigree
was impressive. Josh came from a classic old Hollywood family. His grandfather was "Bernard of Hollywood," the famous pinup photographer who'd discovered Marilyn Monroe. His mother was Susan Bernard, who'd appeared in
Playboy and portrayed the good girl in Russ Meyer's *Faster Pussycat! Kill! Kill!*,
which I'd seen on the recommendation of John Waters's writing. His father,
Jason Miller, was Father Karras in *The Exorcist*. He'd also won a Pulitzer Prize
for writing *That Championship Season*. Josh's half brother was Jason Patric
from *The Lost Boys* and, at the time, more of what we needed in terms of star
power to attach to our script.

Josh drove a tricked-out black Beamer. When he picked me up for one of
our earliest "work dates," he brought me to a screening and lecture by Sir
Richard Attenborough at the Director's Guild. He was playing Liz Phair's
Exile in Guyville in the car. It seemed to come out of three hundred tiny
speakers mounted all over the interior.

Low-fi indie rock is not supposed to sound like this, I remember thinking
as the thrust of the car took over and my head fell back into the rest.

"Marc, I have a question. Is she singing, '*I ask because I'm a real cunt in
spring, you can rent me by the hour*' or '*you can rend me by the hour*'?" I didn't
know or care. I just knew this former child star was renting me by the hour.
And I went willingly. I wanted the director of every film I saw to come out
afterwards, along with the stars, and give me a lecture. Now, that was the way
to see a movie.

Technically speaking, Josh was going to use his connections to "package" the script—to attach actors and maybe even some skilled crew, a cinematographer, a composer. The more he drew, the better our chances of interesting a financier. I was fine with taking that tack. It wasn't like I was even there anyway. Poor Justin had to deal with him day to day—the lunches and the plans. I figured I'd cowritten the thing. I'd done my job. I wasn't a producer and didn't want to be. When they needed rewrites or punch-ups, I'd resurface. In the mean time, what was the harm in disappearing entirely into the Villa Carlotta, with its amber light, cool floors, Nick Drake, and needles? I went on such a king hell bender, I scarred up my lungs and had to carry around an asthma inhaler to jam in my mouth whenever I stopped coughing.

One morning, after a night of getting high, I came downstairs. Justin and Elvin looked ashen and stared at the wood floor suspiciously, as if at any second it was going to allay their balance and swallow them up.

"Oh, damn. Which one of you broke my fucking lava light?" I croaked. It was the only thing I'd contributed to the house, so I was proud of it.

"Are you serious?" Justin asked.

"Why? What's going on?"

"Earthquake," Elvin said. "Earthquake!" He was so freaked out, the Southern drawl he tried so hard to keep down came back. "It was terror-fyin', dude."

"No way."

"You slept through it?"

"I guess I did. Was it the 'big one'?"

"If it was the big one, we wouldn't be here," Justin laughed.

"Is Julie okay?"

They started laughing.

"That's what you have to say?"

"6.7," Elvin said.

"Is that bad?"

Zoe knew I was in love with Julie Bowen. She'd return to LA on breaks or holidays, and we'd go through the motions of being a couple, but I was too depraved and distracted. One night, we watched *Gift*, the film that Perry Farrell of Jane's Addiction made with his then girlfriend Casey Niccoli. It's a pretty funny, if now obscure, film with some really powerful live footage of Jane's. There's also a scene where Perry comes home to find that Casey has overdosed and died among the altars and candles and their live pet chicken. Perry lets out some primal sobs as he cradles her in his sinewy, tattooed arms, and soon I heard similar noises coming from Zoe. I turned to my right, and she was staring at me like I was dead too. She was making her peace with it, grieving over me, with me right there in the room. I don't think we were ever a couple after that moment, although we continued to try. We would drive out to the rink where she had skated as a child, and I would watch her lace up her skates and hit the ice hard, cutting lines in the ice and trying to re- capture some lost, hardcore spirit and innocence too. It wouldn't come with me in the picture, not as I was then. I'd already crossed lines that were be- yond forgiveness: stealing, pawning some guitars that were laying around for drug money, cheating, lying. It was only a matter of time before the guitars were noticed, but I told myself, I'll be dead by then. And yet, amazingly, plans and meetings went on . . . and on. You can't even die if you've got something in development.

Eventually, I'd get so sick of all the hope and struggle to get this stupid movie made that I'd simply leave town. I had no pride in my work anymore. I didn't work. I just wanted junk . . . and Julie. If she was filming some TV show or movie, then there was no reason to stay in LA, especially if I was tasked with being patient while *Gossip* "developed," like some Polaroid of a cock or boobs. So sometimes I just vanished. Justin thought I was out in Venice with Ron, but I'd actually be in Manhattan getting high. The price of a one-way ticket was only a couple hundred dollars, about the same amount that my fa- ther was willing to wire me in case of "emergency" or that I could make sell- ing CDs at our local used record store or, if they wouldn't take any, then at Aron's Records over on La Brea (a long walk from our place on North Beach- wood but doable). I'd pocket the CD cash or pick up the wired racetrack money at the check-cashing place on La Cienega, get a taxi to LAX, and take a cheap flight to JFK. I'd snort some crystallized tar (cooked up in the frying pan, then cooled like poured English toffee and chopped until fine) before boarding the plane and wake up just in time to put on my new favorite song, Liz Phair's "Stratford-On-Guy," in which she talks about descending in an airplane over Chicago and pretending she is in a Galaxie 500 video. I'd pre- tend I was in a Liz Phair video as we descended into New York City. I didn't have any money, so I'd take the subway all the way in, a journey longer than the LIRR ride from Lawrence to Penn Station. I'd walk from Herald Square to the Chelsea, hoping against hope that Jerry or at least someone familiar was behind the glass at the front desk. Stanley Bard would be there in his of- fice, and I'd managed to talk my way in without putting up a credit card or any cash deposit.

"Hey, Stanley?"

"Where've you been?"

"Oh, you know, out in LA. Working on a screenplay. We've got a 'package deal.'"

Stanley, trusting and sympathetic, always gave me a key, even though I had no money. I'd take the elevator up to my tiny room, where I'd fall into the bed face first.

I cannot pay for this room, I'd think as I drifted into a perfect sleep. It made the bed seem that much more comfortable, the quiet and dark so much more peaceful. Usually I'd sleep for a full twelve hours, then get up and walk around the hotel or the neighborhood and exult in being home. I always figured out a way to pay my tab before boarding the plane back to LAX, once the drugs and the borrowed or stolen money ran out and all I had left was enough for another one-way shuttle ticket. Succeeding once, twice, three times, and having Justin believe that I was indeed at Ron's, emboldened me. I knew I was pushing my luck and one day it would run out, but while I was doing it, it felt not only magical but crucially private. Long before smart-phones and texting and checking in on foursquare and GPS apps, it was possible to simply disappear. Nobody knew where I was. Anyone who wanted me would simply have to wait, and for that small, delicious spell, I was somehow myself again—the real me, not the writer me, or the junkie me, or the boy-friend me, or the rock-and-roll kid in all black who knows too much about music.

I never would have figured my luck would run out the one time they stashed me away in another cheap room on a floor where a full film-production crew had set up and was working. If anything, it gave me grounds to complain and imply that I was not satisfied with the accommodations. I couldn't go to the bathroom across the hall without having to wait for some French dude with a walkie-talkie to let me know when I was allowed to pee. Drills whirred; metal poles clacked. And once I entered the bathroom, Gary Oldman would be in there in character, pacing and looking intense and spooky in his tan suit. I wasn't allowed to use the elevator or the stairs to go down for cigarettes until I got the all clear from the French production assistant. As I waited for the elevator, a little girl sat on the floor with her legs dangling over the edge under the black iron railings. She wore a sweater, black choker, and brown engineer boots, which she swung back and forth. She seemed to be concen-trating on remembering her lines. Her lips were moving as she recited them to herself quietly. It was very cute and softened my resentment for these creeps, who'd invaded my much-needed privacy. The film, a campy, stylish, ultraviolent tale about a solitary hit man (Jean Reno) and the little girl he grows to love, is called *The Professional* in America, *Léon* everywhere else. Na-talie Portman was the girl, Matilda. It's now considered a cult classic, but at the time, it was just a pain in the ass. I actually did debate complaining to Stanley Bard. Then I reminded myself that I had $9 in my wallet and another

$16 in my bank account, and if it came to it, I could complain about the noise and refuse to "pay."

One night, Jack and our friend Chrissie, probably the only other Bennington student from the Five Towns (Hewlett to my Lawrence), came over, and we all got high in my room. Chrissie, with her black bangs and perfect facial symmetry, looked exotic, like Anna Karina, and suggested Continental chill until she opened those perfect lips. Then the thick Long Island–ese of Michelle Pfeiffer in *Married to the Mob* hit your ears. Still, she was sexy. We dated briefly post-Bennington, but if I'd known her in the Five Towns, she would never have given me a second look. She probably wore a painted denim jacket back then and listened to Lita Ford. Bennington had arted her up only so much. She may have owned an Ani DiFranco album or two, but she still carried herself like she was concealing a switchblade. We were snorting heroin on the bed, pacing and smoking. Suddenly, I jerked upward and grabbed my leather jacket.

"Okay, we have to get out of here," I announced, and Chrissie and Jack lifted their heads up off their chests at the same time.

"Why? I'm so nice and high. In the Chelsea Hotel."

"I've been dreading this for days, and I can't do it anymore. We have to go. Now that I'm high and have the courage. Where can we sleep?"

"We can go to my place." Chrissie lived down on Waverly off Washington Square Park with a roommate, another Bennington girl named Patricia Ann.

"Okay, good. How do we get out?"

"What do you mean? We can't just walk out?"

"I have no money to pay for the room. I haven't had any money all week. Do any of you have money?"

"No."

"Well, just walk out. Tell them you'll be back later."

"What about my bag. It'll look suspicious." I looked over at my bag. It wasn't a full suitcase, but it was clearly big enough to raise an eyebrow.

"Oh, shit. Right."

"I have an idea," Chrissie said.

"What is it? "

"Gimme another line."

I handed her the glassine bag. I was desperate. If she had said, "Alright boys, first, we're gonna shimmy down the facade," I would have. I was sweating and fretting so much I didn't notice Chrissie taking off her gray sweatshirt and thrusting it under her T-shirt, then putting her cropped leather jacket on. We hit the lobby and pulled open the door. I lifted the suitcase into the air and swung it at anyone blocking my way to the big glass doors ahead of us. At that moment Chrissie let out a torrent of burnt-orange and yellow-brown puke, right there on the lobby floor. From that point on, nobody was looking at the suitcase anymore.

"She's pregnant," Jack shouted as he helped the stricken Chrissie toward the door.

I was already pacing on the hard rubber mat out front. We ran up the street toward Seventh Avenue and hopped into a cab.

"I'm so happy for you," Jack said, holding Chrissie's sweaty forehead in his hands. "You'll name the child after me of course."

As we headed downtown, I looked back through the rear window.

"Now, they will never put a plaque up in front with my name on it."

Some kind of mental egg timer always signaled it was time to return to LA. I had confidence that it would ring when I was needed there. If I needed a push to get to the airport, I thought of Julie Bowen's face. I thought of kissing her, of how she tasted like watermelon and salt and how necking with someone so beautiful felt like a small victory for every awkward nerd kid who ever lived. Julie had her demons. She got into funks. She had, like all actresses at a certain point in their career, food issues. She could be superficial. The town was working its way into all of us, and not for the best. She never seemed to find happiness in conventional relationships. I'd sat through about three "boyfriends" already, and after a point I simply waited for word that they'd gone their own way. I was determined to be a constant in her life. I knew there was no chance I'd ever be one of them, and I was fine with that. It seemed like becoming her boyfriend was the best way eventually to never see her again, and that I couldn't handle. She pulled me back west. I missed her face and the way she smelled. Had I never met her, I might have stayed in New York forever.

There'd always be conditions, negotiations, punishments, small scandals whenever I rematerialized. Justin insisted that if I wanted to live with him, I would have to get a job and contribute, so I took a part-time shift at the Bourgeois Pig on the strip down on Franklin, making espressos and dusting the pool table in the back. From there, I moved laterally to the Daily Planet news kiosk, which seemed a better fit. For a while it seemed like a happy marriage again. The old optimism had returned. We started acting like we were destined to be the indie rock Babaloo Mandel and Lowell Ganz again. Elvin was missing when I returned. Maybe Justin was happy for the company. Living with a gay male couple, I noticed—and I don't mean to generalize—that they sometimes beat the shit out of each other. A guy throwing a punch at his wife or girlfriend is forever cast as an Ike Turner or Chris Brown, but two strapping young dudes seem to have occasional license to vent frustration by wrestling and whaling punches. At least they did in our two-story house on Franklin. Some days I'd be in my room reading the *LA Weekly* or the new *Spin* or an article about Kate Moss and "heroin chic" in an expensive fashion magazine "borrowed" from the Daily Planet when I'd hear a crash. I'd open Justin's door, and he and Elvin would be in the closet rabbit-punching each other.

"Are you guys okay?" I'd ask.

"We're fine!" they'd grunt, as if to say, "Leave us alone, man. We're . . . working it out." I'd walk out of my room again ten minutes later, and they'd be making out. Love.

Ringing up scented candles, fashion magazines, and self-help books was not so bad, and once again I strove to be a mensch—to stay clean, to do penance. About as close to the darkness as I got was playing the *Natural Born Killers* soundtrack at the kiosk. The Villa Carlotta, of course, stood between my front door and the Daily Planet, beckoning, but I held my breath and doubled my pace as I passed it, like superstitious people do when they drive by a boneyard. One day Thurston Moore of Sonic Youth bought a newspaper from me, which I thought a good omen. Whenever geniuses appear, it's inspiring. Another afternoon, I saw Adam Ant and Heather Graham from *Drugstore Cowboy* parking their car. God what good-looking babies they would have, I marveled.

The guy who played Jimmy the Cab Driver on the MTV commercials came in with his dad to buy a copy of the *New York Times*. God, his dad must be so proud of him, I thought. He's on TV every day. He's really funny. His agent is going to get him so much work. All I ever do is ask my dad for money for drugs and plane tickets.

The manager of the Pig next door gave me free coffee, and I gave them free papers for the tables. The nicest of the Pig employees was named James. He'd bring the strong, steaming au laits right to me when I couldn't leave my post. James was a struggling actor with thinning blonde hair and a deep, soothing voice. He was about to get his big break playing Gunther, a coffee shop manager with thinning hair and a deep, soothing voice, on *Friends*. Is that life imitating art? What a strange way to have a career. But at least it was a career.

When rebels are forced to walk the line, sometimes they indulge in small rebellions, little hints or warnings, or perhaps personal reminders, basically harmless, small celebrations of the monsters they used to be. For example, one day on a whim, I dyed my red hair black and painted my fingernails to match with a bottle of polish I lifted from the Walgreens drug store. I'd recently purchased a copy of *The Downward Spiral*, the new Nine Inch Nails album, which was recorded in the house where the Manson family slaughtered Sharon Tate and her unlucky friends. I was going through a Goth phase, edging back slowly toward the heroin I knew I couldn't resist. *The Downward Spiral* seemed to me a very smacky album, and I gravitated toward those the way a golf fanatic might a Huey Lewis and the News album. I bought a copy of *11:11* by Thalia Zedek's band Come because I read it was about dope and never even unwrapped it. It's a form, I suppose, of target marketing.

"This is like that horrible sweater all over again. Do you think they look good? Your fucking . . . nails!" Justin asked me, as I moved my fingers across the keyboard, trying to come up with a follow-up to *Gossip*, anything we could sell. I was content to keep the good ship afloat in the sun, to keep the landlord away. "Really, do you think your stubby fingers look good with black nail polish on them? You're not going to write anything good with those fucking fingers."

The next day I was working at the Planet and Julie Bowen pulled up in her little red Honda with a bottle of nail polish remover. She left the car running on Franklin, walked up to the register, and took my hands.

"Hi," I said, laughing. She didn't speak. She pulled a clump of tissue from her pocket and stripped the Goth varnish off my nails, finger by finger. Then she kissed me, got back in the car, and sped off without saying a word. I guess Justin had called to commiserate.

"You're like our pet," he once told me, "our pet junkie."

I woke up early for work one morning a few weeks later, and I was alone. Justin, now single again, must have gone home with someone. Or maybe he was out shopping. I'd had weird dreams. I put on KROQ, and they were talking about Kurt Cobain, and I already knew what had happened. I listened for confirmation. It was as though all of us were waiting for this day since he'd overdosed in Rome and Nirvana pulled out of a headlining spot on Lollapalooza '94. I called Jack and told him. He hadn't heard, and we were both really sad. I was just putting out the new issue of *Spin* at the Daily Planet, the one with Courtney Love on the cover. I'd once refused to see Nirvana at the Forum with Butthole Surfers because I was all snobby about seeing them in an arena. Back in New York, Herve, Jack, and Tony saw them at the New York Coliseum during the New Music Seminar, and I missed out because I was stuck in LA trying to be a millionaire screenwriter.

"Now I'll never have the chance to see them, ever," I lamented. How bad would it have been at the Forum? Another bad move on my part. Another missed opportunity. I've learned over the years, having been given the opportunity to attend dozens and dozens of rock shows, that you have to get yourself there, no matter how depressed or lazy you feel or how big the zit on your forehead is. If the rock show feels momentous, whether it's the final LCD Soundsystem show or a Yaz reunion, rally, because you will regret it forever if you don't. Get to the shows!

With another massive talent lost to smack, another round of "this is really Marc's fault" was beamed in my direction by friends and business associates. Josh, Justin, and our friend Tracy Katsky, another ex-Bennington student, who was now starting to make some industry inroads, all worried that I was going to pull a copycat and off myself too. Tracy invited us over to the apartment she was sharing with comedian Sarah Silverman, and they all watched me for any signs of despondent, copycat behavior as we listened to one Nirvana song after another on KROQ. I was flattered by the attention but also a little insulted. Why on earth would I want to be an also-died, like Darby Crash, who killed himself hours before John Lennon's murder, almost perfectly ruining any chance that he'd become legendary beyond the Hollywood punk scene? That night, we all went to the movie *Threesome* starring Lara Flynn Boyle from *Twin Peaks*, Stephen Baldwin, and *Dead Poet's Society*'s Josh Charles to take our minds off of Kurt, and for two hours it worked. The film took place at a college and, like ours, seemed to deconstruct the social mores of young, highly sexualized, impressionable kids. It knew it didn't have much of a story, but it had its charm (mostly courtesy of Charles). We all went to the Formosa and discussed whether Lara Flynn Boyle would make a good Mary in *Terminal Gossip*, but the default conversation was always Kurt and dope and death and whether this tragedy would finally push me back into the Villa Carlotta. I was genuinely depressed and thought about it. I wanted to be good . . . but God, Kurt Cobain had put a gun in his mouth and pulled the trigger. What was the fucking point? I found Chris, went out, and copped. It was the white indie rock kid's version of dumping a 40 oz. into the earth in tribute, I guess.

I went out for drinks one night with Julie Bowen a few days before leaving LA for good. Kurt was dead. I was halfway there. She was starting to get real jobs. She was going to have a career. I was going to have a funeral. From a table in the revolving bar that sat atop the Holiday Inn, we looked out at the city—a purple sky, a few stars, a million twinkling lights—with easy-listening jazz on the stereo. This was only the dawn of the age of irony. They hadn't started playing Bad Religion and Dinosaur Jr. or Esquivel in places like this yet. But we liked it as a change of pace from some of the hipper bars in town: The Room, which didn't even have a front entrance, or the Dresden, which had become a scene, like the Formosa and El Compadre, the great Mexican place on Sunset with the live Mariachi band, or the old St. James Club, where John Wayne supposedly kept a horse on the roof, and even the Frolic Room.

"Why am I like this?" I asked her.

"Maybe you are a genius," she said. "But it doesn't matter. You still have to be a person. You have to act like a person like everybody else does. Or you're never going to be happy. You get no pass just because you know how to write."

She squeezed my hand hard; it hurt the bones. My arms were bruised with needle punctures. It was like she was trying to find the real flesh and bone under the yellowy, sweaty flesh and the pose.

"You can do it. You just chose not to."

"That's not true. I can't help myself. I was born like this. I just do what I do. How can you not do what you just do. I listen to the voices in my head."

"Yeah, don't tell anyone else that. You sound crazy."

I felt a tear welling into my eye. I tried to make myself cry. I thought about how I needed an asthma inhaler to breathe now. I thought about Petunia telling me in one of our sessions that nodding was like dying. When you are on the nod, sky high, your body is dying. Sometimes you come back; sometimes you just die. One night, Jack and I nodded out on the tar roof of some apartment down on St. Mark's Place. It was only Jack's craving for a Snickers bar that forced us to get up and shake a leg. In the morning, we learned that two or three junkies had overdosed and died on the same brand of dope we'd been soaring on. I thought about being dead. How lonely it must be. I thought of sad songs. "Hello It's Me," "So Far Away," "Two Out of Three Ain't Bad." I thought of my missing cat. But no real emotions came. I just didn't have them anymore.

"I am crazy," I said. "I'm not normal."

"That's the way you want it. You need a punch in the eye."

"My skin is so bad," was all I said in response. "It's too late to fix anything." There's something about junkies. Even when they clean up, there's a squirre-lyness that never really goes away. You can absolutely turn your life around, but cosmetically at least, you will never scour off the residue of your bad be-havior, no matter how many hours you sit under the sun.

"I'm going to get clean. I'm going to be a success. I'm going to make you proud of me."

"I really hope so. I don't want you to die."

"Do you love me?"

"Well . . . I don't want you to die."

Ironically, I left Los Angeles more or less for good just as we finally started making money. If I'd been a little less proud and gutted it out, I'm sure Justin and I would have had a career there. We'd been introduced, through Tracy Katsky, to the producer Al Burton, an industry veteran who'd had a hand in everything from *The Facts of Life* to *Charles in Charge*. He'd hired us to write a treatment for the pilot of a Telemundo-style knockoff of *Beverly Hills 90210* called *Suenos de Fama* (*Dreams of Fame*). The story took place at a Sea World–like water park and featured an orca that wasn't the famous Shamu. It felt sketchy, and not just because it's kind of cruel to keep a giant wild animal in a fucking swimming pool. Even the whale was B-list, but it was actual work after months and months of theoretical employment.

"These are the kind of jobs you do before you make it," Justin told me.

"Fine, let's take it."

I felt vomit in my throat each time we sat at the desk in the sun-filled living room. I'd get up from the computer and blast the new Green Day album *Dookie* at top volume. Brat music. At the time, the trio was being ostracized for signing with a major label and "selling out." These righteous punks had no idea what real selling out was. Mr. Burton, a perfectly trustworthy and affable old gent, had only one request for the treatment as far as input went.

"I think you need to get an otter in there somewhere," he told us over coffee in his office.

"A what?"

"People love otters. You know, they swim on their backs, holding, what do they hold?"

"Shells?" Justin offered helpfully. "They crack them open. Eat what's inside. Whatever's inside."

We wrote the script and almost perversely omitted the otter. You will not find one in our treatment, and that act of sedition might be the only reason I can still look at myself in the mirror. To Justin's credit, he didn't push it. He knew it was ridiculous too.

Burton never mentioned it again. He paid us, pro that he was, on time and in full. When I cashed the check at the check-cashing place on La Cienega, I took all the money and bought myself a rare steak at Musso and Franks, the famous grill in Hollywood, then stopped into a travel agency in a mini-mall off LaBrea.

Chrissie's roommate, Patricia Ann, had moved to the city for the summer and indicated that I could stay with her again in her basement apartment just up the block from café Sin-é, where Jeff Buckley was discovered. She was keeping a Dr. Who pinball machine in storage for the bar up the street, so we had free pinball but no air conditioning. I never got that. Patricia Ann had more money than even Al Burton.

Her new apartment was about two minutes from my cop spot on Seventh. It would be really easy to spend the rest of my life there. Convince her to take a trip to the appliance outlet on Union Square, cool us off . . . cool us out. The dealers would be out. I could be going to cop within the hour, I thought, as the plane descended. They were always out, despite the weather. Sometimes, when it was hot, they'd just say, "Keep walking, keep walking." Most times, you'd give your order like a motorist at a drive-thru. And they'd give you a foil twist of blow and three glassine bags of smack. Then you'd keep walking, same direction, rather than conspicuously doubling back. It was better to make a full four-corner square, then slip into the bodega on the far corner of Eighth Street and Avenue B. By the time I was in there, pulling a root beer from the cold storage, I knew I was safe. Then it was off to find a dark bar. There was a new bar on Avenue A called Babyland. There were stuffed animals and toys along the walls; otherwise it was a normal East Village dive with a pierced bartender and Royal Trux's *Skulls*, Yo La Tengo's *Painful*, or Cibo Matto's *Viva La Woman!* piped in over the white noise of chattering coked-up or strung out kids. The spot sold both kinds of dope, and the orders would consist of one number, one letter: "two d, three c." But whenever I went for Patricia Ann, I reversed the order, doubling my smack and shorting her on the coke, and blamed the dealer's hearing for the confusion—a failure to communicate. An honest mistake. She'd make due with her single foil of shitty Manhattan gasoline coke, and I'd stash my four bags of smack to last the full week. I was planning on doing the same thing, over and over again, as soon as I could. I had no money for a cab, but you could take the train all the way from the airport to the Lower East Side if you were patient enough.

I never thought I'd be taking the train out to Long Island instead. But something happened to me on the airplane, and I couldn't shake it. I'd met a girl who reminded me that Long Island was no bad place to be sometimes. It produced some good. It produced Adrienne Shelly.

During the last few months I'd started volleying back and forth from the city on a new airline called Jet Blue that had a no-frills shuttle between LAX and JFK—dangerous for someone like me. For $100 I could fly to New York with the same level of commitment as bussing it to Venice. On this flight, I noticed a pretty, pale, blonde girl while boarding, and mid-flight I realized who she was: Adrienne Shelly, the actress. She had one of those faces that popped on screen—the indie Bardot—but in person she didn't assemble in the same way. I didn't recognize her immediately. She looked plainer, with a rounded bulb of flesh at the end of her elegant nose and no makeup to cover her blemishes and lift those cheekbones. I'd had a crush on her since my early days at Bennington. This was largely because of *Trust*, the Hal Hartley romantic comedy she stared in opposite Martin Donovan. Hartley was a hero because he had found a way to make the Long Island wasteland seem romantic . . . a perfect dead-end fit for the coming mutually assured nuclear holocaust. It made his angst seem pure and relatable. The bombs would be falling any minute, so why not be on the Island. It was a terrible place to live but as good a place as any to die. Hartley's characters were no Bruce Springsteen heroes, struggling to get out. They were passive; they'd surrendered, but they were oddly sexy at the same time. Adrienne was clearly his muse for such stories. Her real name was Adrienne Levine. I never knew why or how she came to pick Shelly, the doomed, drowned romantic poet, as a stage name. Maybe it was a family name. Maybe someone else in the Screen Actor's Guild was called Adrienne Levine, and it was merely a practical choice. She'd also appeared on the cover of the April 1993 issue of *Spin*. She was tongue-kissing Evan Dando.

"'S' Is for Sex in the 90s" ran the headline.

Once we landed, she noticed me staring at her while waiting for the bags, so I did something I never do and acknowledged that I knew who she was. After all, how standoffish could she be? She was flying a bargain airline.

"So are you really from Long Island?" I asked her.

"I am."

"Me too."

"What in the world are we doing in Los Angeles?" she laughed. "It's so weird out there."

"I know! Do you live there?"

"No, I'm working."

"How do you think I feel? I live there."

Instantly, I felt like I could talk to her, and that's not often the case with people, much less famous ones.

I asked her if she wanted to share a taxi into the city, and I guess the nice, Long Island Jewish boy wasn't as buried as I'd expected since she extended me some trust. On the long slog in, we talked about Jet Blue ("It's the best flight I've ever taken across country. TV. Blue potato chips!" she enthused). We talked about the difference between New York and Los Angeles ("I know it's a cliché, but Woody Allen is just right.") The fact that I was in a cab with her should have been enough, but I put a fine point on my own career anyway. "I'm with UTA," I said, as I'd said four hundred times before, only this time it felt fake and stupid. "United Talent Agency?" I did not need to elaborate.

"That sounds like you're dating them," she said. She was already a big enough star to not care about "the business," whereas it still secretly (and sometimes blatantly) impressed me. I told her I'd written a screenplay and was working on another one but really wanted to write a good novel. She said she was working on a screenplay as well. I wanted to ask, Why? You're a successful actress. An indie icon even. Writing seemed so lonely and arduous. If you're on a fast-moving train, why hop onto the creeping, crawling donkey I'd mounted? She was polite, but I could tell that she sensed I was scared, in pain, and sick. She was maternal from the start.

"Do you want me to roll down my window?"

Mine was already down.

"It's okay. I sometimes get carsick." And dope sick. I was one step away from another rehab, and this one wouldn't be a cushy Petunia catalog shop, two steps from the cops and three steps from the Leonard Cohen afterworld. I was not the kind of guy you give your telephone number to, but she saw something good in me, I guess. She could still make out the Island in there. We exchanged phone numbers and planned to stay in touch. The sharing of her private digits seemed like a vote of confidence if not a life preserver. I needed someone to trust me.

"Are you okay for money?" she asked me as she got out of the cab.

"I don't know," I said, no longer strong enough to keep up my "we're getting a package deal" bluster.

"Here," she said and handed me the cash in her wallet. It was about sixty bucks, enough for a half bundle of dope, some chocolate and a pack of cigarettes or a decent meal, and a ticket out to the Island.

"Seriously?" I asked, holding the crumpled bills.

She smiled.

"I will pay you back," I promised.

"I know you will," she said.

The cab pulled away. I wanted to see her again as quickly as possible, if only to be reminded that I was still human.

"Where to?" the cab driver asked me. It took me a few minutes to respond.

"Where to?" he asked again, a little impatient. I could hear horns honking around us.

"Penn Station," I said. I was tired of smashing my head on the punk rock. I wanted to go home.

CHAPTER 9

slept for two full days after showing up on the doorstep in Lawrence. I would wake up in fits during this period and not know where I was; when I did recognize where I was, I didn't recall how old I was. If I was home in bed, I must still be in high school? At one point during this prolonged hibernation, my mother woke me up and let me know there was a phone call for me.

"It's Chris," she said. Chris? Did my mother know Chris? Was I still dreaming? Did I leave Chris my family phone number? I must have.

"Hello?" I ran my tongue around the back of my mouth, trying to lubricate it so I could speak. My lips felt like they were flaking away. Chris sounded chipper and up for some bad fun.

"Come over. We're going to pick up."

"Dude, I can't." I didn't tell him I was in my childhood bed on Long Island, and somehow Chris hadn't gathered that the 516 area code was not local.

"You want me to get you some?"

"No."

"Going straight?"

"I think so." Chris did what we all did upon hearing this. He wished me the best of luck with absolutely no investment and went on his way. It was bad form to chastise a fellow junkie who wanted out. Bad karma too. Most of the time these attempts failed, and nobody wanted to be the messenger, resented by the returning partyer on his or her way back into the scene.

Finally, after forty-eight hours plus, I came downstairs and announced that I was hungry. It was true, and it felt good. My mother made me some egg salad with almost no mayo and served it on a bread end with a giant wedge of iceberg lettuce. It was a hostile sandwich.

"I've been on the phone with your aunt Susan," she said. Susan was a shrink. Her husband, Henry, my father's older brother, was a shrink. Like me, he'd declined to become a gambler like my father and his father, and he excelled, most likely because of it. My cousins, Jake and Becky (the latter would become a news anchor for the local station NY1), had grown up in Manhattan and were always subjects of envy. They were just middle-class Jewish kids like my sister and me, but to us they might as well have been Guggenheims.

It was suggested that I be shipped off somewhere. My mother knew what a rehab was by now. I refused. I wanted to stay on the Island, where I knew I was safe. I could escape from a rehab. There was no escaping Long Island. I knew that now. It would always bring me back. Why fight it? We found a local outpatient program.

At night, I slept in my little sister's bed and watched TV. Tupac Shakur was going to prison, and Quentin Tarrantino was headed for the Academy Awards. My sister was off at college, and my stepfather had converted my room into his private TV-viewing and paper-reading "alone-time" den. I didn't fight it. I was just glad I wasn't on my back on the cold clay floor in the Villa Carlotta. My mother took my leather pants and threw them in the garbage. I didn't fight that either. I had no fight in me. When they'd gang up on me at the dinner table, I just mumbled and sometimes buried my head in my hands.

"What happened to your car?"

"I lost it."

"You lost a car."

"I don't know. Yeah."

"In a poker game?"

"Arm-wrestling match."

"I can't drive you to every NA meeting," my stepfather warned.

"That's okay, I'll walk."

I found a meeting up Lawrence Avenue and just across the tracks at the community center in Inwood. And I shared there, smoking cigarettes with the fat, fucked-up Islanders who just wanted to stop being fucked-up. I didn't bristle at their accents.

"Hoy, my name is Paw-luh, and I'm a grateful alco-hawl-ic."

"Hoy, Paw-luh."

I joined in. I clapped. Did my "ninety in ninety" and ate the stale cookies and drank the stomach-rotting coffee piss, and soon I started to feel better. I was taking time off . . . for bad behavior.

While cleaning up, I listened to W-LIR again, the new wave station that I grew up with. It was called W-DRE now, and it played Nirvana and Pearl Jam instead of the Psychedelic Furs and B-52s, which was strange, but the DJs were the same. One day I was making a sandwich, my appetite fully returned, my frame regaining muscle, when I saw a special report. Someone had blown up a federal building in downtown Oklahoma and taken out nearly the entire block, it appeared. I turned the TV off, took my glasses off, and rubbed my eyes.

How am I going to get through the next fifty years in this sick, violent life without something to numb me? I wondered. I didn't have religion, which so many ex-junkie assholes re-embrace. Being an attention-sucking junkie asshole writer *was* my religion.

Ironically, Manhattan had never been safer. Once short on cops and barely safe for tourists, there was a new mayor, and he had launched an organized effort to reverse the perception of the city as a dysfunctional and declining blood letter with thousands of murders a year and tens of thousands of other felonies. Former U.S. attorney Rudolph William Louis Giuliani had run against the Democrat David Dinkins in 1989 and been defeated. Now he was the 112th mayor of New York City, the first Republican in twenty years to hold the position. Dinkins, a Democrat who'd risen over Ed Koch, the mayor for much of my lifetime and a media celebrity, had the backing of the African American community but seemed too classy to rise to the kitschy salesmanship of Koch or to roll up his sleeves and knuckle it out with the NYPD over budgetary concerns. The cops turned on him, whereas Rudy marshaled them like an army. Dinkins was framed as a kind of tennis-playing Nero who'd turned his back as citizens were being mugged at knifepoint and worse, and local business had dried up because tourists were afraid to visit. Rudy was hugely successful at claiming personal responsibility. City Hall would be his command center, but there was a feeling that Rudy and his crime fighters were somehow actually in the streets, like Teddy Roosevelt or Batman, attacking and eradicating the sickness and the violence by any means necessary.

It became fashionable among the Bohemians who remembered the bad old days of "crack blocks" to denounce him, and I am sure I joined in that chorus too once I started my tentative and sober trips back into the city, ostensibly to look for a real job (strongly encouraged by my counselor) and reconnect with Bennington friends. But I was secretly in the Rudy camp as far as what I was really feeling about New York at the time. I had no drugs to provide the illusion that I was surrounded by a force field and immune to street crime. I felt threatened by all things remotely seedy. I used to want a Nan Goldin afterworld. Now, I just wanted peace. I now needed the very cops I eluded while picking up more than I needed the Dart Man, a monster who shot homemade darts at random female pedestrians. If Rudy was Travis Bickles's prophesized "real rain" that would finally wash the city clean, in my fragile state, I was, at the time, grateful.

On days when I was too weak or bored to take the train back to the Island after looking for work, I would stay with my grandmother, who'd sold her house in Canarsie and maintained a small but elegant apartment by Lincoln Center. I had a key, and at night, after she'd fallen asleep, I'd let myself in and watch TV and try to jerk off to the yellow-skinned, orange-haired, aging porn star Robyn Byrd's show (her cheerful, vaguely Ragtime theme song was "Baby Let Me Bang Your Box," which she would dance to with all her naked, younger porn star guests at every climax). My grandmother had MTV, even if she didn't know what MTV was. It was a gift: the comfort and familiarity of *Liquid Television* or *120 Minutes*. She slept with a small pillow speaker tuned to the W-INS news for comfort and companionship, I guess. I worried about falling asleep with the TV on. I was paranoid about autosuggestion. In the morning there'd be breakfast—cereal and bad coffee from the can—and she'd hand me a $20 bill and say, "Don't spend it all in one place, please." I'd tell her about my plans to find a job, and she'd tell me about her day, which consisted usually of a trip to the grocery store by herself, dinner by herself, a few phone calls to friends who were also widows, some knitting, some TV, a few drinks, and then that pillow speaker with its transmission of local car crashes and overseas intrigue, death, and weather. She was grateful for the company and concerned about me. She'd heard about the drugs and had hid the booze in the cupboard, but I didn't want any.

When being a twenty-six-year-old kid chewing the fat with his sixty-six-year-old widowed grandmother got a little too depressing, I would head out to Brooklyn and crash with Ron. He had relocated to Manhattan after losing his job at the food co-op following the big Northridge quake. Ron was one of the most vocal of my friends who detested Rudy. He'd recently been busted in SoHo for pissing on a wall, and in the new New York, that was enough to get you dragged off to the Tombs with the squeegee men and the three-card monte guys and the people who sold bootleg VHS tapes and Yankees hats without permits. Or at least handed an expensive ticket.

"Giuliani! Step by step! Slowly I turn!" Ron would grumble.

"I think he's doing a good job," I'd say, just to bait him.

"Bumbaclat!"

"You know, you're not actually a Rasta."

"White-belly rat!"

"You're from Illinois."

"Fire burn ya!"

"Are you going to eat the rest of that ramen, yo? Yo, Ron. Are you gonna eat the rest of that ramen? Yo."

Neither of us had any money, but it wasn't as bad as Venice had been. It was easier to get by with less in Brooklyn somehow. And Ron was a wizard with ramen. He'd let the foul, powdered-chemical broth simmer for an hour in a dented saucepan as he added eggs, garlic, chili powder, green onions and, finally, the dried, tangled noodles from the packet. He would turn something broken-down and cheap into something remarkable and exotic, and this was exactly what we were trying to do with ourselves and our writing. I didn't feel worldly or progressive crashing with Ron because he was African American. I felt so because of the way he carried himself—how he cooked and dressed, talked to girls, and approached literature and Brooklyn itself. I was fourth-generation Brooklyn, my great-grandparents had lived on President Street, but the borough seemed to belong to Midwestern Ron, and I wondered how'd he managed that. I knew it wasn't just the color of his skin. He was regal, down to the soup, and I studied and copied this as much as I could because I wanted to be regal too—in a constructive and newly positive way. I tried to live in Brooklyn, but it had spit me out, sensing deep down that I took it for granted. Now I was a prodigal son, crawling back with a promise to show it some respect.

Ron took pity on me and gave me a key, and my mother and stepfather agreed to let me stay in the city on my own, just as they had when I was twelve and pacing like a caged lion.

"If he screws up, he screws up," my stepfather said. "He's a big boy."

They let me keep my key to the house on the Island in case I needed a safe place, and for the first time, I didn't take that for granted. It felt good having that key in my wallet. It wasn't a year's chip, but I was determined to stay clean and be humble.

Our apartment was at 261 Flatbush Avenue, just south of the Brooklyn Academy of Music. This was then the low-rent side of the Slope, just at the triangle where Flatbush Avenue turns into Seventh and leads to rows of brownstones and cozy boutiques and cafés. There were fancy food places up on Seventh that wouldn't even deliver to us. But the neighborhood was perfect Brooklyn boho and part of the long tradition of African American Brooklyn bohemianism, from Chester Himes and Cecil Taylor to Spike Lee, Nelson George, and Chris Rock, which is why Ron set his bags down there in the first place. You just had to open the window, and a wave of superloud Reggae, hip-hop, or Soca music would pour in. The stores almost never closed. You could hear music pouring out of the fucking hardware store at three in the morning. The air was filled with the smell of meat pies and cooking from the Halal Haifa bodega just downstairs, which doubled as a mosque. Every afternoon men in robes would face Mecca and kneel in prayer, and Ron and I knew, no matter how badly we needed cigarettes, when it was a bad time to shop.

On our side of the street, there was a video store called Royal Video that specialized in kung fu and porn; a surplus of gold exchanges, check-cashing places, and nail salons; the Chan Yang takeaway and a pair of pizza parlors, Gino's (decent) and Bergen (much better). There was an old-style counter grill and newsstand by the F train entrance, where local drunks and old ladies seemed to spend all day kibbitzing and buying lottery tickets. The movie theater had first-run movies so long as they were action films like *Batman Returns* and *Broken Arrow*.

Given my broke-ass means at the time, my contribution to the apartment was a torn and somewhat lurid Marc Bolan poster that I found rolled up in a cardboard box on Second Avenue by the Gem Spa newsstand and soda fountain. I also brought in a bunch of spell-casting candles from the local botanica a few blocks up. Having temporarily been a Los Angeleno, I developed a torrid love affair with all manner of fetishes, Voodoo, Santeria, and the like. This was hardly a shock since I used to drive to hospital gift shops up and down the Island collecting Christian kitsch. I was an agnostic myself, not an atheist, so I felt like it was a good bet to cover all the bases, spiritually speaking. I was drawn to Jesus because I was a teenage Goth, and even Dracula isn't as Goth as Christ. But it was more than that. I wanted to be the kind of person who could believe in something. I felt cheated. That part of me was, and is, closed. So, as I do, I overcompensated. I believed in nothing and everything. I collected ivory Buddhas, Hindu Ganesh figurines, and incandescent crucifixion holograms in which Jesus's eyes look heavenward, then down in agony. Walking into that particular botanica always made me feel like the "white-belly rat" Ron accused me of being, but I couldn't resist. I'd pretend like I knew exactly what malady or hex had been thrown at us and was shopping for a remedy, like it was dandruff shampoo.

"Hmm, yes, Run Devil Run—that'll do. You see, I'm being chased by a hellhound. How much?"

With Ron's okay, I smudged my sage and lit my Black Cat candles, but with his faux-Rasta status, we were both such spiritual carpetbaggers at the time that we probably did more harm than good. Our only real religion was writing anyway. We both still wanted to be famous and get invited to parties in libraries. But we wanted to be street too, like Jean-Michel Basquiat. (I sometimes called Ron "Ron-Michel," either affectionately or to take the piss, depending on the inflection.) Most nights, we ate what we could, got drunk on beer, twice-smoked cigarettes, and glared at each other.

As it had been when I was younger, my North Star was still the *Village Voice*. On Tuesdays the new issue made its citywide debut at the kiosk on Astor Place by the spinning black "Alamo" sculpture. This was the closest newsstand to the paper's offices off Cooper Union. There was a recession on. Unlucky David Dinkins's campaign had been a year or so shy of the coming

Internet boom, and job opportunities were fading while the population of the city was increasing. It felt crowded and if not like the Third World, then certainly like some depleted and congested Eastern Bloc nation.

People in need of jobs, apartments, or companions started lining up in front of the kiosk like Soviet mothers lining up for bread and toilet paper. Sometimes this line stretched all the way west to Broadway. It took a while to find a job. These were not yet boom times, not like what was about to come, with the Internet explosion. The search itself felt healthy, and I tried to keep a positive attitude. I'd taken to wearing glasses and made a point of shampooing my hair. My complexion had improved, pinked up from its yellow-gray junkie jaundice, which the low, intense California sun could never burn clean.

I mostly sat in the living room of Ron's flat watching coverage of the O. J. Simpson trial. The murder, the low-speed Bronco chase, that all happened while I was shuttling back and forth from LA to New York in the grey blur that comes from mixing black tar and China white. Now that I was sober again, with time to kill, like most of America, I became obsessed with the "trial of the century." It was a perfect distraction for people who had little else going on. I'd never seen news coverage like this before. It was the dawn of the twenty-four-hour cable cycle, the "feeding-the-beast" era, and I basically replaced the smack nod with a clean jack into this new kind of opium daze.

When I got the sense that Ron was growing impatient with my lack of success finding a job, I would leave and spend time with some women. My libido had returned; the death drive and morbid attachment to a single "savior" woman like Julie Bowen was replaced with a healthy sex drive. Sex restored me to the land of the living first, and rock and roll sealed the deal. I still loved it when I was out in Hollywood getting high. Music was good again in 1995 and 1996; there were still "event records": *Wowee Zowee*, *Pinkerton*, *Odelay*, *No Protection*, *The Bends*, *Mellon Collie and the Infinite Sadness*, the first Foo Fighters CD. Even *Sparkle and Fade* by Everclear hit the right spot. I was a sucker for an ex-junkie lament, and leader Art Alexakis seemed to write them in his sleep. I became a dancer in the mid-nineties. When I was high, I never danced, except for that one slow, sweet dip with Julie in the Frolic Room. Have you ever seen a junkie dance? Junkies dance like wet sand dances.

By 1995 every Friday night, rain or shine, all the Bennington kids in the city and some who were still up at school would convene at Don Hill's, the low-ceilinged, bikerish bar west of SoHo on Spring Street, for Squeezebox, a rock-and-roll dance and drag party. Convinced that beer was safe because I didn't like the taste of it, I'd buy a 40 oz. at the bodega on Hudson Street, then sit on the loading docks by the river and pound them before getting in line. I'd often find some Bennington friends doing the same thing. Few of us could afford the high-priced cocktails inside. The line was usually long, and none of us had the juice to get guest-listed, so by the time we made it to the door, the liquor had kicked in, and we were ready to go. Squeezebox was a tonic after several years of junkie death tripping. It was life affirming, rock and roll affirming, and, most crucially, New York affirming. You always left in an up mood, and you never left alone. I'd always wear a T-shirt no matter what season it was because the bar heated up to convection oven temperatures from all the sweaty bodies pushing into each other on the dance floor. The DJ, Miss Guy, was a genius in that he mixed new songs like The Toadies' "Possum Kingdom" or Whale's "Hobo Humpin' Slobo Babe" into the retro glitter rock mix of "Ballroom Blitz" and "Rebel, Rebel" and its eighties compatriots like "Damned Dog," from the excellent *Times Square* soundtrack, and The Cult's "She Sells Sanctuary" or The Smiths' "How Soon Is Now," as if to say, "As long as it's good rock and roll, it's coming on." Most DJs to this day don't employ such a sound philosophy.

Squeezebox, more than anything else, gave me back the postsmack lust for life that Iggy Pop celebrated, and this soon sparked my creative energy. It was, after all, a link to the Warhol promised land that I had sought living at the Chelsea nearly a half decade earlier. Everyone there—straight, gay, bi—was calibrated to a great, sexy Max's Kansas City of the Mind. Even Don Hill, who owned the bar, cut a Warholian figure, with his pale skin, white hair, and taciturn expression. There were, early on, only faithful souls, no tourists, and that's what allowed the gays and the straights, the rich and the poor, the famous and the notorious and the unknowns to dance together and stand in the same interminable toilet line without polluting the joyful energy. Green Door, at Coney Island High on St. Mark's Place, was another great rock-and-roll party, but it lacked the theatricality, the showmanship, of Squeezebox, which was really more of a glitter review, featuring musical and comedy performances between Guy's DJ sets. Mistress Formika, a towering, snappish, and imperious queen, was the evening's host and chief comedienne. Lily of the Valley, the thin and chiseled David Bowie of Squeezebox, and Sherry Vine (whom I once asked out on a date in the throes of spiritual rapture, though I chickened out on the follow-up after he accepted) were among the informal cast of regulars. Squeezebox had its simpatico bands too, like Kembra Phaler and The Voluptuous Horror of Karen Black. Kembra usually sang naked and painted blue. Her guitarist was named Samoa and wore a great, platinum spiked hairdo. They'd play glittered up versions of Chicago's "Feelin' Stronger Every Day" and originals like "Going to Alaska," and like other Squeezebox bands, you could tell they were a little too New York cool and ragamuffin to make it in the pop world, but on the stage at Don's, they were huge stars. The Voluptuous Horror, Guy's own band, The Toilet Boys, and to an extent Lunachicks were the first wave to pay retro tribute to the Max's and CB's era, and the genuine affection drew real life figures from that scene, like Debbie Harry, Joey Ramone, and Jayne County, whose signature song "(If You Don't Wanna Fuck Me, Baby), Fuck Off" was always a show stopper. When you staggered outside after a night in Don's, the blast of air off the Hudson River felt like a new morning. It was how rock and roll should be: loud, trashy, sexy enough to make shy people feel comfortable dancing because they were so inspired.

Amra Brooks had the run of Squeezebox. She was friends with all the performers, and her father, Joseph Brooks, basically invented the formula for the rock-and-roll, new wave glamour party out in Los Angeles with his club Make Up. Amra was Bennington; a few years younger, she was one of the students who had to reckon with Zoe and her glory after Ron, Jack, Herve, and I left. She roomed with Theo from Lunachicks a few blocks from Ron, and I would walk down to meet her for some sensitive, sober fun. We'd lay in her bed and stare at the ceiling, sometimes kissing and tentatively fumbling like little kids as she played her moody indie rock: Smog, Cat Power, all the early Belle and Sebastian EPs. Amra had perfect taste: probably the best of anyone I've ever met. Her record collection was perfect. She would open a Raymond Carver book and point to the dedication he wrote to his second wife, and somehow it would sum up everything both of us were feeling in that moment. She was magical, with her girlish voice, big brown eyes, and retro puff of thick, dark hair. Every man, and probably every woman, who met her fell in love with her, and I was no different. Sometimes she'd make tea in the kitchen, and we'd watch a movie like Terrence Malick's *Days of Heaven*. Amra was obsessed with Linda Manz and did a solid impression of her odd tomboy diction in the film's voice-overs: "I been thinkin' what to do with my few-chuh. I could be a mud doct-uh. Checkin' out da earth." Amra would sometimes let on that she was smitten with other men, and it broke my heart but only in increments. There were times I could simply shrug it off because I never asked her to be any kind of savior. That would have been too crass for someone like Amra. And the "dinner and a movie" girlfriend thing would have been too provincial. Even sex seemed somehow not quite twee enough for our oddly gentle bond; although alcohol (for me, not her) was permitted, and every time we attempted the former, I was inevitably too drunk. Still, her aesthetic, her sadness, and that impeccable cultural taste restored my sense of romance when it came to being saved by movies and music and books and I don't think that can be undervalued as far as keeping me out of the gutter went. If you lose that twee thing forever, as with your sense of humor, most of your soul died, and there, in her Brooklyn bedroom, listening to *Lazy Line Painter Jane* under the covers, I slowly began to get some of my soul back. It didn't matter if she was more in love with Moby (one of the suspected other men) or anybody else. I should say, though, that in the next decade and a half, I would fall in love with about three different girls who were either going out with or crushed out on Moby. And I would interview or hang out with Moby a dozen times and never mention this. It may, however, be why I've never gotten married. I'm afraid no matter how solid our union, my wife, whoever she is and however happy we may be, will eventually leave me for Moby.

Alexandra was another Bennington girl I'd met at one of those rare nights when the entire graduating class was not at Don Hill's, dancing and drinking. She was beautiful, with pale skin and fine, blonde hair, but nearly all Bennington girls were beautiful, so after a point, it stopped becoming a selling point as far as chasing them went. Like the Bennington boys, many of them were artists or art damaged and consequently had some kind of ungainly quality as well, which could be intriguing. Alex had none of that. She may have been eccentric, but it didn't show. She was French but had a British accent, which I found appealing at a time, when I was feeling especially "Wrong Island," and tacky. But if you're thinking Deneuve-ian ice, that's not quite it either. She had a lot of warmth, like she happened to have this Euro thing going on but was, in another life, a Jewish gal from Brooklyn. And although I never had an actual book collection until I was already in my mid-thirties, what for selling them and moving around, it was usually the first thing I checked out whenever I entered the home of someone I'd decided to maybe fall in love with, especially someone younger. Books, records, videotapes. If there was one Seal CD, I might stay the night, but I'd never come back. Hers was not just tight; it was not immediately explicable. I couldn't contextualize a Herb Ritts coffee table book and a copy of *Brighton Rock* with one jaded eye roll. What was that about? I should probably mention that I needed a place to live, and Alex had one in the basement apartment of a townhouse off President Street so soon I was sleeping over. Who knows what she must have thought of me. Like Amra, Alex had known about my Bennington reputation as a writer, but I wasn't a writer anymore, and what did a "Bennington reputation" even get you in New York City? Certainly no donuts or tokens. I was just a scared, ex- and probably future junkie, trying to bank some credit in the straight world. Was that in itself something sweet and heartening to witness, like taking in a stray?

One day, while bored finding work, I called Adrienne Shelly and met her a few hours later in front of her building at the west end of Bleecker Street by

Abingdon Square. She didn't recognize me. I had color in my cheeks, some flesh on my bones. Adrienne was too polite to say anything and sort of patted me on the back with her eyes.

"How are you?"

"Good. Good," I said, trying to play it down and act like I'd always been in such shape.

"Are you hungry?"

"Yes! And not for dope! Crazy, right?" I wanted to say. "Food! It's good."

"There's a new pizza place that just opened up around the corner. I figured we could try it."

"Cool."

Like me, being from Long Island, Adrienne had a discerning pizza palate. The place, called Two Boots, served what I figured was "Giuliani Time" pizza: newfangled, confident, and upscale, offering a gourmet pie with a thin, gritty crust and weird toppings, like tasso, instead of the classic pepperoni.

"What's tasso?" I asked as I stared at the menu. Each pie was devoted to a celebrity, like sandwiches in an old-style Jewish deli.

"Tasso is the future," she said.

Pepperoni had, like Mr. Dinkins, some would say, failed us. I admired Adrienne not only because she was already a famous actress, a success at her chosen art (filmmaking, as she also wanted to write and direct), but because she balanced being a clean-cut Long Island soul with being a real New Yorker in a much more graceful way than I ever had. It wasn't so binary with her, so fashion damaged and ideological. It was more like she kept the Island in a locket, and it remained light, a sliver of photographic paper, locked in a gold heart.

Adrienne was working at the time on a screenplay for a film she was calling *Sudden Manhattan*.

"What do you think of the title?"

I thought it was terrible. *Sudden Manhattan*? There's *Sudden Impact*, and then there's *Manhattan*. You don't want to mix the two. But I didn't tell her that. I said maybe something better would hit her.

It all takes place in her neighborhood in the West Village. She plays a quirky girl, not unlike the character she invented in her work with Hal Hartley, kind of the template for all quirky indie girls to come, from Zooey Deschanel to Greta Gerwig. And by "quirky," I mean she orders a plate of eggs in a local diner and complains that they're "making noise." I know this because I later rented the film. She was protective of the script, or maybe self-conscious, and did not let me read it. I never showed her what I was working on. We just sort of trusted each other—two Long Island kids feeling really lucky that they made it to the city. I could tell by the way she guided me through her far West Village neighborhood that she was proud of it. The West Village wasn't like the East Village. People didn't seem to place a premium on suffering—for art or anything else. Art was hard enough on its own. When she wasn't writing or acting, Adrienne wanted to enjoy life. I learned the concept of compartmentalization from her. I didn't have the complexity required to practice it, but it was up there now, an aspiration and a challenge.

"Have you been to Magnolia Bakery yet?" she asked.

"What's that?"

"Oh, it's so good. Let's go. I am going to buy you a vanilla pudding with bananas."

"Why?"

"Because you need to do something good for yourself every once in a while," Adrienne told me. "It's important."

I hadn't really equated drug abuse with hurting myself. I had wanted and pursued that wretched state of being. It was like shopping for a persona. I'd saved up enough cool currency to purchase it, and I wore it well, until it started wearing me like a punk or a hippie's clothes. The man has to make the clothes, and not vice versa, after all. I thought I was being good to myself, sticking needles in my arm, because for a time that was what I wanted to do and be: a junkie. And because I didn't work a real job and people seemed to indulge my behavior, I believed that I had it made, no matter how sick I felt.

"Good to myself?" She was blowing my mind over pudding.

"Smell," she said as we entered the little corner shop on West Eleventh. The bakery smelled sickly sweet but very clean. There were sacks of flour piled up by the window, which was lightly dusted with it: a different kind of white powder. The cashier was pretty and didn't look like the baker I'd imagined, an old Jewish or Italian woman with a dowager's hump and a chin mole.

"Get it with the Nilla Wafers," she said, and I obeyed. We took our pudding and walked across the street to sit in the shady park.

"Every time you feel like it's getting too much, I want you to go in there and get a banana pudding."

"Okay."

"Promise?"

"Yes."

"That's your big sister giving you an order. Be good to yourself!"

Adrienne frequently said she felt like my big sister. She wasn't that much older than me, maybe a year or two. It used to make me self-conscious, and I wondered why she said it. Maybe she wanted to draw a clear line, so I wouldn't come on to her when I was drunk. She wanted to make sure I knew this was a friendship only, but as far as friendships went, it was special. I never hit on her anyway. She was so small and delicate, I wouldn't have known what to do. She was the one female in my life whom I left alone in that way. Otherwise, I pretty much wanted to fuck every woman I'd ever met, even if there was nowhere to actually fuck them, except perhaps on the docks or in the lobbies of riverside apartments like the tranny hookers. When I went on a date with the actress Annie Parisse, a friend of Jack's and a future star in some of my earliest plays, I had to take her back to my grandmother's. We ended up making out on the roof since it seemed perverse to invite her to stay on the pullout while the W-INS news played in the other room on the little companion speaker. Jack had recently enrolled in the theater school at Fordham after leaving Bennington, and I would sometimes go see him in productions they did of Beckett or Durang plays. Annie, tall with dark eyes and curly hair, was the star in each of them. Everyone knew she was going to be on Broadway some day, and now she is.

I brought Jack and Alex with me to Adrienne's birthday party in a loft in Tribeca, but it soon became clear that my Bennington friends didn't really mix with her indie film gang. As a sort of party favor, Adrienne had hired a fortune-teller to read people's palms. Palmistry was a theme in *Sudden Manhattan*. Louise Lasser, who was married to Woody Allen and starred in some of his early films, like *Bananas* (and played the titular Mary Hartman on television), plays a soothsayer. "Do I have a good long life?" Adrienne asks. Lasser warns Adrienne's character that "horrible torture and then death" await. She advises her to "move to another city." Why the actual fortune-teller didn't warn Adrienne herself of the same thing during the party, I don't know, but I'll never trust those fucking people. They're all over my neighborhood now, and they wave you in with their Crypt Keeper fingers if you happen to make eye contact as you pass by with your groceries. I always want to flip the bird right back, but I'm afraid they'll throw a hex on me (not that any hex has worked yet). Jack and I were too chicken to get our fortunes told and sat in the corner trading barbs with one of Adrienne's friends, a straight-haired actress named Galaxy Craze. Alex, a brave girl, got her palms read. The teller told her that she saw a pregnancy in the future.

"But I don't see a baby."

Fun party.

Eventually, I got a job at Shakespeare & Co. Booksellers on Lower Broadway, right next to the warehouse that used to be Unique, where I bought my new wave T-shirts and sunglasses in the mid-eighties as my bored, slightly disturbed father wished he was anywhere else in the world. The staff were well-read and well-behaved; there wasn't a real rebel among them. Any one of them would chase an escaping shoplifter across Broadway, then deep into Washington Square Park. I never understood that. What if the panicking thief turned and realized you were just a weedy or out-of-shape retail employee making $5.25 per hour and charged back? What if he had a flip knife? Or sharp teeth? Would you shed blood for the store's owners? Not me, baby. I wouldn't even step up to Push-Up Man, the eccentric homeless person who'd frequently wander in, clap his hands, drop, and start doing push-ups on the floor as the startled customers gave him his berth.

The staff rules were pretty strict too. Despite the indie conceits, this was no free-form collective of beatniks. There were floor managers and underlings, just like in any corp. Most of the grunt staff were struggling actors, writers like me, or students from NYU or the New School or the School of Visual Arts. None of us had made it. If we had or were going to, what were we doing there? Making an honest buck, sure, but every employee who didn't seem too like a reject stood out and made you pull the old Billy Joel question, "Man, what are *you* doing here?" Owen, another manager, was one of a trio who didn't seem to be covered in loser dust. He was trim and bespectacled. There was talk that he was wealthy and worked at the store just to stay busy. He certainly had a permanent smirk, the kind of expression that says, "It's cool. I don't need this." Then there was Christina Kirk, a willowy blonde who, like Julie Bowen before her, made my life worth living for a few moments at a time. I fell in love with her immediately and thought of her in the morning when I didn't want to go in. "At least I get to see Christina." If this woman was working in this hell pit, then how bad could it possibly be. Christina was another struggling actress. Years later she would make a name for herself on the New York stage, as would I, but at the time, we punched in and sold books; I killed the time by begging her to get a drink with me, and she killed the time by rolling her eyes and rejecting my boredom-fueled, lustful entreaties. Finally, there was Ron Richardson, who quickly moved up (or down) from sales to management. Ron R. became a book buyer for the store. He was attending the New School and lived nearby in the dorms. Alone by a computer at a desk next to the owners, he was free to listen to whatever music he wanted and provided the store with its inventory: he decided what new titles seemed "Shakespeare" and how many should we order. Upstairs, we were only allowed to listen to jazz or classical on the store's sound system, so the music coming out of Ron's tiny speakers made me float on a Bugs Bunny ether cloud toward his work space, and his good nature kept me close by. We'd chat, and Ron would always refer the conversation back to something called "the Internet."

What the fuck was the Internet? It sounded like science fiction, some-thing out of *Blade Runner*. The Internet? Surely that couldn't be anything good. I still typed on an electric Smith Corona. The blue-screened word processor that I wrote my first novel on was Zoe's. The IBM computer we wrote *Terminal Gossip* on was Justin's.

He'd show me the website for *Paper* magazine, where he was filing book reviews.

"You mean that's *Paper*?"

"It's *Paper*'s website."

"Website?"

"This is the Web."

"Web. Is that like the Internet?"

"The Internet is the Web. The World Wide Web."

"The Internet and the Web are the same thing?"

Explaining the Internet to me in 1995 was like waiting for a duck to roll a blunt with his slick, webbed feet. Ron was patient to a point. Sometimes after work, we'd go grab a pint and shoot some pool at Mona's bar, past the crusty punks along Avenue A. Rudy had yet to start rounding these kids up too. They would sneer at us, with their gray skin and tattoos and studded, painted leather jackets. I hated them. I preferred the squeegee men. I was working eight hours a day selling books. I'd have loved to just panhandle on Avenue A for beer money and conduct myself with an even shittier attitude than the one I already had, but I was sober now. I wanted things. My ambition was back. And I was too smart to be that free.

The worst duty, the mutually agreed-upon short straw, was overstock. I spent entire days atop a ladder, rearranging hundreds of mass-market paper-backs. If you're of a certain predisposition, being surrounded by books can give you a physical sensation of pleasure. Running your hand across all those spines and thinking, I could swim in these pages, is a dreamy act. But over-stock was just fucked. Like the taking of the U.S. census, overstock and in-ventory were abstract projects in a retail universe. They never really had a beginning, middle, or end, but when it was my shift, I was expected to play along and wave my hands around a little bit and pretend to count and record the inventory. The second-worst task was bag check. I would have to sit right by the door like one of those sleepy-eyed French bulldogs in the pet shop windows of the West Village, the ones that whimper, "Please take me home. I hate it here." The main phone was at bag check as well, which meant I would have to answer it every two minutes, then transfer the calls, plus check peo-ple's bags as they entered. There's a presumption of guilt in retail. A manager catching someone on the floor with a bag would assume that person was a shoplifter, and I would catch hell for letting him or her by, distracted by a parade of Hare Krishnas moving down Broadway or locked in conversation with a visiting old Bennington friend, like Chrissie, who'd gotten a job working at *Vogue*.

"How cool it must be to work for a magazine. God, that would be like . . . the dream."

Customers would also come in and ask me if we had a book in stock, like I had the whole inventory memorized. It would be flattering, their assumption that I had such tremendous brain power and recall, if they didn't also treat me like a moron. And why would I be collecting bags if I wasn't one? I'd have to direct them to the big computer at the back where we kept the art books and other items that were frequently jacked. Sometimes I manned the big computer myself when ordered to spend some of my shift at the "information," or customer service, post, and I'd punch in the title or author or ISBN number and wait thirty full seconds for the slow-as-dick software to cough up a title. Oh, to have an ISBN number of my own. At lunchtime I'd go to Au Bon Pain and get the soup of the day and a piece of bread, just like all the other retail kids. I'd drink strong coffee with a lot of cream and sugar and sit alone and read the paper. Broke, with ten minutes of freedom before I had to return to the store, I'd have a smoke and walk around Lower Broadway listening to *I Should Coco* by Supergrass on my headphones. British pop was everything then, and fortunately most of it was inspired. Alex and I listened to it almost exclusively at night and on days when I wasn't working: our romance was scored to Radiohead, Oasis, Blur, Elastica (whom Jack and I saw play Tramps), Pulp, and even Shampoo!

The big book of that season was *The Celestine Prophecy*, a New Age tome that every other customer seemed to come in looking for. We literally could not keep it in stock, even though the customers had no idea exactly how to ask for it. "The Cellophane Prophecy." "The Cellphone Prophecy." I could spot them when they came in, and sure enough that's what they'd ask for. "The Cel-Ray Prophecy." But the only prophecy that still held any water was the aforementioned Travis Bickle prophecy: "Some day a real rain will come and wash the scum off the streets." The city, cleaner than ever and gentrifying with shocking rapidity, was no longer a place for low-renters or fuckups or even barflies. Club kids were bedazzling themselves and acting like they were trust-funders. Crusty punks were now rocking expensive piercing and elaborate tattoo jobs. One couldn't truly slum here, or squat, or troll or cop without feeling conspicuous and a little ashamed. A young man had to have a new hustle and a good, charming racket. I needed to find a new, post-smack, Giuliani-compatible energy from somewhere because I wanted to survive in this Manhattan. Smack makes you tired. It's demanding and exhausting. It takes over your ambition, but it doesn't kill it. Not if you're young. It merely puts it to sleep. Clean up a little, and that hunger, impatience, and frustration can come back in a forceful wave. It's like when you oversleep and then scramble when you realize you're late. You shower quickly, shave hastily, and throw on whatever clean clothes you have to beat back the clock. That's how I felt on Giuliani Time.

I'd taken to going back to the Island on the train a lot more than I used to, without feeling threatened. As drab as it was, it was no worse than a shift at Shakespeare. Some of the edge had been taken off me, and I finally allowed myself to enjoy a little bit of the comfort that big house in the Five Towns offered. After so many Au Bon Pain soup-and-bread combos, a meal cooked by your actual mother tastes really good.

"Does anyone ever come in and sign their books?" my mother asked, searching for safe topics of conversation.

"Sometimes," I said as I dug into my chicken and rice. "The smart writers do, since we can't send them back when they don't sell."

"Wow, you're really learning how things work. That's great."

Yeah, great. Exactly what I wanted to learn. How things work.

"You know, your Grandpa Sam's brother's son is a famous writer."

"Sorry?"

"I think he's famous. Yeah, Gordon Lish." She immediate backpedaled. "Not *that* big."

"Gordon Lish?"

She got up to rinse off her plate and looked like she'd like to jump on a hitched-up horse and disappear in a cloud of high-plains dust.

"Is he published?"

"I think so."

"Gordon Lish?"

"I don't know."

In her fervor to keep the conversation "normal," she'd revealed something strange. I pushed the plate away.

"You don't know?"

"We don't talk about him."

"Why?"

"He's not a nice man."

"He's published."

"I think so."

"Yes?"

"Yes," she said. She looked out the window, wondering if a car might roll up and whisk her far away from the kitchen table and her delicious chicken and her still extremely hungry, young but aging, unpublished only son.

I'd obviously known my mother for over twenty-six years, but in that moment, as she laid out some salmon croquettes and spaghetti for us, it seemed like she didn't know her brown-eyed boy at all. For ten of those twenty-six years, I'd wanted to be a writer. Four of them, I spent studying writing and literature at the college level. My mother had recommended books to me. I'd read her poetry. She'd read mine. And not once had she ever mentioned—not once!—that there was another writer in the family, and he was not merely a very famous writer, he was a figure. A literary . . . fucking . . . figure.

"Have you ever heard of Gordon Lish?"

"No. Why don't I know him?"

"Well, he's not *famous* famous, like Stephen King or . . ."

"No, I mean why don't I *know* him? Where is he? Is he still alive?"

"I'm sure. I would have heard if he'd died."

"Would you?"

"From Aunt Iris, I'm sure."

"So this is a . . . thing. He's something."

"Apparently."

"In New York?"

"I think so."

"Mom? Why. I mean . . . why?"

"We're not close with that side."

"But we're blood. That's close. Blood is close."

Sam was actually my great-grandfather. He was a haberdasher who lost all of his money in the early sixties after people stopped wearing hats and started dressing in a more casual and sporty fashion following the election of John F. Kennedy. With his livelihood gone, Sam became a secret morphine addict, like Bela Lugosi, and, who knows, perhaps the source of my genetic predisposition for opiate abuse (although there was absolutely nothing closeted about my own fervor for the poppy). I didn't get too angry with my mother right there over the croquettes, because I was secretly ashamed that I didn't already know this, that I hadn't even sensed it somehow. I just assumed the Spitzes on one side produced gamblers, bail jumpers, and sneak thieves, and the Lish clan on the other produced parasites. Both sides produced addicts. There were no mavericks in either gene pool and certainly no artists. And when my mother and I were recommending books to each other, I liked to think I was the expert: my titles were from the canon or the avant-garde, while hers were worthy but mainstream fare. I didn't sleep over that night. I was too vexed. As I waited for the train at Lawrence Station, I tried to remember any family gathering where I might have met Gordon Lish: dozens of weddings, funerals, bar and bat mitzvahs, anniversaries. Had anyone mentioned him at school? At work? The next morning, after traveling in to Manhattan on the train, I scrambled into Shakespeare, quickly headed to "information," and looked for his name in the computer. We had nothing in stock.

"Do you know of a writer named Gordon Lish?" I asked Ivana, the on-duty manager. I was secretly hoping she would, since I wanted to be related to a famous writer; I needed to know that such a person was capable of coming from my family and from Hewlett, New York, where, according to my mother, he grew up. It would explain, perhaps, just why I had been so passionate about pursuing this myself.

"Go check the computer," she suggested. I didn't tell her I'd just done that. She wouldn't give a shit about my family history or what it might have meant to my artistic nature. I was just another five-twenty-fiver on the clock. I was afraid to ask the manager, Owen, because if Gordon Lish was indeed a big deal, admitting that I didn't know who he was would give Owen the upper hand (which he already had, having a manager position and a real apartment). But then, if Lish was indeed hot shit, I could impress Owen and everyone else at the store by announcing that I was his blood relation, that his talent had somehow passed through to me and I wasn't just another minimum wage case.

Beginning in college, I'd often fantasized about having a mentor. It must have been something to be Martin Amis and have Kingsley Amis right there in your life. My father and I just disappointed each other. The half day that I spent looking for information on Gordon Lish (back in the day when one could literally walk around for a few days without having a factual question or definition electronically answered) was really just another effort to find a father who made sense to me. What better father figure than a literary figure.

"How could you not tell me that I was related to Gordon Lish. By blood? You've known I wanted to be a writer for ten years!"

I was on a pay phone, placing a heated call to the Island during my lunch break. It really was amazing to me, especially when I was down and really disheartened, that nobody, not my mother or my grandmother, who'd paid for my education, had ever handed me one of his stories and said, "Here. It's possible. Look at him. You're related to this guy. Isn't that cool? Keep going!" If I was an aspiring trumpet player and my great-grandfather's brother's son happened to be Miles, would it not be a little strange not to be informed of this? If I had a seventy-five-mile-an-hour fastball and needed an extra ten miles on my speed, and you knew that my great uncle was Sandy Koufax, would you clam up?

Lish, I would finally discover, was in his early sixties then and was already a legend for his work as fiction editor of *Esquire*. He was a peer of Ken Kesey and a champion of Don DeLillo, Richard Ford, and T. C. Boyle, who was a wonderful writer, even if the one time I attended one of his readings, he was wearing an ear cuff. Most famously, and controversially, he'd been the editor and mentor of the short story writer Raymond Carver at Knopf. Years later, after Carver's career surged, many felt Lish had overstepped certain boundaries between writer and editor and restructured (and even rewrote) Carver's text, but there was no denying the greatness of the work, which I "borrowed" from the shelves at Shakespeare & Co. Lish wasn't just a famous writer or even a literary figure. The guy was a total guru. He presided over an annual writers workshop that was also controversial for its length (up to six hours with no break), secrecy, and his didactic lecturing (no questions, just listening). And yet, once you emerged from one of these summits, there were supposedly no more mysteries about writing. "Captain Fiction," as he was known, taught you how to really write, and from there . . . ? It was implicit that you would have a real career. You would be a real writer. You would get published. Gordon Lish could make you into something. I still carried around the "thanks but no thanks" letter from some *Esquire* editor. When I got clean and before I ended up at Shakespeare, I'd applied there. Whatever job they had handy would do: senior editor. Maybe at large? That way I would have time to ride the trains.

"Dear Mr. Spitz," the response came. "Thank you for your letter. I'm impressed with your credentials" (I'd listed *Suenos De Fama* among my "published works," otter or no otter). "I'm afraid I can't be very encouraging. *Esquire* has a small staff, and I just don't have a role for someone of your experience and interests." My interest was experience, and this seemed to be the brush with luck and authenticity that I'd been waiting for—the thing to unlock it all for me.

"We're not close with them," my mother reiterated, referring to Lish's side of the family. "He's actually your grandmother's cousin. I don't even know what that makes him."

"It makes him a famous writer," I shot back. "Mom, I'm clean. I work in this dump all day, every day. Can you please get his number? An address? Is there someone I can ask? I need to meet him." I felt like someone had just told me that I was adopted and Joni Mitchell was my real mother.

"We were never close with them."

"Mom, you have to stop repeating that! I want to get closer to them. Just get me a number. I'll do the rest."

"Okay, I'll make some calls." My mother knew that reaching out to relatives in Florida would invite a litany of complaints about sore muscles, the heat, the help, but it would be nothing compared the constant hectoring that I was prepared to give her if she didn't turn up at least an address. When the info was found and relayed to me, I froze. I didn't know what exactly to do with it. A letter, I suppose, would be appropriate. And it would have to be well written, persuasive, respectful. It would require a few drafts maybe. It wasn't something I could just dash off. I sat in Ozzie's café on Seventh Avenue in the Slope, sipped strong coffee, and sketched out what I would write to Mr. Lish, my blood relative. I read the finished letter to Alex, and she approved. I tried it out on Ron too.

"Right on," he said. "Not too pushy. It's good. Just take out the 'perhaps.'"

"Perhaps? I wrote 'perhaps'?"

"It's just a preference. I don't like 'perhaps.'"

"Yeah, 'perhaps' is bad."

"Don't sweat it."

"Perhaps" is what nervous people write in book reports when they haven't read the full book. "Perhaps there are elements of homoeroticism in Shakespeare's sonnets." I don't know. I ain't read 'em. I stripped the letter of everything but the gist:

I am a struggling New York writer.
I am the great-grandson of Sam Lish, the grandson of your cousin Reggie.
I would like to meet you and talk.
I don't know how I got here. Maybe you do.
Are you interested in me?
I am interested in you.

I decided not to enclose a sample of the first novel after re-reading the best bits I could isolate and realizing, after the hard look, that it just wasn't up to snuff. It hadn't been published for a valid reason: it wasn't good enough. I was already sketching out ideas for short stories that beat it bad. And *Terminal Gossip* blew it away for authenticity and confidence. Write what you know, and if you want to write something else, go out and learn about it, then . . . write what you know. I should have put it in a drawer, like Hemingway said. Rules. Writers' rules. I needed more of them. And I needed to listen this time . . . to someone who knew what he was talking about.

Lish responded a few days later with a letter and a phone number. He was curious as well. He didn't require the same validation that I did, but the absence of another writer in the larger family history, then the sudden appearance of an aspirant inspired him to grab a pen and find a stamp. I carried the letter around for more than a day, waiting until some voice between my ears indicated that it was the right time to place a call; I got spooky and superstitious about it. I didn't expect Lish to rescue me from Shakespeare & Co., but those long hours working at the bag check or going from aisle to aisle with a drab, gray feathered duster seemed less painful just knowing that I had his private telephone number.

I finally called him from work after bracing myself with a lunchtime shot at the old Jack Dempsey's bar a few blocks east. That bar had a wheel of shots. The tender spun it, and whatever it landed on you got for a dollar. Sometimes it was whiskey, sometimes a vile tropical-flavored schnapps. Dizzy from the latter, I was pleasantly surprised by the way he sounded both familiar and down to business.

"Alright, man, do you know your way around the city?"

"Yes," I answered, quite proudly.

"Are you on the West Side or the East Side?"

Easy questions to answer. I was catching a break.

"Brooklyn, but I can get to you by the F or the 1/9."

Lish carefully gave me directions to a coffee shop on the Upper West Side.

"Okay, thanks. I'll see you tomorrow then."

His voice was gruff but loose in a retro "cool cat" kind of way, very masculine with almost no trace of the Five Towns. The next day, I got there early and waited. It's a practice I still employ when interviewing a really famous rock star, someone whose work has thrilled me, like Morrissey or Chan Marshall of Cat Power or Robert Smith of The Cure, someone who could easily get the upper hand. My plan is as follows: I arrive early and make the location my own, tread around it, lift my leg as it were. I tend to make sure I look better than usual on these occasions. I wear a suit—vintage, usually sharkskin, not a business suit—comb my hair, and shave. Gordon Lish wore khaki. Head to toe. I later learned that he had psoriasis, and it was the only material his tender epidermis could tolerate. When I say head-to-toe khaki, I do not mean a pair of chinos and a safari shirt; I mean a strange sort of beige flight suit, a one piece, topped off with a fedora-style hat. He looked like a bush pilot who'd bailed out and landed at the front of a Pride parade.

"How is your grandmother Reggie?" he asked when we shook hands. "I always liked her very much."

I told him she was well.

"Florida?"

I nodded, knowing exactly what he meant. It's where people ended up after a certain age. Florida and then . . . eternity.

He was at least three inches shorter than I was, but his chest was stout and his posture erect, whereas I slouched.

"Let's walk," he suggested after we purchased our takeaway coffee. The pedestrian sea seemed to part for him as he walked down Amsterdam Avenue. I tried to keep pace alongside him and today recall a feeling of affection for the man. I recognized myself in him, my family, my great-grandfather's face and mannerisms. It was there. We were related. He was great, and we were related. And I loved him then; it was unspoken but intense and, at least for the time being, for those few wondering, tingly moments, it was unconditional.

"Thank you," I wanted to shout. "Thank you for existing."

"I made an arrangement," Lish told me. "Now, you can't tell anyone about this. But I have found someone who is willing to pay your way into my class."

Pay my way? I thought. It seemed a little odd. Why not just let me into the class for free, or cut me a break. I suppose that violated some kind of principle of his. What he had to impart, people had to pay for. He didn't give it away, not even to a family member. It wasn't about the cash; it was about the secrets, the strategies. They had value; they had to be respected.

"I will give you her number," he said of this wealthy mystery benefactor. "You will call her and say thank you, and that will be that. Can you handle that?"

"Yes."

"Don't tell her who you are. Just thank her for paying your way in. I don't want her or anybody else to know you're family."

It was heartening just to hear him confirm this aloud. I left Lish and felt saved. I was going to be okay. I would be mentored. Someone would take whatever talent I had and finally show me what the fuck to do with it. I'd eliminated one very bad habit from my life, and here was an older man, a family member and possibly a friend, who would gently remove the others. Gordon Lish would make me a writer. The following morning, I made the strange call. The woman seemed to be expecting my contact and the mysterious sentiments I expressed.

"This is Marc Spitz."

"Hello! How are you."

"I'm good. I just want to thank you for what you did. And to let you know that it means a lot."

"Oh, well, I'm glad."

The workshop was held in an apartment on the top floor of a building at the end of Fifth Avenue, just off Washington Square Park. After a full day's work, I was exhausted, but I took a bologna sandwich and a green apple to the fountain in the park, sat, ate, and waited for "school" to begin. The living room was spacious and comfortably sat about twenty-five people on couches, the floor, and chairs pulled away from a big kitchen table. Many of them looked like they were about to receive their mantras. I'd heard that sometimes writers flew in just to attend this thing. There was a line for the bathroom, since Gordon did not like to be distracted mid-class by students getting up to relieve themselves. You could go once, before it began; then you had to hold it in while you learned.

Gordon stood, wearing the same outfit as when we'd first met, in the center of the room. His hands were on his hips as he watched us all file in and take our seats. Nobody seemed to make eye contact with him; nor did he say hello to anyone. It was strange. He was waiting for some kind of signal, I guess, some switch to flip in a place deep inside him. Maybe he was meditating. These classes, I'd been told, could go on for hours on end, which is why I took care to eat something first.

I don't want to be one of those whistle-blowers who exposes cult situations for what they really are. Those pieces have already been published about Gordon's workshop. Nor am I ungrateful for my great-uncle's attention at a time when I was desperate, even if he made a point to absolutely ignore me after our one and only private meeting. Finally, I don't want to disrespect the people, and there are many of them, who gleaned a lot of useful tools from his teachings and have produced good and successful work. I will only say that less than half an hour in, I decided that I hated Gordon Lish, wished I'd never met him, and decided someone should punish him. By the fifth hour, I had stopped listening to what he was saying; I'd stopped wanting to be a writer at all. My higher ambitions had melted down. I wanted to quit my job and move to Boise and stare at grass growing and bite into turnips. At one point during his marathon spiel, Gordon told a story about being thrown out of Phillips Academy, the prestigious private school in Andover, supposedly after having a fight with another, anti-Semitic student. Humphrey Bogart had also been expelled from the institution. "Don't tell me about Phillips. I don't wanna know about Phillips," he raged.

I ask myself now why I couldn't just let the old man talk his talk. I've since read some books on the craft and found them absolutely useful. Stephen King's *On Writing*?—I read that shit three times. More screenwriting bibles than I can count too. Field. McKee. *Save the Cat*. Yes, Lish was what King calls in his book (although not Lish specifically) a "literary gasbag transcendental asshole," but I was already the bigger asshole at a third his age. And what had I done to justify it? He discovered Carver. Yes, he was frequently hostile, but he'd pulled those certain strings and got me there. Perhaps Lish was indeed offering a shorter route toward being good. Lish was an ass, but I, like my old man, was a punk. And being a punk is worse. You can reform an ass, but you can't tell a punk nothin'. As Joey Ramone declared, he doesn't want to be learned, and he doesn't want to be tamed.

My father was a punk in the same way. Once, while driving home from the racetrack on one of our shared Sundays, we were listening, as usual, to CBS FM, as we did, and "It's My Life" by the Animals came on.

"This great part is coming up. Wait for it," he instructed as I studied the lyrics and nodded to that simple and sinister riff. I waited. "You can't hold me," Eric Burdon screamed as the rest of the Animals changed the chorus behind him. "Don't push me!"

"Don't push me!" my dad echoed, and from that point on, all authority figures—rabbis, high school teachers, cops, college professors, even the doctors who told me to quit smoking or drinking (and certainly the rehab counselors who insisted that I would end up in jail or dead if I didn't stop)—were the real pushers. "Don't push me!" Gordon Lish was pushing me.

When the time came around for week two of his workshop, I debated blowing it off. I simply could not imagine sitting through another round of it all. Six hours of pushing. Gordon had made it very clear that he saw both absence and tardiness as not quite an insult but rather evidence that one was not serious about the class. I was serious about the class. I seriously hated it.

A Bennington friend had actually attended Phillips Exeter, the sister school to Phillips Academy, or maybe her dad went there. She owned a school T-shirt, and one druggy, drunken night, by chance, I'd borrowed it, and as with everything I borrowed, it became mine—one of my favorites too. It was broken in, soft, good for little else but lounging around Brooklyn . . . until now. I don't think I'd even washed it. It still smelled like sex and smack and the beach. I had the notion to do what I was going to do. I tried to talk myself out of it. I failed. This once harmless bit of stolen property had already transformed into something else. It was now a banner, a song, by the Animals. It was "don't push me." A weapon that I had to use because it was there. I wouldn't go out and find an Exeter shirt, but . . . I had one. As when I made the choice to get back on dope, I instantly felt powerful again, heading toward what may have been certain doom, if not the end of yet another promising shortcut toward a career as a real writer.

I didn't eat anything before class this time. I knew that I wouldn't be staying long. I stood outside and smiled at the other students as they filed in. We all were familiars now, having been in the shit together a week previous. Some gave me sympathetic looks, as if to say, "God, what are we in for this time? Ha ha." Others couldn't get upstairs to suck off the great man's ego fast enough. Again Gordon stood, hands on khaki hips. He nodded serenely as the room filled up. When his internal buzzer rang, he began the evening's lesson. I waited about an hour as he talked, and talked, and talked, and talked. But this time, with each bit of wisdom, I smirked and shook my head. I tsk-tsked and rolled my eyes. I knew he could see me, but he was ignoring me, just like he had the first time I entered the living room the previous week. Just like he had this time. Still, I could tell he was losing control of the once rapt room. Nobody did this. A politely asked question would sometimes be met with a vicious cutoff. He had the floor. He had the voice; we had the ears. But I was filling his with a lot of raspberry.

Some of the other students started giving me disapproving looks, but Lish wouldn't acknowledge me. I wouldn't reach him. He refused to allow it. It was an unspoken battle of wills.

"Take it easy. People will hear about this. He's a Lish," I told myself. "Same last name as your great-grandfather. He's family." But my "self" wouldn't listen. My "self" was going to pull the pin out of the grenade. Maybe I didn't have faith that he would stick by me. My old man certainly hadn't, and although things were still in the pink cloud with Alex, no woman had either. It's also possible that I knew I didn't have a publishable book in me yet. I wasn't ready. I mean, if I were close, no way would I let anything get in the way of having it read. Or would I? Just how sick and self-destructive was I? I'd stuck needles in my arm. So what if I wasn't using them for anything but ruination; my balls were bigger than his. I hated him. I hated writers. I hated myself for aspiring to be one. Aspiring to be an even bigger ass. I hated that after he got famous Raymond Carver left his wife and found a new one. I hated that everyone leaves. "Be the punk instead. Rip it up, pull the pin, destroy . . ."

The room was hot—body heat and now temper, nerves shooting up and down a dozen spines. But my great uncle Gordon, editor of Raymond Carver, "Captain" of the good ship *Fiction*, owner of the scoop on how to write well, kept his cool. He went on, talking, ranting, cracking wise, glaring, throwing rhetoric around; not one person in the room challenged anything that came out of the man's mouth. I decided I'd it was time for detonation. I unbuttoned my leather coat and took it off with a flourish. I sat there with my skinny, tattooed arms, in my funky, stinking, gray, stolen Phillips Exeter T-shirt. The lettering was large and maroon: it was impossible to miss the message. It was like red paint on a fur coat.

Someone gasped, but Gordon still went on. But I could tell I had him. I'd fired the proton torpedo at the Death Star's thermal exhaust port and was merely waiting to see if it hit the money. He talked and talked and talked, but he wasn't listening to his own words anymore. I'd taken him back to school. Back to a memory that he had no use for. He finally looked me in the eye, for the first time since he had sized me up in that coffee shop and we had both tried to gauge just how familiar our respective features were. His black, furious eyes—eyes that had seen their way out of Hewlett, eyes that had scanned the flawed text of Raymond Carver—locked on me now. "Out," was all he said. One word. Well chosen. I looked around.

"Now," he said.

I nodded, smiled, and grabbed my coat. Before leaving Lish and his disciples, I took care to put on my sunglasses, found my pack of Camel Lights and slowly put one in my mouth, and made my way toward the door. It was the best-tasting cigarette I'd ever enjoyed. I could have written a book about the first inhale, and in that moment I knew that one day I would be published, if only because I was not supposed to get there without the Captain's direction. I didn't know when, but I knew it would happen someday because I absolutely would die trying to prove him wrong.

I took solace in what was becoming a real romance with Alex, the first with post-Bennington domestic qualities. In Hollywood, I didn't even have a lamp or a night table. Now I did garden work out back. We'd take long walks up Seventh Avenue and share an ice cream at the Häagen-Dazs shop, sitting on a bench in front and slowly spooning it out, one for me, one for her. We took the train out to Coney Island and spent a day eating fried food, playing ski ball, and taking Polaroids in front of the freak show billboards. We'd browse the flea markets and collect clothes and knickknacks to decorate the apartment. Alex and I shared a sort of pack-rat aesthetic, and she also had a tendency to paste her heroes to the wall, postcards of writers and artists she admired. We didn't need the city most nights; we'd get drunk and have sex— on the kitchen floor, against the washing machine, on the bathroom floor. We'd play music and watch movies. One weekend, we took the F train out to Coney Island and ate greasy food and posed in front of the old-style banners and advertisements for the freak shows. She could keep up with my drinking and never judged me when I got sloppy and inevitably morose and angry. Domesticity was, like sobriety, a project, and I'm not sure I was motivated to slow down and tuck in for the right reasons, like, well, love. It was more like . . .

vanity. I was getting old; slowly and incrementally, but it was happening. That had never crossed my mind before—that it would happen to me. I was absolutely going to die young. You couldn't tell me different. I hadn't considered what, if I somehow survived, might happen to my hair, my teeth, my skin, my dick, my clothes. Oh, man. Was I going to become that guy in sweats? One day, while buying candy on Eighth Street with Alex at one of those nut shops where they hand you a shovel and point you toward a series of bins full of toxic jellies and cheap bulk chocolates, I noticed my hairline had started to recede ever so slightly.

Oh, God, I'm going to look like my father when I'm old, I fretted. I'd better get used to it—wrap my head around the hard truth that junk is easy, but aging is not for pussies.

As if I needed all this rubbed in, the old man called me at work one afternoon and told me that he'd be coming through town.

"For a race?"

"Saratoga." He never came to town just to be in town anymore. He lived out in Chicago.

"Why don't we get a drink?" I suggested. I was about to talk up the merits of the Holiday when he offered to take us to his favorite bar: Billy's Topless, over on Sixth Avenue. It was a small titty bar with a half-moon stage and some ringside seats (where you had to tip) and a back bar (where you could just drink and watch). Red lit and I suppose as classy as a place like that gets, Billy's was famous. I'd been there with the old man before. Alex seemed curious, and Ron was absolutely down, so Billy's it was.

I gave her a look like, This is my blood. Are you sure you still want to be with me?

They were playing Motley Crue when we walked in, "Dr. Feelgood." My father broke a hundred at the bar and got much of his change in singles. He carefully handed a stack to Ron and a stack to Alex. Then he put his arm around me and handed me a stack too.

"She's pretty," he said of her. "You thinking about settling down?"

"No," I said. "I don't know. I mean . . . we live together but . . . "

"Do you love her?"

"I don't know, Pop. Jesus."

"What happened to the other one?" He was talking about Zoe.

"She's gone."

"What about the cat?"

"Gone."

"That money I sent you?"

"Gone."

"You're doing good. How's your mother?"

"Why don't you ask her?"

"How's your sister?"

"Why don't you ask her?"

"Well, give them my love."

"Okay, Pop."

"You look good," he said by way of consolation. "Gotta stay away from the drugs."

"I know, Pop."

All I wanted in the world at that moment was a bag of heroin and a Slayer CD to snort it off. I would crawl into a turtle's shell, and none of this would rattle me at all. I'd go broke in there. Bald in there. I'd write the great American novel in there and creep over to Gordon Lish's door. He'd open it and say, "What are you doing here, turtle?"

"Changing the face of contemporary literature." The voice would echo from under the carapace. "Glurg, glurg, glurg."

A few weeks later, Alex met the other side of the family. I took her out to the Island on the railroad for Thanksgiving dinner. She charmed my family with her crisp accent and attentiveness. My mother was, and remains, a sucker for kitchen sink dramas and *Brideshead Revisited* and now *Downton Abbey*. You could natter on like a chimney sweep, and she'd kvell. Even my emotionally distant stepfather, Al, was doting on me in a way he'd never done before with the guests I'd bring back; granted, many of them were highly stoned Bennington boys, holiday orphans just looking for a piece of turkey and a warm bed. Alex and I kissed and huddled as we waited for the train back to the city, our bellies stuffed with turkey and my mother's leaden noodle kugel.

"I like your family," she said.

She seemed to beat away all the loneliness that lived at that train station, when I was coming back from the city late at night, sneaking away to Manhattan when I should be at school, never talking to anyone. It'd be nice to have a family of my own—to almost insure that I'd never be completely lonely. I mean, my father was basically a sociopath, and he still had me. Gordon Lish didn't know me at all, but when he received my letter, he'd had to reckon with me. It's what you do. Family is a powerful thing.

I had no idea that we'd already started one.

Alex and I adopted a dog that winter from the shelter up in Spanish Harlem, a mutt we named Odessa after the coffee shop on Avenue A. I would rise from our warm bed and walk the thing in the tundra of Park Slope every morning before getting ready for work. By the spring, the dog was fully grown and began walking me instead, pulling me up the block and barking its head off. Maybe it had been abused, but it seemed eager to be getting somewhere and couldn't wait for my deliberation or abide any street traffic.

After feeding her and kissing Alex goodbye, I'd grab an onion bagel and coffee on the corner and ride the train in over the bridge with every other office worker and retailer. At least things at Shakespeare had taken a turn for the interesting. Chris, the general manager, had brought on a kid named David Greenberg, who quickly became my favorite staffer and one of the more interesting downtown figures I'd ever meet. David was just wired differently. He didn't have a low gear; he was just quick, cruel, and hilarious, like the Warhol stars of my teenage fantasies. He knew all of those folks too, the ones who were still alive. I'd only ever gawked at the likes of Viva. He'd had full conversations with Gerard Malanga—about art. He could talk about art. And like me, he had an encyclopedic and effortless pop-music data base in his brain: session players, B sides, release dates. I was dispatched to show him the ropes.

"Whatever you do," I said, "don't plan on staying here too long."

David had been involved with Allen Ginsberg. I don't know if it was a boyfriend situation or just an intense connection. He never went into detail but certainly made sure that everybody knew about it; it was part of the myth he was quickly building. Ginsberg was not Ginsberg; he was "Allen." He also knew "William," "Gregory," and "Patti." Oh, and "Marianne," as in Marianne Faithfull. And they knew and, it was implied, respected him as a kindred spirit, a like thinker, an artist. What the fuck was he doing in a bookstore? He was a musician too. I only had the facts, he knew how to play, how to write original songs and great lyrics. His band was called Pen Pal, and they already had a record in the shops at HMV in Midtown. After work one day, we went over to the Pink Pony, the café down on Ludlow Street, and I watched in awe as he played a note-perfect version of U2's junkie ballad "Running to Stand Still."

"You know I took the poison from the poison stream and floated on outta here," he'd sing with soul and feeling, which seemed to come from nowhere, given his ironic conversational style. Like Dylan, Bowie, Bruce, and Axl, he had at least three amazing rock voices in his arsenal and he could do dead-on impressions of his heroes. His rendition of "Queen Elvis II" by Robyn Hitchcock was uncanny and immediately made you want to find the CD and replay the original a dozen times. Whenever I'd come to him with a great musical discovery, like Ben Lee's "Song 4 You," David not only had already heard it but could also sing it back to me.

David was the ultimate "Man, what are *you* doing here?" Shakespeare employee—that is, until Suchi materialized from . . . well, nobody really knew where, or why this woman was working in a bookstore on Lower Broadway. Suchi was slim and Asian. She styled her long, hot pink hair in bangs and wore the kind of outfits that only a famous person, or someone within close proximity to the famous, would dare wear: white leggings and flowered frocks and odd jewelry. When the reunited Sex Pistols came to town to play the Hammerstein Ballroom, I fretted loudly about not being able to afford a ticket.

"I'm going," Suchi said. She came back the next day raving about the show.

"What's her story?" I asked around, as we did whenever there was a new hire. Everyone, starved for distraction, had to know the poop.

"You don't know?" David said. "That's Iggy's wife, man."

"Iggy Pop?" As if there were any other "Iggy."

"Yep."

"Well, what the fuck is she doing working here?"

There was no way Suchi Pop was pulling down more than we were, and we were on Maggie's Farm, none of us clearing six bucks an hour. I'd already been there a year—marked time there. For example, I heard the "Trial of the Century" verdict come over the airwaves while walking the floor and straightening the personal growth section. Customers gasped as O. J. was found "not guilty." I knew the smell of the place. I knew how to lift a ten from the till for lunch when I was broke and not have it show up in the end-of-shift count out. I'd tagged the bathroom and stockroom with my nicknames. I had "staff picks."

"She's in bag check," I marveled as Suchi, looking perfectly serene and content, handed out little numbered chits to the dickheads who filed in off Lower Broadway.

I decided I had to find out what her story was and asked her to get a drink after work one night. She agreed, but even after spending the night gabbing with the woman, all I could pry out was that she lived nearby. Even full of whiskey courage, I didn't have the balls to come out and say, "So, the kids say you're Iggy's wife. Or ex-wife or something. That true?" When she invited me up to her apartment, I jumped at the chance to investigate further, but even when we were making out on the thin rug in her oddly lit, tiny living room, I had no idea what was up. Was Iggy going to bust in? Was he out of the picture? Was I committing some kind of punk rock sacrilege? Getting it on with the Godfather's woman? I looked around and wiped the kissing film from my mouth. Cigarettes, spit, sex. There were no photos of Iggy. The weird light was coming from one of those Brion Gysin revolving dream machines in the corner. It turned like a bingo hopper and threw black-and-white shades on the wall hypnotically. I zipped up and told her I had to get back to Brooklyn. At work, we never once discussed our clinch. And I never knew exactly why Suchi Pop was working in a bookstore for a hair above the minimum wage. Years later I would come to interview Iggy more than once, and I never brought it up. And I never even boasted about it in the bars for fear that some punk would jump me in the name of The Stooges.

David Greenberg was not impressed with fame, and I found that admirable, even if the source of this was a delusion (or a utilized illusion) that he was already terribly famous. And on the Lower East Side, he absolutely was. He and I together ruined the perfect order of the smoothly running indie bookstore. We were the termites you needed to burn out, or the whole structure would collapse. I started chipping again, hiding the smack use from Alex and everyone else, and he was the only other employee who knew his way around the bag. I'd cop a bag over on Clinton Street, and we'd share it at work. I'd head down to the bathroom and do a line, then pass it to him and relieve him at bag check as he attended to his own bag. It made a weeknight shift go by quickly. We also muscled over the "jazz" and "classical" rule by using our serious rock-snob skills to argue that trip-hop (Tricky, Portishead) counted as jazz. Sometimes we just ignored the rule completely and played the brand-new Oasis album, *What's the Story Morning Glory*, as loud as the stereo would go. David had a perfect ear. The first time he heard "Wonderwall," he knew it was the single and a future classic. Famous people would say hello to him when they wandered into the store. One day, a spaced-out, skinny Jeff Buckley stood at the bag check engaged in a deep conversation with him. Everyone drew closer, trying to eavesdrop, and David loved the attention. He introduced me to "Jeff," who was sweet and funny, if a little bleary. He'd come in to buy the new Marlon Brando memoir, *Songs My Mother Taught Me*, and I grabbed a copy and handed it to him.

"Just take it," I said.

"Cool."

When he left, the store seemed a little smaller; the air had gone out of the room.

That guy is so lucky, I thought. He is going to have a life. I am never going to get out of this place alive.

Alex came in one afternoon, smiling and pleasant at first. People who worked there were used to seeing her, and she had the kind of face that just made you want to greet her warmly and ask if she fancied a cup of tea.

"Can I talk to you a minute?" she asked. It's never good news when someone says that. Never.

Can I talk to you a minute? Insert disaster.

"Sure."

I got someone to cover the register, and we walked outside into the bright
sun.

Alex was pregnant, had been for a while, but there was still enough time to
do something about it if that's what we chose to do. She just wanted to tell
me. Then she left to do some shopping. I'm not sure why she had to tell me in
the middle of my shift. I couldn't leave to shop or drink or throw myself in
the East River. I still had to stand there and ring up stupid copies of *Griffin
and Sabine* or Ross Reports for aspiring, audition-minded actors with their
sad, hopeful faces.

"We could have it," I whispered late one night while we lay on the bed with
the dog. I felt guilty. I had no money, but maybe my parents would help. Her
parents? If I'd been less of a junkie loser fuckup out in Hollywood, I'd be able
to raise a kid, send him or her off to Bennington one day too. I would have
some money in the bank. Pride. A career. Now, I was getting older. My father
was getting older. It was time to have a kid. This was the moment, wasn't it?
And I wasn't ready. She was even less ready. She'd only just graduated.

"We're not going to be able to do all the things in life we want to do," she
sobbed. I don't think she even knew what those things were beyond some
mental list she'd run down in her head, and "being a mother" was not high on
it. Not immediately. Not now.

"But we could." We fell asleep without deciding. It wasn't my decision
anyway, and I felt some relief in that. I was terrible with decisions. I just
steeled myself for whatever it was she decided.

"I want to go home."

"Why do we have to do it there?"

"I just want to."

"Okay, I'll get off work."

"You don't have to come."

"Are you fucking crazy?"

London. The abortion had to be in London. There were clinics in Brooklyn. There were clinics in the East Village. We could have taken care of it in
an afternoon and then tried, somehow, to rebuild to what was essentially the
most solid relationship either of us had known. But she was scared. She
wanted the comfort of England and her family. This had all gone down in

Brooklyn. Brooklyn was tainted, and, now, so were we. We were getting rid of the kid. Neither of us knew if it was a horrible sin, and I still don't know how I feel about it all morally, but I know it certainly felt like one. We were broken. Suddenly the sex was gone; the poor dog looked vaguely shamed as I walked her in the morning, as if she were trying to say, "I know, I'm not a baby . . ."

After she got pregnant, we didn't fuck anymore. Didn't play music anymore either, and music in 1995 was as good as it was in 1965: a golden age. Pulp had released *Different Class*, which was even better than *His and Hers*. Radiohead had just put out *The Bends*, and Blur's *The Great Escape* was a perfect continuation of the peak they'd hit in *Park Life*. Don Hill's was still open to us every weekend. Suddenly I realized how good I'd had it. Yes, I had to toil in a bookstore, but at least there were no abortions. She went over first. We couldn't fly together. That night I went to Don Hill's. It was Jack's birthday, and I told him I'd make an appearance. He was the only one I'd told.

"Maybe they're killing that baby right now, Girl," he said as DJ Miss Guy cued up the new Soundgarden song "Pretty Noose."

Things ended with Alex soon after. The procedure in the hospital there was complicated, and she got very sick. This isn't some comment on the National Health Service. I just know she was healthy going in, and within an hour she was pale and sweaty and vomiting, unable to keep down simple beef consommé as she shook and moaned under a sheet. I paced and chain-smoked in the waiting room and, once it was clear she would have to stay overnight, had an awkward early supper with her mother.

"So, what year did you graduate?" she asked.

"Um . . . '92."

"Ah."

The rest of Britain seemed obsessed with who was going to win the singles-chart battle between Blur or Oasis. It was on the evening news. I couldn't give less of a shit. Once Alex was released from the hospital, I would lock myself in the family's little bathroom with its weird porcelain tub and hand-held shower, bury my face in my hands, and sob. I was on heroin again inside of a month. Alex dumped me. She was intent on starting over, and I understood. It was painful just staring at each other in the kitchen over the *Post*, much less entertaining any thoughts of fucking or even kissing. If I'd had anywhere else to go, I would have left her. The only thing that went through my brain when she sat me down and kicked me out was relief. I wouldn't have to hide my smack anymore.

I had no other way of coping with the bumps in life and no real faith in anything else. I always told myself that I sought drama to have something to write about, but I sometimes think I found myself back in trouble as an excuse to get back to the drug.

For the rest of the summer, my heroin use got bad again, but at least I had that perversely pleasurable feeling that I was punishing myself every time I vomited or coughed or got sick and walked Avenue B with nowhere to sleep. It was a reckoning for killing the kid. I missed Alex, and all the promises I'd made to the dog, well, I broke them. Like with Heaven, the cat Zoe and I'd had, I wasn't around to take care of Odessa; she had to be put to sleep after attacking a stranger on the street. I couldn't care for another living thing. I would have killed a cactus plant. I would have found a way to kill a Pet Rock. I was bad company, til the day I died, and surely that day was coming on soon.

I was sleeping on the general manager Chris Peterson's floor. He was out of town and gave me his key. I would let myself in, place the couch cushions on the floor, and cover myself with a towel. I had no idea if and when Chris would come home. It was an uneasy sleep. I knew some old Bennington people who were working and mostly eating E in the back of "House of Trance," a ridiculous DayGlo-painted record and rave equipment store on St. Mark's Place, where they would strut around like drugged-out Miro roosters and listen to Aphex Twin's drippy ambient music, Goldie's jungle tracks, or the first Atari Teenage Riot album at ear-pureeing volume. Inside, there was the constant thrum of a 250-bpm drum machine loop. You just got used to it.

"What's up, yo?"

Bmmmmmmmmmmmmmmmmmmmmmmmmm!

"How you doin' man? Long time."

Bmmmmmmmmmmmmmmmmmmmmmmmmmmm!

"You know maybe a place I could crash out? I'm beat."

Bmmmmmmmmmmmmmmmmmmmmmmmmmmmmmmmm!

"Aw, lemme think."

Bmmmmmmmmmmmmmmmmmmmmmmmmmmmmmmmmmmrrrrrrrrrrrrrrrrrrr!

"Cool."

Bbbbbbbbbbbbbbbbbbbbbbbbbbbbbrrrrrrrrrrrrrrrrrrrrrbbbbbbbbbbbbbbbbbbbrrrrrr rrrrrrr!

I'd sometimes borrow a key from one of them. I often had no idea whose apartment I was letting myself into and what would be going on once I was inside—who was going to come home, whom I'd be facing when I woke up. I tried just to sleep, or nod, and as a point of pride, not steal anything.

One day David left Shakespeare & Co. for lunch and never came back. I couldn't see myself working there without him, so I knew I would have to find a way to leave as well, but I couldn't quit. Chris was mad at me for drinking all his vodka, and there were rumors I was stealing from the till. One day he sat me down.

"This isn't working. Right now, as it is, I will give you a recommendation wherever you go. But if you stay, I can't promise that."

"Okay."

I'd been there three full years—a big gap unless I listed it on my resume.

"So, Bennington. Nice. Los Angeles. What was that like? Hmmm. There's a gap here. What were you doing between 1994 and 1997?"

"I'll tell you what I wasn't doing: heroin and getting abortions."

I went looking for work, but mostly I'd hang out in House of Trance, bum cigarettes, and watch my friend Ian do the robot dance under the black light. Sometimes he'd power-down and sit in front of the computer, watching messages pop up.

"What is that?" I asked.

"It's a chat room."

"Can I chat?"

"Okay, but don't flame."

"Flame?"

"Keep it cool. Don't write anything in all caps. That's like shouting."

Nobody ever came into House of Trance. I'm not sure what exactly they sold. It was just a house . . . of trance, so hours and hours would pile up. Sometimes I'd be on heroin, sometimes not, but I'd be sharing my problems with total strangers, and it became addictive to the point that Ian had to ask me to leave.

"How do I get into a chat room?"

"They're everywhere."

I just walked around. I had no idea full conversations were going on in the ether around me. It was a new world, and it gave me hope. There would be new books, maybe even new girls, more chances to get it all wrong. I was twenty-eight. I was still not published. I was still broke. I was still broken-hearted, but at least I'd made it past the stupid club-admission age.

I was at Don Hill's one night waiting in line for the bathroom and accidentally burned Chloë Sevigny with the cherry of my cigarette. The minute it happened, something flashed in my brain: I'm burning Chloë Sevigny with a cigarette. Not I'm burning some blonde chick with my butt. Nobody else looks like Chloë Sevigny. Nobody has her nose, her forehead, her shoulders . . .

There are men and women and Chloë. She's pretty unique—unmistakable. I'd seen her before at the Brian Jonestown Massacre show at Coney Island High and other "place-to-be" events, always looking a little spaced-out and unapproachable, maybe to cover shyness, maybe not, but I hadn't dared approach her. Now I had no choice.

"Oh, man, I'm sorry. Are you okay?"

She nodded. The burn wasn't so bad. Just a quick jolt of pain. Nothing that would leave a scar.

"Let me buy you a drink, okay? I really am sorry."

We continued to wait for the bathroom. I had a choice then to make conversation or just go outside and pee by the river somewhere. There'd be a long wait to get back into Don's. There always was if you weren't famous like Chloë or connected like Amra Brooks. I was a regular but got no special treatment. I decided to stay, which meant I was obliged to make some kind of conversation, or else the moment would be even more awkward. And so, even though I knew the answers, I asked the ice-breaking questions: What's your name? What do you do? She said that she was an actress.

"Oh, yeah? Theater? Film?"

I pretended I had no idea. She'd already been featured in *Sassy*, which Jack and I still read every month. Jay McInerney had dubbed her the new "it girl" in *The New Yorker*, which Jack and I didn't read. But we had seen her in the Larry Clark film *Kids* at the Angelika. It had the opposite effect as *Trainspotting*, which had made us a little proud to be junkies and want to go out and cop and find a bench in some park and stare up at the stars. *Kids* was like being trapped in a room with your younger, stupider self (if your younger, stupider self was a white b-boy skater). It made me want to get an AIDS test and go home to Long Island forever. She went to the bathroom, and I went to the bathroom, and when I came out, she was gone.

If I find her again, it's meant to be, I told myself. At Don's in its packed prime, this was not a given. People got lost forever in those throngs. Sometimes you'd come with a party of a dozen and leave all alone, wondering if you'd imagined the earlier part of the evening. But after a few quick sorties around the dance floor and the row of cocktail tables along the front wall, I found her cooling herself by the open door exit, the street breeze coming in.

"Hi, I've been looking for you," she said.

"Really? You want that drink?"

"Sure." Again, I had to keep her on the line. Hookups were sometimes foiled just by the wait for the bartender. It wasn't as bad as the Holiday Cocktail Lounge, but there were nights where you could feel yourself get older as you tried to order your vodka tonic.

"Do you dance?" she asked as we sipped our cocktails by the bar. Miss Guy was, as usual, inspired. One song after another made you happy to be young and alive and pretty in New York City. I nodded.

"Are you good?"

I shook my head.

"Me neither."

We pushed past the sweaty bodies onto the floor and did the white kid new wave movie hop, which I could do pretty well. You basically dance like they do in the montages in *Sixteen Candles*, *Valley Girl*, *Hot Dog: The Movie*, or any number of eighties flicks. Guy was playing "Girl U Want" by Devo and "Never Say Never" by Romeo Void; then without warning, he segued into the much slower "How Soon Is Now" by The Smiths. It cleared some of the floor. I gave her a look that asked if we should stop, but instead, she put her arms around me, and we began to slow-dance more conspicuously. I began to wonder if any of the crew I came with were watching me now. She was tipsy or clumsy, and we melted into each other like we'd been dating for years. At the end of the night, we didn't kiss or anything. She left before I did and wrote her number on my hand.

"Call me, okay?" she said.

"Absolutely."

I watched her go and immediately exhaled. Did that really just happen? I tried to keep the digits from fading with sweat. This was, again, years before you could just text someone your number or, even faster, ring them on your phone so they'd have you on their call records. I kept blowing on it and holding it high above the increasingly drunk and swaying crowd.

When I found my friends, Jack had indeed been watching me out on the floor.

"You can't be dating no Chloë Sevigny with no job. She's the it girl, Girl," Jack whispered to me as we went up to the bar and counted out our singles. Neither of us could afford to drink much at Don's.

"Thanks a lot."

"I'm just giving you the truth." He was right. But I had a little indie film cred, didn't I? I still had a screenplay making the rounds out in Hollywood, and I could summon that illusory Hollywood thing at will—I'd been there long enough. I'm talking about that sense of "becoming" something. You can't dismiss someone who may be "becoming" a star because you never know. You never know . . . It's why people whisper their gossip in bars and restaurants there. Adrienne Shelly notwithstanding, I never mixed with people on their way up anymore, but I had a lot of friends who were expert at faking it. David Greenberg acted like he was already a rock star. Jack had a good rhythm too.

He'd get drunk at Max Fish, where we were faces, then head to the Boiler Room, a gay bar on Second Avenue, where he was an even bigger "star." There were nights when I had to drag him out of that place so he wouldn't go home with someone sketchy.

A week or so later, I called Chloë from a pay phone on the corner of St. Mark's and Third Avenue. The right pay phone was key when it came to building confidence. I'd scout them out. This one was right in front of a news kiosk and across from the seedy St. Mark's Hotel. It seemed cinematic. I was worried that she'd given me a fake number and a brush off, but the way she held me seemed to indicate differently.

The thing is, take away Don's and the crowd and the loud music and the gorgeous Smiths songs and the *New Yorker* profile and all the fashion, and sometimes you just have two incredibly shy people in a bar booth. Without all the white noise, we both determined that we actually had to drink until we could talk, one Greyhound after another at the Holiday, which seemed doubly lit to pick up every pore; it was one of those dates.

"We should do this again," I said as I walked her east toward the apartment she was crashing in. It belonged to the actor Michael Rappaport. We finally kissed before she went inside, and it was drunken and sloppy and sweet, but it didn't go further. Chloë was crashing with friends, and so was I. Where was I going to bring the "it girl" to seduce her further? Up to my grandmother's roof, or to some stranger's house to raid the fridge and watch *The X-Files* on a snowy TV with a bent antennae? Or to House of Trance? I wasn't equipped for this. I was too insecure, too broke. It was bad timing, and I knew it, even as I tried to preserve that "I just kissed someone" adrenaline rush as I walked home alone.

We had one more date, the "it girl" and I. I took her, perhaps unwisely, to Max Fish, the hip bar on Ludlow Street between Houston and Stanton. Max Fish was the postwork junkie hipster square dance. It was full of beautiful boys with greasy Joe Dallesandro hair and too-tight leather jackets and beautiful girls with Japanese-style bobs, thrift store dresses, and combat boots with thick white socks. It was like a Bennington house party, complete with bad pop art (which lined the walls) and lots of sex (mostly in the spacious, graffiti-strewn toilets, where glassine bags and spunk covered the floor). The front half was full of pinball machines, but the best seats were either at the bar, staring at the TV and the Julio Iglesias promotional installation light box altered to make Julio look like a burn victim, or the table just by the jukebox so you could commandeer it and play "Bathosphere" by Cat Power, "Sugar Water" by Cibo Matto, and "The Model" by Big Black or Jonathan Fire*Eater's EP over and over again and try to cadge free drinks off Harry, the lank-haired, friendly bartender/painter. Max Fish was a bathosphere, giving all who entered a sweaty, sexy hipster soaking. Bringing Chloë Sevigny there was like taking Derek Jeter to a sports bar on the Upper West Side. I could feel all the eyes on her, and it made both of us tense. Max Fish was best for one-night stands. Often you'd get picked up by a girl and dragged up the street to fuck in her apartment, then find yourself back at the bar or playing pinball, literally without ever knowing where exactly your dick had just been. Never, never take a potential girlfriend in. Especially not an "it" girlfriend.

CHAPTER 10

"**W**ind the record back."

Like this?

"Yeah."

Jmmmmrrraaaaawwwwwwwdrrrrrrrrrrrrrrrrr.

"Now stop, which you do by hitting the button that says 'stop.'"

Obeyed.

"Now you are what we call 'cued.' When you are ready, hit the button there that says 'play.'"

I look over at the silver button on the silver-and-black Technics turntable. Sure enough, it says "play." I hit it, and the twelve-inch Fugees single of "Ready or Not" begins to fill the spacious, vacuumed room, with its tan banquettes and polished bar.

"Cool."

"Now, you are a DJ. Don't be nervous. You'll do fine."

"That's it?"

"Well, no, when the song is over, you will have to hit 'play' on the other turntable, fade the Fugees out, and fade up . . . What are you playing next?"

"Portishead. 'Glory Box.'"

"Fine . . . Do it."

I hit the button.

"This is not supposed to be this easy."

"It's our little secret."

She kissed me for luck, and then she was off to her date, or appointment, or wherever she had to be, and I ordered a vodka grapefruit from the bar to kill my nerves. The waitress brought it to me and didn't ask for any money. I was going to like being a DJ. My Jedi master was Bonnie Thornton, and the venue was a posh restaurant and bar in the Gramercy Park area called Granville. It drew beautiful women and wealthy men, and wealthy women and beautiful men, and on that night one very jittery, scruffy DJ. At least I had something new to tell people when they asked what I did for a living. DJ sounded a lot better than failed author and bookstore clerk. Lord knows, I had the record collection. I convinced my parents to drive out to Park Slope with my crates in the back of their new SUV.

"Why do you need your records now?"

"I can make money with them, Ma," I promised.

"Selling them?"

"No. Playing them in bars."

"Someone's going to pay you to play your dirty old vinyl for them?"

"Can you believe it?"

Bonnie was a pioneer. She'd cracked the code. You didn't even need to count beats or have perfect rhythm to DJ. All you needed was taste. This blonde scientist in low-rise booty pants had found the angle, and because she was such a stellar selector (and was drop-dead hot), she almost single-handedly opened a vast market for live, on-site spinners and indirectly fed a whole lot of junkie ragamuffins who knew the two good songs on albums that only had two good songs. Suddenly, every bar and dining establishment worth a mention in *Time Out* had to book a live DJ. It was the perfect way for an aspiring writer, actor, painter, rocker to make an extra $100, which was the equivalent of about $500 as far as getting through a city week went at the time. She could have been greedy and gobbled up every free slot, but she shared the wealth. Once the owners of these new, upscale bars got over their disappointment that you weren't a hot blonde in a low-cut blouse, they paid you just the same and sent over free drinks and sometimes a meal.

Bonnie knew everyone downtown, from Parker Posey to Huey, from Fun Lovin' Criminals to the photographer Ellen Von Unwerth. She also co-ran her own weekly club. It was called Cheetah and resembled Sasso's disco in *Carlito's Way*. The era of "bling" was upon us, and you weren't nothin' if you didn't have a chilling bottle of vodka or Cristal in front of your leather banquette, blinding gold and diamonds on your fingers and in your teeth. Jack, who dubbed her "Hot Bonnie," would never go near Cheetah because we had no money, and the clientele intimidated us, even if we all grooved to the same music. We weren't about beveled glass, chrome, and neon. We skulked in dark bars and smoked in alleyways. Grungy Don Hill's was more our speed.

Technically Bonnie was my boss, but none of us really did much work at NaNa, the punk rock shoe and consignment clothing store on Prince Street in SoHo. Like Max Fish, it was more of a weigh station for people as they moved on to better things. It was a place to skulk around for a few hours every week and not really assist any customers. It reminded me of the staff at Flip, the boutique on Eighth Street in the eighties. I'd become one of those ambivalent, unhelpful, and icy retail punks I'd marveled at as a teen. The unspoken rule was that you showed up, you tried not to steal or get into trouble, you put your hours in as best you could and pulled your paycheck, and then you could focus on whatever it was that you really cared about. Yolanda Ross, my other boss, for example, went to auditions. Now she's a regular on the David Simon show *Treme*. Bonnie ran her club and collected vinyl. There was an artist kid named Jared who was planning a gallery show. Only Thomas, one of the long-term sales people, seemed remotely content to work retail, but even he had higher aspirations. He was working toward purchasing the Vivienne Westwood suit that had been haunting him. Nobody wanted the Saturday shift, since that was the only time the store got seriously busy with tourist traffic. It was the short straw. You actually had to work. Sometimes my day would consist of walking down Houston Street to El Sombrero, the Mexican restaurant on the Lower East Side that served takeaway margaritas. Other times, Thomas would give me $5 from the till and send me off to find a packet of those sickly sweet sugared nuts that the vendors sometimes sell by Union Square.

To go out with Bonnie after work was to feel like the chick in the relationship. All the doormen knew who she was. She never paid for a drink. She'd eat oysters at Blue Ribbon, and we'd get the check, and it'd be all zeros with no numbers before them. Free. She had her real side too, which came through after a few whiskeys. She was also the sensitive Florida girl who came to the city to escape an unhappy childhood (is there any other reason to come to the city?). This girl would emerge as the music on the jukeboxes we always bum-rushed grew more and more melancholy. Our favorite haunt was Milano's, a hole in the wall on Houston Street. We took comfort in the songs that either predated or ignored rock and roll. Rock and hip-hop called the tune daily; it was the rhythm of the city. But it was nice once in a while to get drunk and just let Frank Sinatra's "One for My Baby," Tony Bennett's "I Wanna Be Around," and Julie London's "Black Coffee" work you over while you stared across the elevated cocktail table at a Southern girl of the Cheap Trick variety. As will happen when two rock geeks put their heads together, Bonnie and I started making each other mixed tapes. I think she probably has fifty of mine, and I have nearly as many of hers.

Some songs will only ever be "Bonnie songs": "Sleepwalk" by Santos and Johnny, "I Saw the Light" by Todd Rundgren, "Imagination Is a Powerful Deceiver" by Elvis Costello (I believe it's a *My Aim Is True*–era B side; well worth seeking out), and for some reason "Bad" by U2 (the studio version, not the more iconic live rendition). Bonnie and I kissed to that one as it played on repeat (studio version, not the more iconic *Wide Awake in America* live version) for an hour one night. "Skyway," too, by The Replacements. Once I was walking home from the Atlantic Avenue subway stop to Ron's place at three in the morning, listening to a Bonnie mix. Just as it started to flurry, "Skyway" by the Replacements came on, and it seemed like we were sound-tracking our respective New York City movies somehow. I didn't have to do that alone anymore. I had finally found someone whom I trusted with the controls. It was a relief not having to know everything, not having to be the biggest rock-and-roll egghead in the room.

Soon, I added playwright to the business card I'd never get around to printing up. DJ and playwright sounded better somehow than poet or convicted felon. The more titles I added, the smaller junkie would become, and as thirty approached, I desperately wanted to shrink that bitch. When I wasn't at Ron's, I was up in Hell's Kitchen. Jack, whom I quickly taught to DJ as well, was crashing with me in the apartment of his friend Andie, whom I was dating at the time, even though most of my romantic thoughts still concerned Bonnie.

Andie was an eclectic mix tape of a girl, cool California jazz one minute, crunchy Denver noodling the next. She was an earthy hippie type who wore essential oils but plucked her eyebrows into movie star arches and wore fur coats. She was an actress and a singer who mostly made her living doing voice-over work. I still get stopped cold sometimes in a drugstore or in front of a TV when I hear her voice (that impossibly smooth Stepford tone) encouraging me to purchase peas or yogurt or tampons. "Oh, God, that's Andie," I say, and until the spot is over, I can't move my feet or hands.

Well-to-do, Andie owned two apartments in a building on Ninth Avenue in Hell's Kitchen, walking distance from the Fordham campus, where Jack was still in the process of getting his degree in theater studies. The neighborhood was quickly gentrifying, but it was still on the rough side. Andie slept in the railroad apartment, with a shower in the kitchen and a big back living room. Although it was humble in size, she decorated it like a Miami Beach condo with pristine white couches, a shag rug, an expensive stereo and TV, and a very eighties glass-and-chrome coffee table, perfect for snorting drugs, which I probably did the very first time I met her on one of my final Liz Phair–soundtracked trips out of LA. I barely remember it, but apparently she gave me a blow job, I fell asleep, then in the morning, after snorting up all my drugs outside the laundry mat and spending all my money, I hailed a cab and reluctantly returned west. Hardly a romantic comedy–style "meet-cute," but the next time we met, I was a New Yorker again, relatively clean, and in need, as ever, of a place to live. Andie, prone to taking in strays, gave me a key.

She had a little black pug named Zelda. I once asked her if she'd named it for Zelda Fitzgerald, but she'd named it for the video game character. This was the difference between Andie and Alex, but on the compatibility scale, Andie had something over my last girlfriend: she wanted to be famous too. Ambition: it's infectious, especially in Manhattan. And what she lacked in cool-kid taste, Andie more than made up for in drive and talent. She had an *Idol*-finalist worthy singing voice, smoky and elastic, easily as marvelous as the soon to be megastar Christina Aguilera. She could sing pop, but she could also sing standards. Sarah Vaughn had, well, maybe a little on her, but only just. For some reason at the time, however, Andie only wanted to sing shitty alt. rock.

When she finally played me her demo, I was dismayed to hear she sounded exactly like Alanis Morissette (who, for the record, I don't consider shitty, but the Alanis clones who got deals after *Jagged Little Pill* and trekked across America that summer on the inaugural Lilith Fair tour were not for me, and probably were not supposed to be). Andie had even imitated Alanis's broken notes (notes she was too technically skilled to break herself), the hard *c*'s of her phrasing, and even the Canadian "oots."

No, really? Why? I was thinking, but of course, I said, "I love it," instead. Polite, sure, but mostly desperate. She had *two* apartments. I had none. It was winter. And who could fault her for posing as Alanis? She was the biggest pop star in the world in 1997. It'd be like faulting a band for sounding like The Beatles in 1965. Was I any different, scheming to write like Irvine Welsh or Nick Hornby, the two hottest, most pop-savvy novelists of the day?

The nineties were the decade when my generation stopped doing street drugs and began its ongoing love affair with prescription meds. Elizabeth Wurtzel had published *Prozac Nation* in 1994, and that seemed to be the beginning of the end for copping. Heroin was, as the Dandy Warhols sang in the summer of 1997, "*so passé.*"

Too many deaths, too many busts, too dirty somehow in the "bling" zone. Instead, we hit the Xanax bottle Andie kept in the underwear drawer. When Andie's demons would flutter around her like fruity bats, she'd get a look in her eye, and I knew when to either beat it or open the pill drawer, divide one of her meds, and suggest we mutually calm the fuck down and enjoy the city.

She'd say something like, "Everything's gone awry!" which was a signal to head downtown and give her some space or run the tap, get the "palindromes," break one in half, and swallow. I'd still pick up a bag of street dope from a dealer who worked the bank near Stuyvesant Park, but mostly I was drugged like an upstart mental patient: suspended animation, chemical style. It made it okay to be going nowhere slowly, as Diane Lane once complained.

Andie was the one who finally got me actually writing again after over two years of selling other people's books and after the debacle of Gordon

Lish's workshop. She was a good manager, even if she couldn't really direct herself out of some deep funks and into her desired superstardom. I'd never given up on the dream of being a real writer. Even when my mother suggested, as she did ten thousand times and still sometimes does, "Why don't you become a teacher?"

"No."

"But you're so smart."

"What would I teach? How *not* to get published?"

"You could recommend books. You were always so good at that."

"I worked in a bookstore! That was my job."

"You'd get benefits. Summers off."

"Mom, teaching is what people do when they don't make it as an artist in New York. They go to Seattle, or they teach."

I already had a few Bennington friends who'd headed for the Pacific Northwest never to be heard from again. Others went to Austin. It felt like surrender. They didn't want fame or drama or a little brush with death here and there any longer, and I couldn't relate. They might as well have been on whatever Pluto is now. A sad space rock. Teaching? With me instructing the nation's youth, the country would be in worse shape than it already was.

"Hello, class. My name is Mr. Spitz. S-p-i-t-z, as you can clearly see on the board. Please open your books to page . . . You know what? Nevermind. What's the fucking point? Do you mind if I smoke? Cigarettes are cool. Write that down. Only thing that gets me through the day. With liquor. Okay, all the women over eighteen raise your hand. Say, is it lunchtime yet?"

As I said, Andie took damaged people in and fixed them. It was rich-girl guilt—and perhaps a by-product of her Mormon upbringing, although she never tried to convert me in any formal sense, gathering perhaps that I hadn't much of a soul to save. She'd meet someone without a work visa and get them the work visa. It's virtually why she kept the second apartment, for her human projects. She'd grown sick of my moping. I needed to write. Physically, I needed to type, or I was not myself. All I did was chain-smoke and eat Xanax and watch MTV and *Ally McBeal* and play with the dog who would never know that she had a much cooler namesake.

The Verve were on heavy rotation, with Richard Ashcroft singing, *"Try to make ends meet. You're a slave to money, then you die."* It's one of the saddest pop songs ever. Sometimes my fear of heights was the only thing keeping me from jumping out the window onto Ninth Avenue.

One afternoon, Andie took me up to Barney's and purchased about $1,000 worth of clothes for me. The idea, I suppose, was to jack up my self-worth via Dolce & Gabbana and Matsuda, but I never wore any of it. It was too nice—

and not really street enough for me. I wore the same black Gap T-shirt, skinny black cords, and battered wing tips every day, leather cuff, vintage wristwatch.

"We should do something about your skin too," she fretted. "Oof."

"I don't need a facial."

"Oh, you do, honey."

"I need a typewriter."

"Really? Why?"

She got excited.

One day Andie announced we were going to get me a computer. She looked like a child who'd just worked out a spelling bee puzzler. She had the correct answer. It had come to her in the night.

"Typewriters are stupid. It's 1997! You should be writing on a big computer! So here's what's going to happen. I'm going to buy you one."

"Oh, no. You don't have to."

"You have to start writing again, Marc."

"I don't know."

"You're not writing because you have nothing to write on. It's so simple, I can't believe I didn't think of it sooner. A writer needs something to write on. So stupid."

"Are you sure? Computers are really expensive."

"Stop it. We're getting you a computer, and that's that. You can pay me back with your first big check."

"Really?"

"Yes. You are going to have the equipment that you need. And you're going to write something incredible on it. Promise me."

"Okay."

"You promise?"

"I promise."

"It has to be incredible."

I'd made her a vow. Now, if nothing else, I *had* to work. I'd lost a lot and stolen even more from others, but that thread of morality, the one tied up in the ethics of artists and patrons, was still there, resilient as a fishing line.

We looked in the classifieds of the *Press* and eventually drove out to Queens and purchased a used IBM computer from a bearish guy who rebuilt them using spare parts. He assured us it worked fine, even if it was a little beat up. It was one of those hulking, grade-school-type machines, a tiny monitor with a blinking green cursor set on a massive cream-colored plastic cabinet with a mouse plugged into the keyboard. There was a basic word-processing program and, to Andie's delight, some built in software like a home *Jeopardy* game.

"Let's play another round!" she'd beg.

"Andie, I'm working on a play!"

"Oh, please."

"Okay, just one."

I never planned on writing a play. Few of my literary heroes were play-wrights. I was aware of David Mamet because he was Jewish and seemed tough and secure, like he always knew what to order off a menu. The only other playwright who seemed as cool was Bill Murray's character in *Tootsie*, the one who wanted a theater that was "only open when it rained." I'd taken a playwriting workshop up at school, and my experience as a screenwriter out in Hollywood had given me some game with dialogue, but I'd also gone to school with Jonathan Marc Sherman and didn't want to be number two as far as Bennington dramatists were concerned. Sherm was hard to beat.

He was a prodigy; he'd written a play called *Women and Wallace* in his teens that'd already been produced Off-Broadway and garnered a positive review in the *New York Times* by the time I got to Bennington. I'd actually appeared in one of his plays at school. It was called *Nothing to Say*. I had to show up at the theater space in VAPA at a certain time every night and walk across the stage as essentially myself, a black-clad poseur boy, and Justin Theroux would call me a "fucker." I was flattered to be asked, but I could hardly say I caught the theater bug. Justin, by the way, never really considered me a "fucker," even if I was essentially stunt-cast. We were friends. He painted a hip-hop graf-inspired mural on my wall up at school, and every time I ran into him in later years, either in Washington Square Park with our dogs or at the Chateau Marmont, we'd hug and briefly catch up, with him always leading with the same salutation: "Question, Marc." It's in the delivery. Theroux gets a lot of shit, from people who don't know him, for appearing slick, with his motorcycle and leather jacket and punk rock T-shirts, all black, but he was exactly the same in the early nineties when I met him, the coolest guy in a room full of cool guys. Maybe he's upgraded from Dickies and Docs, but the aesthetic is as unchanged as it was in 1992.

The title *Nothing to Say* was pretty apt, and I'm sure even Sherman wouldn't rate it among his best, but it gave me a little bug, seeing it all up close and backstage, and soon I took a playwriting workshop led by a tower-ing, granite-carved playwright named Gladden Schrock. With his smoked leather skin (it seemed he favored generics, which simply said "cigarettes" or perhaps "tobacco" on the design-free packs) and deep voice, Mr. Schrock was our equivalent of Sam Shepard or even Sam Beckett. Gladden instructed with his own language.

"What you gotta do there is mind the ploys and shards!"

"Um . . . okay."

"You don't wanna let the hog onto the picnic blanket there, yes?"

"Of course not."

Soon the director of *Nothing to Say*, a pierced, punk Drama Fuck named Owen Kane, was directing my own offering, *Cool Baby*. It concerns a "fucker" of a poseur writer and his descent into hell, which is filled with even more (and greater) poseur writers, some of them appearing as contestants on a brimstone tinged version of Chuck Barris's *The Dating Game*. The audition flyer read in part, "PS: if you feel like you could be Jack Kerouac, Sylvia Plath or Ernest Hemingway, please come and try out."

Sherman was even harder to beat in late nineties New York than he'd been up at school in the late eighties. At the time I began my "second" play, *Retail Sluts*, Sherman had cofounded a theater company, Malaparte, with the movie star Ethan Hawke. He had budgets, press, fame, everything Jack and I lacked. But I had one think that Sherman didn't: a bête noire and the absolute sleep-sucking, spleen-bleeding spite that it engendered in me.

It's name was . . . *Rent*. God, I hated *Rent*.

It was playing just a few blocks from Andie's Hell's Kitchen halfway house. My mother got tickets. Everyone got tickets to that fucking thing, and out of curiosity, I agreed to join her and my sister for a matinee. I did this a few years earlier when Bobbie Poledouris, Zoe's mother, scored a trio of tickets to see *Blue Man Group*. I hated those blue cocksuckers too, with their faux naïve expressions and all that hippie circle drumming. It reminded me of being back at The Kitchen, starving and burning, as every tourist offered up his stored-up travel nut to be taken in by these ping-pong-ball-spitting charlatans. If you can tie your dick in a knot or make noise with two garbage can lids, there will always be another load of bus-mooks who will line up to share their wages. It's enough to make you hate culture. When I was a kid, I saw *Little Shop of Horrors* at the Orpheum down on St. Mark's and Second Avenue, and Sandra Bernhard's ingenious *Without You I'm Nothing*. Then *Stomp* came in and put a stranglehold on the place. I still sometimes motivate myself to write a new play by thinking, This is the one that's going to evict *Stomp*! Fuck *Stomp* (I've never seen it).

"I've read all about it," my mother said excitedly, as we took our seats at the Nederlander, just a few paces from where Andie, Jack, and I were living. "It's just like your life, Marc."

I'd read all about it too, and the parts that seemed similar to what I'd gone through (struggling for shelter, AIDS panic, the cafés, the heroin, etc.) only made me hate it even more.

The playwright, Jonathan Larson, was getting tons of press for his retelling of Puccini's *La Bohème*, but it's hard to get *bohème* right, and I was only there because I was hoping he'd misstep somehow. Not that I could tell him this. Larson had also bettered me in my ambition to be a great dead writer. He'd perished from an undiagnosed heart ailment, and it's only in hindsight, a decade and a half later, that I can finally see that as tragic. Back then I was too bitter, and even though he was unreachable, I was gunning for the poor guy. The lights came down. The head mics filled with spit. My mother's and sister's teeth came out in wide, fully entertained grins, and my wildest hopes that *Rent* would (in my opinion) blow were met.

What a cloying load of pigshit, I thought as I shifted in my theater seat and the spectacle began. What would Antonin Artuad make of *Rent*? I wish he were here. We'd throw tomatoes. This isn't the New York City I know—junkies and people dealing with HIV and bills with humor and pluck. There's no fucking pluck! Artists don't have pluck! Fuck pluck! This is a fraud! A fraud!

Rent ran forever. *Rent* won the Tony. *Rent*, like Shakespeare, Miller, Sondheim, will be revived as long as there are stages. And nobody will ever know, and few will care, that *Rent* also birthed my career in the thee-ay-tuh. As we filed into the lobby, my mother grabbed me and whispered, "That one guy had a wallet chain, just like yours!" That's all it took. From that point on, I was a playwright. I would not rest until I got "downtown" right. I would steal it back from Larson like U2 stole "Helter Skelter" from Manson.

"No more fucking *Jeopardy*, Andie!" I insisted. "I've got to finish this play."

I wrote *Retail Sluts* in a day and a half in a furious burst of resentment. It concerned a store called Jet Boy, Jet Girl (after the Eton Motello song that Plastic Bertrand sampled for "Ça Plane Pour Moi"). Jet Boy is a store like NaNa in SoHo (although I stole the name Retail Slut from an actual store in Los Angeles) and its staff of fuckups who are all, as I was, pushing thirty: Dommy, a hunky actor who tried to make it in LA before coming back to Jet Boy; Clarence, a gay junkie whose sugar momma buys him Prada and tries to convert him to Christianity and save his soul (by fucking him); and Tony, the manager, who's so tightly wound, he polices the local playground. All three are stuck wondering why they never made it, why they are clocking in and earning minimum wage, how that places a value on them in an expensive and rapidly gentrifying city, what trouble they can get into with such a miniscule sense of self-worth, and how they both hate and need each other. Once I started writing plays, I began to explore the drama section of bookstores, stealing or simply standing and reading whatever I could before being noticed. Joe Orton and Christopher Durang became my two favorite playwrights, so I made sure to scatter a lot of sex and pop commentary throughout the whole thing in search of the right winking, farcical, and brutal, but still affectionate, tone. I basically threw all my anger, jealousy, and frustration into it, and soon that blinking green cursor was moving overtime, skipping across the screen and making a reactionary, punk rock, black comedy: the anti-*Rent*.

When it was finished, I showed it to Andie first. I watched her read it in her faux fur coat, her pretty, light eyes scanning the lines and the stage directions. When she laughed, the weight of the world lifted, then descended until she laughed again. When she nodded, I felt cleaner. When she smiled, I felt like I could possibly purge the junk and slack from my veins and fuck her again.

Jack was next. I was a little nervous, even with Andie's declaration that while not yet "incredible," this was the perfect start. But Jack was actually studying theater. He'd read all the plays I never did. He knew all about *Angels in America*. He was directing plays over at Fordham. Annie, the best actress in school, was devoted to him.

"This is not bad," Jack finally said as we sat in the diner, my turkey meatloaf and mashed potatoes getting cold as I nervously moved the fork around in the pile. Jack hated *Rent* too, even if he knew and could sing its songs verbatim (and on key), like an unofficial understudy.

"Really?"

"It needs work, but . . . it's very funny."

"Oh, whew."

"We should do this?"

"No."

"Yeah, it's good. I can see it."

"Seriously? Where? How? At Fordham?"

"No, they'd never do this at Fordham. Please."

"You mean on the street."

"This is an on-the-street kind of play, Girl."

From the start, we had no class . . . and that was part of our appeal.

In 1998, there was really only one answer if you had a good piece but not a lot of money. We decided to take it over to Aaron Beall, already a downtown legend. We knew of Aaron because Max Fish was basically our clubhouse, and it was just up Ludlow from Aaron's headquarters. Aaron, who was about ten years older than us, had cofounded the Fringe Festival, then expanded his influence outward to include the production office and a series of storefront venues along and around Ludlow. There was the House of Candles, the Piano Store (where the offices were held), and the most famous theater space, Todo Con Nada, where John Leguizamo did many of his early performances.

I saved *Retail Sluts* on a floppy disc and took it over to Kinko's to be copied, then proudly delivered it downtown and left it for Aaron with a note and my voice mail number. I still kept one so that my parents or Bonnie could reach me. I had no phone of my own, but you could maintain your own answering service for about $10 a month back then, and sometimes a message was the only thing that kept me alive. It was never bad news, only good—a girl, a DJ job offer—since I only gave it out personally. It was unlisted. I checked it every day. Aaron never called, so a few days later, I followed up in person, and he happened to be there.

"*You're* Marc Spitz?" he asked.

"Yeah."

He looked me over. "I was hoping you'd look like this."

I wasn't sure what that meant. Apparently Aaron saw my junkie scrawniness, black leather jacket, tight Levi cords, and pointy shoes as marketable.

"I read your play. It's good, but I lost your number."

I looked around at the desks in this narrow storefront. Papers, bills, takeaway containers—utter mess. Suddenly I felt a little better. These people were as messed up as Jack and I were.

"How do we do this?" I asked, perhaps a smidge too eager.

"Why don't we go to the Pink Pony? Have you eaten?"

We went for coffee. Aaron was short, nervous, and fey, with glasses and an impish, bemused, slightly unstrung series of facial expressions that somehow made his conversation partners feel at ease. There were traces of the sixties and seventies hippie-minded theater scene in his aesthetic, his clothes, his demeanor: Richard Foreman, the Living Theater . . . he was old-school but also very Lower East Side hard. He was of Ludlow Street at the time, and that meant hard drugs, fast sex, and glamorous indie rock—an aesthetic a bit harder and less avant-garde than our downtown black box forbearers. Aaron Beall was not unlike like a high school drama teacher gone urban decay—purposeful but a little flaky.

As creative director of his own establishment, he had to support you. It wasn't really about the money or renting the theater. If he liked you, he'd give you the space, and you'd split the box. It was that simple.

"We'll go look at the calendar."

"That's it?" I was going to get to put this up?

He nodded.

"How long did it take you to write?"

"A week?"

"Do you have more?" he asked.

"No, but I have a few ideas."

There was a staff of dedicated theater geeks busying around the Piano Store who didn't seem to have day jobs either. One of them, a director named

Ian Hill, occasionally even slept in one of the prop storage cages in the basement of Todo Con Nada, I suppose to keep out the rats. The space was infested with them. It had been five years since Bennington, and for the first time, I felt like I was back. Only this was better. It was New York City.

Jack came down to meet with Aaron and check out the space. He knew by this point how to get a show from script to stage, how to cast it, and what else we would need: props, a set designer, a stage manager, a light plan. All these things were absolutely foreign to me. He asked the staff every question that needed to be asked. I just sat in Max Fish and nursed my vodka tonic, stared up at Julio, and waited for Jack to join me, only this time we wouldn't be playing pinball or trying to hook up with sex partners; we'd be "producing." Our crew of mostly Bennington kids would provide, as ever, true strength in numbers. But now, instead of bumming out cigarettes or loaning us cash or messing around in some drunken corner, these ex-classmates would operate the board, print up the programs, all of us suddenly feeling newly vital and useful. The industries we'd tried to storm, they'd never let us in, so we would make our own productions. That's how it's done on the Lower East Side after all. It just felt right. Like the B-12 liver and iron shots my grandfather used to boot into my old man's arm. We were energized and free to make something other than a hangover or a bad decision.

By the time we had a production schedule, a cast, and an opening date to work toward, we'd gotten close to some of the key Piano Store people. Ian Hill was friendly and brilliant in his way—a theater visionary who would later excel over in Brooklyn at the Brick. Art Wallace, an eccentric, bearded chap could always be found in the bar next door when we needed some wires connected or had other technical issues, and Kirsten Ames, then Aaron's girlfriend, was working closely with some of the new "alternative comics" who'd frequently perform at the Luna Lounge on the same block, people like Marc Maron. They weren't judgmental. They seemed to appreciate our bad behavior and the fact that we were writing about things we'd actually done. I'm not sure Jonathan Larsen had ever copped a bag of dope. It sure didn't seem that way. One night, during rehearsal for example, I staggered, bloody and dazed, into the Piano Store offices, my shirt torn from my chest and the knees of my cords ripped open. Kirsten was at her desk doing some business.

"What happened to you?" she asked.

"Oh, I fucked some girl I shouldn't have, and I just ran into her boyfriend. He beat me up a little."

"Where?"

"Under the bridge."

"Jesus, do you need a drink?"

"I need a Band-Aid. And a drink, yeah."

I'd slept with the girlfriend of a good friend. It was a shitty thing to do, but she'd more or less initiated it, and it's nearly impossible to say no when that happens, even if I knew I would probably end up paying for it if it got out (and it always gets out). People can't just shut the fuck up about sex, just have it, then forget it. Sure enough, one night I was imbibing peacefully under the melting Julio Iglesias sign at Max when the now hip and furious boyfriend, my new ex-pal, showed up with a purposeful smile on his face.

"Come on," was all he said. I knew it was time to face it like a man. The sex had been really good, and so the punishment was bound to be really good too . . . just not for me.

He marched me out there after finding me at Max Fish, knocked me to the ground, threw some punches, and spit in my face. I remember shouting for help and hearing my voice travel out over the water and grow thinner and thinner. Nobody was coming to help me, so I just closed my eyes and took it.

"If I ever see you again, you're gonna get the same thing," he promised, but that wasn't going to happen. We both drank at Max Fish. He would probably see me again the next night.

I knew Aaron was going to hear about this from Kirsten and that it would only enhance Jack's and my image as authentic, rough-and-tumble artists. We were bad people who under different circumstances would sneak-thief away with the box office, but it seemed like maybe we'd found the one place where we could stay a while, do some work for the first time since Bennington, and not get chucked out after four years, just as we were peaking. Todo Con Nada . . . the Ludlow Street theater scene was like our graduate studies program; Aaron, Kirsten, Ian, and Art were our new shambolic but righteous faculty. And a half decade after my sputtering attempt to take it whole, all of New York City was suddenly available again.

"You're not a very good person are you?" Kirsten laughed. I shook my head. "You're lucky you're funny."

I was funny alright, born funny, brought up funny, but I never considered myself all that lucky, what with one failure after another. All that was about to change.

CHAPTER 11

The way in is almost never the way you think it's going to be. Growing up, music was all I really cared about. I treated even a Top 40 radio hit, say, Laura Branigan's "Gloria," studiously. But I never thought I'd be a rock writer, even as I read *Rolling Stone* and *Creem* religiously. I was fiercely proud of my record collection and could shoot my mouth off about which were a certain band's best and worst albums, who had the best count in ("1-2-3-4") of all time, and all manner of rock boy trivia and ephemera, but there was a long and lingering self-consciousness there too. The rock writers I grew up reading—Lester Bangs, Nick Kent, Nick Tosches, Cameron Crowe, Dave Marsh, David Fricke, Chuck Eddy, Jaan Uhelszki, Anthony De Curtis, Kurt Loder, Jon Savage, Julie Burchill, Charles Schaar Murray, Paul Morley, Lisa Robinson, John Pareles, and, of course, "The Dean," Robert Christgau—all seemed like other voices in my own head. I got it. The sound and attitude and style of rock and roll were so satisfying and natural to me that I always assumed I would be a musician. I had the anger, and sometimes only facts and thoughts about bands could quell it—even when I was five or six and made mental notes about which Beatle sang what.

> John: "Please, Mr. Postman"
> Paul: "All My Loving"
> George: "Don't Bother Me"
> Ringo: "Boys," "I Wanna Be Your Man"

The Fabs weren't even that far away from the 1970 breakup. Lorne Michaels hadn't offered them three grand to reunite on *Saturday Night Live* yet. In my childhood bedroom in Queens, The Beatles had never split anyway. They were as alive as they'd ever been to me. I lived in that fold-out poster that came with the *White Album*. I was eight, and we'd just moved into the bigger house in Lawrence when I saw the crawl across the bottom of our TV screen

208

one afternoon announcing that Elvis Presley had been found dead in Memphis. I was watching *The Creature from the Black Lagoon* on the brown, shag carpeted floor and eating a Twinkie.

"Elvis is dead!" I shouted as I ran up the stairs. "Elvis is dead! Mom! Dad! Elvis! Elvis!"

But Elvis remained a living thing, or living King, in my bedroom as well. So did Brian Jones, Janis Joplin, Jimi Hendrix, Sid Vicious, and Jim Morrison. When I was eleven, Jim was on the cover of *Rolling Stone*: "He's hot, he's sexy and he's dead," the infamous tagline ran. No, he's not. He's right here. His face is red, and he's staring at me from the cover of The Doors' *Greatest Hits*. My friend Jim. Mr. Mojo Risin'. I could identify the sound of Stevie's harmonica versus Bob's versus Bruce's and was proud of that when nothing else made me feel proud.

I had a rock-and-roll taxonomy that helped me understand the world as much as my parents (then still together) or teachers did. I had all the Stones records too. One year for Chanukah, my mother and father gave me a new LP for each of the eight nights. Of course, the Stones were still active, still making hits. *Some Girls* had just come out, and "Miss You" was on the radio all summer. Growing up in the seventies, it was impossible not to be swept up by these absolutely enormous personalities. Mick Jagger, Paul McCartney, Elton John, Alice Cooper, Freddie Mercury, Donna Summer, KISS, and even Sha Na Na, whose variety show I never missed, seemed colossal, like superheroes or Japanese movie monsters. The next logical step would be to pick an instrument and learn to play, then to open my throat and speak to the beat, maybe find some friends who felt the same way and give ourselves a name . . . put that name on the kick drum, and it would be accomplished. But I had no talent as a musician. None.

I took one and only one drum lesson at age fourteen. My teacher was a longhaired classic rock fan who played a Keith Moon–style vintage Premier kit in a soundproofed studio in the back of a small music shop over in Hewlett. Nobody but him could sit at that one, but the kid had a smaller, red Pearl kit, which was relatively new. That's what he gave lessons on. My mother drove me over. She figured it was a healthy way to vent aggression, to bang on something again and again and again. When she picked me up an hour later, however, and asked, "How'd it go?" I flatly informed her that I was never going to see that bastard drum teacher again.

"I don't like his attitude," was all I'd disclose. The truth was, he intimidated me. He kept a pack of cigarettes rolled up in the sleeve of his T-shirt, and they shifted as he played a simple beat on his tom.

Boom bap bap. Ba-boom-bap bap.

Then he handed the stick to me and said, "Do what I just did."

I guess he was testing my ear. I had, and still have, good recall for a beat or a hook and easily duplicated it.

Boom bap bap. Ba-boom-bap bap.

I handed the stick back to him proudly. I was that much closer to rock-and-roll stardom.

Then he added the hi-hat cymbal, and that's where my career in percussion went off the radar, never to be detected again.

Boom bap bap. Crash. Ba-bom-bap bap. Crash. Ba-boom-bap bap.

"Try it a little fast this time, okay?"

Boom bap bap. Crash. Ba-bap bap. Crash.

"Okay, one more time."

Boom. Crash. Boom boom boom boom. Bap.

"Are you a lefty or a righty?" he asked.

"I'm ambidextrous," I answered.

"I don't think you are."

I felt like a piece of shit and began to sweat.

"Are you coordinated?" he finally asked after seventeen attempts to get me to combine more than one piece of his rudimentary kit.

"What do you mean, like sports?"

"Do you play sports?"

What did sports have to do with anything? I wanted to play rock and roll because I didn't like playing sports.

"It's okay," I told my mother. "Most of the bands I listen to program all their drums anyway. I'll just get a synthesizer."

"So, you'll take piano lessons," she said, and patted my shoulder to try to cheer me up. "I took piano lessons."

"Synth."

"Isn't that a piano? I mean, isn't it the same thing?"

"A synth can sound like a piano, but a piano can't emulate the sound of a synth."

Suddenly I was John Cage or Philip Glass . . . an expert and a visionary.

With piano lessons, the teacher came to you. We already had the Steinway piano in the living room. It had belonged to my grandparents, Reggie and Charlie, and was the very same instrument that my mother had taken her lessons on as a child, but it had been furniture, and nothing but, for twenty-five years. My mother kept potted plants on the thing. It wasn't in tune. It was just furniture. My mother found a reasonably priced piano teacher through the

Pennysaver, and happily my attempt to master the 88s lasted much longer than the drum lessons—that is to say, for four lessons.

My teacher, Mr. Lawrence, was in his sixties. He had so much hair coming out of his nostrils that he seemed mustachioed even though he was clean shaven. He had onion breath and wore the same tan corduroy sport coat, blue shirt, and navy tie each time. The ensemble smelled like cedar. He brought his own sheet music in a leather folder. He removed the pages and spread them on the wooden stand. The first song we learned was called "Start Today."

"It's appropriate, yes?" he joked.

Whatever, I thought, as I followed his fingers across the keys, and again my recall made it seem deceptively easy at first. As my mother eavesdropped from the nearby kitchen, Mr. Lawrence sang the words with onions, and we played "Start Today," again and again. I read the lyric sheet as we "jammed."

"Sing a tune . . . play a tune," the song went.

That's not really a rhyme, I thought, and lost my bearing. Rhyming 'tune' with 'tune.' You can't rhyme a word with the same word. It's bullshit. Bullshit!

I was bored. I wanted to hold the synth cord in my mouth like Jimmy Destri of Blondie in the "Heart of Glass" music video. "Start Today?" "Heart and Soul?" These songs didn't rock. And the lyrics were just lazy, weren't they? Lyrics are important.

I always felt more comfortable with a song's words than its music and already sensed that a witty turn by, say, Steely Dan ("Don't Take Me Alive," "Hey Nineteen"), Randy Newman ("My Life Is Good," "Short People"), Elvis Costello (everything), Warren Zevon (*Excitable Boy*), and my favorite songwriters, Chris Difford and Glenn Tilbrook of Squeeze (*"I'm playing your Stereogram, singles remind me of kisses, albums remind me of plans"* is still one of the top-ten best lyrics ever written, if you ask me) were literary. Soon, Morrissey and the early hip-hop of Run-DMC, Slick Rick, and Beastie Boys would deliver similar and even more tangible thrills. I understood where these words came from—I got the mentality and agility behind them—whereas I couldn't keep a simple drum beat or master Hamlisch's "The Entertainer," the theme from *The Sting* on the 88s.

More than anything else, people writing to me via my website or social pages ask, "How did you become a rock critic, and how can I break in?" Some even find my address and send me handwritten letters. I never really have an answer because, in my head, I'm not a rock critic, even though I've "been in this business a minute," like Jay Z says. In my head, I'm just another failed musician.

It seems preposterous today, and certainly wasn't the case in the sixties and seventies, but in late 1997, being a rock writer could be a career: with a salary, health insurance, expenses, and a 401(k). Lester never had that option. I doubt even Jann Wenner had that option when he began. But when I got in, it was a job-job, and Lord knows I needed one.

In mid-fall of 1997, Andie, through her many record-industry connections, got tickets to see a taping of a show called *Sessions at West 54th Street*. It was kind of a New York version of *Austin City Limits*: highbrow singer-songwriters playing in an intimate setting for well-connected urbanites. Beck and Fiona Apple were going to be playing the next series, performing in an intimate round at the Sony Music Studios. I too had dived deep into Beck's last album, *Odelay*, as every good hipster was almost obliged to do, and Fiona Apple, what can you say about her talent? It was the kind that caused hushes. While waiting in line, I noticed Ron Richardson, my fellow ex-employee from Shakespeare & Co., and went over to say hello. It'd been well over a year since I'd left in disgrace. He'd graduated from the New School and was working at *Spin* (Fiona was currently the cover star) in a department then mysteriously referred to as "new media," the way one today might say, "Black ops."

"You mean like chat rooms?" I knew what those were. Chat rooms. Message boards. Green-lit friendly zones where you didn't "flame," or shout, when killing time in House of Trance wishing you had heroin instead of bad E and Gatorade.

"Kind of," Ron said, as ever, with total patience.

"Anyway, it's good to see you. Let's stay in touch."

We exchanged numbers and promised to follow up, but I didn't think much of it. People did this all the time in Manhattan, and in the days before Facebook, they almost never actually kept in touch. I didn't anyway. It was too hard tracking someone down, finding a quarter, leaving a message, getting a message. You needed . . . a quarter. A phone. Plus, Ron was my past. When you've moved on, you don't look back. Ron was good people, but if I wanted to drink with him, if it was important to my soul or my career, I figured, I'd have long ago found him, and I'd be drinking with the guy. I'm sure he felt the same. New York was too big and fast.

But a few days later, Ron actually called my voice mail number and asked if I was interested in interviewing for a job at *Spin*. Donna Moran, the *Spin* radio news editor for the brand's recently launched radio and website ventures, the latter called *SPIN*online (which only AOL subscribers could access at the time), was overtaxed and had reached out for some kind of gal Friday. Ron thought of me, but I'm sure I was not his first choice. He knew how I'd behaved at Shakespeare. I was unmanageable, termite-like, wild and disrespectful. But given our postwork conversations over the jukebox at Mona's and the Holiday, he also knew that I was nice on the mic when it came to the rock knowledge. The Other Music clerks had little on me. In his mind, I was a risk, but I was also a steal. Ron Richardson had his eye on the twenty-first century and secretly fretted that Donna, cheerful and competent as she was, was more *Circus* 1977 than *Spin* 2000. AC/DC, Zeppelin, Thin Lizzy, these were her favorite bands. And the one closest to her heart, the one that stood above them all, was KISS. No wonder she needed a break, filing stories about Sneaker Pimps, Marcy Playground, Our Lady Peace, and Snot. In fairness to Donna, KISS had recently reunited with Ace and Peter, in full makeup, and they'd been the cover stars of the August 1996 issue of *Spin*: four different covers, one of Ace, one of Paul, one of Peter, and one of Gene, in tribute to their four 1978 solo albums.

Walking into the *Spin* office on Eighteenth Street between Fifth and Sixth Avenues was a strange experience. Peering through the various old issues that lined the hallway, some of them already iconic, like the one that declared J Mascis (no longer Eric Clapton) God. Another nodded to Juliana Hatfield's celebrated virginity ("Like a Virgin Juliana Hatfield Gives It Up"). Neil Young's artist-of-the-year cover. Perry Farrell's. I had bought every one of these issues the week they hit the stands and committed much of their contents to memory. I studied the mastheads: Burroughs, Tosches, Terry Southern, Elvis Mitchell, Elvis Presley (he'd been named the "advice editor" because of the *Dear Elvis* column that ran in the eighties), Chuck Eddy, Michael O'Donoghue . . . fuck. I thought of the swimsuit issues, where stars like LL Cool Jay (on a surfboard), The Weather Girls, and Johnny Cash mocked that whole Sports Illustrated jock and babe mentality. Tom Tomorrow. Little Sutty. Cisco and Egbert. Henry Rollins on the glory of 7/11 ("How many people can you depend on 24 hours a day, 7 days a week? Cyndi Lauper? Nastassja Kinski? Do they have a 16 oz. coffee with your name on it?") How many artists I had never heard of in the eighties and early nineties until *Spin* folk like Bonz Malone, Richard Gehr, John Leland, and Jonathan Bernstein told me about them. The Mary Chain, Fela, Camper Van Beethoven, Mojo Nixon, John Trubee, and the Ugly Janitors of America (whoever they were, it didn't even matter). Morrissey was on one cover. Robert Smith was on another. Much of my teenage sensibility had been formed right here in this room, I thought.

Actually, the room where my teenage sensibility was formed was a few floors up. The magazine offices were divided into two separate floors, each the size of a loft apartment.

Wow, these rock critics are really well dressed, I thought, as I made my way through the cubicles and saw various slick-looking, very adult folks in power suits walking around busily, cell phones pressed to their ears. I was so green, I didn't realize that they were ad salesmen and executive assistants. Magazines run (or used to, anyway) on cigarette and sneaker ads and buys from record companies looking to sell the new Veruca Salt or Built to Spill album. And here I was inside. Perfect from now on, indeed.

Nobody looked up at me as I took my seat in the conference room, but it didn't matter. I'd entered the sixth dimension. I wasn't leaving without its secrets. Ron Richardson came in with Fred McIntyre, a neat, stocky man who looked like the kind of guy who signed for merchandise at a grocery store or hardware store in some fifties TV show—rolled-up work shirt, chinos, unflashy brown shoes. Fred was an old-school punk who would play Operation Ivy and Fugazi out of his little office. He'd figured out how to earn a living without giving that up: put on a tie. Just put on a tie, get a haircut, and there you were, closet punk with salary. Even before the coming Internet boom had fully detonated, you could be a comfortable iconoclast with a dental plan.

Fred and Ron had found a way to rebel without starving, and I wanted in. The conference room's windows were covered with boxes and boxes of back issues and merchandise: T-shirts, visors, beer coasters, mouse pads, key chains, and office supplies.

"Ron tells me you're a talented guy and you know the magazine real well."

I looked over at Ron, who was giving me a "Don't fuck this up, I'm sticking my neck out" stare. He really had no idea which Marc Spitz was going to show up: Would this be some ultimate act of self-destruction, or would I check all that attitude and just be myself for ten minutes? Was I smart enough to do that? Ron's eyes scanned my hairless jawline. I'd shaved. Good sign.

"Yes," I finally said, "I've been reading it since I was sixteen. Every issue. Never missed one." This was not my jaded Jim Carroll voice. I was keeping that tamped down, in the same way I once trained myself to not talk like a "lawn-guyland-uh."

There would be plenty of time to be a punk rock dickhead if I got in. I just needed the key: the path out of the cold and into wherever it was these two dudes ate their lunch.

"Me too," Fred said.

"Even the Charlie Sexton issue?" I offered, pushing it perhaps a bit too far.

"Hey, don't knock Charlie Sexton," Ron said and laughed nervously. Was I taking the piss?

"Oh, I'm being totally sincere," I insisted. "'Beat's So Lonely'? I still DJ it all the time."

Ron looked relieved again.

"Oh, you DJ?" Fred asked.

"Yeah. Vinyl only." Fred looked impressed. All those nights lugging my crates up the stairs or feeling the leather strap of my DJ bag dig into the flesh of my shoulder, they'd all been worth it. I looked Fred in the eye. I could count on one hand how many people I've made eye contact with in the past decade.

"I don't really know what you want to achieve with the site, but I can promise you that if you give me this job, I will work hard for you every day," I told Fred.

"Good," Fred said, then turned to Ron.

"Let's get him squared with Donna."

What did that mean? That was good, right? Fred stood up and offered his hand. I shook it and nodded respectfully. Fred left, and Ron and I sat there.

"What was that?" Ron asked.

"Did I do okay?"

"Yeah," Ron laughed.

"Cool," I said, Jim Carroll's drawl slowly returning to my voice. I had to exhale and let him back in. He was a feisty foe.

"So, what the fuck kind of job is this anyway, man?"

Ron frowned and nodded his head. "He" was back.

"Content generator. Increase traffic."

"Right." I had no idea what that meant. Content? Traffic?

"We're looking for counterbalance," Ron said. "We can be a miniversion of the magazine, but what's the point? We can be so much more. The Web gives us the freedom to be a bit irreverent."

I could be irreverent. I didn't revere anything.

It seemed like the print edition of *Spin*, thicker than ever with the afore-mentioned ads still fueled by the post-Nirvana big-money alt. boom, was concerned about either being upstaged or scooped—or worse, made to look uncool—by the lowly website. New media was, at the time, just some slimy lamprey sucking on the big, sleek, modern rock shark as it cruised the ocean looking for ad buys. There was no money in it. No prestige. The business model of the record industry didn't support it. Maybe some of the smarter editors were prescient and saw technology bending away from the classical model, but they certainly didn't treat Ron like someone who was about to come into power. It might have been a case of "Let's all keep our jobs for another few years, shall we? Maybe this thing will pass." Herve's beloved hypertext, after all, was supposed to change publishing, then turned into a footnote or a fad. Virtual reality was supposed to enable us to dine with Gandhi or have sex with Jayne Mansfield, but that never really took off either. Nobody was quite sure where the new technology would take the magazine, if anywhere at all. It was an era of healthy suspicion. All eyes were on The Prodigy that very autumn as they were supposedly going to revolutionize music with their aggro electronica, but what if they didn't (they didn't). Madonna signed the trio (fronted by the pierced, snarling cyberclown Keith Flint), but despite excellent singles like "Smack My Bitch Up" and "Breathe," they didn't break in America. Neither did the equally worthy Daft Punk or Chemical Brothers.

The best-trafficked rock-and-roll websites of the era, *Sonicnet*, *Allstar*, and even the soon-to-be-iconic *Pitchfork*, were still finding their feet, and *Billboard* was mostly a repository for straight trade and business stories and stats. There was no *Gawker* or *Huffington*; music blogs like *Gorilla Vs. Bear*, *Aquarium Drunkard*, *Stereogum*, *Brooklyn Vegan*, *Miss Modernage*, or *ProductshopNYC* were far over the horizon. All "new media" bets, as far as I could tell from my short time inside the bubble, were either off or being seriously hedged. Nobody wanted to be a Luddite, but they weren't exactly throwing loot at the *Spin* site either.

I was hired to blog, only I didn't know it at the time. There was no formal word describing my job. But it was a job. A job at *Spin*. I wasn't expecting anyone to congratulate me in the hallway or on the way to the elevator. I was half hoping to run into Julia Chaplin, the cool hunter I'd met at the Holiday Cocktail Lounge four years earlier. "Look," I'd say. "I made it. I'm in too!"

But she wasn't there, and nobody else looked up. My life had just changed. And nobody cared.

I wandered into the trendy but empty Coffee Shop and called my mother from the pay phone by the toilets, which reeked of ammonia. She wasn't home. Then I called Andie, but she wasn't home, and neither was Jack. I thought about calling Julie Bowen or Justin, but that seemed a bit much. If I gloated, maybe Ron or Fred would pick up on the bad karmic vibe and call my voice mail to tell me they'd had second thoughts. I didn't know what to do. It was like being drugged. I walked around the Virgin Megastore to escape the cold, and browsed through the new CDs, thinking about the stacks of free, promotional CDs on Ron's desk, and action figures, books, videotapes. It was like Christmas every day in that office.

"I just got hired by *Spin*," I said as shoppers milled through the aisles. "I just got hired by *Spin*." Nobody paid any attention. I needed to tell someone, so I called Adrienne Shelly and let her know that I would finally be able to pay her back the money she'd loaned me two years earlier.

"*Spin* magazine." You know the magazine you French-kissed Evan Dando on the cover of? That one. That one!"

"Congratulations."

"I want to break up with my girlfriend! Did I just say that?"

I blurted it out. I didn't even know it was coming.

"Huh?"

"Nothing, sorry. I'm . . . scattered."

"Why don't you come over?"

We went to sit in the small, sunny park across from Magnolia Bakery, facing a local playground full of slides and monkey bars. We drank coffee and watched the happily playing toddlers.

"God, those kids are cute." I loved the world. I loved coffee. I loved New York, and the sun for giving us warmth and light. I hated my girlfriend. I didn't hate anything about her in particular. She was beautiful. Kind. Encouraging. I hated myself for being there in the first place . . . for having needed someone beautiful, kind, encouraging. I didn't anymore.

"It's better to end it now," Adrienne said.

"But am I not being a dick? I just got the job. Isn't that like the guy whose band goes platinum and he dumps his longtime girlfriend for Winona Ryder overnight?"

"She's not your longtime girlfriend."

"It's true."

"And she's not your wife. Look at those people." We saw a mother and father pull their kid off the ground and simulate flight, the mother grabbing the right arm lovingly, the father grabbing the other as the kid let loose a whoop.

"You don't have that do you?"

"No. I mean, I'll miss her pug."

"Pull off the Band-Aid, Marc," Adrienne advised. "She'll respect you for it. And you'll be doing her a favor."

I figured that maybe one day, in the distant future, that might be true, but for now I knew I was in for a battle. Whether I was up for it or not, I wasn't sure. *Spin* had given me back my balls in a flash. Did I have to get them kicked in on the same day?

"You're not taking those. You're not taking anything. In fact, you're not leaving!" Andie screamed.

"Oh yes I am."

It got bad very quickly, then worse once I'd told her that I got hired . . . and that I was moving out that night. I'd already packed, but she pulled the sweaters out of the bag, along with everything else she'd bought me and some clothes I'd acquired myself.

"This isn't working. Come on. You know that."

"Oh, now it's not working? It was working yesterday when you had no *Spin* job."

"No, it wasn't. We were just pretending."

"You gave me AIDS."

"We slept together twice. With a condom. Also, I don't have AIDS."

"You have something. You look like shit. You're doing heroin."

"I'm not."

"You're stealing from me. You're taking my money and buying heroin drugs!"

"No."

Yes. But not anymore. I was gainfully employed. The future was happening now. Everything was different. On the cab uptown, I actually buckled my seat belt! I had something to lose.

I knew I had to get out of there. Finally I just made a mental commitment to fuck the clothes. Fuck everything. Just go. I left in my stocking feet—well, one stocking foot. I'd find another shoe somewhere. I'd buy one with my first *Spin* paycheck. I knocked on Jack's door.

"I'm leaving," I said.

"I hear." The whole building could hear. I'd have asked him if I could crash, but she owned that apartment too.

"You wanna go up to the Bronx?" I asked, wondering if maybe I could stay with him and his mom for a few days.

"You better call Tyrone," he said, reading me with a bit of Baduizsm. I called Bennington Ron instead. His door was always open. It was back to Brooklyn, but that seemed okay this time. My life seemed to have changed in an instant after that simple meeting, and I had no idea what was going to happen next. "I love waking up in the morning and not knowing what's going to happen," Leonardo DiCaprio's Jack Dawson, the Bohemian tramp steamer traveler, tells a table full of stuffy first-class passengers in *Titanic*. He's in a borrowed tux and clearly out of place, but he's convinced Kate Winslet's Rose not to jump overboard, and so he's being rewarded with a dinner before being sent back to steerage. "Who I'm going to meet. Where I'm going to wind up." Sitting in the theater in Park Slope, only days into what would end up being a full decade at *Spin*, I felt the same way.

CHAPTER 12

Spin was in transition as well when I arrived in the winter of 1997. Bob Guccione Jr., the founder and editor in chief, had just sold it and many of the original staff, including well-known writers like Legs McNeil were no longer there. A freelancer, Staci Bonner, who'd worked there in the early nineties, filed a lawsuit claiming harassment and discrimination and the court case that spring drew tons of negative publicity and a split verdict on a series of charges. Nobody spoke of the suit despite the surplus of press when I first arrived; either they were sworn to silence or most likely simply wished to move ahead, salvage the magazine's reputation. A new editor in chief, Michael Hirschorn, who'd been at *New York* magazine, was hired to take the magazine, founded in 1985, into the twenty-first century. Always brattier, funnier, and smarter than most music magazines, *Spin* under Hirschorn would be even more of an upstart affair. It'd be the smartest kid in class, the one you kind of wanted to beat on but who also helped you get through the day with its insight and wisecracks. When I got there, *Spin* was literally taking *Rolling Stone* on, publishing in its March 1998 issue an unauthorized *South Park* cover story set to hit newsstands at the same time as *Stone*'s sanctioned feature. Ours featured the hit Comedy Central show's Chef character grabbing portly Cartman's boy boobs in a parody of *Stone*'s famous Janet Jackson cover from the fall of 1993. *Spin* took its cues from eighties cultural piss takers like New York's *Spy* and San Francisco's *Might*. The unspoken message was that we were taking the piss out of it because we loved it. The magazine was growing a little more sophisticated with each issue under Michael and his editors, like Dave Moodie, the darkly handsome, puckish and wry features editor, who was actually a cofounder of *Might* along with Dave Eggers. While I still dressed like an arrested art school boy, Moodie, Hirschorn, and writer-turned-editor Craig Marks dressed like urban preps. They always seemed to be smirking at some inside joke that nobody else would ever get, and I wanted to hear the punch line too. Hirschorn's new batting order also included a half dozen genuine rock writer stars, and I'd read incredible stories by them all. Sia Michel was lithe, blonde, and intense. She had written one of the last profiles of Biggie Smalls before he was shot in March of the previous year. Her then boyfriend Charles Aaron was the archetype of an astute indie rock writer, a young iconoclast in his academic glasses, flannel shirt, and carefully chosen merch T-shirts, like he threw away nine out of the ten that were sent over by the labels because they were insulting. Charles had interviewed Bob Stinson of The Replacements shortly before he died, and as with Sia and B.I.G., nobody would ever be able to make that claim again. He took the singles column over from John Leland, another "Classic era *Spin*" legend, like Legs. The power structure was shifting from those who were there at the beginning to those who either freelanced or worked their way up the masthead during the first part of the nineties and now had offices and real say as far as what went in and what didn't. I studied each new issue, which I now got weeks before any of my friends, wondering how one became "one of those guys." There were articles on trepanning (literally, drilling a hole in one's skull), fashion spreads with themes like flies and Jesus, and lots and lots of Radiohead coverage. They were making the jump from Britpop also-rans to game-changing futurists in the wake of *OK Computer*. Missy Elliott and Timbaland were doing the same for hip-hop. I wanted to be a futurist too, like Simon Reynolds, who was around as well, pale and bespectacled and boyish. Simon used to write for *Melody Maker*. He'd actually covered the Stone Roses and Happy Mondays at their peak. Sometimes a writer whose name I recognized from the masthead would wander in for a meeting with an editor, and I'd linger and eavesdrop: Oh, that's what Mike Rubin looks like. Look! There's Jonathan Bernstein or Kim France.

Going back down to the online hub was painful. No legends were eating lunch there; there were barely any employees. Here's the thing about a place like *Spin* or any supposedly cool or enlightened public brand and private community of like-minded artists and writers, a place that from the outside looks like the best record store you could ever hope to work or hang out in, where the records are all free and sometimes the artists themselves come and give them to you: it's still fucking high school rules. The cool kids (in this case, the editorial staff and art department) only mixed with the other cool kids both in the office and at night at rock shows and bars. And when they dealt with the publicists, they only dealt with the cool ones from major labels like Interscope, Columbia, Warner Brothers, or the big indies, like Matador or Sub Pop, and the independent publicity firms, like Girlie Action and Nasty Little Man, who had major artists like Beastie Boys on their roster.

It's why eventually, we, the established print rock press, were all sucker punched by the blogosphere bands. Nobody saw them coming because the old, rigid high school cool system had not been fully torn down yet. And so the labels did what they always did: they scrambled to sign everyone, but by that point everything there was to know about Beirut or Clap Your Hands Say Yeah, or whoever the fuck else was known and had been heard. *Spin* of the early 2000s had no idea whom to cover, how much space to give them, or even if they were any good or particularly cover worthy. People can dispute this, but I was in those meetings. We were asking interns what was cool. The confidence was gone. But back in 1997, short-lived as it was destined to be, it was there in abundance.

The high school social hierarchy naturally left dozens and dozens of disenfranchised writers, freelancers, and publicists for smaller, less cool labels like TVT or indies like Shorefire standing hungrily at the window, smelling the pie and wondering how they were going to tell their artists that they weren't going to get a feature in the April issue. Once I got to *Spin*, and the website slowly became a bit more readable and funny, they could say, "But I got you the next best thing . . . a full interview in *SPIN*online. How about that! *SPIN*online. It's their 'website'!" A small posse of the ambitious but unwanted nursed each other through this culture of rejection and this became my first social circle as a rock writer. The only thing we had in common, besides the slow realization that our collective dream jobs of working in rock were not going to necessarily satisfy us, was that we all bowed to Marti Zimlin. Marti was the Queen of the Modern Age's cusp and she taught me the basics of the high school-ish rock business with speed and precision like a Kung Fu master instructs on razor star throwing. In a word, Marti taught me "juice." Juice kept the big machine humming.

"You have no juice, Marc Spitz," she observed early on. She always referred to me by my full name said as if it were one word: Marcspitz. "Got no j-you-ice. That's your problem. You need to get the juice, Marc Spitz."

Marti had worked at the music site *Sonicnet* for three years and had amassed the connections through a combination of charm, persistence, and a little intimidation. She was just fierce and the idea of saying no to her was enough to set even the hardest rapper quaking. She spent all her money on clothes, and her style, big black glasses and loud voice, put rock stars at ease. She was as big as they were so they could relax. That was the key to juice: size and symmetry. You can't make a rock star feel self-conscious about being mega. Marti picked up friendships with members of Depeche Mode, the Cure, and the Wu Tang Clan. Sonicnet had their shit down, in part because they were conceived as a web entity and not an offshoot of an established print brand, trying to thrive in the shadows. In Marti's eyes, Ron Richardson wasn't floundering in his attempts to get respect for *Spin*'s "New Media" because it wasn't the future; she knew it was. She had no problem telling the purists who were holding out for print coverage, say Richard Ashcroft from the then surging Verve, that they were fucked in the brain and were going to get left behind if they didn't start behaving like Radiohead right quick. Ron, according to Marti, was failing because he lacked the "juice, man."

So how does one acquire the juice, once you understand its necessity and respect it's power? Well, you have to attract raw attention, be big, move big, spend your paycheck at boutiques a la Marti, look sharp, and act like you know even if you have no idea. This wasn't the Holiday bar or some Brooklyn kegger anymore. This was the show. None other than Courtney Love had offered Marti a job as her personal assistant, but she'd turned it down because she didn't wanna pick up "Courtney laundry."

In the old *Spin* offices on Eighteenth Street between Fifth and Sixth Avenues, the online department was such an afterthought that we weren't even on the same floor as editorial. We shared space with accounting and ad sales a flight below. Any excuse I could find to go up to the edit department, I would take. I delivered messages and mail. Sometimes I'd just take the elevator up and say to whoever happened to pass, "I'm going on a coffee run. Anybody want anything from the bodega?" It seemed so much more exciting up there. The light was better, the music louder, the people more glamorous. I befriended a pair of research department editors, Greg Milner and Andy Gensler, and was soon comfortable sitting in either of their desk chairs, chatting on my breaks and sometimes when I should have been trolling the Web or calling publicists for news stories. Always the hooky player . . . always looking for something better, I guess. From this vantage point, I got the lay of the open warehouse space with its multiple cubicles and closet offices.

I could see into Hirschorn's office, past the desk of his beautiful and hip assistant Victoria De Silverio. I didn't need a reason to come into work every day, as I did at Shakespeare & Co., but on days when even the dream job felt like a grind, I thought of Vicki's face (as I had of Christina Kirk's a few years earlier). She was petite and dark haired, with a desk full of monkeys. Vicki collected them: monkey key chains, monkey mugs. She was seriously dating Walter from the post-hardcore band Quicksand at the time and seemed utterly unattainable. So, of course, I began to obsess. I was finally off the street. I was writing—all day, every day—and getting paid for it. But because it

wasn't on a piece of glossy paper, and because Dr. Dre's and Metallica's publicists didn't say hello to me when they came into the office, none of it
seemed legitimate. It was like getting just the bread, none of the meat and
cheese. You can technically survive on it, but everyone around you is enjoying sandwiches.

A dozen times a day, I filed copy over to my boss, Donna Moran, the KISS
fan, who would edit it and post it on the site. It was clean, but the voice wasn't
necessarily mine. This was pop pap, meant to be read by chinless DJs clad in
the merch Charles Aaron sent back. They'd read my words over the airwaves
on the one hundred different "alt. rock" stations that had popped up in the
mass-format shift that preceded grunge and then pop punk and whitey ska.
Once Nirvana and Green Day and, most recently, No Doubt started selling
tens of millions of records, light, classic rock, and Spanish stations suddenly
started getting hip to Dickies and wallet chain rock. Now swing was the in
sound, but it was almost a given, even among the most culturally thickheaded,
that this was not built for longevity. Those zoot suits were going to look
pretty silly in a few months.

Everything that went on the site or over the wire had to be qualified:
   "Aging Jewish folk-singing legend Bob Dylan . . ."
   "Headband-favoring dead guitarist Jimi Hendrix"
   "Deceased junkie poop-eater GG Allin . . ."
   "Son of God, Jesus Christ . . ."
   "Legendary rock wild man Iggy Pop, who has acted in films such as *The
Crow 2* and *The Color of Money*, will make his outer space debut on *Star Trek*
spinoff *Deep Space Nine.*"

Now, one could describe Iggy Pop in a lot of ways, and surely "legendary
rock wild man" is one of them, but really, would you want to write twelve of
these sound bites a day? Every once in a while, I'd be steered toward a band I
would otherwise have ignored since it was enjoying big hits: Marcy Playground, Gin Blossoms, and because our AOL point person out in California
clearly had a crush on Johnny Rzeznik, the front man for the Goo Goo Dolls,
who had the same hair as Jennifer Aniston from *Friends*. To be fair, they did
have the biggest hit in the country, the ballad "Iris," from the soundtrack to
City of Angels, the crap Hollywood remake of *Wings of Desire*.

   "I have a scoop for you on the Goo Goo Dolls," she'd e-mail me. "Johnny
Rzeznik makes a really delicious lemon-drop cocktail."

   "Kill me."

   "Run with that, okay? I was backstage, and I had one."

Drill a hole in my skull, I thought.

And this counted for political:

"Pop sensations Chumbawamba used their performance on *Late Show with David Letterman* to air some political grievances. The anarchist group chanted 'Mumia Abu Jamal' at the end of their appearance, causing the show's producers considerable stress."

Pop sensations? I adored "Tubthumping" for the fluke hit that it was, but "pop sensations"? Once qualified, everything had to be hyphenated, pre-chewed, and placed on the shit conveyor belt. There was no j-you-ice to be had churning out this rubbish.

There was nothing "ur" or "meta" about it either, and I wanted to be ur and meta too, just like my new writer heroes one flight above. I didn't even know what "ur" or "meta" meant; I'd only overheard Dave Moodie use it in sentences. Still, I was grateful and a good soldier for our little reserve army. I went for sandwiches and supplies for Donna and sorted through her mail and promotional CDs to figure out which she would want to keep and which to sell at the Academy Records store directly downstairs. I even accompanied her to a guitar show where Paul Stanley was signing autographs. Donna wasn't the problem. She was perfectly nice, if a little intensity deficient. When you go to an arena rock show and look back at the rest of the crowd, you will see fifteen thousand Donna Morans. She was a basic, good-hearted, sincere rock-and-roll fan who could have just as easily worked for an insurance company by day. She didn't seem to live and die for it. It didn't haunt her the way it plagued Jack and me.

I also cleaned and organized all the cardboard boxes in the conference room where I had my interview with Ron and Fred. When Snoop Dogg came by for a Web chat, I'd run out to fill his rider: orange soda, Pizza Hut. When nobody wanted to interview the band Pee Shy (yes, Pee Shy), I took their CD home, read the bio, and prepped so many notes and wide-ranging questions that the two women in Pee Shy (once again, yes, Pee Shy) were genuinely shocked and a little bored after a while.

Sometimes I'd be dispatched to post fake questions on sparsely attended Web chats, especially when they weren't featuring a famous pop star but rather a solid editor or writer like Will Hermes.

"If I find myself attracted to the pretty Backstreet Boy that looks like a blonde chick, does that make me queer?"

Another thing I noticed about *Spin* magazine once I was on the inside: nobody was very rock-and-roll. Only the art department smoked, and nobody seemed to drink or do drugs, unless it was some underwritten field trip to some corporate rave. Then they'd ride around in limos and "cut loose," maybe end up in a hot tub with Moby. It wasn't a lifestyle I aspired to, as it had already been with me and my gang for a decade. Losing the *Cat in the Hat* hat in favor of some Prada or Miu Miu didn't qualify as evolution. I spent a lot of time out on the fire escape, blowing smoke into the air and wondering to myself, How does one get discovered here? Zev Borrow, another star writer who probably knew how to use "ur" correctly, would get expensive sushi with the holy Radiohead. I was twice as "rock" as Zev. Why did I have to sit across from Steve Perry, the lead singer of Cherry Poppin' Daddies, drinking Diet Coke and holding a microphone while he waxed philosophically about music, freedom, and why zoot suits are here to stay. Or wait an hour and half to interview Steve Poltz, the singer-songwriter who cowrote Jewel's "You Were Meant for Me" and was putting out an album of his own. Steve Poltz? This is why I quit dope? To costar in the rock-and-roll equivalent of *Broadway Danny Rose*? Puppets. Jugglers. Bring them on, was our philosophy.

At least I was slowly learning how to conduct interviews and picking up little tricks. For example, I didn't know how to ask people questions without looking them in the eye, so I wore what Jack and I called "St. Mark's sunglasses" to every interview (Kurt Cobain wears a similar model in white in a few iconic photos). The vendors sold them along with incense, pot pipes, and bundled, bad-vibe-scattering sage along St. Mark's Place between Second and Third Avenues. Having a slug or two of bourbon always helped too. I sometimes carried a dented silver flask that I'd found in the Salvation Army on Eighth Street. One gulp of whiskey made talking to Nigel Pulsford (the bald guy in Bush who's not Gavin Rossdale) a lot easier. Yes, the bald guy in Bush who wasn't Gavin made me nervous. He might as well have been Dylan or Tom Waits. When the lead singer of Candlebox told me how he was going to make it rain onstage on their next tour, I nodded enthusiastically and imagined I was interviewing Prince. I sat dutifully at Cipriani's waiting for Geri Halliwell to make a brief appearance while launching her ill-fated post–Spice Girls solo career, and when the record label tool implied that she was going to enjoy a career on par with George Michael after he left Wham.

Still, I was not ungrateful and still years away from being dangerously jaded. I still remember the first rock show I ever got listed for on my own: The Danielson Familie (the spooky, blonde brothers and sisters who played indie gospel in white robes or matching uniforms) at Threadwaxing Space downtown. The first promotional CD ever sent to me was Rick James's comeback album *Urban Rhapsody*. I stared at the middle-aged, way-past-his-prime Superfreak on the cover of that album for an hour, thinking, Someone wants me to have this. Someone cares what I think about this. They sent me this CD for free. Other people will have to buy it at the local record store.

Even more happily, some real heroes from the days of W-LIR were now at a point in their careers when coverage from *Spin*'s website was welcome. The big print mags were no longer interested in running features on them. I got to sit with Richard Butler's brother Tim and talk about the Psychedelic Furs.

"Why did you go and rerecord 'Pretty in Pink'?" I asked, finally having the chance over a decade later to air my grumbles. He looked sheepish. The answer was obvious: money. I interviewed the B-52s at a recording studio, and we talked about "Party Out of Bounds" being used by my hometown's beloved new wave station, W-LIR, as the theme for its weekend dance party. It was LIR's equivalent of Loverboy's "Working for the Weekend."

I am talking to the very man who shouted, 'Surpriiiiiiiiise!' I thought. This was fucking Fred "The Cancerian from New Jersey" (as he sang in "Songs for a Future Generation," my favorite B-52s song). I cleared off piles of promotional CDs so Green Gartside from Scritti Politti could have some perfect desk space to sit while I interviewed him. I went down to the bodega to buy a packet of chocolate donuts for Andy Partridge of XTC when he needed a chocolate fix after coming in to preview the band's comeback album, *The Apple Venus*. I sat across from Robert Smith in a hotel suite and chatted with him for a half hour. He was in full fright wig hair and smeared lipstick but spoke like a regular bloke. I stared at Andy Fletcher of Depeche Mode in another hotel suite while he read an article about cloning in the *Independent*. I went up to the Paramount Hotel in midtown to interview an extremely surly Jesus and Mary Chain. They were frightening; it was barely noon and they already had pint glasses in their hands. "What is it like being the coolest band that ever lived?" I asked the Brothers Reid in the children's room surrounded by stuffed animals. "I think the Velvet Underground would have something to say about that," Tim Reid responded, never lifting his sad Scottish mug from the lager foam at the top of his glass. The only God from the eighties I didn't meet was Morrissey, but that would be remedied soon enough.

One night after work, I went for a beer with Ron Richardson at our old haunt Mona's.

"You don't seem happy," he said. "I'm a little worried."

Ron knew what happened when I wasn't happy in the workplace. Things started to disappear, things . . . people . . . and in their place, trouble.

"I'm sorry," I said, "I just hate writing this watered-down crap and having to keep a smile on my face talking to all these losers. Why does edit treat us like shit? Why can't we work together, online and print?"

Ron nodded in sympathy. It was a question he'd been struggling with for over a year. We were all *Spin*, all part of the same entity. And yet there was almost no solidarity. We might as well have been emptying their wastebaskets.

"Nobody hired you to write watered-down crap," he said. "I hired you to be you."

"LA calls and complains if I'm not respectful," I whined.

Every single time I deviated from the format or screwed up a fact, or the spelling of some star's name, I'd get a call from headquarters.

"Write what you want. Just don't curse."

It seemed fair enough. If I didn't say "fuck" or "shit," I could let the readers know "this is a column." And "I am a writer of this kind of lame column." I created the illusion that I was dispatching from a busy news bureau: "What's that? I'm being handed a bulletin . . . ," when I was really sitting in a corner of *Spin*'s b-floor, where they stored the things they didn't want to reckon with. Nobody knew or cared who came up with the rock news; it was aggregated by robots as far as a radio listener or Web surfer knew or cared and remained that way for years. There were no "voices" and few "personalities." I would make sure they knew that Marc Spitz was filing the news. And he was flesh. He was horny. He was as bored with some of these stories as they would soon be hearing them. When he went to the bathroom, he didn't just take a break; he wrote about it at the end of a news item, essentially conveying, "Hang on, I have to take a leak. Back in a minute." Instead of writing about the soundtrack to a new Drew Barrymore movie, he wrote about how he needed to write a script for Drew because, at the time, she hadn't made a good movie since *Mad Love*. When Eddie Rabbitt (of "Driving My Life Away" and "I Love a Rainy Night" fame) died, he wrote about it as if Paul McCartney or President Clinton had passed on. When Rush got snubbed by the Rock and Roll Hall of Fame voting committee (really, guys, vote them in already), he held his Sugar Ray news tidbit and instead filed a rant on why Rush deserved induction. When I say "he," I mean, of course, me, but it all came through a character I invented to jazz up these freeze-dried bits of meaningless "info" and allow myself to stand by them without feeling like a veal cutlet. I was absolutely convinced that every one of these missives was going straight into the void—space junk, read by nobody out there. Who was out there? I didn't hear any feedback unless it was from a furious radio employee out in LA demanding that I "clean up" my items and get "professional." Maybe there were comments or stats, but I wouldn't have known where to find them. I didn't even have Instant Messenger until about two months in.

"Wait, you can talk to someone at their computer too? Instantly?" I asked Ron.

I really had no idea of the scope of the Internet. I figured this stuff was reaching some bored college kids somewhere. I didn't even know that it was being read inside the *Spin* offices, that my sardonic daily news blurts were being photocopied by an obsessive Pearl Jam fan named Jessica and circulated among the editors upstairs whose attention I coveted. This was fortunate because I'm sure I would have clammed up and been much less free and funny.

Sometimes I had to borrow money from Ron Richardson just to afford a liverwurst sandwich or some soup. I still had no money—I was barely making enough for lunch and subway fare—but I was finally writing in a way that felt fun and rock-and-roll. It was the wrong medium but the right stuff and about five years too early to leverage into some kind of power play. It didn't matter anyway. I didn't want to be a pioneer. When given the chance, I readily threw it all away to join the cool kids upstairs.

One day I was at my desk eating lunch and reading the *Post* when I got a call from Dave Moodie.

"Can you come up?" he asked. I flew from the desk chair and walked toward the elevator. Ron was in his office playing "Getting Jiggy with It" by Will Smith over and over again. He and his cubicle partner Susan were having a staring contest, only instead of staring, they were playing "Getting Jiggy with It" and daring each other to break (which meant pleading for it to be shut off or replaced with the new Cornelius or Add N to (X) or Modest Mouse CD).

"Don't freak out," Moodie said with a mischievous smile. "But I heard you used to be a heroin addict."

"Um, no. Why? Who told you that?"

Instantly, I ran through a variety of possible finks and came up with nobody. I'd shared a cigarette with Victoria, Michael's assistant. I had a huge crush on her. Maybe I let it slip to make me seem more interesting. Was it Julia Chaplin? How would she know? Did she see us try to gank some of her roommate's CDs and assume we were strung out? What else would we be stealing for? Dope! Or maybe Moodie could tell by my pallor and posture and took a shot in the dark. I didn't press it because of what he said next.

"I need someone with experience to work on a story for me."

"Oh, oh yeah. Well, I don't like to talk about it, but yeah, I know smack."

I know smack? I guess I always called it smack. It had that sharper inflection, like a wet fish hitting a deck. Everyone looks. Smack.

Moodie was putting together a story with a writer named Lily Burana on ex-junkie chic. He asked if I could find people to talk on the record about how perception of them as one-time junkies helped them socially—this, of course, in the wake of River Phoenix, Kurt Cobain, Hole bassist Kristen Pfaff, and the Smashing Pumpkins keyboardist Jonathan Melvoin, who'd recently overdosed. Kate Moss's skin and bones beauty had changed the pop aesthetic and helped make self-destruction and addiction seem cool again for the first time since the early seventies. The health club craze and big money "Choose Life" eighties thing was over and Moodie was wondering, as he did, if its opposite end had finally mainstreamed to the point where you could actually get ahead by suggesting a familiarity with King Heroin. As I walked back to the elevator, I thought, Okay, this is what we are here. I get it. We're skeptics! *Spin* had always been skeptical and some of its most powerful exposes hinged on that quality, whether it was tracking the money raised through Live Aid or Celia Farber's writing on the AIDS crisis.

I immediately got on the phone and asked David Greenberg, who was a living, raging Wildean quote machine. David jumped at the chance to have his name appear in *Spin*. He gave me a great quote, so bolstered, I asked another mutual friend, a Max Fish habitué, sometime dominatrix, and full-time junkie named Bernadette. She said she was reluctant to talk on the record, so I asked if I could quote her using an alias, and we came up with Rhonda Weiss, god knows why. Her quote was excellent, no need to push or prompt. She got it instantly: "Everyone's got a vomiting story. I walk around with people, and it's like, I vomited there, I vomited there. Like I'm a tour guide. I don't feel like I earned the depression that resulted, but yeah, I feel like I'm queen of the underground." Both David and Bernadette (under the pseudonym) made the story. It ran in the December 1997 issue, with Dave Matthews on the cover, his potbelly peering out from the waistband of his white trousers.

"Is being an ex-junkie, or rather, being an ex-junkie holding forth with sordid, graphic, near-pornographic recollections of your former smack habit and maybe popping off a book, movie, or talk show to highlight such shocking erstwhile depravities . . . the next junkie chic?" ran the lead-in. At the end of it said, "*Additional reporting by Marc Spitz.*"

It was the first time I'd seen my name anywhere in print.

"*Additional reporting by Marc Spitz.*"

And yet, I was still not "made." An additional reporting credit? An intern could get one of those, I'd later discover. One issue would pass without another assignment. Then another. Then another.

"How do I get in here?" I asked Andy Gensler over lunch one afternoon. Andy laughed at my naked ambition. Most people wondered this very thing but never came out and said it. I was too old to be patient or cool. I'd tasted the ink. I wanted more.

"Do you play hoops?" he asked.

"Hoops?"

"You're tall."

There was a basketball team that played other magazines, and I quickly signed up because much of the edit staff was on it, including Andy and Greg, my lone pals. Both were among the only people who would say hello to me in the hallway or the elevator when I loitered upstairs. Our boss, Michael Hirschorn, was on the team too, as was Thomas Beller, another star writer and, as far as I could tell, the only baller with any real game. I didn't care that the only skill I had was the ability to rebound. I had a mental block about dribbling, so I was the grab-and-pass man. I didn't even mind taking my shirt off for a shirts-and-skins game (our customized jerseys were supposedly on order and, to my knowledge, never actually came). Up and down the court, heaving with smoker's lung, I would grab then pass, grab then pass, and really put my all into it, red faced and determined. During one furious drive play, I was following Hirschorn down court. He turned to call for the ball, and I buried my entire head in his sweat-covered torso. It was like that Richard Pryor bit where he talks about his father punching him and his entire chest enveloping his dad's fist. Only the fist was my face.

"Good hustle," Hirschorn said, and he helped me out of his flesh. He patted me on the shoulder, laughing. At least he knew who I was now. I was the guy who entered him reverse-John-Hurt-in-*Alien* style. After the game, we'd go to a deli or diner and hang out and talk, and I'd always shoot my mouth off to let them know I was reading the magazine and listening to new bands, but I still wasn't getting any work. On Mondays, I'd be back at my desk, writing about Robbie Williams for goons in Toledo to read out over the airwaves.

Financially, at first anyway, there was very little difference between working for *Spin* and working nowhere at all. I was still always broke, borrowing money from friends or getting advances on my tiny paycheck from the accounting department or sympathetic people like Michael Bryant, the magazine's general manager. Some writers could count on the expense accounts of major-label press reps to eat and drink, but I wasn't one of them. I was the

Web guy. They'd have to write "future" in big red letters on the back of their receipts when filing their reports to justify all those vodka tonics.

Nobody among my Bennington crew knew how little "j-you-ice" I had. They only knew I was working at *Spin*. On the weekends Ron Shavers and I would go to Brooklyn house and roof parties full of grads and recent grads. They were basically college keggers in slightly more funky living spaces with slightly more evolved music (*The Miseducation of Lauryn Hill* and *In the Aeroplane over the Sea* instead of Young MC and Ugly Kid Joe), and those kids only knew that I was a rock writer now. I felt like the king hell indie nerd, someone who could walk proudly into Other Music on East Fourth Street, stare at the racks, and say, "Well, let's see now, I already have that. And that. And that. And *Urban Rhapsody* by Rick James. Have you heard it? Freaky?" I shot my mouth off, and nobody showed me what that hole was for. Some of these parties had live bands. The spaces out in pre-gentrified Williamsburg, Greenpoint, Bushwick, and Red Hook were large enough to throw festivals in before the rents shot up. There was a kid my age, maybe a little younger, whom I kept seeing at these parties. Jack, Chrissie, and I called him "Midget Elvis," because he was small and wore his blue-black hair in a Goth-Presley quiff. He was amazing on guitar, but every band he was in was full of sucking beardos, which I had no trouble telling him after a few beers. Eventually "Midget Elvis" found the right band. They were called Yeah Yeah Yeahs, and by the time I drank with him again, I had a tape recorder in front of me.

Still, I was healthier. My posture was better. I flirted with more ease. When people asked me what I was working on, I would say, "Beta Band" and never mention that it was a news blip on Beta Band for the website. For all they knew, I was hanging out with the members of Beta Band themselves; I'm not sure if Beta Band even knew when they were hanging out with Beta Band. One day Ron Richardson handed me the new Beastie Boys album *Hello Nasty*.

"Wait, this is the new . . . new Beastie Boys album? Like this is it? Here?"

"Yeah, can you listen and write something up on it."

"This is it. This CD? Has the new Beastie Boys album on it. In it."

"Yeah, that's it."

"No way."

"That's it."

The Beastie Boys took years to write, record, and release a new album, and whenever one came out, it was, hands down, the event record of the moment. As with my Bennington acceptance letter, it wasn't supposed to simply be handed to me. Where was the pageantry? The slow, patient crossing off of the days on the calendar?

"Okay . . ."

Take away the anticipation, and unfortunately, you lose a lot of the verve too. I became a different kind of listener and fan. I felt a weird remove that I couldn't place. The pursuit, the focus one needed to keep during the work-day, the time and effort one had to carve out to budget in, find, and take home a record, that was all part of the listening experience. I missed it, and I think it's why I was never much of a critic. You can be a great rock writer and a shitty rock critic (one who described PJ Harvey songs as "Primatene Misty death blues workouts"). There were hugely talented record reviewers at *Spin* and *Rolling Stone, Village Voice, Melody Maker,* and *NME* who managed to work through this handicap. I was not one of them. I'd been on the street too long.

Still, the prestreet date privilege bought me a lot of goodwill with my friends. I brought Bennington Ron Massive Attack's new album *Mezzanine* (still my favorite of theirs). A great fan of their also-perfect first two albums, *Blue Lines* and *Protection*, he was very excited, which made me feel proud to be able to give it to him for free, and prerelease, as a sort of "Thank you for letting me sleep on your floor for, I don't know, five years on two coasts." It wasn't a Cadillac, but it was something. I'd also put these songs on mixed tapes for Bonnie before anyone else heard them.

"What's that one song at the end?" Bonnie would ask.

"That's 'Like a Friend,' by Pulp."

"It's good."

"I know."

I went to every show. Every morning I'd wake up with a stamp on my hand or a wristband on my arm, and I'd keep them both there. It was my signal to the world: I work by night. I'm on the list. I rock. I have juice. And if it wasn't exactly true, my clout was slowly increasing. I found myself on the general-admission floor of venues less and less and grew accustomed to the view from the mezzanine at Roseland or the Hammerstein Ballroom or the Bowery Ballroom. And from there, it's the side of the stage, then backstage, and before too long, you're onstage, sitting next to the drum kit, watching the crowd from the band's perspective. I wasn't quite there yet, but the rock stars were getting close enough to touch—and occasionally alarm.

In early 1998, I flew out of New York City for the first time under some-one else's sponsorship. It was my first business trip, and I was not high on heroin, not listening to *Exile in Guyville*, not running away from anything. In fact, I was heading toward something. The destination was Chicago, where *Spin* was cosponsoring a concert with some beer company . . . and where my father had been living for a decade. The event was at the Aragon Ballroom, a cavernous Deco-era dancehall downtown. Our hotel was a posh W-style chain nearby, and the *Spin* crew, which included Ron Richardson, were given high-rise business suites with views of the whole city. Once we checked in, I called my father from my room.

"Where are you staying?" he asked.

"The W something," I said. "Maybe just the W."

"That's a nice place. You could have stayed out here." In the suburbs. Park Ridge, out by the O'Hare airport. He was missing the whole point. He didn't even offer to come in and see me. There were races to go to instead. I had to suggest it.

"I can get you into the show if you want. Do you know Garbage?" He didn't.

"Are they good?"

"Yeah, they're really good. The drummer produced *Nevermind*."

"What's that?"

"Nirvana?"

"Oh, yeah." Even my parents knew Nirvana. "I have to get up early."

I guess I hadn't given him much notice, and even if he did come in, his mind would be on the ponies.

"Why don't we get breakfast," I helpfully suggested.

"Great."

"Great."

I opened the minibar and started sucking the little bottles of vodka. I'd never stayed in a chain hotel before, only the Chelsea Hotel, and I'd had drinks at the revolving Holiday Inn in Hollywood. This would be the first of about two dozen nights on hotel sheets for me, but I was already picking up on just how lonely they can be once you've taken in the view, put your clothes and toiletries away, called the people you know in the city or town or country. People die in hotels. Janis. Belushi. Michael Hutchence. They find bodies in closets and under the bed. This is why: heartbreak.

I just wanted the old man to see me in this nice, clean room, with the view and the minibar and the little shampoos and soaps and free towels, and know that I didn't need his money for dope anymore. I had my own money for dope. I was in Chicago because someone had flown me out here to interview a band. I shouldn't have let his tepid reaction ruin the experience, but of course I did. That night I was supposed to walk around the Aragon, getting quotes from fans about how cool it was that Garbage (who'd been a mystery guest until all attendees were already inside) were playing. But I just kept drinking. I never got one quote. After the show, when Garbage held a meet-and-greet with the press after the show, everyone there asked serious questions; I was the only one who was drunk. All the other reporters, many of them local, a few from websites, seemed to be asking such well-thought-out questions, the kind I had bombarded poor Pee Shy with only months earlier. Not only did I have nothing to ask, but I lost my balance. I actually fell off my chair, causing all the reporters and the band to look at me.

"Are you alright, babe?" Shirley Manson, Garbage's Scottish lead singer, asked me sweetly.

"Harmph," I coughed, then got back into my chair and sucked on my pen.

My slip briefly upstaged the rock stars, and I sensed the power of being seen as a total car crash, in sunglasses, smoking in a no-smoking building: more rock-and-roll, somehow, than the rock-and-roll star.

In the morning, hungover, I dragged myself down to the lobby to meet the old man. He wasn't alone. He'd brought a racetrack buddy with him, Frank. I had no idea why. Maybe they were en route to the track that morning as well. I would be a detour, as usual. I'd met Frank before. Frank was older, Italian, and rich. He had a wickedly dirty mind, which he expressed in that tight, clipped Illion-oyce accent.

"Your father says he's got a big dick. That means you got a big dick. You got a big dick? You ever choke the chicken?"

"You look good," the old man said.

"You're losing your hair," Frank noticed.

"I am not," I said, and ran a hand through it.

"You will," he said. "You got less hair than the last time I saw you."

"I was nineteen!"

"Gonna be bald. Better get ready."

We sat and ate breakfast, but I couldn't eat my pancakes. I just kept picturing myself bald. Bald in rock and roll. Moby was cool and certainly had something on me when it came to some of the women I'd loved, but both Billy Corgan and Michael Stipe started sucking fast when the hair went. And the guy from Midnight Oil was never very cool. Who knows how big The Screaming Blue Messiahs could have gotten if their lead singer'd had hair. Or Bad Manners.

"You're not eating," my father observed.

"Are you proud of me?" I asked him glumly.

"What?"

"I said, 'Are you proud of me?'"

"Yeah. You're going good," he said.

I wasn't sure what I had to do to get a reaction. He seemed just as unexcitable as the *Spin* edit staff when it came to me. And unlike my mother, he still loved rock and roll. Getting drunk and falling off the chair? That seemed to be the only thing that worked as far as gaining attention. This stuck in my mind.

Some weeks later, Spiritualized, the druggy, art rock band lead by J. Spaceman, late of Spaceman 3, played Windows on the World, the restaurant and bar on the 106th floor of the North Tower of the World Trade Center. Apparently Spaceman wanted to play "the highest place in the world." Their current album, *Ladies and Gentlemen, We Are Floating in Space*, had been released some months earlier, and I guess they wanted to actually float in space while playing it entirely to a crowd of well-connected ladies and gents.

I brought Bonnie Thornton as my date and got drunk quickly: open bar syndrome, or O.B.S. as I diagnosed it. One had to be careful not to contract O.B.S. or they might end up doing something foolish like passing out in front of Shirley Manson. It was a dangerous disease, but then, isn't rock and roll all about danger? Perhaps O.B.S. was both the affliction and the answer, like getting tanked up with snake venom before a trip to the jungle? I mean, all those rock writers who didn't pass out in front of Shirley Manson, where were they really going? To the next bloodless promo event? The next junket. To ask the next rock star, the next pre-planned and meaningless, bullshit questions. Where would they be in five years? What would they be? Not Lester Bangs. Now that guy had some tenacious O.B.S.

With full-blown O.B.S., I spent much of the night with my head on the cool, glass pane of Windows on the World, looking down on the clouds and blinking lights. My old man looked older. I was getting older. I'd be bald by the time I was thirty, according to his gambling buddy Frank. I needed to find out about Rogaine. How did that happen? Life was short. The view, from up there, seemed infinite too, like life seems when you're in your twenties, but that was a lie too. There was an end, always an end. I was twenty-nine now. This was the time to fuck shit up. This was the time to rock the fuck out. It might be the last time I'd ever get, certainly with the safety net of the twenty-somethings right there, ready to catch me if I truly fucked up.

At that moment, a thousand feet above Wall Street, I decided that I would no longer be grateful just to be off the street or working at an institution like *Spin*. That was a sucker's game—acting careful and friendly forever and towing the line. There was no reward for good behavior in this business. And if it's truly whom you know, then the trick was to make everyone know you first, then sort out whom you wanted to keep as your friend and ally. What was the worst that could happen? I'd lose my job. I'd die? Wasn't making the same junkets to ask the same stupid questions just a living death anyway?

"How is this record different from the last record?"

"So, we gonna see you on tour this summer?"

"What can we expect next? Another record?"

What would Lester do? What would Jesus do? No, no forget that. What would fucking *Batman* do? According to Black Grape, Jesus *was* Batman anyway. In that moment, I decided that I would become a rock writer super hero; ridiculously costumed, numbed by drugs and O.B.S., and yet with a wintry focus; committed to the pose with sociopathic fervor. But I would need a sidekick.

CHAPTER 13

I was at my desk when I received an instant message from someone named Ultragrrrl. I usually ignored these solicitations, which tended to pop up in the middle of a thought. Most of the time, they were porn sites fishing for suckers. I don't know why I clicked this particular box. Ultragrrrl sounded like a porn handle if ever there was one. Maybe it was the three *r*'s in the middle. Porn sites weren't hip to Riot Grrrl were they? I opened the box.

"Hi."

"Hi," I typed.

If I had ignored this "hi," I truly believe the downtown rock-and-roll scene of the last fifteen years would be unrecognizable to us today. Maybe Ultragrrrl would have tried another rock writer, but I doubt he would have opened the box either.

"Who and what is an Ultragrrrl?" I was bored. It was lunchtime, but I wasn't hungry, having crammed a large coffee and a half pack of Camels into my bloodstream already.

"She needs a job," she wrote. Not bad—refers to herself in the rapper third person. Maybe this was a kindred spirit here, a self-created freak.

"I love you. Please give me a job."

"Love?"

"I read the site every day, and I love what you are doing. But you need me."

"Why?"

"Because I'm Ultra!"

She was funny and bold, and I thought, Well, if I were Ultragrrrl, what would I want the me to do in this situation? A year earlier, I *was* Ultragrrrl, just looking for a hole in the fence. So I went to tell Ron that maybe we should hire her as an intern.

"We need an intern," I said. Ron lowered the volume on the You Am I CD playing on the stereo.

"We do," he agreed, in that slow, suspicious way of his whenever I came to him with an idea or a suggestion, as if this would be the one to finally capsize the ship.

"She loves my stuff, so you know she's got good taste."

Ron rolled his eyes.

"Forward me the info."

"Okay, but can I tell her you're going to follow up?"

"Fine."

"That means you have to follow up."

"I will follow up."

When I got back to my desk, I typed, "Okay, send me your info, and Ron Richardson, who's my boss, will be in touch."

"Thank you! Thank you!"

"Where are you anyway?"

"Tenafly."

"Where the fuck is Tenafly?"

"New Jersey."

One glance at Ultragrrrl in the flesh, and it was clear that the anonymity of the Web, with its flashy handles, was her generation's equivalent of War-holian reinvention—a way to be larger than herself. X-ers had nowhere to hide, so we had to eat drugs and wear sunglasses. Y-ers had the Web. Ultra was no anime robot slayer in a PVC jumper, no Aeon Fluxx, but rather a cute, slightly chubby, teenage New Jersey virgin with orangey bleached hair and no eyebrows. Most of the time, I still felt nineteen too. I never paid much attention to the fact that there was now a generation going to and graduating college—that it had been a full decade since Sara Vega first handed me that copy of *Maldoror*. That there were fewer than eighteen months left in the nineties. But once I saw Ultra in person, I realized that I was no longer inventing the future. Not only did Ultra know all about the bands I grew up with—The Smiths, Joy Division, New Order, The Cure, Depeche Mode, and Siouxsie and the Banshees—but she knew two dozen brand-new bands none of us had ever heard of. Like so many of us, she was a combustible force that just needed the oxygen of the *Spin* brand to ignite. At home, in her bedroom, all this passion and knowledge meant nothing, but touch it to the magazine and the Web, and it had serious power. I paced as Ultra had her interview in Ron's closed office. When she came out, she gave me a hug, and I could feel her enormous breasts against my belly. Ultra barely came up to my navel.

"I love you," she said.

"I love you too."

Outside of her little instant message box, she was soft-spoken and polite. I just shrugged in my shades and stared at her rack and her fanny-packed behind as she skipped to the elevator. Ron noticed this.

"So?" I asked.

"I hired her."

"Oh, cool."

"Don't sleep with her." He warned. "Seriously. Don't sleep with her." I'd slept with coworkers at the bookstore where we'd toiled—another small, gossipy world. A lot of them. Ron knew it. He was protecting me from myself probably. I was a horrible flirt. Like any New York rock and roller born between 1969 and 1980, I made out with her a couple of times, but she was and remained a virgin for years once we brought her on.

Of the three production coordinators I filed my news reports with and was basically chained to all day, I only slept with one after a night drinking at Max Fish, but she'd already left *Spin*. I went home with two assistant editors. Made out with an editor's assistant. But never Ultragrrrl. Wait, that's not true. I suppose there *wasn't* a rock boy south of Fourteenth Street who hadn't sucked face with her at least once. I thought that I was the exception, the one who'd brought her into this world and turned her, like a vampire host, but there was this night . . . in a cab . . . Anyway, it's dicey stuff, getting intimate with coworkers, shitting where you eat, even in the relatively loose world of rock and roll . . . and *Spin* had just been through a scandal. I figured any bad behavior was all in the name of "hip," but I still heeded his warning as best I could. Sex, however, was everywhere. When we broke from AOL and launched as an independent site at what was at the time the biggest party of every South by Southwest convention down in Austin, I made sure I was safely hidden behind the amps while I got my hand job from a cute Texan girl who looked like a brunette Drew Barrymore circa *2000 Malibu Road* as the Flaming Lips played "She Don't Use Jelly." She was one of a pair of twin sisters and a coworker of mine, whom I happened to be sharing a hotel room with; I had sex with the other sister in the bathtub. This got around. When Sia Michel heard, she kept referring to us as "Sister Lovers," after the classic Big Star record. It was attention. I wanted more. All I had to do was fuck strangers and get high? Done and done.

Ultragrrrl and I gave each other something much more valuable and enduring than any cheap carnal thrill. We gave each other encouragement. Ultra existed to validate my ridiculous rock-and-roll behavior and vice versa. While she was a decade younger, we were both at about the same level of maturity, sexually and emotionally. When dressing up and acting out, I was grateful to have a sidekick.

There were other stimuli to egg us on. VH1 had started running its *Behind the Music* series around this time, and I was riveted to the classic three-act stories: the rise, fall, and resurrection of Def Leppard, Aerosmith, Iggy Pop, and the greatest *Behind the Music* stars of them all, Motley Crue (whose episode is the *Raging Bull* of BTMs ("We want to fuck all the girls. We want to snort all the drugs!" "We're shooting alcohol! What are we doing? We could just drink it!"). MC Hammer and Milli Vanilli made me envious of a less restrained time. I'd missed the era of gross excess by just a few years. It was on the wane, still detectable, but someone had to seize and slurp it down while they still could, and nobody seemed to have a taste for it. But "Rock Boy" and Ultragrrrl did. We drank ourselves witless, and there was no outfit too ridiculous for us to model in the office, at interviews, at record company parties, and on the subway. I wore a black feather boa and a Velvet coat. I was back on heroin inside of a month. I'd cop a bag or two, go to the bathroom in the *Spin* offices, and sit on the toilet. I'd dig my finger into the bag and just hit myself with a taste. Occasionally a coworker would come in and take a piss or a shit, and I'd freeze, but once I tasted that back drip from my nostrils down to my tongue and throat, I didn't give a shit. I kicked open the stall doors and stumbled to my desk.

It was dicey doing smack on the job, and at my age. I mean, how much luck are you gonna push? But I convinced myself that it wasn't actually me doing it. You can trick the brain that way.

"If you are killed in the Matrix, do you die here?" Neo asks Morpheus in what was soon to be the new age's biggest hit and signature film. *Spin* magazine was my Matrix, and I was gambling on the answer being no. I wanted the red pill, all the way.

Besides, the *Spin* bathrooms smelled of pink hand soap and always had fresh TP and seat covers. None of the toilet stalls I'd snorted drugs in before, with their filthy hand dryers and piss-covered tanks with antisocial graffiti everywhere, had housekeeping. You can't get strung out when there's housekeeping. I kept the hard drugs away from Ultra. She didn't eat pork or shellfish, and so I figured heroin was *trayf* too. Besides, I didn't want to do drugs with my sidekick, and she didn't want to do them with me. We both wanted to do drugs with rock bands!

Only rub was, at the time, there were barely any American bands behaving in such a fashion. The only hedonists were DJs like Fatboy Slim, who probably kept a bottle of something by the decks. "I Hate My Dad" rock seemed to rule the day. Apologies to their fans, but we considered these chubby gloom-pots, who simmered then screamed in loud-quiet-loud grief over basic hip-hop beats—Korn, P.O.D., Papa Roach, and the biggest and baddest (not bad meaning good but bad meaning bad) of them all, "The

Bizkit"—utter nightmares. Maybe not Korn. They had a few good songs. "Freak on a Leash." But Limp Bizkit was the bête noire of our smart little indie rock world, where Belle and Sebastian were our friends and Thom Yorke and Björk were godheads. I first saw Fred Durst and Co. backstage while covering the Ozzfest for the website. It was an otherwise great day. I actually got to stand inches away from Lemmy, with his warts and white cowboy boots, and get paid for it, but discounting Ozzy, most of what passed for metal didn't sound like metal anymore, just as country music didn't sound like country anymore. They'd all taken really unfortunate turns. I wonder if Ben Stiller regrets appearing in a Limp Bizkit video now? Or Halle Berry. It's hard to explain to people who weren't around at the time just how un-avoidable Limp Bizkit was. We had to cover them. Ben and Halle had to make the scene. The only thing that kept me from Plath-ing it in my oven was Kid Rock. At least he was intentionally funny and had a genuine sense of rock-and-roll badass. Most of these bands didn't even seem to want girls at their shows.

A few rungs down the ladder, commercially speaking, there were a few exceptions, but none of them were big enough for a feature. The Unband was one of these glorious beacons of real, sexed-up, druggy, life-affirming R-O-C-K. I didn't understand why they weren't as big as Tool or any other sports-arena-filling powerhouse. Too drunk? Definite possibility. Too ugly. Probably. Still, even at their little club shows, as with The Ramones or Motor-head before them, when they plugged in, you just started to smile, your body churning, "Yes! This is fucking correct. This is why we fight!"

The Unband! Google them. Matt, Mike, and Eugene. What a perfect name for a good rock-and-roll band in 1999. They were unlike just about every other joyless combo out there, a faux-stupid trio who sang witty anthems like "Rock Hard" and "Drink and Rock." I snorted half of Bogota in the bathroom of the Lower East Side rocker hole Motor City with them one night and closed down another bar called the 2B on another while conducting a never-published interview. It went a little something like this:

Marc: *Have any of you ever choked on your own vomit?*
Matt: *Not to the point of dying.*
Marc: *Nobody ever talks about that—choking on your own vomit and surviving.*
Mike: *Sleep on your face.*
Eugene: *Hey, does anybody else have a hard on right now?*

For whatever reason, Ron Richardson refused to run the full transcript on the site, and I dared not pitch it to the magazine, but it's still one of the best things I've ever done and could have been my very own *"Frank Sinatra Has a Cold."*

There were others who gave me hope and didn't seem at home in the soggy, safe, and joyless rock realm circa 1998. One night, I took Patricia Ann, who'd been chucked out of Bennington for poor grades (an impossibility I used to think, since they didn't give out grades, only written comments) to see The Dandy Warhols play at Irving Plaza. The Dandys were pre–"Bohemian Like You," their crossover hit, and were still at a level where coverage on *Spin's* website was a big deal. After the show, we went backstage, where Zia, the keyboardist, was laying out long rails of blow. It was like seeing rain clouds after a year's schlep through the nu metal desert. I said I was from *Spin*, and Courtney latched onto me.

"Hey, *Spin*," he said, referring to me by the name of the mag. "Are you here to see some real rock-and-roll action?"

"Yes!" I confirmed. "Yes, I am."

The Dandys didn't care about curfews or security or cameras. They were rock-and-roll posers, living how they imagined it would be if they ever got to make records and go on tour and pretend they were the Stones in 1969 and 1972. I wanted them to be my best friends, all of them, even the drummer who didn't talk to me.

"Listen, *Spin*. We're at the SoHo Grand. Be there tomorrow at ten when we leave, and we'll take you on the bus," Courtney told me at the end of the night.

"Seriously?"

"Yeah, just be there, *Spin*," Zia said.

"We're not gonna wait for you, *Spin*. We're leaving at ten, *Spin*."

I called Ron Richardson from the phone booth of the Holiday after taking the edge off the rock star blow binge with a few vodka tonics.

"I have a scoop. I'm going out on tour with the Dandy Warhols."

"That's not a scoop."

"Okay, technically no, but you know something crazy is going to happen."

"I would think so, yes."

"So I can go? I don't know how long it'll be. A few weeks."

"I would think so, yes."

"Right, so I can go?"

"Sure," he said, before adding, "but you can't come back here if you do."

They left without me, but soon I'd develop a friendship with another, even more dangerous rock star—you could argue, the very last real rock star. I opened my inbox one morning and there was an e-mail from someone claiming to be Courtney Love.

I already felt like I knew Courtney Love. From the beginning of the decade, Zoe and I had followed her band before they were famous, and then,
after they were notorious, they just got better. We remained fans. I even had
trainspotted them, buying pricey rarities like the "Retard Girl" single or the
Beautiful Son EP (the one with a childhood photo of Kurt on the cover and
songs about Yoko Ono and rehab). I was at the Hole show at the Hollywood
Palladium in 1994 when Courtney brought her baby, Frances Bean Cobain,
onstage and held her up at the end of the show like she was a lion cub. LA
was spooky that night. You had to pass through metal detectors to get into
the club; police helicopters circled in the air. All for Courtney.

I'd reviewed for the website, again inexpertly, Hole's long-awaited follow-
up to *Live Through This*, the sunnier, poppier *Celebrity Skin*, and Marti Zimlin had e-mailed her a copy of it. While the album would go on to sell over a
million copies and yield two big hits, the title track and the acoustic ballad
"Malibu," she was insecure about it. Billy Corgan, her ex-boyfriend and the
scene's new alpha talent in the wake of Kurt's death, had helped her write the
record and contributed the title track's blunt riff, which made it a big radio
hit. "I've got to find life in this hack song of mine," Courtney wrote to me as
the band was about to start a long promotional tour in support of the album.
"I feel like Steven Tyler, man. It's just so hack that fucking riff." She wanted
to be a star on her own but wasn't sure it was even possible, not in any way
that wouldn't leave her ill and driven to distraction. "I am nervous," she confided. "I do not like living on Nirvana money. I hate it. It's obvious from the
way I spend it that I hate it." Hole's new sound was California music made by
a former indie rocker whose fame now overshadowed her band and the entire
scene itself.

Courtney was a movie star too, having appeared in *The People Vs. Larry
Flynt* the previous year. She was dating costar Ed Norton. But as much as at
least one element of her personality wanted Hollywood and Malibu, the real,
shy, rock geek Courtney wasn't happy in the sun. I never expected to even
meet her, much less become, for a time, a confidante and new liaison to the
still powerful world of *Spin* magazine, but circumstances made it so. She'd
appeared, along with Hole's enchanting, red-haired new bassist, Melissa Auf
Der Maur, and skeletal cofounder Eric Erlandson (then dating the real Drew
Barrymore), on the cover of the October 1998 issue. The tagline read, *"She's
been called sellout, bitch, killer. But will Courtney Love have the last laugh?"*
Around the time the shock and sadness of Kurt Cobain's death was finally
fading somewhat. It literally took years—that's how powerful his persona and
Nirvana's music had been. Now, with the rise of the Web and its easy ano-
nymity, there were whispers that Courtney had had something to do with

Kurt's death: cowardly, whispering conspiracy theorists winking and warning. Courtney herself was mortified that *Spin*, with which she considered herself beyond simpatico, would even acknowledge these creeps by using the word "killer" on the cover.

"Craig and Michael fucked me so hard that I've been crying all day . . . My own people put 'Killer' on the cover," she wrote me, instantly putting me in the awkward position of having to defend bosses I barely knew, the same ones who refused to acknowledge my existence. Where did my true loyalty lie? *Spin*? Courtney Love? I was hardly a diplomat, but I did my best to smooth things over, or at least change the subject. I already knew about her problems; you only had to pick up *Page Six* or read The Velvet Rope, the smarmy music-biz gossip site, to hear about her problems, so I bombarded her with mine: how I was chipping dope, how I couldn't get any print work or respect from the people upstairs, how I couldn't figure out just how much eyeliner to apply; the perfect balance was elusive, especially while high. I did whatever it took not to set her off on a rant. Sometimes the rants came anyway, and it felt as if Courtney could be writing to anyone—like maybe she'd forgotten midway through the letter exactly whom she was talking to. She was just getting her yayas out, making herself feel less violated and pained. Other times, she was incredibly sweet and big sisterly, as Adrienne Shelly had been. "Do not wear eyeliner around me," she warned. "I almost sent [ex-Nirvana guitarist] Pat Smear back to the SST store when he got Kurt to do that." And while she still carried around all the baggage of the dying scene, and most of America associated her with hard drugs, she begged me to steer clear of backsliding into smack addiction. "Don't do heroin. It's passé. I killed it. It's over baby. Stop it right now." She was parodied on *Saturday Night Live* for being a stumbling train wreck, but Courtney was whip smart and could put a mutual friend or public figure into a perfect box. "She's so Betsy Johnson. He's so Kim's Video." I appreciated the dichotomy in her personality—the too-smart and sensitive indie kid and the flaming, hack-riffing, firebrand and shit magnet. Sometimes the former would recommend albums to me like Echo and the Bunnymen's *Porcupine*, which I had, or The Zombies' *Odessey and Oracle*, which I didn't, and which became one of my all-time favorites ("Get that Zombies record or perish!"). Other times she'd lose me ("We went to a baby shower at Spago"), but I never felt anything less than pure joy on seeing her name in my inbox and reading her mail, always signed "CL." It's weird to be friends with the most famous person in the world, and weirder still to see a side of her that most everyone else in the world does not. She was like a Bennington art school girl who referred to herself unironically and accurately as a "millionaire cultural icon." She even confided to me that she "used to dream of going to Bennington." I thought of Zoe, up at school, styling herself after Courtney Love, when all the while Courtney just wanted to be a Bennington girl.

I pushed to meet her in person. Hole was playing the 1998 Video Music Awards out in LA, and I asked her to get me tickets. "These tickets are totally hard so don't get your hopes way fucking up." I didn't care about the show. I just wanted to hang out with her. I was lonely, and Courtney, for all her critics, was perfect. But you can't be friends with the most famous person in the world, as much as the most famous person in the world almost always needs a friend too.

Now that I had something in common with Courtney's writer-friends like Craig Marks, or David Fricke over at *Rolling Stone,* I liked them a lot better. He wasn't as threatening to me. He even smiled at me once while I was chatting with Victoria outside his office. Craig, for whatever reason, was playing "One Week" by Barenaked Ladies extremely loudly and happily bopping his head to the goofy, Canadian beat. Being smiled at by Craig or Michael as I walked through the front office and toward my desk in my black suit, black eyeliner, spiked-up hair, and feather boa, a cigarette unlit in my lips and my bug shades pushing up my bangs, was better than being winked at by a pretty girl. I knew what that was like, getting the attention of pretty girls. Improbably, I'd gotten good at it. But I'd been hopeless at attracting editors. Thing were changing.

"There's crazy Marc Spitz, with his dangling cigarette and his sunglasses indoors and his black clothes, weaving on drugs like Nick Kent. He's friends with Courtney Love," I imagined people saying as I staggered past their glass office doors. "What can we use him for? He's got to be good for something. And where's his sidekick Ultragrrrl? She's a fuckin' kook too."

Tracey Pepper was a new editor just hired away from *Interview* by Michael and Craig to start a "front-of-the-book" section. The front of the book includes the pages of small pieces that warm you up before getting into the features well. Every magazine has them. *Vanity Fair* calls it *Vanities*; *The New Yorker* calls them *Talk of the Town* pieces. *Spin* didn't have anything of the kind, and so Tracey and Sia Michel put together a blue print, which included a gossip column called, slightly embarrassingly, *Backstage Pass*. It wasn't a very *Spin* name. It had none of the punk rock, postfeminist enlightenment the magazine was famous for. It suggested blowjobs for access, and wasn't there something inherently tacky about gossip? One day I looked up from my desk to find Tracey hovering, all kinky red hair and burbling impatience.

"You go out a lot, right?" I nodded my head. "Friends with Courtney Love?"

E-mail friends, but I didn't correct her.

"I've been to Moomba," I answered, referencing what was then the hottest nightspot in the city, a beckoning two-tiered outpost for the rich and famous on Seventh Avenue. Moomba, like the other hot bars of the period, Spy and Wax, was about perception versus reality. It was supposed to be hot and so it was. One imagined miracles inside: free coke, Charlize Theron, a yogi walking around handing out flowers and whispering the secrets of the cosmos. Once up in the VIP area, after a forty-five-minute wait and extended negotiations with the maître d', you'd find some glowering *Saturday Night Live* cast member like Chris Kattan eagerly watching the stairs to see if you were someone glamorous coming to join him and be semi-famous together. It had its mini-myth, but it was about a month away from the tourists who didn't seem to mind the crushingly antiseptic vibe.

"Right," she said, unimpressed. "Here's the thing. My gossip columnist is leaving, and I need a new one. Can you write this for me? You want to be my new columnist?" She was all but tapping her foot, like she didn't wish to spend any more time breathing in loser dust in the online "pod" than she had to. I noticed Ron skulking around wondering what a print editor was doing on his turf. I absolutely did not want to be a gossip columnist. The only rock-and-roll gossip columnist I knew wasn't even a real person: Father Guido Sarducci, who wrote for the Vatican newspaper, in all those old SNL skits. When I thought of gossip columnists, I thought of bottle service and hair mousse and A. J. Benza's catchphrase, "Fame . . . ain't it a bitch."

If I was going to put away the smack, like Courtney Love suggested, that soul crush would have me back on in the length of one Descendents song. But it was print. A permanent edit gig. My name . . . every month . . . in *Spin* magazine.

"Yes, totally," I replied. Tracey didn't smile. I could tell she wasn't fully sold on "Rock Boy." She thought I was a dick. I thought she was stuck up with nice tits, but maybe we needed each other somehow.

"Good. I'll e-mail you. We'll go over everything." She sped off.

In truth, I'd only been to Moomba twice, both times with my friend Patricia Ann, who was friendly with Kevin Cadogan, the blonde guitarist from Third Eye Blind, then one of the biggest bands out there thanks to their multiplatinum debut and KROQ smashes like "How's It Gonna Be" and the eternal "Semi-Charmed Life." I was a theater geek, putting up *Retail Sluts* for a scattering of Bennington friends and other theater geeks, drinking in Max Fish, and trying to get my new play off the ground. This stuff does not a savory gossip column make.

I was also distracted, as I'd begun, at Aaron Beall's behest, work on another play called *The Rise and Fall of the Farewell Drugs*. They considered *Retail Sluts* a "hit" over at the Piano Store and wanted more. Jack and I were more than happy to keep going. If *Retail* was all pre-*Spin* struggle, *Farewell* . . . was post-*Spin* all the way and powered by the budding cynicism of someone who's had a peek at real fame and an insight into how the culture moves. It was about boy bands. As if nu metal wasn't enough of a drag, the other genre of music that was selling millions and millions of units was a new type of saccharine pop music lead by the Backstreet Boys. I thought, What would happen if one of those bands was fabricated from a Lower East Side junkie 'pig-fuck' or 'skronk' combo that just happened to be cute, like Jonathan Fire*Eater or Jon Spencer circa Pussy Galore? What if they took the bait? Would they be able to hold the ruse together, or would their worse demons win in the end? These were the Farewell Drugs: Reed Kidneyfailure, Johnny Klonopin, Chimpy Phister, and Sloane Ranger. They'd become the squeaky clean "Skatekeys." I'd been meeting a lot of people in the music industry, and they were great characters: cynical publicists living high on expense accounts, band managers, who were one rung up from the publicists (who really only served to take a request to management and almost never made a decision on their own), band friends, hangers on, makeup artists, photographers, and eminently corruptible journos like myself.

In early 1999, *Spin* moved its offices from Eighteenth Street to a nondescript two-story complex in a building on Lexington Avenue, adjacent to the *Vibe* magazine offices. *Vibe*, a respected hip-hop culture magazine, owned us at the time and had the bigger and, by the sound of it, much more socially garrulous offices. At the *Spin/Vibe* joint holiday parties, the *Vibe* staffers seemed to be the only ones having fun, dancing and drinking to booming Jennifer Lopez and Destiny's Child hits while the indie rock nerds flinched in the corner, discussed the Elephant 6 collective, and wondered if the open bar was dry.

I'd finally moved out of Ron's and into Bonnie's old studio on Christopher Street between Bleecker and Seventh Avenue, a loud, touristy strip where, in addition to the St. John's Lutheran Church, there was a pool hall (Fat Cat Billiards), a barbershop that catered to gay men, a famous gay bar called Boots and Saddles, a fetish gear shop called London, and the famous Village Cigars smoke shop. I didn't have much furniture: a mattress and TV in the bedroom and the red dinette set that Bonnie left behind in the tiny kitchen. I wrote at the dinette table. At night, I could hear the majestic black trannies off the Path train screaming at each other and "reading" the neighborhood dogs. "Woof, woof woof!" they'd bark back on their high heels, as the alarmed pooches sounded off.

I was back in Manhattan and finally on the edit staff. Things were looking up. Working for Tracey enabled me to attend the all-important editorial meetings, and slowly Tracey and I developed a partnership of sorts that led to other, smaller pieces and a strong voice for the front of the book. Her tough exterior was persona as well. She was a Valley Girl, just like Zoe. I didn't need to look beyond the complete set of boxed Spice Girls action figures to suss out that she was not as brittle as she acted. Of course, when I filed my first bits of copy to her, they had the anarchy and infinite space of the Web. I'd submit sixteen hundred words when assigned five hundred. I didn't know what a thesis was.

A nut graf.

A lede.

A pull quote.

I just blurted. What would Lester do? I wrote long, like I filed my online news and e-mailed Courtney Love. I had no sense of restraint or the finite space of a print page. I didn't see words and grafs in shapes. I saw them for what they could do for me, how they could make me feel better inside. I saw them as things that had to come out so I could move through the city faster. Still, Tracey heard a voice that she could train with a little patience. You can't give someone taste and style if it's not there, but if they have it, you can gently instill in them a sense of grace, or at least tell them to dial it the fuck back if necessary. And I'd completely lost my fear of rock stars. I walked right up to them.

"Tommy Lee, that's Tommy Lee," the voice in my head would signal. "I'm talking to Tommy Lee. Hey! Tommy Lee is talking back to me. He said something. Ask him another question."

Michael Hirschorn left *Spin* at the start of 1999 and was replaced by Alan Light, who'd been at *Rolling Stone* and was the editor in chief at *Vibe*. Alan was soft-spoken and, like most of the major editors in the business, improbably clean-cut and an Ivy Leaguer. He was careful and not threatening to the advertisers, but he knew his history and had guts. He'd written the Ice-T cover story circa Body Count's scandalous "Cop Killer" single, after all, and most recently, a massive oral history on Beastie Boys for *Spin* ("The Story of Yo"). I was a fan of his work, but it was dizzying. I'd just gotten Michael Hirschorn to know me by name and ridiculous visage. Now I had to impress someone entirely new? Introduce him to my superhero alter ego?

It didn't take long. Once I showed up for one of those edit meetings in big shades and a feather boa and threatened to light a cigarette, Alan Light knew who I was. One day I went to lunch and left my sunglasses on my desk by the phone. When I came back, they were gone. I trailed into the art department to see if anyone had borrowed them and saw taped to the wall a series of Polaroids of half the art staff . . . and Alan Light, my new boss, posing as me, in the glasses, with one of my cigarettes dangling out of their lips. The art staff all smoked, sometimes in the stairwell of the office, ashing into a paper cup half full of water, so I knew them all. It was usually where I'd hang out when the online pod got too stuffy. If I wasn't there, I was upstairs in the fashion offices, trying on jackets and thumbing through the new issue of *The Face*. I realized that most of the edit staff I so envied were actually awkward around the artier members of the staff or the high-fashion-acquainted editors like the super hot Daniela Jung who wore librarian glasses and spoke with a German accent. But they all liked me and vice versa. I didn't go to journalism school. I went to Bennington. Art and fashion were second nature. It was yet another gadget for my utility belt.

The column started off well and soon developed a signature tone. We had the stars we loved (The Donnas, Rammstein) and the ones we loved to take the piss out of (Carson Daly, who was dating Tara Reid and had a dog named Stoli, always got an extra "hiccup" in the caption copy I filed to Pepper). And while it was a thrill to be back in Manhattan after a half decade in Brooklyn, the city changed a little for me once it became a beat. I liked East Village bars with jukeboxes and pool tables, not horrible clubs in the Flatiron or Chelsea that smelled like Fred Segal candles and felt like prisons made of blonde wood and mirrors: Lotus, Eugene, *feh*. The big record company parties after the Grammys or the Video Music Awards (when both events were in New York and not LA) were always the most decadent. The industry was flush. Sean Fanning and Sean Parker were tinkering at that very moment with the file-sharing software that would, within a year, begin to corrode the nearly century-old business model, but nobody knew it at the time. People still paid cash for music, and lots of it. The label-funded parties served live lobsters; rose petals were strewn over the marble steps of four-star hotels. I attended one after-party in an industrial art space, which featured half-naked women in Plexiglas cubes dangling from the ceiling. Out in LA, the Standard Hotel was becoming famous for live models similarly contained, like pet shop turtles in Plexiglas people-quariums. It was an era of putting flesh under glass and hot lights. I still never had any money myself, but I finally had the "j-you-ice" to get invited to parties where I could eat and drink for free. I lived off flogging promos. As when Jerry the desk clerk had been absent from the Chelsea Hotel, when Moe, the one clerk at Disc-O-Rama on Christopher Street who seemed to like me, was not in the house, sometimes I didn't eat. Like my rock-writer forbearers in the junket-happy seventies, post *Rumours* and Frampton, I too used these fat record company parties to fill the pockets of my black velvet jacket with pieces of salami, cubes of cheese, and little pieces of bread. I'd have jammed a live lobster in my pants if I could. I sometimes wondered if I'd missed the golden age of *Spin* and of rock and roll itself by just a few years.

At the end of the century, the biggest artists, all of whom appeared on our cover under Alan, were Creed (an oily, bare-chested Scott Stapp to the front), Papa Roach, and Matchbox 20. Alan was in the unenviable position of having to stand by these choices and took a lot of unfair flack. Whenever he had a chance, he put Eminem on the cover because it always sold, and he was an artist we all agreed was worthy. Eminem alone. Eminem with D12, his supergroup of Detroit rappers. Eminem as artist of the year. Eminem in a boat. Eminem with a goat. Everybody revered Radiohead as geniuses, the most important and progressive rock band since Nirvana, but they didn't sell magazines.

It didn't take me long to realize that in rock and roll, the VIP room was never the VIP room. It was always a decoy. There was always a "real" exclusive area, which the genuinely famous people seemed to know about. You'd have to sit in the actual VIP room and notice several of your fellow beat reporters there too before realizing the ruse; then you'd escape and go find the real mother lode. But it was always vaguely disappointing when once you got to the *Indiana Jones and the Last Crusade* grail room, there'd be no proof of God's existence but only Tom Green eating cold mini-quiche off a paper plate.

Still, I'd finally upgraded to the "cool kid" publicists; some of them had actually worked with Nirvana, which, a half decade after Kurt's exit, gave them immaculate cred. Nobody's managed to replace him. The best of these press folk, I quickly found once they started talking to me, had the same patina of glamour and real-deal rock and roll as the rock stars they represented (and as Ultra and I were trying to cultivate). Chloë Walsh, Mitch Schneider, Dennis Dennehey, Jennie Boddy, Jim Merlis, Steve Martin, Bobbie Gale, Ambrosia Healy, Brian Bumbery, Nils Bernstein, and Rick Gershon all come to mind. Each of them had been around since the Kurt and Courtney days or longer. Some of them even knew and worked with Kurt and Courtney, which gave you a perma cool, like having an association with the Decca era-Stones or Bowie during his MainMan phase. They all had that jaded rock-and-roll energy that Ultra and I cultivated for ourselves. After a point, this became the only energy I was truly comfortable around. How could I explain what I did for a living to my old Bennington friends or family? It was such a weird gig. When I didn't want to see them, I would always say, "I'm on deadline." What did that even mean? I was always on deadline. "I have an interview." They never asked, "Who with," but if they had, I'd have been stumped.

Even Jack and Bonnie didn't really get it, and every night when I came home to Brooklyn when living with Ron, it was like returning from the front. I slowly replaced most of my Bennington friends and old work friends with people in the "media world": fellow rock writers from *Rolling Stone* like Rob Sheffield, whom I recognized in a bar from a caricature that the magazine ran next to his byline, Austin Scaggs, who smoked a corncob pipe and seemed literally to glide through every party he entered, and Jenny Eliscu, who was friendly with Britney Spears and didn't get annoyed when I asked, "What's Britney really like?" We all did the same thing. We knew the pressures and the perks. It was just easier to talk shop. The *Spin-Stone* rivalry didn't really concern us. Everyone at *Rolling Stone* read *Spin* and vice versa.

Soon, I was bossing publicists around and acting like an utter diva, especially once I determined that they could not handle their charges. All someone had to do was treat the gig like a job and not a calling, and I was on them like a bitch on toast. I was writing a piece about Slipknot, the extreme metal band whose gimmick was that they all wore masks. I was backstage at the Roxy trying to get a quote from the kid who played Anthony Jr. on *The Sopranos* (he was a champion of the band), when someone grabbed me. He was wearing a clown mask.

"Do you want to trade punches in the face?" he asked.

"Pardon?"

"You get to punch me, then I get to punch you."

"I really don't."

"If you knock me out, then I don't get to punch you. See?"

"I do."

A fresh issue of *Spin* was a passport to the good graces of my family. Traveling to the Island on the train with an advance copy in my bag was a great feeling and key to getting whatever I needed: a loan, a trip to the drugstore or the thrift store, or a smile from my mother and a little bit of forgiveness for my past transgressions.

"Oh, how exciting! Are you in this one?"

"Yes, I have a column."

"What page? I can't find it. Find it for me. Oh, there you are! There you are!"

She didn't know a thing about any of the bands I'd written about, but that didn't matter. I'd lowered the bar so much during my time in Los Angeles that just not being dead or in jail or in a coma in some hospital sucking fluids through a tube was a win.

I got even more of a freak pass when I could call my mom up and say, "Turn on VH1 at 7."

"Why?"

"Why do you think?"

"Are you going to be on television? What channel is VH1? How do I find it?"

Spin's media-relations heads, Jason Roth and later Adrienne D'Amato, considered me some kind of mascot mouthpiece: the black clothes, the fey drawl, the shades. I never said no. I even went on some demeaning "rap session" with MTV's faux-stoner, contest-winning VJ Jesse Camp. We'd done a cover feature on him, outing him as secretly smart, but he seemed pretty thick to me. After the taping, he asked me if I was gay.

I grew to hate being on TV. They never gave you makeup, as if rock writers weren't entitled to it. I always looked fatter than I was. And they'd talk to me for a half hour and use a ten-second non sequitur. Plus, we never got paid. It was considered part of the job, with the wink-wink coming from the TV people that it was good exposure. And it certainly was if you were one of the dozen irritating stand-up comics who depended on it, but I was a writer. I saw it as a racket and still do. Rock and culture writers have more dignity than they receive and shouldn't mug. The good ones—Rob Sheffield, Ultragrrrl, Joe Levy—can place a quip the way Roger Federer can place a tennis ball, and there's something to respect there, but I still think they're lowering themselves somehow whenever I see a friend like that on the telly. They're much funnier and more natural in the bar booth, believe me. After a point, it has nothing to do with writing. It's all shtick—never ending shtick. And I had my own shtick-hell to raise.

As the century drew down, culture was eating itself. Those days of sitting in the cocktail lounge with Julie Bowen, listening to actual cocktail lounge music and not "cocktail lounge" music, were over forever. Everything was ironic retro, or meta, or ur. Sincerity would have one last gasp with the whole emocore movement and the brief superstardom of Dashboard Confessional's Chris Carraba, before everything was wholly consumed by a pandemic of ironic, too-hip, too-smart-by-half disconnection. Besides, once you do one of these talking head spots, you're pretty much on the hook to do them for the rest of your life. Unless you sass them. I don't know if it was the hangovers or some Paddy Chayefsky sense of righteousness (it was the hangovers), but I eventually began showing up hostile.

"Could you please take the cigarette out of your mouth. We can't show you smoking on camera."

"It's not lit."

"I know, but come on. How about the shades?"

"I'm an albino."

"Really?"

"I don't wanna scare the kids."

"Come on. You're not albino."

"So?"

"Okay, leave the shades, but the cigarette. Please. Come on, bro. Bro? Do it for me."

"I don't know you."

Just like you're nobody in sports until you get that ring, you were nothing as a rock writer until you got your first cover. The hall of fame voting committee would only ever use the lack of cover stats as a strike against you. With the column and the TV spots and the first name basis with the Nasty Little Men and Women, I was heating up, but it didn't matter. I'd never be a big gun—a Zev Borrow, or Maureen Callahan, or Sasha Frere Jones, or Mike Rubin, or Chris Norris—without a cover story. That year, a mystery document called "The Rock Critical List" began to circulate. While most attribute its authorship to Charles Aaron, he has to my knowledge never copped to it. The subtitle read, "Squirming in a Box Marked Fucked Since 1998," and the text by Jo Jo Dancer (the titular character of Richard Pryor's biographical film) called out all the big rock writers of the day: Touré, Joshua Clover, Neil Strauss, Eric Weisbard, Simon Reynolds, Danyel Smith, Joe Levy, and Robert Christgau (of course). It took to task not only them (Strauss is called a "balding dickless imp"; Ethan Smith is referred to as an "*EW* sniglet editor") but the validity of the form itself: "I can assure you that music criticism, like all criticism, has more often than not sucked the ass of a lubricated goat." Still, I was envious of those who were mentioned, and I'm sure those who made the list were at least partially flattered.

I'd scored some quality front-of-the-book pieces, which got a lot of attention. Jeff Buckley had been dead for a couple of years, and in that time, his beautiful voice and perfect features, now frozen young forever, had made him some kind of surrogate boyfriend to a generation of young men and women whose fear of actual intimacy was already being encouraged and abetted by the Web. Shortly after the odds-and-sods collection *Sketches for My Sweetheart the Drunk* was released, I wrote a *Talk of the Town*–style piece on the posthumous cult of Jeff Buckley. I sat on a bench in Tompkins Square Park with his still-grieving guitarist, Michael Tighe, who now spoke about Jeff as if he were some kind of angel. I never told him that I'd met Jeff at Shakespeare & Co., and he was just another good-looking, talented, East Side stoner. I didn't give away the angle of the piece either. I'd gotten adept at gently misleading my sources. Nothing I wrote was ever mean-spirited, and it was rare that anyone was truly hurt or offended. Stephen Jenkins of Third Eye Blind rang up once and demanded to speak with any editor who had the power to fire me. He was politely told where he could put his suggestion. Patricia Field, the fashion maven, called me "nasty" in *The New York Post*'s gossip column *Page Six*, but otherwise I knew where the line was and what to reveal or keep breasted. I'd been to the river where Jeff died on my very first road trip. I made out with a sweet-faced indie rocker on those muddy banks in my Tom Waits porkpie hat, my first tattoo still scabbing on my right upper arm.

In the spring of 1999, Tracey and I had worked up what we thought was just another similarly astute front-of-the-book piece, drawn from studying the newspapers and websites of the day, like my old man used to study the racing form, until something popped.

"Where the hell is Axl Rose?" I asked Tracey over our sandwiches in the conference room. "Do you realize it's been over five years since Guns N' Roses released a new album?"

"Really?"

"1993." I remembered buying it at Aaron's on La Brea Boulevard in Hollywood. *The Spaghetti Incident*. Not the most triumphant swan song in the history of rock, although it has its moments.

Most of the band had been fired or quit in exasperation as Axl and a slew of producers holed up in some expensive Los Angeles studio tinkering with the mystery album that was either going to be the greatest rock-and-roll record ever written, an utter fiasco, or simply a never-heard legend like Brian Wilson's *Smile* was at the time. As the nu metal mooks continued their whiney reign with their clean white kicks and their potbellies, the rock world seemed somehow less dangerous and fun and exciting without Axl, Slash, and Izzy in it.

"Where's Izzy?" Fuck that. Where's *Axl*?

There were no rock stars like Axl in the age of "I hate my dad" rock. It was unpopular to like them back in 1992, when a furious Axl was allegedly instructing Kurt Cobain to "shut his bitch up," but now even Hole were covering "Paradise City." There was a danger deficit in rock. A cold November rain had doused all the sex and fun and heat, and I for one was turning my lonely eyes to Guns. The first Guns N' Roses *Rolling Stone* cover story back in 1988 made me want to drive my Toyota fast, while drunk, and set my school and my stepfather on fire. That's what rock and roll should be like, I figured. Axl had somehow taken that with him when he vanished. The biggest star in rock and roll simply disappears . . . and nobody was asking why, or where to, or what was next. Tracey brought the idea to the features editor, Rob Levine, who took it to Alan Light, and Alan quickly assigned me to my first *Spin* feature after a year and a half of struggling to get into the well: a rise and fall story, *Citizen Kane* in a Stephen Sprouse kilt.

What did the new album sound like? Who was in the band now? What did Axl look like five years after his last big promotional tour? Nobody knew. The biggest rock star in the world slowly receded from public view, and somehow few even noticed, what with his successors shooting themselves in the head. Pre-TMZ, pre-twenty-four-hour news beasts, there were still mysteries and no sinking sense that everyone out there was wise to everyone and everything.

I got access to some Sunset Strip scene luminaries through Amra Brooks, and indirectly her well-connected father, including Brendan Mullen, the punk impresario who once booked Club Lingerie where Guns got their start. I went through aboveground channels to reach people like Tom Zutaut, the old-school A&R executive who signed Guns to Geffen (Inger Lorre of the Nymphs famously urinated on his desk). When Tom sat me down in his office and told me "the real story," I kept staring at the desk, wondering, Is this the one she whizzed on? I mean, if it were my desk, I'd keep it. I paid a bartender to pour extrastrong drinks and flirt with another source, the writer Lonn Friend, who dished everything on the band: Axl's temper, the drug use, the whole inside skinny. It was enough to fill a feature in itself. Friend called the next day horrified, and I felt guilty so I took it off the record. I was still learning the whole ethical scope of this thing. I had a source up in Canada whom I'd never met and rarely spoken to on the phone. Her name was Sorelle, and she only communicated via Instant Messenger. She was persistent and dangled bits over my head that I couldn't verify but that seemed plausible. I went to Rob Levine and got her hired as an additional reporter. Some of what I was uncovering was crazy. Axl was obsessed with dolphins and had become a practitioner of past-life regression therapy. It was all building up to something huge and bizarre . . . not unlike the "Estranged" video.

One night Alan Light got a call at home from W. Axl Rose—Imagine it's 11:30, you're in your sweats, ready for *Letterman*, and the telephone rings. Alan had no idea how Axl Rose had got his home number. The rock star spoke calmly, hitting none of his famous high notes. He told my boss that my story was going to derail the album (which would be publicly known as *Chinese Democracy*). Axl then proceeded to tick off every incident where the media had fucked him over, from a botched *Rolling Stone* photo shoot to a Jon Pareles review in the *New York Times* of a GN'R live show. He quoted the Pareles review verbatim. Alan stared at the tape recorder by his phone and wondered if he should hit record. He opted not to and instead calmly explained to Axl that *Spin* was being aboveboard. We were not trying to hide the story or railroad him. As soon as it was bumped up to a feature, we had gone to his Geffen Records publicist, Lori Earle, to inform her. Axl was invited to participate. Alan would do the interview himself. Axl indicated that he would think about it since Alan seemed like a reasonable guy. Alan took a suitcase to work the next morning, ready to fly to Los Angeles at a moment's notice.

Part of me was jealous. Why hadn't Axl called *me* at home? I was the one writing the fucking story. The other part of me was, of course, flattered: fucking Axl Rose knew I was writing about him! When I saw how rattled Alan was, I was mostly just grateful. It was intimated that if we ran a story now, we'd have no access when the new album came out. If we held it back, we might get an exclusive when the time came, especially since Axl now liked Alan. My career was basically in Axl's and Alan's hands. An on-the-record interview would be huge. Alan had to decide if it was worth trusting him or trusting me. There was no guarantee there'd be a record, and if there was, Alan was savvy enough to know that Axl'd go to *Rolling Stone*, which was twice as big as *Spin*, anyway. Oh, and *Rolling Stone* never printed a conditional interview form that GN'R supposedly made any potential journos sign (under the headline "No Appetite for Criticism"). Axl Rose also never implied in song that Jann Wenner was upset because his "dad" got "more pussy than [him]," as he did about *Spin*'s founder Bob Guccione Jr. I sat at my desk down in the online pod and chain-smoked in the hallway with the art department staff.

"What've you got so far?" Alan asked when I was finally called up.

I certainly had enough A-list stuff to justify a cover, whether Axl spoke or not. I had Lars from Metallica (along with Noel from Oasis and Gene Simmons, the best interview subject anyone could ask for, just turn on the tape recorder). I had Nikki Sixx, Alice Cooper, and Moby, who'd been tapped to produce the album at one point. I had the psychic who talked about Axl's past-life regression therapy and obsession with dolphins. I had the engineer who described the recording of "Rocket Queen" and Axl actually fucking some girl in the studio to get the right orgasmic squeals. I was getting paid to discover things about records that I played in my car in the eighties. I even had a wild account of Shaquille O'Neal rapping with the band in the studio.

"Shaq?" Alan asked.

"Shaq."

Alan sat there at his desk, the biggest in the building. He watched me and I watched him for what seemed like an hour.

"Okay," he finally said. "I'm pulling the trigger on this."

He took a huge leap of faith and told me to keep going. He was the metal Jason Robards, and I was the metal Hoffman and Redford.

"But you better get Slash."

"I'll get him."

It was intense and high stress, with Rob and me working through the weekend and there first thing Monday morning when everyone came in. I had no idea what I was doing, and Rob gently kept the piece on course. I loved how the rest of the world seemed to melt away; the little things like answering e-mails and shaving just took a backseat. It was almost like being back on heroin—the tunnel vision and the singular goal. When I saw the mock-up of the cover, I nearly cried. "What the world needs now is Axl Rose," it said, with a beautiful photo of a young Axl in leather pants, sitting on an amp.

It was the first buzz issue of the new, new *Spin* and, I believe, among the first high-profile instances of pre-Millennial retro fixation as far as pop went. The future was unknown and probably terrifying, but the past? God, wasn't that sooooo much fun? The computers might fail on December 31, with planes falling from the sky and wealthy and credit all reduced to zero, but . . . "Paradise City," dude!

As expected, the Axl story got a lot of attention for the magazine. It was one of the first of its kind, looking back, as the century ended, to a time that was already seeming so much easier and pure and innocent. A flood of theme and list issues would follow it. Alan had taken a chance and triumphed. I was soaring, brought back to earth only by one letter to the editor.

Brendan Mullen, one of my sources, posted a cranky missive, complaining about the way I'd quoted him in the piece . . . or misquoted him. I was afraid of Brendan Mullen. He had a reputation as a crank, one of those angry punks who never got over it, and loudly derided all the younger punks who came next. I didn't even do the interview with the dude. I farmed it out because I was intimidated. Some of my other LA sources had warned me about his temper. But when I read his letter to the editor, I had a drink or two for courage, then, before bed one night, wrote Brendan back via e-mail and apologized, explaining that it was my first major story. I was juggling a lot and overwhelmed, and I'd gladly run some kind of correction or retraction for him if he felt his reputation had been severely damaged. As with Ultragrrrl's e-mail, I could have easily let it alone—ignored it or asked an editorial assistant to respond. I don't know why I engaged him, but it too would change my life . . . eventually. As the months went by and the issues shipped out, my suspicion that Axl was a fluke was confirmed. I didn't expect to move to the top of the batting lineup overnight, but I was still a little disappointed when no other assignments came in. Hadn't I hit a clinch homer for the team? It was back to the front of the book for me.

I'd read about a Punk Rock Hall of Fame awards ceremony out of Los Angeles, and Tracey gave me a few hundred words. The piece would demand that I fly to LA on my own, rent a car, and check into a hotel. Most reporters have their own credit card. They travel on it, then submit the receipts. In twelve years of rock reporting, I never had a credit card—and still don't. I've just never had good credit. Nobody's ever issued me one. I've applied. Even when I had a lot of money, from a large advance, I paid for everything with cash or a debit card. I wasn't going to let this stop me, however. I rang Justin, my old screenwriting partner, who basically agreed to drive me everywhere, very relieved, like my mother and father and anyone else who ever really cared about me, that I wasn't in the ground. If I didn't have to pay for gas, I could afford to stay in a relatively cheap hotel like the famous Hyatt on Sunset, once the "Riot House" where Led Zeppelin raised hell and Keith Richards and Bobby Keys threw the TV set from one of the famous cement balconies, now a Hyatt Hotel like any other. Bands still stayed there—you'd often find a tour bus idling in the circular driveway—but they usually behaved themselves. Everyone did in the late nineties. Still, it was great to return to LA on someone else's dime and to know that I was in the land of theoretical creativity on real, concrete business. I had deadlines. I knew when this piece would run. It wasn't a pipe dream; it was just work.

The Punk Rock Hall of Fame Awards was basically a museum exhibit of old LA punk memorabilia. A few of my favorite bands from junior high and high school, like X, The Plugz, and Devo, were booked to play, and various scene luminaries like the elfin DJ and former club promoter Rodney Bingenheimer and Paul Reubens, aka Pee Wee Herman, were to be given lifetime achievement awards. I knew there was a chance that Brendan Mullen would be there too. Maybe he'd be able to ID me from the contribs photo and push me into a corner, wag a finger in my face, and make me piss myself. I only enjoyed confrontation when I was drunk. John Roecker, who was coordinating the event, was a wry, gay, stylish artist who was best friends with Exene (they ran a vintage store called You've Got Bad Taste). He knew Amra and liked the idea of the event getting national coverage in *Spin*. He was sweet and protective as he led me around and helped me gather my quotes.

"This is Ann Magnuson." Wow, I thought, Ann fucking Magnuson. She was one of the stars of that downtown NYC art and performance scene that preceded our arrival in the city. Zoe also loved her band Bongwater, founded with Mark Kramer, the producer of all that Galaxie 500 greatness. We played *Double Bummer* all the time.

"That's Pleasant Gehman. Let me see if I can find Paul. Don't call him 'Pee Wee,' okay?"

"Is Brendan Mullen here?" I finally asked him.

"Ha," he laughed, as if to say, "Rest easy. We all know Brendan's reputation out here."

"No, Brendan told me to go fuck myself when I invited him. He thinks I'm a carpetbagger. Too young to be a part of it. I wasn't really there."

That sounded familiar. He'd indicated that I had no right to profile Guns if I wasn't there. As if Doris Kearns Goodwin wasn't allowed to write about Lincoln because she wasn't in the box at Ford's Theater.

"Some people want to own the punk rock," Roecker quipped. "I was at nearly every Whiskey and Starwood show. But what right do I have to celebrate LA punk?"

Oh, Jesus, I thought. If I ever run into this Brendan guy, I'm doomed. How fast can I get the fuck out of LA? Surely he's waiting out in the parking lot with a tire iron. In my head, Brendan Mullen was still twenty-five years old, rangy and speeding, in a vintage suit.

Justin picked me up at the gallery once my reporting was done, and we went to dinner at La Poubelle, our old candlelit hangout on Franklin. It hadn't changed at all, but we had. The sit-down was a little stiff. Justin was doing well and seemed proud, but a little surprised and maybe a smidge envious that I'd gotten somewhat successful and hadn't overdosed or wound up in prison or rolling around in a wheelchair after falling off the Brooklyn Bridge.

"You know, Josh is still trying to get that movie made."

"Isn't he too old to play Shaky now? He'll end up playing the elderly black jazz professor at this point."

I didn't care about movies anymore. I only cared about rock and roll, and rock and roll was protecting me from the past. I felt like you could hit me over the head with a bottle of red wine, and I wouldn't feel it. I'd been inoculated against Los Angeles.

The following night I met Julie for a drink at Bar Marmont, next to the Chateau Marmont hotel. Julie and I drank martinis and talked about the old days, and sure enough, as with my parents and Justin, I'd lowered the bar so much that not dying was a triumph and being gainfully employed was a big deal.

"You look good," she said. "I'm so proud of you."

"You look good too," I said. She didn't look so good. She still had those Lloyd Cole *"cheekbones like geometry and eyes like sin,"* but her complexion was no longer perfect. She was skinny and seemed nervous and strung out. But it was still Julie. After drinks we went back to her house up in the hills. She was doing well too, getting lots of work. She had a nice back deck and a pretty view. We fell into the couch and began to make out like we used to. I was wearing another weird agnès b. sweater and worried that it smelled from my travels but decided I should table my self-consciousness and see where this was heading. It never went very far with Julie, but this seemed different. I pulled off her pants, and she made a comment about how there were pigs on her underwear. Indeed, there were. I'd never seen her in her underwear before. Had there always been pigs there?

"Why have we never done this?" she asked, as I pulled my pants off. If I'd had an answer, the last half decade and more would have been very different. She was naked now and looked at me. I tried to smile.

"You're still wearing clothes." She went into the bedroom, and I followed her, and we fell into bed and started fooling around again.

"Oh, would it be so bad?" she asked.

"No." What was I supposed to say? Yes, let's wait another ten years?

The next thing I knew I was inside her.

"Stop. Wait," she said and got up and stared at me.

I knew it, I thought. Something's wrong. What's wrong? Something's always wrong. But she didn't stop. She just calmed herself, stared for a minute, and then resumed.

"What do you want?" she asked me.

"This is good," I said. What was she talking about? Then it occurred to me that she was asking what I wanted to do in bed, like, anything freaky or different. I didn't know what to say. This was pretty much all I'd ever wanted, and when it finally happened, it was almost like I was watching myself. I couldn't feel much in my extremities. I almost preferred the moments when we kissed because it took me out of my brain having someone else's brain so close by. Did it mean we were a couple now? No. Did she like it? Maybe. She seemed to. I sensed this was it, like the elimination of years of sexual tension just happening because it finally did, nothing more, nothing less. When it was over, we lay in her bed and listened to the crickets.

"Tell me a story," she said.

"Do you want to hear about the time I shit my pants?"

She giggled. "Yes, definitely."

I told her about living with Alex in Park Slope and trying to be domestic, walking the dog we'd adopted and doing the grocery shopping and the wash.

"I can't picture you walking a dog or taking care of anything," she said.

I told her that one day I was out running errands on Seventh Avenue, and I felt an extreme gastric disturbance. I was three blocks from home, with a handful of shopping bags, and I tried but failed to get there before spontaneously evacuating. I described how I had washed my soiled black corduroy jeans, then my only pair, in the washer, dried them, put them back on, and nobody was the wiser. How I felt like relationships were full of these lies and illusions and tiny deceptions and that everyone was figuratively and literally full of shit and scurrying to and fro to hide it from their partner. It was a way to signal to her that I wasn't going to cling. She kissed me, satisfied with the story, and we fell asleep. In the morning, I asked if we could do it again, sensing that it would be a very long time, maybe forever, before we'd ever have sex again.

"I can't. I'm sore."

My suspicions confirmed, I walked out onto the porch and listened to the bird in the heavy morning smog. So it was black coffee—she was out of milk—then an awkward drive back to my hotel, with *Morning Becomes Eclectic* on KCRW the only conversation. I kissed her and that afternoon flew back to New York City. I wondered if I would ever see her again. I would.

Having escaped Los Angeles without being throttled by Brendan Mullen and filed my story on LA punk, I figured that the genre and one of its furious pioneers were long behind me, but I opened my e-mail one afternoon in the new media pod, and it was from an old Bennington friend Matt Ellis. He was back from a few years in Prague. About two dozen of us Lit Fucks had made beelines to that city once the Cold War ended. Matt was now working for Carol Mann, a boutique agency in Greenwich Village. One of his colleagues was looking for someone to do an oral history about Darby Crash from the Germs, and was I interested in meeting him. His name was James Fitzgerald.

"Sure," I wrote back. "Give him my number."

James Fitzgerald filled a room in the same manner as Gordon Lish. Both seemed like they came out of a more romantic time when literary men were just bigger. They were survivors of the real counterculture, during a time when acting the way that I did so blithely all over downtown Manhattan could get you beaten up or thrown in jail or shot at. It had given him that "Alright, impress me" air. Coupled with a deep, gruff voice, unruly graying hair, and a theatrical limp, he was a pretty unnerving character, but a few whiskies put me at ease during our first meeting in the old Cedar Tavern, then on University Place just south of Union Square. Over a hundred years old, the Tavern had switched locations over the years but always drew heavyweights from the world of art and letters: Pollock, De Kooning and Franz Kline, Kerouac, Ginsberg, and Corso had all sat in the thick, dark-wood booths and eaten the chili and the burgers and drunk the beer. I guess James, whom I almost immediately started calling "Jim," was impressed that I was able to drink and smoke the way I did (i.e., they way they did). I also knew everything there was to know about baseball and Bob Dylan, our mutual hero.

Fitzgerald had been an editor at Doubleday when Jackie Onassis worked there in the eighties. Jackie O. used to bum cigarettes off him. He'd worked at St. Martin's (which rejected my first novel *Loose*) and had a hand in some already iconic rock books, including Jon Savage's *England's Dreaming* and Johnny Rotten's *Rotten: No Irish, No Blacks, No Dogs.* He was friends with Dennis Hopper, Merle Haggard, and Ed Sanders, who was a Fug and wrote *The Family*, the great Manson tome. He represented Hells Angels, Black Panthers, magicians, and crackpots; anything outside the law and the establishment seemed to genuinely thrill him. Darby Crash was a perfect Fitzgerald subject: dead and spooky. He was a junkie, closeted, possibly a genius; he'd studied Scientology and nurtured a Family-like cult of LA punk girls in the late seventies before overdosing on December 7, 1980, the day before John Lennon's murder, which all but reduced his carefully planned suicide to a footnote. People carried signs that said "Imagine" and "Give Peace a Chance" that week; few of them brandished their cigarette-inflicted "Germs burns." I didn't even own a copy of the Germs' lone album. I knew Darby from the Penelope Spheeris film *The Decline of Western Civilization*, in which he cooks breakfast and plays with a tarantula. The Germs' music had aged well though and found a new audience in the nineties with the rise of BMX and skate culture. The band was second only to X and Black Flag in terms of sturdy West Coast punk iconography. There'd been a tribute record in 1996 and rumors of a film titled *What We Do Is Secret* (which would finally be released a decade later).

I found the Darby myth fascinating. I liked that he was considered a prophet by some, a fraud by most, and a deluded, tragic drug casualty ultimately. But I knew that I was firmly East Coast. What would Brendan Mullen say if he knew I was writing about Darby Crash. He'd have me scalped.

Because of the LA-centric nature of the Axl cover story, James Fitzgerald just assumed I knew my Pacific Coast. But I'd only lived in LA for a few desperate years. Fortunately, we talked about Darby for all of five minutes when we met at the Cedar Tavern. We basically discussed everything but the book, including the Yankees and the Red Sox (I was a fan of the former, he of the latter). After drinks, I followed him woozily back to the office on Fifth Avenue between Eleventh and Twelfth, just across from the Forbes Building. Nobody on the street looked like Jim. And he moved through the Village like someone who had been there since the Lenapes rowed canoes in the Hudson. Jim was more like a boxing trainer.

This is more like it, I thought as we rode up in the elevator. Here is the kind of agent that a real fucking writer should have. Hard drinking, short-tempered, someone who could put the fear into an editor. Not only would I follow this guy into the publishing world, I'd want him with me in a bar fight.

At Carol Mann, I said hello to Matt, awkwardly asking how Prague had been, even though he'd been back for a few years. That's just the way with

Bennington people; you can not see them for a lifetime, but as soon as you do, it's like you saw them last week.

"Do you think this book'll find a publisher?" I asked Jim before I left.

"I don't take books on that I don't get published. The title is key. Let's really nail this title." We shook hands, and I left.

Does that mean I'm going to get published? I wondered as I crossed town back to the *Spin* offices, cutting through Madison Square Park. At least I had an agent again; it had been about five years. Back at the office I printed out all the Germs lyrics I could on the Web and faxed them over to Jim to see what jumped out at them. He e-mailed me back a few days later. His electronic transmissions were as to the point as his personal manner.

"*We All Swim.* There's your title."

We All Swim? I didn't even know that song. I looked back through the print-out packet and discovered that Jim had taken a random snippet from the lyrics to the song "Our Way": *"Against the current we all swim. Cageless wonders of sometime when the paper icon's chase will end."* I had no clue what it meant. As I said, I was barely a fan. We all swim. Where do we all swim? Sooner or later, we all swim alone? And I swam, I swam so far away?

"Okay, Jim," I wrote back. "That's the title." And I, a writer with the same name as an Olympic hero, began writing up the proposal for my first book, entitled . . . *We All Swim.*

CHAPTER 14

Ok, what happened was . . . the century ended, and people just stopped listening: "Did you say something?" Snnnnnorrrrrrrrrrrt. "You wanna know the weird thing about religion?" "I haven't heard this record in years. Was this a 4AD?" "Close those blinds, and I'll tell you." "Those aren't birds. They're not birds. Tell me it's not sun . . . rise . . . time." Snorrrrt.

Discounting the experimental scattering when I first got to Bennington in the eighties, I swore I would never do coke because of the old man. That was his drug. I had mine. Boomers did coke. X-ers did smack and hated coke-snorting boomers. I was an impatient person by nature, and it seemed silly to want to speed that shifty-twitchy feeling up. Whenever I did coke after graduation, I'd inevitably find myself in some terrible hotel for days on end, staring at some Alicia Silverstone movie that wasn't *Clueless* on television and afraid to move or pick up the phone. Whether it was the low-rent, angry, flimsy St. Mark's Hotel downtown or the chilly, creepy, high-priced Paramount uptown, the result was always the same: paralyzing fear, a cruelly diminishing golf ball of shitty East Coast blow, and either *Excess Baggage* or *The Crush*. Heroin slowed the spin of the globe down to a very pleasant tugboat chug. But if the nineties were about smack, the 2000s were all about coke. It turned out the Internet, which I was convinced was a fad back at the old House of Trance, was not a fad. Who knew? Now it was producing twenty-something millionaires and multimillionaires, and same as it ever was, the fastest and easiest way to telegraph your status was with a little amber bottle of blow. People never whipped out smack to say, "I've made it, check me." Coke and cell phones and Metrocards—that's what had changed from one century to the next, as far as I could tell. One day nobody had either; the next, a bunch of rich dicks were motormouthing into their Samsungs.

Why was I doing coke too as the millennium ended? I was no Internet millionaire. I wasn't even an Internet thousand-aire. I just spent time with their likes in bars and at clubs and rock shows and parties, writing my column and afraid of sleep because, as Shakespeare (and Nas) said, it's the "cousin of death." I was working out of my apartment now, only coming in for edit meetings. Alan had put me on staff, and I was finally able to leave the online pod. Between new plays down on Ludlow Street and *Spin* deadlines, there wasn't much to do but play air guitar in my kitchen. When I wasn't writing furiously or furiously high, I had to face myself, and I simply did not want to.

I waved good-bye to my twenties with a party at Don Hill's in October 1999 (attended by Greg Dulli of Afghan Whigs for some reason) and the aforementioned Wall Street douches; thus, coke was it.

"Hey, Greg Dulli, I'm thirty. Want some blow?" (I don't recall what he said, but you can probably guess).

Coke gave me ultraviolence too. I lost whatever mensch was left inside me. The gak placed ten thousand baby hornets in my bonnet, and I could not go to bed until the buzzing had stopped. I sent a lot of hate e-mails before bed and often woke up to the digital equivalent of that old joke about the snail that gets thrown out of the garden, and ten years later the guy who threw it hears a knock at his door, and the snail says, "Hey, what was *that* about?"

I would go see a band with Victoria De Silverio, my *Spin* coworker, and the woman I'd pledged the end of my youth to, and I'd seethe at the afterparty as I watched one of the band members flirt with her. They always did. They couldn't help it. She was gorgeous. She never invited it, but she didn't exactly discourage the flattery either. I'd make mental notes to trash them in my column.

"The Drunkenness Monster [from the Canadian rap band Len of "Steal My Sunshine" fame], you just made the shit list, motherfucker. Signed, the Cokeness Monster."

My plays got a lot more nihilistic with the influence of coke and unrequited love. ". . . *Worry Baby*," the next production that we did at Todo Con Nada, was directed by another Bennington student, Carlo Vogel. It was about a couple of yuppies, Dexter and Donna, who venture down to the Lower East Side because it's supposedly "safe" now, thanks to Rudy and his quality-of-life police. They encounter a white B-boy named Larippo, who's been shot in a drug skirmish, and he holds the wife hostage while the husband goes for help. ". . . *Worry Baby*" was a politically incorrect, super-sexed-up, carnage-drenched hell trip through a dangerous kind of New York that was growing less and less familiar with all those aforementioned tooting yuppies flooding into the newly safe Lower East Side. Of all my plays, it was the most offensive and the most successful, very nearly making it to a big-budget Off-Broadway (as opposed to our usual "Off-Off") production. That one extra "Off" equals about 200,000 in production. I'd been paired with Andy Goldberg, a director from The New

Group, and he brought major comic actors like Tina Fey and Paul Rudd to read. Justin Vivian Bond, the genius cabaret performer, read Mrs. Normandie at one gathering. Swoosie Kurtz read her at a larger one at the posh Ars Nova space in Midtown. It still freaks me out, the idea of famous actors reading my stuff. Sometimes, when I watch *30 Rock* re-runs, a decade on, I am still reminded that the person playing Liz Lemon is the same person who read aloud, "*I wanna go where you're going. I want to leave this world wrapped in your arms. And you can fuck my bullet hole while we're dying.*" Most of the time, she's just Liz. It was so surreal seeing these real actors read our demented little downtown plays for real producers and wine-and-cheese theater types. It must be how a punk band feels when they sneak a bona fide hit onto the charts. *The Farewell Drugs* and "*. . . Worry Baby*" now established some kind of sensibility we were grasping at. We even had a publicist this time, Timothy Haskell at Publicity Outfitters (kind of like Urban Outfitters . . . but not). In his release, Tim described the play as *Who's Afraid of Virginia Woolf* meets *Reservoir Dogs*. Soon the *Village Voice*, my high school lifeline to New York City culture, expressed interest in doing a profile in the theater section. I would no longer be just the guy who read about artists in the paper; I was now becoming one of those artists people read about, maybe even kids trapped out on the Island, yearning for a more exciting life in the city.

Jack and I did an interview with Alexis Soloski, one of the *Voice*'s theater critics. She was bespectacled and blonde and I found her attractive, but if I was flirtatious, it wasn't because I wanted to get her into bed, necessarily. I wanted her to tell me what the hell I was really doing with these plays. I had no idea. They felt good, and people seemed to like them, but I was winging it. Watching the plays, all of them, from the dressing room (I could never sit in the seats at Nada), it seemed like someone else had written them. I wanted her to profile me so I could figure out who I was. A few days later the photographer doing the photo shoot had me pose on a stoop outside of Nada. I put my hand down on the pavement to brace my body and nearly punctured my palm on a discarded hypo. When I saw the profile (headline *Sad Cat, Pop Dog*), I was excited, but it wasn't enough. I needed more from my first critic. I wanted to follow her around so she could tell me who I was as I bought a turkey sandwich at the bodega, or waited at the walk/don't walk signal, or flossed my teeth. I wanted to move in with her and have her tell me what every word I wrote meant, what every move I made signified. I could live my life, and she could review it.

The New York critics seemed to find our arch rock-and-roll pose a breath of fresh air. Our audiences were loud. They drank and smoked while the play unrolled and sometimes utterly unraveled. *Time Out* called us the "hottest theater scene in the city," but I had no idea what I was doing, or how we got there.

We also started appearing in *Page Six* around this time, which made the plays even more notorious. My friend Chris Wilson, a decadent and dastardly writer/reporter who worked at the *New York Post*, along with a friend of mine from Bennington, Jared Paul Stern, found our drunken exploits amusing and threw us a few breaks on slow news days. At Bennington Jared, like my first roommate Dan, had been obsessed with Brett Easton Ellis. Despite his modern taste in literature, he also had a weird fetish for the club aesthetic and turned his little card room into something resembling a wood-paneled gentleman's lodge. He was the kind of guy who wore an ascot unironically, but we liked each other fine. He later made the tabloids himself for allegedly trying to extort money from the billionaire Ronald Burkle. I felt bad for the guy once the scandal broke and seemed to dwarf him and all his charming affectations. Chris was tougher stuff. I once spent a day working alongside him at "the *Page*," filling in for one of his reporters during the holidays. Richard Johnson, then the editor of the section, was away, and I sat in his chair and answered his phone. It was then I realized this was "big gossip," not the safe little indie rock page I put together every month. There was an entire culture of obsessive scoop suppliers who lived to be sources. Who knows if they made the shit up or actually saw their "exclusives," but they all wanted credit for bringing the dirt to the door. It was overwhelming, even by rock-and-roll standards. I was pretty jaded, but I didn't know how poor Wilson slept at night, having to wade into that world every day. Actually, I knew pretty well how he wound down. A hard drinker, he frequented Siberia, the tiny bar in the Fiftieth Street subway station that I'd only ventured into before or just after shows at the nearby Roseland. To this day, a text from him will make my liver and spleen shake. And yet, I'm always happy to see him, and he really threw me a bone when I was a young playwright in the city. Everybody read *Page Six* in the years before *Gawker* and *Vulture* and all the other major culture sites. They read *Page Six* in LA. They read it in London. To make "the *Page*" was to be noticed by your snooty aunt and uncle up on Central Park West and your street-rat Max Fish junkie friends. It brought in the audiences at our crumby little Ludlow Street black box. Soon, amazingly, we were too popular for Nada. We literally could not seat the number of people who wanted to see our shows or sustain a longer run that might accommodate them at our Fugazi-like ticket prices.

Aaron Beall's empire, once the engine of the Ludlow Street theater scene, was fast going down the toilet anyway, a victim of post-Giuliani gentrification. The hero mayor I'd hoped would save us all from the Dart Man had done his job perhaps a little too well. We gave him an inch, and he took away our dancing and our homespun art scene. New York was "safe," and bank accounts were full. The Yuppies got in like dry rot and wouldn't leave until the entire Lower East Side looked like the Green Acres Mall in Valley Stream. Subsequently, Aaron Beall had lost his block of theater spaces, and for personal reasons, most likely stress related, he'd dyed his hair clown colors. He and Kirsten Ames, who was now acting as my manager, what with all the press we were getting, had long before broken up. She took a path toward legitimate theater, booking my plays and her artists, like Marc Maron, over at the spacious Westbeth, by the West Side Highway, off the Hudson River. Aaron, by contrast, began referring to himself as "Le Star Bang," some bastardization of Lester Bangs, I suppose, and convinced me to take on the title "Pure Pop Playwright." I'd always loved the Nick Low album *Pure Pop for Now People* and was, with the coke and the *Page Six* mentions, at the height of my egotism, so I agreed. My work was to be the centerpiece of the new "Pure Pop Festival," a Nada-centric event that would, I suppose, somehow raise enough money to push back the hordes and preserve the Ludlow Street theater scene and rival the annual Fringe Festival for prestige. It was a lot to lay on me, and Jack and I pretty much knew it was a plan doomed to fail. We were loyal to Aaron and agreed to put the productions together, but once the till was full, our efforts only provided a Band-Aid. Poor Aaron was hemorrhaging with debt. Few wanted to work with him because of rumors that his theater empire was insolvent. Soon even Jack, Carlo, and I were following Kirsten west. Maybe it would be nice to do a show somewhere with a clean toilet in the dressing room. I felt guilty until one night at the Westbeth we were asked to vacate our dressing room so that the performance artist Karen Finley, also performing there at the time, could enjoy some private time. The esprit de corps of punk rock theater only extended so far, I guess.

We needed a new producer, a real one, for our new play, *I Wanna Be Adored*, and found one in the form of Bob Rake, a gnomish man with an evil glint in his eye. Bob wore a beard, a ball cap, and sportswear and always traveled around with a tall, statuesque friend. He had a wife out in New Jersey. He was a legit producer with a keen ear for good theater but also quite possibly the devil himself. He liked the play, which imagined what would happen to Ian Curtis's soul after the Joy Division lead singer's suicide in May 1980, on the eve of the band's first U.S. tour. I have him descending as far as purgatory but being barred from hell by the devil himself (who is concerned that Ian will make eternal suffering seem glamorous). Bob worked out of New York Performance Works, a massive theater complex off Chambers Street in Tribeca, the sight of an old bank. We got the medium-sized black box and immediately began putting a production together, with our regular set designer, Andromache (another Bennington student whose mother is the great stage actress Kathleen Chalfant), building a northern England home that switched during a blackout to a Weimar-style cabaret. I even bought a gorilla suit, a sort of tribute to Marlene Dietrich in *Blonde Venus*, and Sarah Gifford, who'd been Hella Hecht in *The Farewell Drugs*, played a dancing ape.

We found John Del Signore, our Ian holding auditions basically looking for someone who could do a sustained and credible Manchester accent. John supposedly spent most of his time then frozen in public squares, covered in silver paint. He was one of those robot street performers who give me the creeps, but he nailed the Manchester accent.

Given our press, my directors, Jack and Carlo Vogel, and I now had the courage, with a real producer and some good press notices, to go to the Bennington people who'd already made names for themselves in the downtown theater world. Jonathan Marc Sherman, who'd so vexed me in the fall of 1988, having already made a career for himself at nineteen with his play *Women and Wallace*, read the script and agreed to play the devil. As I mentioned, post-Bennington Sherman had started a theater company, Malaparte, with Ethan Hawke. Now, he was going to do one of my shows. How did that happen? Peter Dinklage was on board as well, as the sort of narrator, a vulgar borscht-belt comic named Bobby Lemondrops. Like Justin Theroux, Pete was a working but still un-famous actor. He'd already done that classic scene in *Living in Oblivion* that reduced all surreal dwarf appearance to instant cliché. Annie Parisse, the big theater star at Fordham with Jack, was to play Ian Curtis's Belgian mistress.

Doing shows with Sherman and Dinklage at Rake's New York Theater Works put us on an entirely new level both of debauchery and proximity to real fame. I was starstruck and nervous every night, wondering which famous and semi-famous actors would RSVP and, of course, what they would think of our street-level theater (which was no longer street-level). Josh Charles, who'd failed after Kurt Cobain's death to console me onscreen in *Threesome*, and his girlfriend, Jennifer Connelly. We'd go to a bar and Liev Schreiber, probably the best theater actor of my generation, would show up and shoot the shit. One night we all went to a bar called Halo around the corner from my apartment, and I noticed a pretty girl with short hair staring at me. I was pretty drunk, but I soon realized it was the actress Toni Collette. I'd written a short piece for *Spin* on the Todd Haynes film *Velvet Goldmine* in which she played a character based on David Bowie's wife Angie. Normally, I would never let on, but like I said, I was pretty drunk and surrounded by famous people, so it didn't seem as weird. She told her friend (not famous) she thought I was cute (the almighty "cute") and then, right there in front of me, entered into a debate with this woman about whether or not I actually was nice looking.

"He is."

"No, he's not. You're crazy."

"I think he is."

Drinking with famous people was more like being back in high school than working at *Spin* was. Toni Collette won the debate, and we made plans to meet the next day for coffee at the Espresso Bar across from my apartment. I got there on time, and she'd already called to say she'd be running late. "You know Toni Collette?" the barista gushed. It was then that I got extremely un-comfortable. I was sober. Bars were dark. The Espresso Bar was natural light.

Toni Collette, sly and blonde, showed up, and we shared a few coffees and some awkward conversation. Finally, she asked where I lived, and I told her my apartment was right across the street. She came back and sat in my dirty kitchen—where I wrote and played air guitar—and, I guess, waited in vain for me to make a move. That's the thing. My rebel persona, my cool invention, my boa-necked rock Batman, my "guy who drank" . . . whatever he was, he never materialized when I needed him. He was there 99 percent of the time— when it was inappropriate. I never heard from her again.

When the cast and crew weren't at the bar on Duane Street after the shows or in the West Village apartment of our friend Brendon Blake (who strummed and sang an acoustic version of The Stone Roses' "I Wanna Be Adored" as the audiences filed into the theater most nights), we were at Rose's Turn, a piano bar in my neighborhood. Sherman was the gayest not gay per-son ever, and I knew he wasn't gay because I'd kissed him on the mouth. Sher-man was mad for truth or dare, and out of the four shows a week we did, at least half of them ended with his presiding over marathon sessions in one ex-Bennington student or another's apartment. One time we even did one in the basement of the Paradise Club, a strip joint near Madison Square Garden. Rake liked to unwind after a show by hitting the titty bars, and every so often, he'd spring for the cast and crew to join him. Everyone but Sherman and I ended up naked that night, strapped to one apparatus or another. There we were, two chaste playwrights in an empty room lit only by a fish-tank lamp that was full of water but void of fish. They'd clearly and wisely fled. We were there with two strippers, one blonde, the other African American, both at-tractive, both naked, and what did we do? Truth or dare.

The only person I ended up making out with that night was Sherman (on a dare). There was no sex in the champagne room, and there were no fish in the fish-tank room. It was a long way from quiet, old Franklin house, where we'd first met up at school. He still takes time out of his life as a husband, father, and much more famous playwright to appear in my shit. He doesn't have to, but then, he never did.

After *I Wanna Be Adored* performances, we'd sometimes go to the Slipper Room, a new bar built largely with Internet bubble money. The owner James was another Bennington figure who'd studied painting and sculpture as a graduate student. Handsome and dandy, James had dated Patricia Ann and was friendly with Zoe and Chrissie, my fellow Chelsea Hotel escapee (who was the bartender, along with another Bennington boy, a painter named Douglas). James styled himself as a sort of bon vivant who dressed like an invited guest on *Playboy After Dark*, all iridescent suits and vintage shoes so ugly they were beautiful. As with most Bennington students, he dealt in absolutes when it came to art and style: Norfin trolls were good; Barbie dolls were tacky. The bar was decorated as such: ornate, with a tin roof and red walls, gold-framed photos, and a Balthazar of champagne, or maybe it was a Rohoboam. It wasn't Max Fish, with its punk rock art. This was the new burlesque. There was a big stage at the back with lush, velvet theater curtains. There was a DJ console to the side of the stage, where I started DJing for free drinks. James had recently married (on the roof of the Chelsea Hotel) a willowy blonde Razorfish employee named Camille, who wore horn-rimmed glasses and vintage clothes like her husband. Camille frequently go-go danced at the bar as I spun. On Friday nights, there'd be a review of locally famous burlesque stars who carried themselves like international superstars, as my beloved Warholian and Dreamland actors had done: Dirty Martini, Lady Ace, Murray Hill, the voluptuous Bob, a Marilyn Monroe look alike, Richard Fox (who'd perform as a demented child star named Albino Andy), Bradford Scobie (who'd prance about as Dr. Donut), Julie Atlas Mewes, who was hands down the smartest and most inventive of the lot, Scotty the Blue Bunny, and Austin Scarlett, who didn't perform, but I suspect every time he left his flat, he was on stage.

I'd had enough backstage theater experience by then to not be fazed by the view into the dressing room from the DJ booth. Tits were no longer things to stare at, as they'd been back when Adam David and I traveled to Times Square as teens. DJing was a job, and cueing up a bump-and-grind number for performers who just happened to be pulling things out of their vaginas or buttholes was no different from playing Abba for a drunken tourist per request. I'd have to squeeze past them to pee and whip my dick out simply because the song was about to end. Only Scotty the Blue Bunny, a comic who hosted the show some nights in a blue latex rabbit suit, was hard to work with, waving his dick at me from the tiny room as if to say, "Hello, Mr. DJ!" And a few years later, whenever Miss Rose Wood, a towering transgender performance artist, performed, I'd always duck behind the cabinets because inevitably everyone in the front row would get splattered with some form of fluid. It may have looked like the cover of Tom Waits's *Small Change*, but most of the time, it was just another Thursday night, with free drinks and, if I was lucky, cab fare home, usually alone.

When we weren't at the Slipper Room, we were around the corner at the Library bar. The Library, formerly one of my old smack pickup spots, called Psycho Mongos, had a great punk/hard rock jukebox, both vintage ("The Ace of Spades" by Motorhead, "Where Eagles Dare" by Misfits, "Bad Luck" by Social D, "Who Was in My Room Last Night" by Butthole Surfers) and current ("Feel Good Hit of the Summer" by Queens of the Stone Age, essentially our design-for-living anthem with its chorus of *"Nicotine, Valium, Vicodin, marijuana, Ecstasy and alcohol"*). Yes, please. There were cobwebs on the walls. It smelled like stale beer, puke, and mold, but it was dark and oddly womblike. Anton Newcombe, the lead singer of Brian Jonestown Massacre, was usually glowering at the bar, ready to get into a hostile conversation about politics or the music industry or The Beatles. Nick, the owner, had put a big TV at the back. Like me, he'd gone to the Ritz as a teen in Connecticut, and before every show, the Ritz would show clips of cult movies and cartoons. Nick wanted his own little Ritz there and amassed a collection of video-tapes—although bartenders only seemed to play *The Toxic Avenger*, *Brain Dead*, *Basket Case*, or *Bloodsucking Freaks* (most of the time it was just *Blood-sucking Freaks*, which would play until the tape unspooled, rewind automati-cally, and then play again).

Nobody hip drank there; it had just opened and was always empty, so our little social crew annexed it, and the rounded table in back was off limits to other customers. It was so dark you could get a hand job under the table without anyone noticing. I know people who've fucked in the booths while the bar was open. On Halloween the first decorations went up and have not been taking down to this day.

I Wanna Be Adored was even better received than "*. . . Worry Baby*," with *Paper* magazine now giving us a historic context and not just a review. I even got a profile in *Paper*, which, along with the *Voice* and *Details*, had provided me with a window on the art scene from my painfully distant bedroom out on the Island in the early eighties. "Now, Spitz looks ready to cross that major threshold of all emerging artists," wrote the late Tom Murrin, one of our early champions. "He and the actors in *Adored* will actually get paid. 'It's what I al-ways wanted, to write and get paid for it,' he says. 'Jackie Mason's on Broad-way. Why not us?'" One night Liev pulled me over at the Duane Street bar and whispered to me, "You're good. Be careful who you work with," intimating that I might want to stop doing theater with friends and drinking buddies if I really wanted to make it. I appreciated the advice, but I was having too much fun to heed it. Plus: cred! Besides, some of my friends and drinking buddies were starting to get genuinely famous. Peter Dinklage killed every night ad-libbing and breaking up the crowd as borscht-belt comic and Hades MC Bobby Lemondrops. One night I was walking along lower Sixth Avenue with him and someone shouted out, "Bobby Lemondrops." It's still one of my proudest moments as a writer.

When the play closed, I took my gorilla suit, went home, and slept for two weeks. Nicole Barnette, from Bennington and the Formosa Café posse, had moved to New York; Julie had come to visit her at her apartment in Hell's Kitchen, and we all had dinner at Pastis. Julie was dating another straight, clean-cut, faceless guy who did something or another in some business or another. She didn't seem happy. I called her a few days later and we went over to the Cinema Village to see the documentary *American Movie* together. I imagined what it would be like to be her real boyfriend. Anyone's real boyfriend, making plans, seeing movies, going to dinner, talking about wine. It seemed like hastening death, or at least middle age. We parted and made plans to get coffee, which I never expected would actually happen. It was just something polite to say when you walk away from an old friend in a city. But the next day, she buzzed me from the street. In the daylight, she seemed thin, withdrawn, and disoriented, but my apartment was so small that to stand in the kitchen was to virtually be in the bedroom so soon we were making out. My closet was open and she noticed the gorilla suit from *I Wanna Be Adored* hanging with my sharkskin blazers and old overcoats. She smiled, got up, and grabbed it, and soon she was wearing the thing.

"Careful, there are pins in it," I warned.

"I don't even care," she sighed. We flopped on the bed and started fooling around again, but I stopped it. She looked depressed and a little lost.

The truth was, sleeping with Julie once was all I'd ever really wanted to do. It's all I knew how to do: kill the curiosity, gather the details, then write about it later. It was writer sex—passionless, dreary—but better than none at all. There really wasn't anybody I could imagine myself with on a regular basis—a girlfriend or a wife. And once anyone expressed any emotional neediness or vulnerability, I ran. It was not part of my movie.

CHAPTER 15

I had a meeting about *We All Swim* with a yet another prospective editor. Her name was Carrie Thornton, a feisty Southern gal who seemed quite different from the other editors I'd sat down with. Foremost, she was young and could reference nearly all of the new bands, as well as The Smiths, The Cure, and the Mode. She had a vaguely new wave hairdo but was clearly comfortable in the buttoned-down world of big publishing. We both had a similar sense of raw ambition. Carrie had been given the power to buy books only recently, and I'd been encouraged to write them probably around the same time. Neither of us had anything to show for it yet.

Our first date was in Hell, literally: a gay bar in the West Village called Hell. She was determined to drink there, but at first neither of us could find it. At the time it didn't strike me as strange that I was lost in my own neighborhood or that Carrie felt like a bar she'd been to once (and one she didn't realize was a gay bar) was the perfect place to get acquainted.

Oh, God, this is not going well, I worried, as I scanned the blood-red walls and the empty bar stools. Happy hour in Hell was not swinging. Slowly, as I sat and chatted with her, I found myself speaking honestly for the first time since meeting Jim and entertaining the possibility of publishing again.

"Can I confess something?"

"Please."

"I absolutely understand why editors have been skeptical about the commercial . . . what do you call it? . . . of a Darby Crash biography. Appeal? I'm skeptical about it. But I think Legs McNeil and Gillian McCain left a huge fucking opening for an oral history of West Coast punk rock. Have you read *Please Kill Me* recently? I just re-read it for the fifth time, and they all but ignore it. They don't even talk about Black Flag. In a punk rock book! Would you be interested in something like that, or do you have your heart set on Darby Crash?"

She thought about it for a moment. I tried to look competent and sipped my Greyhound.

"I mean, then you would be able to include new wave and power pop. The Knack. I love The Knack. Devo, who came out to LA from Ohio. Same with The Cramps. Well, they didn't come from Ohio. They came from . . . somewhere. Here probably. The Go-Go's. The Plimsouls. Um . . . Josie Cotton. The whole *Valley Girl* soundtrack."

I still couldn't quite place the haircut, but I was praying now that it was new wave. A lot was riding on the inspiration for that tonsorial choice.

"I would be more interested in buying that book, actually," she finally said, and we immediately began reconfiguring *We All Swim* right there—in Hell. I didn't even know I could change the gist of a book once it had been proposed.

"And while we're at it, can we talk about that title?" Carrie said.

I walked her up to the train on Fourteenth Street, extremely buzzed. Once the buzz wore off, I started to worry. What if I can't work with anyone? The book had been passed on eleven times after all, and part of me had already written it off as more evidence of bad karma. I'd done too many selfish and evil things to deserve a book deal or a cool editor with a Tracey Thorn haircut. A few days later, Carrie and Three Rivers Press, a division of Random House, made an offer. We got dinner to celebrate and get to know each other better.

"I can't believe I'm going to have a motherfucking ISBN number," I gushed over my vodka in the Jane Street Tavern, a cozy, Bohemian hole-in-the-wall a few blocks from my apartment. "I can't tell you how many ISBN searches I did at Shakespeare & Co. I wonder if they'll stock the book." I'd sent her a selection of alternate titles, cribbed from various songs from the region and the era, and we'd decided on something tough but absurd in the vein of *Please Kill Me*. My first published book was going to be called *We Got the Neutron Bomb*. I felt even more confident in my relationship with Carrie after our second meeting. It was odd. She was nearly a half decade younger than I was, but part of me shelved "Rock Boy" in her presence because she had a maternal, almost delicate air about her. I felt weird cursing in front of her. Maybe it was the Southern thing; it conjured the gentleman out of scoundrels like me. Something told me I shouldn't rattle her, and so I never brought up the fact that I had almost no contacts in LA and virtually no idea how I was actually going to write the book. Monetarily, the pressure was not high. The advance was meager, but again, it was our first shot at the title. A title anyway. *We All Swim*?

One night just before Christmas 1999, Jim Fitzgerald took me to a party at the photographer Bob Gruen's apartment in the Westbeth Building by the West Side Highway. Gruen had a hypnotic gaze and a mop of kinky, silvering hair. He was a *Please Kill Me* cast member and had taken several iconic photos, including the famous 1974 shot of John Lennon posing in his New York City T-shirt. The apartment was small, every inch lined with books and photos, but Gruen and his wife put out a banquet on the order of the INXS "The One Thing" video. All these great downtown rock legends were meandering around: Tiny Weymouth and Chris Franz of Talking Heads and Tom Tom Club; Roberta Bayley, who took the cover photo for the Ramones debut album; Penny Arcade, a performance artist and another *Please Kill Me* cast member; Archie Freed, who signed The Stooges and MC5 and, along with Iggy, was really the star of *Please Kill Me*; Victor Bockris, whose Warhol biography was never far from my reach. And there, with long, greasy hair and wearing a leather jacket, as if ready to perform, stood Legs McNeil, my teenage hero and the paradigm for much of my adult professional life.

"Legs, meet Marc. Marc this is Legs," Jim said. "He's going to take up where you left off."

I was a little embarrassed to realize that while a decade and a half younger, I was dressed just like the guy: leather coat, tight black cords, pointy boots, greasy, almost wet hair, all of us bathed in smoke. Legs's writing partner, Gillian McCain, must have noticed this too. She was frosty with me, but Legs just took it as flattery.

"I've signed to do a book on LA punk rock. But I'm a little lost," I said, moon-eyed and drinking warm whiskey with no ice from a plastic cup, the rim all bitten and rough.

"Just write about who was fucking who," Legs laughed. "Seriously." Later he took me aside and said, "If you ever need any help, just ask. Jim will put you in touch." It was one of the happiest nights of my life. Legs McNeil had offered to mentor me. Legs McNeil—from *Spin*. Mentoring me. Marc Spitz. From *Spin*.

I'd already had some subjects on tape. The Go-Go's, for example, had recently reunited for a tour to capitalize on their excellent episode of *Behind the Music*. I found myself having breakfast with all of them one morning in the café of the Marriot Marquis. And there I was eating eggs and home fries with Belinda, Charlotte, Kathy, Gina, and, of course, Jane (long my favorite Go-Go and the one I wanted to go to cool places with). A friend of mine named Danny Athlete, who didn't work at *Spin* but somehow showed up at all our parties and events, had helped me coordinate and conduct an interview with John Doe of X. It was a key interview and could easily fill the tank with gas or run the car off the road. I had been an X fan since high school. "I must not think bad thoughts" was one of my senior page quotes. The album the song came from, *More Fun in the New World*, was never too far from the tape deck of my car. Same with *Los Angeles*, *Wild Gift*, and *Under the Big Black Sun*. The near-perfect first four X albums. As far as I was concerned, X was the most important band ever to come out of LA, more important than Love or The Doors, and I had absolutely no idea what to ask John Doe. I didn't know a thing about what it was like coming up on the Hollywood club scene in the late seventies, and there was so little out there to educate me. There was Penelope Spheeris's aforementioned documentary, *The Decline of Western Civilization*. There was a paperback called *Make the Music Go Bang*, which was sort of thin and hacked out. And there was the art exhibit catalog called *Forming*. *Details*, in yet another of its ever-changing incarnations, had run a piece on Hollywood punk. Someone faxed it to me, and I pressed it into the blue Five Star spiral notebook where I kept my handwritten wish list: Rodney Bingenheimer, Kim Fowley, Penelope Spheeris, The Dickies, Pat Smear, Don Bolles, Lorna Doom, Charles Manson, Chuck E. Weiss, Ray Manzarek, David Lee Roth, Kinman Brothers (The Dils), Top Jimmy, Geza X, Gar Panter, Tomata Du Plenty. I didn't even know that Tomata had died. I was in the tall grass. And John Doe, innocently promoting one of his low-key solo albums, probably figured we'd be talking about . . . one of his low-key solo albums.

> Me: Um, so uh, whatchamacallit. So, they told you what this was about, right?
> John Doe: Untitled book on the history of LA punk. Deadline not available. Size of piece inclusion in book. Phone number 718. Are you calling from Brooklyn?
> Me: No, I'm calling from Manhattan.
> John Doe: Wait, Manhattan has 718 now?
> Me: Um . . .
> John Doe: Just take out the long pauses and the places I get mixed up.
> Me: So, can you talk about the earliest stages of your relationship to Los Angeles.
> John Doe: The earliest relationship to Los Angeles was through books. Charles Bukowski . . .

At that point, I knew I was going to be okay. I'd found common ground. Very few people on the LA punk scene were actually born in LA. John Doe came from Baltimore. Plus you can't really do worse than leading off an interview with the word "whatchamacallit."

Still, I sensed I needed a partner. Legs McNeil had Gillian. Jean Stein had George Plimpton. I knew from how nearly the Axl feature in *Spin* had nearly murdered Rob Levine and me that a large-scale oral history was *Butch Cassidy and the Sundance Kid*, not *Taxi Driver*. God's lonely man could not get it done. Feeling like I couldn't tell Jim or Carrie that I wanted a partner without flagging the now officially "untitled book on the history of LA punk" as a problem child, I'd sit in the Library bar, drink whiskey, do blow off the hand dryer in the bathroom, and brood to Patricia Ann. My deadline was approaching, and I already knew from *Spin* that you can act a fool and wear feather black boas. You can smoke in the stairwell and chip heroin out of a glassine envelope in the downstairs toilet. You can excuse yourself from an interview with Dean and Gene Ween to go vomit in the sink. But you do not ever fuck with a deadline.

"I need help. And another round."

Danny Athlete had a real job at some website and knew less about LA punk than I did. One night I asked Amra Brooks if she would write the thing with me. She had West Coast cred to share, thanks to her father, Joseph, and his nightclub promotion. She'd helped with the Axl story. But we'd had a relationship. We were a little too codependent to produce a big book. Sometimes she'd buzz my apartment unannounced and give me a heavy look, so we'd go to the bedroom and just lay there in silence, hiding from things that neither of us would ever reveal to the other. I loved her. I was wildly attracted to her, but she was fragile. She was always talking about some rare berry pies she was going to someday bake. This would be bloody. I needed stronger stuff in my camp, someone who loved a fight.

"Why don't you ask Brendan?" she suggested.

"Are you kidding? He wants my head. I barely got out of Hollywood alive the last time I was there."

"Well, appeal to his sense of historical perfectionism. Call him and say, 'If you know so much about the scene, why don't you help me tell it right?'"

It was not a terrible idea, but I was way too chicken shit to even entertain it. Sober, anyway. One night, drunk and a little more courageous than I might have been sober, I e-mailed Brendan Mullen and asked if I could hire him as a consultant. Then I passed out.

Typically, in 2000, I woke up in the morning and did my Roy Scheider routine with the Visine. Coming to after sleeping off a bender was always an "oh no" moment. You check the room to make sure you're alone and not naked next to someone else naked, someone frightening. Then it's, "How's my head?" Most of the time you knew when the hangover was going to be incapacitating. You felt the spike in your skull before even really coming to. Other times it was a walking lethargy, a functional flu that could be minimized by a makeshift Russian bath in the tub, running the shower spray and inhaling the steam until little yellow beads formed on the bathroom ceiling. Some Chinese hot-and-sour soup from Sammy's Noodles or a line of blow, and I was back.

"It's showtime folks!"

But it didn't end there. This was the era of drunk dialing via e-mail. Then, putting the world to right, the "whom must I apologize to today" review. I was, as I mentioned earlier, a cokey, late-night e-mail score settler.

That morning, I remembered what I'd done and rushed to my computer to see if I couldn't unsend the e-mail. Brendan had an AOL address, and at that time, you could unsend mail that had not yet been opened on the recipient's end. Sure enough, there was a reply from Madscot21 in my inbox. Not only had the fucker opened my invitation, he had written back quickly. And he was interested! Of course, not as some "bullshit paid consultant." No, Brendan wanted in fifty-fifty. He wanted to write the thing with me.

Jim of course hated the idea.

"Who the fuck's Brendan Mullen?"

"Brendan is LA punk. The guy opened The Masque."

"What the fuck's The Masque?"

Jim, as any good agent would, was protecting me from myself, but I was already convinced that this was the only way "Untitled LA Punk Book" was going to get done right. I told him the only alternative was to give the money back and squelch the deal, so he initiated negotiations with Brendan, and I waited as sparks flew. As was his habit, Jim cc'd me on every e-mail, and it was like being a kid in the middle of warring divorcés all over again. Neither wanted to give an inch. The letters were especially ferocious for some reason, as if they'd come from warring clans who'd been spitting and slugging it out for centuries.

"Fitzgerald. Listen here, Irish pig. Just try and write this book without me. See how well you do. Nobody's going to talk to your boy."

"I don't respond to this." Click.

Only now there was no going back. I told Jim, ordered him really, to stop negotiating.

"Offer him half."

"But you don't even know what he's . . ."

"Half!"

But that still wasn't the last of it. Brendan didn't want to pay any expenses and didn't want to split the cost of photographs, which the author always has to pay for and which, in addition to taxes and commissions, takes a serious piece out of what initially seems like a large advance (not that I'd even gotten a large advance).

"Fuck it, let him have everything he wants," I shrugged.

"But . . ."

"Please! Everything!"

Once the negotiations were done just before the Christmas 2000 holidays, Brendan's entire demeanor changed. He suggested I come out to Los Angeles immediately.

"I don't really have a place to stay," I protested. "Keith Morris from the Circle Jerks said I could sleep on his cot." I thought that would impress him. It was true. I'd talked briefly with Morris, who was the original vocalist in Black Flag before leaving to found Circle Jerks and growing enormous dreadlocks. Like a lot of punks whom you'd assume would be snarky and mean, Keith was sweet, smart, and nothing like his punk rock image. Marilyn Manson is the same when you meet him in person. Most of the supposed boogie men are. Still, it just felt weird. There was no context. And where was that cot? In the living room? In his room? Did Keith Morris snore? I know I did. *When* I slept.

I always felt like writers should write in hotels when away from home. They should write in rooms that look like hotel rooms when at home. But there was no money for any of that. This would be rough travel—hard trodding in unfamiliar territory. Even with Brendan Mullen as the punk rock Sherpa, I had no illusions it would be a cakewalk.

"You can stay here. There's an extra room," Brendan offered in his stuffy voice.

"Serious?"

"It's the office. You can sleep in the office, Marc."

"Okay, thank you." At least I knew where the bed would be. And Brendan and I, if nothing else, had a context.

I was going through a period where I didn't want to fly. I'm not sure why. I just felt something dark when it came to flying in 2000.

"Don't get on airplanes, man," that self-preservation voice (all too faint in my life) constantly whispered to me. Sometimes I'm fine flying; other times, I feel incredible dread and foreboding, and you can't drag me to a terminal. This was one of those times. I spent the last of my initial advance on a sleeper cabin aboard the Super Chief, and Brendan agreed to pick me up at Union Station. I spent much of the three-day trip in the smoking car underneath the train or eating cheap ham-and-cheese sandwiches and drinking whiskey and Cokes in the dining car. I had nobody to talk to, so I eavesdropped on conversations until it seemed like I wasn't traveling alone. I'd write down things I overheard.

"I don't need a woman to give me pain," one old black dude said. "I can do it myself with a bottle of Jack Daniel's. Only takes me two days to recover ... instead of three years." I raised my Jack and toasted him, but he'd never know it. I knew the train was nearing LA, and I began to pace. I was still terrified of meeting Brendan Mullen. Even on the phone, he sounded imperious with his still pronounced accent. He called punk "poonk."

The man waiting for me at Union Station on that too-sunny morning was nothing like the photos I'd seen or the images I'd concocted. Here was a schlumpy, soft-spoken, absent-minded, middle-aged man with a shaved head full of silvering stubble, covered with a cloth fishing hat. Like my father, he'd reached the age where being a dandy, in an iridescent jacket with zebra fur lapels (as he was wearing in another vintage photo I'd seen of him) just wasn't worth it anymore. He wore a clean, navy polo shirt and chino pants and seemed cheerfully stoned, almost like a hippie.

"Is that Marc?" he asked.

"Hi, Brendan." I offered my hand and we shook.

"Alright, Marc. Glad you made it."

He did seem genuinely happy, now that we'd gotten the business out of the way. I looked at his face, trying to make out the young, angry punk who'd once inhabited it. There were patches of stubble and patches of clean-shaven skin, as if he gotten lost in thought mid-razor stroke and never returned to the task.

We got into his beat-up car, and he spent five minutes trying to get the station to come in. Someone had bent the antennae in half. We drove to the nondescript suburban block in West LA where he was living with his pal Jim, a strange, tall man who worked a day job. It was strange that he still had a roommate at fifty-one. I began to understand just why he was taking such a hard tact with my agent. Brendan didn't have much, for all his legend. His archives were collected in boxes lined up around a long, wooden kitchen table. His records were in storage. His ride was a beater too in a city where a man's wheels mean everything. His glory days as a club promoter, performer, and DJ at Club Lingerie in the eighties and the Viper Room in the nineties were long over. As I put my suitcase down in the anteroom where I would end up sleeping for the next month and a half, I realized that if Brendan was going to help me with my first act, I was going to help him with his second. He'd been waiting for me too. We needed each other. From that point, I began to love the guy. And I think he warmed to me fast. We ended up taking a long lunch at Denny's, which began a kind of tradition (sometimes we'd go to Canter's on Fairfax). I'd sit in the booth, and Brendan would give me history lessons about the dark side of LA: Manson, the Process Church, L. Ron Hubbard, the Hillside Stranger, the murder of New Wave Theater host Peter Ivers. It was like eating Moon Over My Hammy with Kenneth Anger or James Ellroy.

Brendan, a wake-and-baker, was a terrifying driver, and that is something in a land where drunk drivers were divided into bad, conspicuous drunk drivers, who got arrested, and decent drunk drivers, who got home to the Valley or Silverlake. This was pre-GPS, and Brendan's cannabis-fuzzed sense of direction was better in theory. Once we drove all the way to Pasadena to interview Peter Case from the The Plimsouls and Dave Alvin without headlights. He'd forgotten to turn them on.

Lucy's El Adobe, an old-school, low-lit Mexican place near Brendan's house, was our command center when we had money ("The Eagles used to eat here," he'd sneer). We'd eat Astro Burger when we had none (which was most of the time). We'd fuel up, go over our hit list, and then spend the next ten hours excavating the LA punk past.

Another time we staked out a junkie hangout looking for Rick Wilder of Berlin Brats. Brendan couldn't pass a house without pointing out some grisly mishap that had taken place inside.

"Hillel Slovak overdosed there. That's where Sal Mineo was stabbed. Peter Ivers got his head bashed in right up there . . . Oh, and we have to write about Jane King. Jane King was an actress who used to hang out at The Masque, and one day she disappeared, and they found her by an overpass. She'd been murdered, Marc, by the Hillside Strangler. I had to hire security at The Masque. Can you imagine, Marc? Security? At The Masque."

Imagine was all I could do. In the introduction to the LA punk book, which I lobbied to call *We Got the Neutron Bomb* after a Weirdos song (Brendan always hated the title), I wrote self-consciously, "One of us was there, the other spent the 70s watching the Muppets, but we shared a common goal. To give Los Angeles punk rock the respect and consideration it's due." This isn't entirely true. The Muppets part, yes, but I was not evangelical about giving LA punk its fair shake. I just wanted an experience, and a first book, which would lead, hopefully, to a second book. It's amazing that *Bomb* is as good as it is, regarded now as a classic in the rock-and-roll canon, because it was such a cluster fuck of motives.

"Have you ever heard this? The Weasels. It's called 'Beat Her with a Rake," Brendan would chuckle as he pulled an old 45 from one of his dozens and dozens of crates. "Oh, oh, this one's great. The Rotters. 'Sit on My Face Stevie Nicks.'"

Years later, when he moved to a more spacious house in Silverlake, he'd fill an entire garage with record shelves. I only knew the big guns of LA punk. I'd never heard The Screamers; they never recorded. The Alleycats, The Eyes,

The Controllers, Top Jimmy and the Rhythm Pigs, Black Randy and the Metro Squad. Before we wrote a word, I got the full-on crash course. When it was my turn to play a tune, I always went for the familiar: *Beauty and the Beat*, particularly track five.

"This town is our town," Belinda Carlisle sang. *"This town is so glamorous, that you'd live here if you could and be one of us."*

Brendan once let slip that he'd slept with one of the Go-Go's. As much as I begged (and I begged constantly), he would never reveal which one. Something in him bristled each time I played *Beauty and the Beat* though. I figured if I spun it enough, the town would become my town again. But in Brendan's eyes, I was always the New Yorker. When we fought, we fought like sports fans. Brendan was not anti–New York, but he was certainly committed to ripping down the NYC exceptionalism with regard to popular culture and certainly punk. As much as he reviled the Eagles, he would have taken them over nearly ever New York City band that was not The Ramones. They got a pass.

"Legs McNeil is a provincial cunt." When Brendan said "cunt," it came out "coont." "There were punks in LA long before there were punks in New York City, Marc. Believe that. Frank Zappa. Phil Spector. Charlie Manson. Jim Morrison. You know who was in the crowd when The Doors came to play in Detroit, Marc? Iggy Pop. Looking up at Jim Morrison like a fucking hero." He wiped his nose and tried to calm himself down.

Brendan never got over the fact that the failure of most of the New York punk bands to score hit records after the signing bonanza of the mid-seventies and the flameout of the Sex Pistols on their 1978 American tour had ruined any chance for his friends out in Hollywood to get major-label attention. Only the snotty, poppy Dickies were signed by a major.

Even the Go-Go's, who'd hit number one in 1981, were on IRS. X was on Slash, which didn't get major-label distribution until 1982 or so. Much as when I represented *Spin* magazine in my e-mail exchanges with Courtney Love, I was the surrogate villain, in this case, the New York carpetbagger trying to pass as a native and in private getting all kinds of shit on behalf of Stiv Bators and Richard Hell. Only Joey Ramone, rumored to be very sick at the time, got a pass. Brendan loved the Ramones, and their multi-album live release *It's Alive* was a constant as he went through his photo archives or searched for old addresses and phone numbers, while I drank whiskey and transcribed interview tapes (Brendan typed about thirty words a minute).

We became, against the odds, a really good two-man army. Brendan would prep me for each interview. "Rodney [Bingenheimer] will just say, 'Yeah, yeah,' to whatever you say, so if you want him to say, 'The glam kids from the

English disco formed their own bands because they wanted to be David Bowie and Iggy Pop. But they couldn't be David Bowie or Iggy Pop, so they became punks instead," just say, "Rodney, did the glam kids from the English disco form their own bands because they wanted to be David Bowie and Iggy Pop, but they couldn't be David Bowie or Iggy Pop, so they became punks instead?" "Yeah. Yeah."

When Ray Manzarek was truculent because I'd asked him a question that he'd clearly explained in his own book, Brendan neutralized the situation.

"It's called *Dance on Fire*. You didn't read it did you? When you're going to interview someone, you should think about buying and reading their autobiography first."

"We will, Ray. We'll drive to the Virgin Megastore and buy it today."

If I taught him anything, it was how to hit record before doing your telephone interview. Brendan could be absent-minded. There were times when he'd come out of the office after doing a key interview and hand me a tape to transcribe (Brendan didn't transcribe), and it'd be white noise.

"Fuck, Marc. That was a great interview."

"Go write down what you remember. Quickly!"

Sometimes we'd take the night off and get Japanese food with Brendan's pretty, brunette girlfriend, Kateri, then the managing editor of *LA Weekly*, and a revolving array of cult-hero friends of theirs, like Genesis P-Orridge. At the time, Genesis was feminized, bleached blonde, and intense but had yet to embark fully on his gender-switch art-life project. As with Keith Morris and others, he was much gentler and more humorous in person, and we hit it off enough for him to call on me some months later to DJ his birthday party at The Slipper Room. Genesis, a founder of the protoindustrial combo Throbbing Gristle, sent me a request list, and I was amused and a bit relieved to see that it consisted mostly of sixties nuggets by The Who, the Stones, and The Kinks. David J of Love and Rockets, Tones on Tail, and the legendary Bauhaus was another guest, one who made me a bit more nervous. He rang me as well when I was back in the city, but I was too starstruck to follow up with him.

I felt like I was crashing Brendan's high school reunion. Some of his old punk friends were doing really well, like KK and Trudy Barrett. He was a member of The Screamers back when, and she was his girlfriend. They were the scene's trendiest couple and now lived in a big house on a cliff. KK was doing art direction for Spike Jonze. Others hadn't changed at all. When we went to interview the writer Pleasant Gehman (who also appeared in the Axl feature and was a *Spin* contributor who wrote the artist-of-the-year story on Nirvana in 1992), she looked more or less the same as she did in the countless black-and-white, glossy photos spread across the dining room table in Brendan's house. Brendan was twenty years my senior almost to the day; both of us were Libras.

Pleasant Gehman was only ten years older than I was and, despite the years of partying, didn't look it. She'd discovered belly dancing a few years earlier, and went from taking to eventually giving lessons and performing. I'm not sure I would have lasted out in LA among all the boomer punks without discovering Plez. I say "discovering," because back when Justin and I were trying to make it as screenwriters, we lived about four houses up from Pleasant on Franklin and didn't even know it. I'd passed that house on my way back from the Pig and Villa Carlotta five hundred times, mostly high, sometimes not. There'd never been any activity during the day and only the flicker of the TV and some loud music by night. I figured some hippies lived there. When Brendan pulled into her driveway, I couldn't believe it.

"You know, I used to live on this street!" I shouted. "Right there. Like right over there."

He looked at me like he couldn't believe it either. To Brendan I was only ever a New Yorker.

I followed Pleasant Gehman around like a puppy after our interview for the book and each time I returned to LA on assignment for *Spin*. It was half out of lust for her tan, voluptuous body, full lips, and thick, black hair and half out of a feeling that I could be a portal to this long-gone Hollywood nighttime world that I was attempting to recapture without ever having been there in the first place.

I would have been Plez's friend had I grown up in Hollywood and been ten years older. There's no question. We became friends right then, with me returning again and again to that house just to hang out with her, listen to music, get fucked-up, and be less alone. I made out with her one night on the balcony of my room at the Riot House, but it never went beyond that. Her choice. I would have probably married her. I loved that slow, spaced, Southern Californian drawl. We had a lot in common. We both liked drugs. We were both gossip columnists. (She wrote a longtime gossip column in *LA Weekly* called *La Dee Da*. Crispin Glover reads from it before nearly kicking David Letterman in the head during his notorious 1987 appearance). We both had a fear of puppets (she'd later send me a zine she'd written called *Puppet Terror*). But every night I sat on her couch, in her kitsch-filled living room, drinking wine and snorting coke and filling the ashtray with cigarettes, I couldn't wrap my head around the fact that Jeffrey Lee Pierce had done the same. Like most junkie art school kids, I worshipped the late Gun Club singer, and the band's debut *Fire of Love* was never too far from my CD player. My copy had razor blade scores on the jewel box. Now that I'm the same age Pleasant was when I met her, I understand well why she wouldn't let me sleep with her, despite our mutual attraction. I was a living, walking, snorting reminder of time the avenger.

"Tell me more about Rankin' Jeffrey Lee . . . snifffff."

I used to try to enter the TV set when I was a kid. I'd place my face all the way up against what was then a convex, not a flat, screen until the people in the movies and sitcoms were fishy. One night, Brendan went to meet a guy about a DJ job at an old Hollywood bar called Boardners. Like me, Brendan was picking up some extra coin here and there by spinning records for the hipsters in the clubs. Already drunk on the half pint of whiskey I always kept in the pocket of my leather jacket, I wandered out into the street and found myself on Hollywood and Cherokee, right where the entrance to The Masque used to be. I placed my face up against the chain-link fence and stared down into the alley. I tried to imagine a young Brendan and his friends, Darby and Belinda and Lorna and Don and Pleasant and Alice, suburban kids excitedly staggering down there, into the smoky air, in their spikey hair and skinny ties and garbage-bag dresses, posing up against those graffiti-covered walls and trying to be something bigger and braver than they actually were.

CHAPTER 16

On September 7, 2001, I went with Maureen Callahan, now an editor at *Spin*, to Madison Square Garden. This time, we were going to see Michael Jackson's *30th Anniversary Concert* tribute to himself, produced by David Gest, then Liza Minnelli's waxy-faced new husband. Maureen and I both grew up in the eighties, a period when if you liked punk, heavy metal, new wave, reggae, or adult contemporary music, you also liked Michael Jackson. If you roller-discoed in spandex tights or smoked pot in the parking lot in a painted denim jacket, if you were a cheerleader or a jock, a preppie or a Goth, you owned a copy of *Thriller* (well, maybe not the Goths). We were both morbidly fascinated by what Michael had done to his face, his skin, his hair, and his career. Maureen and I watched these changes, separately and then together, while working at *Spin*, with a pop-culture obsessive's attention to detail, and every phase of the mutation meant something to us. We took him seriously and personally. The destruction of Michael's *Thriller* face, no longer even his *Off the Wall* face, seemed to us, by the late nineties, no different or less tragic than the erosion of the ozone layer, the deforestation of the Amazon. Michael—just Michael, no need for a surname—was America to us. He was the world, we were his children, and the news that he was back performing live surely meant that a brighter day was coming.

Maureen and I shared what we called a "pop-culture duty." A pop-culture duty was essentially a religious rule. If a movie came out—say, the unnecessary Tim Burton remake of *The Planet of the Apes*—neither of us really wanted to see it, but we felt like we had to "cover it," not necessarily for *Spin* but also out of a general sense of pop-culture duty. This applied to new R. Kelly records and even TV, like MTV's *Fear* or *Big Brother*. Maureen read every British "red-top" tabloid: the *Sun* and the *Mirror*. She subscribed to the *National Enquirer* and assumed any item she read there was the absolute truth. This wasn't escapism. We took this shit very seriously.

We didn't have tickets but decided to try our luck with the scalpers outside the Garden in front of the very same steps where we would both emerge as kids after traveling in from the Island.

"They're probably going to be nosebleed seats. Really expensive nosebleed seats," I worried. "Maybe we should just bag it."

"Come on," Maureen said. "Liza Minnelli?"

In the future, no matter what the debate and regardless of whether Liza Minnelli is in any way involved, I suggest using "Come on, Liza Minnelli?" as your closing argument since it's impossible to refuse. Eager to erase all memories of his child-molestation scandal and remind people of his past, Michael had called in all of his famous friends and some worshipful new pop and R&B stars like character witnesses.

"Marlon Brando?" She kept throwing out names. "When are you ever going to get a chance to see Marlon Brando and Beyoncé on the same stage?"

Outside, on Seventh Avenue, Maureen and I easily found a pair of tickets for $100 each, only two bucks over cost. We rode the escalator up to the cheap seats, got a couple of beers, and settled in for the ostentatious pop wax-museum and Vegas-style pageantry. The show didn't disappoint. Brando didn't sing or dance, but he did deliver a monologue, while seated in an easy chair on stage, about children who were being "hacked to bits" somewhere in a less fortunate part of the world. It was not unlike the "inoculation" monologue from *Apocalypse Now*, and the sight of a "fat guy," as Brando called himself that night, onstage in full recline was in its own way one of the most "rock" performances I've ever seen. I may have never caught Nirvana, but I saw Brando. Liza Minnelli came out in her *Cabaret* sequins and sang "Somewhere over the Rainbow," her mother's signature song, for no apparent reason. Destiny's Child performed "Bootylicious" for a very apparent reason (it was their new single). Gregory Peck, Atticus Finch himself, appeared on a screen and called Michael a *monstre sacre*, or "sacred monster." This was supposed to be a compliment.

The only performer yet to show his destroyed face was Michael himself.

"What's happening?" I asked Maureen. "Dude's in the building, right?"

"He's coming. He'll be here," she promised. Maureen was a Catholic, and I drew my strength and patience from her. We would soon be delivered, pop culturally: restored to a glorious 1983 of the mind, our sins washed away with lemony Pepsi and happy tears. Finally, nearly two hours in, Dame Elizabeth Taylor emerged, glittering and unsteady, and introduced the Jacksons.

"Jacksons?"

"They're going to do the full Jackson 5, Motown 25 thing, aren't they?" Maureen said, shaking her head, impressed by their audacity. "And then Michael is going to recreate his solo moment."

"You think?" Some of the Jacksons had thickened in middle age. All of them seemed older and slower. To tackle such a moment in American pop history was just insane. The *Motown 25: Yesterday, Today, Forever* television special, was broadcast on NBC in the spring of 1983, just as *Thriller*, already a smash, was really going supernova, was becoming our moon landing. Some audio-video club member actually wheeled an old Trinitron into the classroom to show it to me and my classmates back at Lawrence Junior High. This time, however, Michael needed an oxygen tank. It made me feel old too, and a little sad. The things that used to thrill so effortlessly and genuinely were now somehow kitsch.

Shortly after brushing the brothers off the stage, Michael got out the glove. By the time Quincy Jones and Kenny Rogers materialized to lead the crowd in a rendition of "We Are the World," I felt like I needed to go somewhere and take a punk rock shower. I turned to Maureen, who was wiping tears of laughter out of her eyes, and said, "No wonder the rest of the world hates us."

The next three days seemed hopeful. There's a point in September when you can feel the always-harsh New York City summer fade and the fall come on. Fall is a good writing season. I write best when I can wear suits without sweating. A writer should either wear a tweed or heavy wool suit, drink whiskey, and not sweat—or a white linen suit, drink gin and tonics for the quinine, and sweat a lot. I preferred the former archetype. Women dress up in the fall, dudes can wear leather jackets, nobody on the New York City streets is showing you their gnarly toenails, and people get enthusiastic about going out again—drinking cocktails, smoking cigarettes, talking about books, movies, TV shows, and ideas. I'd started a new play and was looking forward to the publication of my very first book that November. It had been a rough ride, doing all that research on the West Coast, butting heads with Brendan Mullen, making a hostile stranger a trusted friend somehow. Now it was time to exult in the attention, to think about future projects, and, most crucially, to rock out.

I went to bed early on the night of September 10, thinking I was just about to make it through another motherfucker of a New York summer. It had been a rough spell of warm weather and untimely death. On tax day, Joey Ramone had passed. He happened to be on the cover of *Spin*'s "Twenty-Fifth Anniversary of Punk" theme issue (which excerpted *Neutron Bomb* under the title, to Brendan Mullen's absolute and loudly expressed horror, "Sit on My Face Stevie Nicks"), and I was told that he was shown the cover while on his deathbed, which made me very proud. Just a few weeks before the Jackson concert, Aaliyah and her entourage died in a small Cessna crash in the Bahamas. She was just twenty-two. We gathered in a banquette at The Slipper Room and mourned her, DJing her music and comforting ourselves that the worst was over. The bad juju was lifting with the change in the weather. It had to.

I think the explosion might have woken me up, but I didn't know I'd heard a noise. I only realized that my eyes were open, and it wasn't the usual gradual come-to. It felt like a stuck snore that catches your passages and jams your breathing. You feel like you are swallowing mud and just shoot awake—all the blood rushing to your eyeballs, prying them free from the lids, your brain shouting, "What? What. What!" I'd fallen asleep lazily and drunkenly with the TV on—to Conan O'Brien's *Late Night* on NBC, I guess—and now Katie Couric was on the *Today Show*, covering some accident on the West Side downtown. The first reports indicated that a small plane had crashed into the North Tower of the World Trade Center. This had happened before in the city, I reasoned. Hadn't I read about a small plane hitting the Empire State Building once? I pulled on my trousers, grabbed my cigarettes, and walked outside, up Christopher Street toward Sheridan Square. People were pooling, and the traffic had stopped. I heard a second noise, a high-pitched, terribly quick *skreeeeeee*, and before my brain could make out what was happening, it happened. A second plane hit the South Tower. From the distance up Seventh Avenue, the violence of the impact was not really detectable, but abstractly, the visual was unmistakable: planes were crashing into our buildings. I allowed myself to think this was a terrible coincidence, something to do with an air traffic control mishap. Nobody was running or fleeing. It wasn't raining bombs on us. We were all just . . . still. I don't think I was particularly frightened—just sort of in a prolonged state of blank denial and feeling a little unsettled that I couldn't work out just what was going on. New Yorkers like to be clued in, and this was a sucker punch.

I noticed the guy from my newsstand on Bleecker Street. He was smiling, pumped with adrenaline and probably just grateful for a break in his grind, not harboring any "death to America" sentiment.

"Why the fuck are you smiling?" I asked him coolly. "This is bad. You understand 'bad?'"

He looked shamed.

"I'm sorry," he finally offered.

I would have never thought to talk to him that way before. Plus, I liked him. We had one of those New York relationships where you depend on the person, you see him every day, you always exchange a nod and a pleasant look, but you never know his name. I'm the customer, or boss, or "my friend," or the guy who buys the Camel Lights, the *Post*, and the occasional pricey British music magazine. He's the guy who sells those to me and gives me my change. He's "man," as in "Thanks, man."

And now something was breaking us apart.

I returned to my apartment. No neighbors were about. They were probably watching the events on TV. I thought about asking the super what was going on, but this was no busted pipe or mouse invasion. Asking him would only make it worse. Best to just silently deduce it all.

I turned on the TV, and it was obvious then that we were being attacked. I sat on the bed smoking and watching the towers smolder. I didn't know what to do. Another plane had crashed into the Pentagon in DC, and there were others in the air, nobody could say for sure how many. We didn't know where the president was. We didn't know anything and just sort of froze. About an hour later, an hour that seemed to creep as the suspicion dawned that some, perhaps a great many, of our fellow New Yorkers were dead or dying, the South Tower, the second to be hit, collapsed. White smoke erupted out of a hole in the world, an apocalyptic dust. I lit another cigarette, pulled on my leather coat and wrapped my black scarf around my neck tightly, and went back outside, but I continued to duck back into my apartment to watch what was happening on the television. It didn't seem real unless I saw it on TV. It's just the way my generation was bred. Whenever something important happened at school—Reagan being shot by Hinckley, the Challenger exploding, or even Michael appearing in *Motown 25*—they wheeled in the tube. The TV had to confirm everything—even at sporting events, you see the old people watching the field, and the people our age watching the giant Diamond Vision screens above it. But this was difficult to process even when the TV was telling me, "It's true." Giuliani was on now. Shaky handheld cameras were following him; covered with dust, he looked shaken. It was odd seeing such a warrior appear that way, but still somehow heartening; as was the resolve of the cops and firefighters at the scene. Whatever was going on, he would figure it out. My secret support for him seemed somehow validated. He was a leader, and suddenly not being able to dance in a rock-and-roll bar didn't seem like such a grave issue. People were leaping to their deaths from ripped windows—in the very building where I once temped for a week in a data-processing office, eating lonely lunches and tentatively mixing with the permanent staff. The same windows I'd leaned against and stared down at the seemingly infinite, dark blue below at my first posh *Spin* party four years earlier, when I'd decided I would leave any trace of myself behind and inhabit "Rock Boy" until I was a star. Spiritualized had played its *Ladies and Gentlemen, We Are Floating in Space* as we watched in amazement. Windows on the World—now, it was vapor? Gone? Dust. Death. Memory. *Death* . . . hallowed ground. It didn't seem real. I wasn't afraid, yet, or even sad. I was just stupefied with disbelief. Certain New York landmarks seemed immovable. To take them away would surely produce a mass phantom-limb syndrome.

I didn't know one New Yorker who hadn't passed through the World Trade Center at least once if they'd lived here long enough; even the art kids like Ron Shavers and Camille and I had temped there. It was New York and while I still have neighbors whom I've shared a roof with for five years and never talked to, we are all part of that weird, unspoken brother- and sister-hood. We have a reputation for being hard and insular, but when one of us perishes, a little bit of everyone in this city dies too. We were all in shock. "How can this happen? We made it here from where we started out? That's the battle. Not this!" whatever this was.

The North Tower fell what seemed like fifteen minutes later. I saw it crumble, this time from the street while my neighbors and I—my fellow city dwellers, all of us too busy to die, too purposeful for this, whatever this was—stood there, smelling death smoke, straining to believe what was happening. I stood in the middle of Seventh Avenue and watched the survivors and by-standers begin their slow crawl, covered in ash.

At around noon, after a fourth plane, United 93, crashed in Pennsylvania, I finally thought about work, story deadlines, life, family, friends. I checked my e-mail. The managing editor of *Spin* had sent out a note that essentially said not to bother coming in or filing. I checked my phone. There had been spotty service all morning, but suddenly there was a slew of backed up mes-sages: a half dozen messages from my mother and father. I sat on my fire es-cape and stared down at Christopher Street. A smell like burning chemicals and meat and tire rubber started to fill the air. The weirdest thing about Sep-tember 11 was that the stores were open. I never kept food in my fridge, and by two in the afternoon I felt like I needed to eat, so I walked to Gourmet Garage on Seventh Avenue and bought a salad and a muffin, while people were still making their way past toward St. Vincent's Hospital like zombies in a Romero movie. I ate my lunch and called my mother and father. My father, who hadn't lived in New York in years, had clearly left a piece of his guts here and kept prying for details.

"Did you see it?"

"Yes."

"Are you okay?"

"I don't know." I really didn't. I wanted to be okay. I told myself I was going to be okay. "Are you?"

He was in Chicago. For all I knew they were flying planes into the Sears Tower or Wrigley Field. He was fine but shaken. It was a little weird in that moment, one so confusing, to have a flash of calm and realize that I was the New Yorker now, not the old man. The guy who first brought me there was asking me about the city. And I didn't know what to say. I'd worked so hard to become a real New Yorker. I had gone to bed a real New Yorker, and since waking up that morning, I didn't understand the city anymore. This wasn't New York anymore. New York wasn't this vulnerable, was it?

Brendan Mullen rang from LA. Were they destroying buildings there as well? *We Got the Neutron Bomb* was finished and in galleys.

"Is anybody going to care about LA punk now?" I asked, trying to manage a laugh.

"They didn't care about it before," Brendan assured me. "Don't worry. Is everyone you know okay? Friends? Family?"

It was odd to hear him speak warmly about New York. If anyone was going to have a hand in destroying Manhattan, I was sure it would be Brendan.

I finished my salad and, for some reason, put on the new Radiohead album, *Amnesiac*. It wasn't as good as the previous album, *Kid A*, and certainly not in the same league as their 1997 masterpiece *OK Computer*, but one song, a woozy ballad that builds to a thundering drone, titled "You and Whose Army," seemed to place everything that had happened in a kind of temporarily workable context. I have no idea why it was comforting, medicinal even, but every time Tom Yorke sang, "We ride, we ride tonight!" I felt a little less terrified and . . . terrorized. Now when I hear it, I think, "Well it's clearly a Smiths rip. 'Death of a Disco Dancer.'" But on September 11, it was a lullaby.

Tracey Pepper, who had been stuck downtown at a doctor's appointment, called me when she finally got back to her apartment, a Deco doorman building on West Sixteenth and Seventh Avenue. I walked up there to be with her. As I passed St. Vincent's Hospital, which was surrounded by police cars and news vans and pandemonium, I wondered why there weren't more ambulances and screaming wounded and realized that could only mean that there weren't a lot of survivors. Dazed people wandered into the emergency room, and bodies on stretchers were loaded out of ambulances and rushed in past them. When Tracey greeted me at her door, she was pale and just kept shaking her head. Her green parrot, "Mr. Green Jeans," usually squawked abruptly every time I ever went over there—a loud jungle cry—but the thing was dead quiet.

"He knows something's going on," Tracey explained.

I would have paid to hear that nerve-jangling shriek again, to have things be predictable. Nobody knew what else was in the sky.

"Let's go up to the roof," she said.

"I don't wanna go up there."

Twenty floors above Chelsea, we had a full 360-degree view of the city. We could see the Statue of liberty, the Chrysler Building, the Empire State Building, and there, where the Twin Towers had been twelve hours earlier, a massive plume of light-black smoke, wafting up into the otherwise perfect blue sky. I had passed those towers every day. They were the gateway to my nights out. I'd crossed Seventh Avenue on my way from the West to the East Village, and they'd loomed watchfully overhead, as if to say, "Don't get into trouble, now." How could that view, that relationship with a horizon, be gone? My friend Damien, an artist and a bouncer at the Library, e-mailed me.

"I liked that view," was all he said.

We went up to the roof of her building; some of her neighbors were drinking cold Chardonnay and watching the pit smolder like it was just another late-summer day. We just stood and stared at it. There was nothing else to do or say.

"Is it over?" I asked.

"Is what over?"

I didn't know how to say it at the time, but I was wondering if anybody was going to give a shit about the new Basement Jaxxx album again. Would we all be living underground by the weekend? How were we going to get back to whatever it was we were just complaining about yesterday?

An e-mail went around letting us know the office would be shut down for the immediate future. As missing-persons flyers, some Xeroxed, some laminated, began to cover every free area, I walked around the Village in a daze, and when I wasn't doing that, I was glued to the TV looking for any info. President Bush gave a speech that night and assured us that our military was "powerful and prepared." It felt good to hear, and I wanted to believe that he was in control. I didn't vote for him, but at the time I was glad he was the president and Rudy was the mayor.

There were people in the streets shopping and driving. The bars were open, and I'd meet friends for drinks. We'd play the jukebox and smoke cigarettes and flirt, six of us cramped into a booth at 119 around the corner from Irving Plaza or down at the Library like scared puppies in a crate, journalists, artists, rock stars, nobodies, all unified by our dumbstruckness. I remember Melissa Auf Der Maur, the bass player from Hole and Smashing Pumpkins, now embarking on a solo career, all hollow eyed and talking wistfully about her native Canada. How it was safe and sane up there in the Great White North.

I was not sane. I was angry. I wanted bloody revenge. I closed my eyes and imagined fighter planes locating this new enemy and carpet bombing them. I wanted to see their heads on spikes. I hated myself for feeling this way but the air still smelled like burning rubber and metal and flesh, and the idea that just breathing it was eventually going to kill us all was tricky to shake off. But

I wasn't going anywhere, up to Canada, down to Mexico, or out to Chicago or LA. If more attacks were coming, I would die with my fellow New Yorkers.

I knew things would recover when I started receiving e-mails from impatient publicists on the West Coast.

"Hey . . . I know you guys are going through a hard time over there, and I'm really sorry, but I'm just wondering if you've had a chance to listen to the new whatever's album."

Real eggshell walkers, those LA flacks, but in a way, I was grateful. Their needling e-mails were like green shoots. The writing staff convened, and it was discussed just what, if anything, *Spin* was going to say about what had happened. Opinions differed. Some thought it would blow over and we should solider on as usual. Others figured that was daft, and we should have a theme issue. *Rolling Stone* put the date on the cover. Were we really going to put Pink or Sum 41 there instead?

Humor and sex helped us as much as anything else. I recall walking into The Slipper Room and smiling as James, the owner, dropped the needle on "Bombs Away" by The Police, then segued into "Life During Wartime" by Talking Heads. Then there was the unintentionally funny Mariah Carey film *Glitter*, which Tracey Pepper and I rushed to see. I kept dates with girls. If there were going to be attacks (and at one point the Empire State Building was evacuated, and for a week we had to open our daily mail wearing rubber gloves so as not to touch any spores), then we New Yorkers were going to drink and smoke and have as much sex as possible before it all went to hell. I picked up a pretty blonde artist named Erin, and on our first date, we sat in a bar on the Lower East Side called Welcome to the Johnsons. It was tricked out like a seventies living room. We watched George W. Bush give the address that confirmed what everybody already knew: the attacks were part of an Al-Qaeda plot. Those countries that didn't renounce the extremists and hand over their known operatives would be considered terrorist states. When the speech was over, my thoughts returned to how I was going to get Erin into bed.

They'd roped off downtown, and you had to show your ID at a checkpoint to get above or below Union Square. Nobody knew if we'd ever get back to where we'd been. Selfish concerns, plans, upcoming book releases, impending deadlines—all gone. We just drank and listened to music and tried to make each other laugh and forget sad things and remember the nineties, when everything had been so much easier.

The Who's four-song set at the Concert for New York City some weeks later snapped me out of my numbness. They played four songs I'd heard all my life, but there in my little bedroom with Patricia Ann and Gideon Yago, the MTV VJ she worked with, something happened. I saw camera sweeps of the crowds, cops and firefighters who'd rushed to the towers that day, and they were not healed and never would be fully, but you could see relief and defiance in their eyes.

Rock and roll is important, I told myself. Rock and roll matters. Al-Qaeda had tried to destroy my city, and now The Who (with John Entwistle still in the band, but not for long) was absolutely thrashing "Won't Get Fooled Again." It was time to get back to work.

Gideon Yago, nearly a decade younger than me, was already an emo heart-throb to millions of smart, sad kids, but it didn't go to his head. He became, like another MTV star I'd met through Patricia Ann (who did makeup at 1515), a semi-regular drinking buddy of mine. Cocktails and rock trivia: none of us could take on Matt Pinfield, a college DJ turned on-air personality. Matt was an autodidact, but it was fun trying and vying for jukebox and trivia dominance. Like me, Gideon found it bluntly amazing that anyone was paying us to do what we would do anyway: write, scarf down culture, go to rock festivals, absorb New York City, be ourselves . . . whatever that was. Most days, the money—and the booze—still made it impossible to figure out.

CHAPTER 17

"St. Christopher be my guide," I'd say while strapping in, the old wanna-be Catholic in me roused to the front after 9/11. Some people I know stopped flying for good. I was never *not* on an airplane. Sia Michel had been appointed editor at *Spin* after Alan Light departed to start up a short-lived classic rock magazine called *Tracks*. Sia was more of a gambler. She liked my persona and felt it was a good match for the more adventuresome and dangerous bend she envisioned for *Spin*. No more safe Eminem covers or soul-crushing forays into Nickelback land. We would go back to our roots as a bold and bratty "new rock" bible, play up our strengths, and find our groove again. I was to be a major part of this campaign and felt flattered.

Under Sia, I started flying all over the world, and it beat the increasingly angry and sedentary drinking a lot of my friends were doing on the Lower East Side, as the firemen and volunteers worked the pit and the CIA went looking for Osama bin Laden in the mountains of Afghanistan. The feeling of movement—of just going forward, forward, forward, lifting from the tarmac and landing somewhere strange, checking into an anonymous, clean hotel, and taking a taxi to the recording studio or concert venue (then completely and neatly reversing these steps)—was somehow comforting, as if looking back at what my own city used to be was just too depressing.

It wasn't all smooth and clean. The wait to get onto an airplane was nail-biting. You sized up your future fellow passengers at the gate. After 9/11, if you saw someone with brown skin or a beard, you felt frightened, and then guilty for feeling frightened, and then angry at him or her and at the entire situation. But once in the air, the sheer propulsion was liberating. "I go all over. I take people to the Bronx, Brooklyn, to Harlem. I don't care. Don't make no difference to me," Travis Bickle says in his *Taxi Driver* voice-over, and I felt the same way. I'd get a call or e-mail from Sia every few weeks, throw a few pairs of socks and underwear, a pack of cigarettes, a pad, a pen, and my CD Discman into a bag, and I was off. I'd never even owned a passport before and had to get one rushed, but such hassles were few. I just had to fall into a glossy, black town car in my dark glasses and T-shirt, get to the airport, fall into another taxi wherever I landed, check into the hotel, find the rock star, and figure out something interesting to say about him or her. I could drink while doing all of this. I could smoke (except on the planes). I could take drugs. I could jerk off. I didn't have to shave. And I got paid well. I had no girlfriend, no pets, no mistress, no plants, nothing in the fridge that would spoil. I'd become perfectly and permanently a rock-and-roll passenger, empty inside and running—perhaps too old to be living this way, but feeling no pain in the moment, which was all we felt we had in the fall of 2001.

I did Weezer's first major U.S. cover story shortly after 9/11. The band's leader, Rivers Cuomo, was one of the few pop songwriting geniuses in "modern rock" capable of an emotionally true ballad and a crashing, power-chord rocker. You could identify a Weezer song among two dozen KROQ sound-the-sames. They had a style. They were the real thing. Weezer had been successful since 1994, when I was working at the Daily Planet in Hollywood, but by the time I started getting published, they'd long since disappeared after their second album, *Pinkerton*, flopped. Written in part while Rivers was attending Harvard, it's now considered the band's masterpiece and one of the holy trinity of touchstones (along with The Smiths' *The Queen Is Dead* and Fugazi's *13 Songs*) for the emo movement of the late nineties and early two thousands. Rivers took the initial failure of *Pinkerton* personally and badly. My first genuinely good scoop as a rock-and-roll gossip columnist was about him. I'd been told by a source that he'd grown a long mountain-man beard and spent long days doing nothing but bouncing a pink-rubber Spaulding ball against the wall, over and over again. Bonk. Bonk. Bonk. For hours on end. He seemed like our generation's version of Syd Barrett—increasingly unreachable, off somewhere in inner space. Bonk. Bonk. Bonk. I ran the story, and it got a lot of attention. Later, his publicist, Dennis Dennehey, confided to me that it really shook him up to have that image out there. It got him back to work. About a year and change later, the band finally released a solid comeback album. Though it was simply called *Weezer*, fans referred to it as "the green album" (their debut, also titled *Weezer*, is known to all as "the blue album"). They were now fully back in a groove, creatively at least, and were already recording a follow-up, titled *Maladroit*, when negotiations began to put them on the cover of *Spin*'s July 2002 issue. Weezer didn't do a lot of press in general and had done none since their mid-nineties hey-day, but they'd agreed to talk to *Spin*, and I suppose because of the story I ran, Rivers agreed that his first interview since the *Pinkerton*-triggered breakdown would be with me. I flew to Los Angeles, where they were finishing up the record at

Sunset Sound Records in Hollywood. I'd already checked into the Hyatt on Sunset. It was still a haven for mid-level bands, and a Prevost tour bus was frequently parked in the semicircular drive. I was changing out of my travel clothes when Sia called and said Rivers had changed his mind and wasn't sure about the interview after all.

"Seriously? I'm already here."

"I know. I don't know what to do."

"I'm in LA! I'm on the balcony, staring at the smog. What the hell? Does he even know what a pain in the ass it is to fly now?"

"You have to talk to him. He likes you."

"You want me to beg?"

"I don't know. I'm at a loss here. Just . . . do something. Get the story."

I could feel my heart beating rapidly under the clean, white bath towel. I lit a cigarette.

"Can you get a message to him?" I asked Sia.

"Yes."

I paced on the balcony, smoking, and stared across Sunset Boulevard at the billboard that faced my room. It was a promotion for the film *Donnie Darko*; a dour and demented, silver-blue rabbit, staring back at me as if to say, "Give 'em hell." Most journalists don't push rock stars around or really demand much of them. The rocker always has the upper hand. Maybe it's because they have the money and the minders, but I had the power of bullshit on my side.

When I arrived at *Spin*, I could barely converse above a whisper when sober and would studiously avoid going to the bathroom at the same time as a co-worker for fear of stumbling into conversation, but I had patiently and carefully designed my work persona to be the social aggressor and this applied to dealing with the rock-and-roll stars as well. It had only been five years but I was a galaxy away from the Long Island kid who cowered from Nigel the bald guy in the band Bush. I was writing features now. Cover stories. Two or three every year. On the high school scale, I was one of the popular kids; a jock. And I could stare down any rock star no matter how famous (just as long as it wasn't Morrissey . . . more on that later). And after a point, I could even do it semi-sober, with just a lung-full of nicotine and my trusty dark shades for support. I tested myself. It was necessary to get harder and harder at the level I'd reached at the mag. Fear was for freelancers or the fuckers who did charts for the front of the book, not the masthead's stars. It's like that scene in *China 9, Liberty 37* when Warren Oates says, "There are no soft gunfighters, boy."

This was a new century and a new reality, and it was a harsh one. So I made myself harsh and hard. Our Sylvia Plath books and cardigans and Belle and Sebastian albums wouldn't help us anymore, but our acid tongues and our two fists, our leather jackets—these were the new rock writer tools.

"Okay, please tell Rivers fucking Cuomo I do not fucking fly. I have a great fucking fear of flying, okay? But I took a Valium, and I got my ass on an airplane, and I flew all the way across the fucking country to talk to you about your new album. Now, are you going to tell me about your new album, or do I have to get right back on a plane. Because if that's the case, then you are going to have to find me some more fucking Valium. I ate 'em all." This was my boss I was talking to, remember.

Sia laughed. She loved it.

"I'll get them the message."

An hour later, a call came into my hotel room from Rivers's assistant.

"We were just about to order dinner. Why don't you come over now?"

All the posing, I should mention, goes out the window during the one-on-one interview. It has to. It's too quiet, too real. Just you and the subject, usually alone in some room. If someone's lurking outside, a publicist or the other, less interesting band mates, it's usually detectable, but it does little to mess with the intense intimacy. It's like being in bed with your girlfriend—for twenty to thirty minutes after sex. There's no hiding, no real looking away. Both of you know what's happened, what's happening. That it has to be done . . . to sell records, to sell magazines. A lot of jobs and money are riding on this quiet conversation in a little room.

That afternoon, I first found myself in a situation that I would experience again and again in the new decade. Me. A rock star. A couch. Twisted posture. No eye contact. That's both our postures and both our eyes. Rivers was shy, and when I wasn't drunk or bluffing, I was even more so. It was like being on a date. I knew what I knew about the rock stars, and they knew what they knew about *Spin* or "the press," most of it coming from either personal experience or the film *Almost Famous*. My approach in these situations (again, not drunk) was to sort of indicate, "Come on, I know this is ridiculous, but I'm here and you're here, and we have to do this. Let's make the best of it." I would sometimes, as I did with Rivers, talk about my analog tape recorder and how I am paranoid about losing audio. Rock stars, especially the ones who produce, can relate to that. I would sometimes reveal that I had a drug problem. Occasionally (possibly always) I would hold an unlit cigarette in my hand. I wanted them to know that I was as damaged by rock and roll, and as saved by it, as they were. I wasn't even remotely square. These conversations were very soft-spoken. Sometimes whispered.

I found the more talented the subject, like Rivers or a little later, Trent Reznor, the quieter the exchange. I knew I had a privileged view. Most people didn't get to sit on the couch next to Trent Reznor and have him literally whisper calmly about trolling around scoring drugs, and being miserable while playing Madison Square Garden, and getting clean. When they saw him, he was on an arena stage screaming "March of the Pigs" or "Head Like a Hotel" with a gang of Goth droogs behind him. But I saw rock stars' flaws up close: their weird teeth and zits. None of them, not one, had good skin. Not Green Day or Dave Grohl. It was a sacrifice they made in order to live a free life on the road, and I had the same spots on my face. Maybe a little less.

As with my best drug snorting and spontaneous blowjob receiving, I did most of my best note taking in toilets. I felt comfortable sitting on a top-down seat and scribbling into my knee over any free sheet of paper: napkins, stationary from hotel pads, even toilet paper or the little squares of cardboard on the flip side of a matchbook. I got good at collecting novelistic detail: what was on the shelves, what was playing on the stereo, what a rock star whispered to someone else when he or she thought I wasn't listening. I was always listening. Always. And missed nothing. I couldn't wear a wire, so I took my notes *All the President's Men* style, in piss-smelling bogs, Porta-Johns at festivals, or tour bus loos, which were like airplane toilets. I also took notes in airplane toilets. I did this because I was usually very drunk or high on the road and feared forgetting a good detail, but I was almost always able to decipher the scribble when safely back at my kitchen desk in Greenwich Village. I didn't write in cafés and had no private office at *Spin*. When back from a gig, I'd unload the matchbooks and hotel pads and put the piece together. I wrote in my tiny, filthy, roachy kitchen in my one-bedroom apartment with the red-tagged, useless stove and one stick after another of Egyptian musk smoking in the cheap wooden incense burner to cover the smell of cigarette smoke and whatever band I was profiling blasting out of my red Sony boom box, over and over again.

"What does the guy in apartment four do for a living?" new neighbors would ask the super, who lived across the hall. "Is he going to hurt me? Are my kids safe?"

"Yeah, no, he's just a rock writer."

Deadlines kept me alive. Deadlines kept me out of the bars and away from the dealers. I never took my feet off the rail if a piece wasn't due, especially since I knew all the card checkers and bouncers at most of the downtown bars at this point. They'd let me stay twenty-four hours a day, and I'm sure I'd still be there, coked out and ready to greet the noon barflies when they reopened, if I didn't have 750 words on Kelis and Tenacious D due by ten o'clock.

As 2001 wound down, some of my friends turned to Celexa to get them through the day. I turned to The Strokes.

By 2002, rock and roll was finally changing, and it was definitely for the better as far as I was concerned. Those bloody kvetching nu metal and rap rock bands that we had to cover at *Spin* only because they all sold millions of copies of their cynical, formulaic CDs were out of vogue now, and a new, sexy garage rock was starting to gain real traction. The new bands' sales would never equal those of their predecessors, but they had a cultural heft that would soon change the way people dressed and behaved in addition to what they sang in the shower.

A lot of these bands formed right under our noses in Lower Manhattan or Brooklyn, and with all eyes on New York City in the weeks and months after September 11, they now had the floor. Smoldering, paranoid New York had become the new Seattle somehow. Typically those in my profession have always looked to England for guidance as far as new music goes. *Spin* could never compete with *NME* and the late, lamented *Melody Maker*, whose enthusiasm for the next new thing bordered on pathological. Now the roles were completely reversed. I'd see bits of interviews I'd done for my column showing up in the pages of *NME* as their "world exclusives." (And because it was *NME*, they could steal these bits outright, and I would say nothing. I was flattered). The twenty-two-year-old kid interns who worked at *Spin* now had it better than the top editors at IPC over in London simply because they were here in the city, and soon the company that put out *NME*, *Uncut*, and other quality music publications were sending young reporters to the East Village to embed. Nothing but nothing seemed to be happening anywhere else, but here in Manhattan and Brooklyn, a half dozen readymade media stars like the Yeah Yeah Yeahs, Interpol, The Realistics, and even the wryer and campier electro-clash acts like Fischerspooner were readying for their stardom moments. None of the Squeezebox bands primed to blow up nearly a decade earlier had done much: Psychotica, Toilet Boys, even Lunachicks and The Voluptuous Horror of Karen Black, whose stage presence didn't seem containable by anything less than an arena, ended up, like the Ramones and The Dead Boys before them, moving their targets a bit closer. Jonathan Fire*Eater, who'd set the Max Fish scene wild with envy after signing with Dreamworks for a reported million-dollar deal, had fallen apart. Even Pavement had quietly broken up—a scoop I ran in my *Backstage Pass* column after interviewing Stephen Malkmus about his first solo album with his new backing bad, The Jicks. We were so passionate about Pavement. It was strange to hear the news of their demise in such a casual, impassive, "Oh yeah, I guess we broke up" fashion. I thought about Herve. Was he crushed? Had he moved on too?

The last band from the city to get big was the fucking Spin Doctors. In order for it all to coalesce for New York, there had to be a Beatles or a Blondie or a Nirvana: one band that was undeniable enough to come up from the street, and everyone else would then follow. The Strokes were already the best and most transformative band of the new rock scene, but they also had that quality. *Is This It* was a perfect album, from the opening title track to "Take It or Leave It," which the band routinely closed its live shows with (never returning for an encore).

When Courtney Love took Winona Ryder to a Strokes show, she supposedly became quite flustered. "Her eyes glazed over and she uttered, barely audibly, 'Jesus, not since The Replacements,'" Courtney recalled. Courtney would write a song about Julian, their lead singer. We were all fascinated by this new group that seemed to materialize from nothing and make all the new metal and boy bands seem lumpy and foul overnight. Within a year or two, Justin Timberlake would leave 'N Sync and be hanging with them. Who of our generation didn't want to be a part of that band? Skinny, bleary, writing songs like "I Will Dare" and "Unsatisfied." It had been a long time since there'd been a band you fantasized about being a member of. Kids wanted to be like the Strokes, a few adults too, but their appeal in the rock press was even more intense than that. We were proprietary, competitive even, especially those of us who'd been following them for a while, drinking in the same bars, attending the same rock shows at the Bowery or the Merc. We vied for ownership of their story, which was only just being written, and mostly by goo-goo-eyed Brits.

"That is my band there," Gideon would say as we drank in the Library together. He had it over me in that he was already friendly with a few of "the guys" and was dying to write about them too, but he didn't know what he was dealing with as far as balls-out ambition went. Gideon may have covered Korn at MTV, but he'd never had to write about those fuckers. I was not going to let him cut in line. The Strokes were my ticket, and I would have punched any rivals in the eye, even if we were matey.

"I'm going to write the first big piece about them," I vowed. "Me."

"Already pitched it, dude," Gideon gloated.

"You're not a writer. You're a talking head."

Gideon was actually a very good writer, and a fistfight between the two of us would probably be a draw, if not a knockout in his favor, but again, I had my eye on the prize and "the guys."

The Strokes seemed like the band to finally make the last seven years of my life feel real—a chance to go back in time to an era of rock journalism when Nick Kent tangled with the Pistols and Bangs traveled England with the Clash or Vivienne Goldman went down to Jamaica to hear out Peter Tosh. They were one of those bands: Big Star, The Replacements, R.E.M., Black Flag. Future rock history. We could all feel it.

I'd been their champion at *Spin* even before Sia became editor in chief. I'd ruined the good cheer at the 2001 holiday party by getting very drunk and loudly scolding my boss for giving band-of-the-year status to U2.

"U2? What is this, 1987? They are *not* the band of the year. The fucking Strokes are band of the year!" It was my Sister Souljah moment. As I said, even before I was a music journalist, when I was still merely a *Spin* reader, Jack and I took band or artist of the year, as well as album of the year, very, very seriously. When Teenage Fanclub's *Bandwagonesque* was voted album of the year over *Nevermind*, years before I'd have ever even dreamed of working at *Spin*, we were (like most of the rock community) pretty outraged. Rock and roll was important. "God parted the heavens and gave us The Strokes. They're a gift from God. To New York. And to *Spin*. We've been waiting for this band." They seemed like part two of The Who–kindled rebirth.

A little under a year later, in the late summer of 2002, Sia called me and asked if I would be interested in going on the road with The Strokes and writing their first American cover story. She'd chosen them as *Spin*'s band of the year. Finally! Gideon may have had the youth, the better salary, and the little emo girls drooling over his bespectacled charm, but I had the gig. This was essentially The Strokes' victory lap tour. They'd already gone from a residency at the tiny Mercury Lounge bar and rock club on Houston Street to a split show at Radio City Music Hall with The White Stripes. They'd returned triumphantly to the Mercury with a secret show under the name "The Shitty Beatles" (a *Wayne's World* nod) and were now headlining large clubs and theaters on their own. They were also opening three East Coast dates on The Rolling Stones' "40 Licks Tour." I had visions of traveling on the bus with the band, becoming a part of their inner circle. I have to confess that I'd already started dressing like them, not that the way I'd dressed since college was that far removed to begin with.

"You can have total access, but you'll have to drive behind the bus; there's no room on the bus itself," I was told by Charles Aaron, the veteran *Spin* writer and editor who would be bringing in the piece.

"Behind the bus?"

I guess it was better than nothing. I didn't even know if I remembered how to drive a car. It had been about seven years since I'd sold my 1987 Toyota for heroin money out in Hollywood. Driving, to me, was Long Island. I was a Manhattan kid now. Permanently. Worse, I'd be going through DC, where the band had one of its dates, and someone was picking off random people at gas stations. They called him the DC Sniper. One minute you're feeling the pain at the pump, and the next, you're just feeling the pain. The Strokes had security. I just had my romantic fantasies about Lester Bangs and the Clash. I was nervous as I piled into the white Ford and tooled out toward the West Side Highway. I had no idea how to get to Portland, Maine, where I would be meeting up with the touring party. I only knew I needed to be there—as with Bennington, as with the Chelsea Hotel, as with Max Fish, and as with everywhere I've ever thrown myself in an effort to become . . . someone.

Turns out, a car is like a bicycle. One does not forget how to drive. The autumn air in Portland was cold and wet. My quaint little hotel was right next to the theater, which the band had sold out. Maine reminded me of Bennington. Portland was another near-rural but gentrified and fully modern New England town. Little hipster girls in vintage gear were already lined up outside as I walked in, made my way backstage, and introduced myself to Ryan Gentles, the band's wiry manager, who like me had the build and wardrobe of a Stroke. They were all watching the opening band, the power-pop group Sloan. I went out into the crowd during the show. It's good to do this sometimes, even if you have a VIP all-access pass or sticker. You have to experience the show like a fan. I never understood writers who didn't do this. It's a different show from the balcony, behind the velvet ropes, with people taking your drink order. You're not really there. You might as well be in your living room. The crowd was very young, kids out on a school night, boys and girls, all of them ecstatic to be there. Here was a band absolutely at its peak, enjoying its moment.

After the show, I waded into the dressing room, but as always there was a warm-up period—that blind-date awkwardness. I know some rock writers instantly go "bro" and can avoid this period, but that in itself is a shtick. It's nice to not have to deal with shyness, I guess, but I just hold up the wall and try to observe and sometimes have a couple of beers before I engage. Julian Casablancas, the lead singer, was the first to talk to me. He was wearing a white belt (a look already being copied by a million hipsters across the world) and a crazy vintage jacket with a family crest on it. If he weren't a rock star, you'd cross the street to avoid him. Julian challenged me to a game of pool and kicked my ass over and over again. He was a hustler. The girls were let in and waited patiently for autographs. Albert, the guitarist, cranked up Nick Cave on a boom box, and Nick Valensi called New York to hear all the details about the White Stripes show in Union Square, a show all of us were sorry to miss. As was my procedure, I ducked into the bathroom and scribbled, then ducked back so as not to look too conspicuous, but Valensi, the tallest, skinniest, and probably the smartest of the group—certainly the most suspicious— caught me. To this day, he's the only rock star subject ever to call me out for my mental recording of a scene while I thought nobody noticed. "You're getting all this aren't you?" he asked. "You know, you don't have to do that in the bathroom. We know we're all 'on.'" I couldn't really win with Nick. Interviewing him a few days later in Philadelphia also marked the second and thankfully last time I passed out mid-question while attempting to conduct a q and a. Actually . . . that's not quite true either. Three years later in Paris, I passed out while interviewing Bob Hardy and Nick McCarthy of the Scottish band Franz Ferdinand, but I chalk that up to jet lag, as I came to the festival grounds where they were performing straight from the airport. We had to make that interview up the next morning over breakfast, where the band's lead singer, Alex Kapranos, joined us for cold pancakes and eggs, weak coffee, and burnt toast from the kind of buffets I seemed to live on at the time. Besides, this was only quid pro quo. I had bands falling asleep on me all the time. Once, mid-question, Peter from Black Rebel Motorcycle Club took off his jacket, crumpled it into a pillow, and took a nap in the booth we'd been sharing in some downtown restaurant. Then the others followed. I called their publicist, Jim Merlis, and said, "Um, Jim maybe you can come and wake up your band?" I suppose the journalist is obliged to remain conscious and upright. Valensi didn't judge me too harshly though.

"It's my birthday," I told him—a tacit message: be nice to me. It's the kind of thing a homeless guy on the subway says in an effort to extract some more hand outs, but this time it was actually true. It was past midnight and I was officially thirty-three. Lester Bangs died at thirty-three (and I know Jesus did as well, but Lester was more important to me than Jesus), and I was finally getting my Bangs-worthy assignment with a band that would still be talked about in twenty-five years. They were already that band. It was apparent to everyone, even The Strokes.

The next day I drove to Boston, behind the bus, and checked into my hotel, took a walk down to the harbor, and stared at the water, killing time. That's the thing about these on-the-road assignments. Nobody ever tells you about all the crushing waiting. If you arrive in a strange city on a budget (gas, food, basics) at say nine o'clock and aren't scheduled to go to the venue until at least seven or eight in the evening, that's ten hours that you have to fill. You read magazines and *USA Today*. You shower, shave, and get dressed hours before going out. You eat lunch alone, no old friends or relatives to call up. Then you get to the venue, and it's dead empty. The band is wandering around backstage; the crew know you're a journalist, so most of them clam up. The caterer won't let you near the food. You're basically a standing lamp until the doors open. Then the crowd comes in, the band's nerves get the better of them, and they are grateful for the strength in numbers. At that moment, you sort of become part of the crew, especially after a few dates. You wish everyone a good show, and once they're on stage, you eat a little of their food, steal a bottle of Jack Daniel's, and watch from the side of the stage. Maybe you get wrecked with them at the afterparty, but you always, always end up lonely in the morning, some times on the cold, title floor of your rent-a-room. Being in a foreign country is worse. It can be the loneliest existence of them all, especially if there's no porn. Happily, The Strokes and their manager took pity on me. Or perhaps they'd seen *Almost Famous* too and liked the idea of taking "the writer" on their adventure. I quickly started receiving calls in my room during the day. The band was to be honored by the *Harvard Lampoon*, and I was invited to meet them at the bus and come along. Finally, I was being welcomed onto the bus.

Although the ice had been broken the night before, with The Strokes actually singing happy birthday to me, the band was still standoffish on the bus. They didn't completely trust me. And they talked in code; for example, they called the coke that someone was coordinating for the evening's festivities "Dr. Zhivago," like Christian Slater does in Tarantino's script for *True Romance*. I picked up these inside jokes and made it clear that I was a different type of music journalist than perhaps they were used to—the type that actually would very much like to share some of that coke—and that it would be okay to get a little high in front of me and not worry about it getting into the piece. Especially if they shared the coke. The Strokes were the first band to make me feel comfortable doing my note scribbling in the open; ironically, they were the first band I spared out of a certain sense of esprit de corps. Somehow, I didn't want to fink on them. I wanted them to like me. I wanted to be a Stroke. I threw a good measure of my journalistic integrity out the window of that bus as it rolled toward Harvard Square.

The Harvard guys completely lacked the kind of collegiate cool I was used to at Bennington. The *Lampoon* staff were all socially awkward and vaguely hostile nerds. They watched the band and me at the cocktail party in the library like we were the ice sculpture, slowly melting. Nobody knew what we were doing there. This silly, tense meet and greet was yet another product of this first real fame that the band was experiencing—like when the keys to the city are produced and other celebrities approach you like they've known you all your life. No wonder someone placed a call to the good Dr. Z. The Fleet Center was probably their largest solo show yet. I caught it from the back of the stage, kneeling on the stage floor to the side of drummer Fabrizio Moretti's kit. It was the optimal perspective for a journalist, a band's-eye view, watching the audience watch The Strokes as they played one of their biggest shows to date.

The line on The Strokes was that they had an easy run; they were children of privilege but were sometimes an authentically angry crew. It was hard to predict their moods. At the Boston show, for example, Julian picked up the mic stand at the end of "New York City Cops" and threw it across the stage. I wrote "Eddie Vedder" down in my notebook, as I'd seen Vedder pull the same move. Julian had told me earlier that the Pearl Jam song "Yellow Ledbetter" had made him want to be a musician. He probably saw Eddie Vedder do this as a kid, but now he was doing it for the same reason I did basically everything I did— because someone I admired had done it first—and this helped him make sense of terrifying things like being an overnight idol to a million cool kids.

"What album is the song 'Goodbye Yellow Brick Road' on?" Albert Hammond Jr. asked me, all sleepy eyes and kinky hair. He was fiddling with the bus's stereo.

"Um, it's on *Goodbye Yellow Brick Road*."

We were in the VIP parking area of the Fed Ex Field stadium in DC. The sniper was still at large, but he'd spared me so far. The Strokes were opening for the Stones but didn't seem too interested in Mick and Keith.

When the Stones came on, Julian and I watched in the pit, passing a bottle of red wine back and forth.

"How could you not like The Rolling Stones?" I asked Julian, who was becoming more and more drunk.

"I just don't."

It was a strange feeling, being ten feet away from a strutting Jagger in a venue where people had paid hundreds of dollars to sit a hundred yards away from the band.

"Not even *Exile*?"

"I don't know, man."

I noticed Julian exhaling cigarette smoke, then cupping the blue vapor with his hands and pulling it back from the air into his face, as if he was washing himself in a sink.

Rock stars, I thought. I just love them.

I grew up in the seventies and eighties when The Rolling Stones were still a powerful band and a going concern. There would be other generational divides, subtle things that made me realize that perhaps, one day, I would be a little too old to do this credibly. That this might be the beginning of the end for me as a young, brave music journalist, and like the Stones, I might start to look a little unseemly wearing certain things, moving in certain ways, and traveling in certain shadowy social circles. The next night in Hartford, for example, Peter Wolf of the mighty J. Geils Band ambled backstage to wish The Strokes well. He huddled with Julian in the locker room area of the arena for about ten minutes, discussing how to handle sudden fame, then returned to the VIP area and the crowd.

After he left, Julian approached his manager Ryan and asked, "Who was that guy?"

As the resident Gen Xer, I patiently explained the significance of the J. Geils Band to The Strokes: kids in eighties T-shirts and jackets who were too young to remember some of the cultural signposts of the decade.

"'Centerfold'? No? 'Freeze Frame'? No? Come on. Um . . . 'Love Stinks'?"

"Oh yeah, from the *Wedding Singer*," Julian finally deduced.

It had happened, maybe a few years late because of the pace I'd been keeping and the fact that rock and roll keeps you young through your thirties (that and Kiehl's and Rogaine), but time, the avenger, first in the shape of Peter Wolf, of all things, had finally begun to catch up. Things moved quickly in the modern age.

If the J. Geils man pinned me, Andrew W.K. held me for the one-two-three count. As with The Strokes, I was the first American journo to interview Mr. W.K. extensively. It was I who introduced the hard line according to A.W.K. (in the March 2002 *Spin*, should you try to disprove this claim). That interview became a sort of anti-touchstone for me: the moment when, after five years as a well-paid music journalist, with two books under my belt, basically living the fantasy, I finally exhaled and realized that one day, probably soon, I would have to figure out how to become a real person because I no longer understood where this rock-and-roll jive was heading. Whereas The Strokes had a laconic cool that I naturally understood, Andrew was like a pony on the mark, just ready to run and kick. Listening to him rant into the end of my phone about smashing himself in the face with a brick to get the right sleeve photo for *I Get Wet* (the right amount of blood, that is—in the end he resorted to pig's blood), I felt like Don Draper when he first hears "Tomorrow Never Knows" in Season Five of *Mad Men*; like, "Okay, yeah, it's been a good run, Spitz, but it's over. You are officially old and in the way."

When I first got to *Spin*, I was twenty-seven, and there were people like Charles Aaron and Will Hermes and other writers I respected who were in their thirties and seemed dignified. Rob Sheffield and Joe Levy over at *Stone* were about five years older than I was, and so was Alan Light. But even Sia, who would actually go drinking with Ultragrrrl and me, didn't commit to the rock lifestyle like I did. There was no map for how to do that and sustain it into your thirties.

Pretending I was young and nothing had changed in me left me open to gaffes on the order of Jack Lemmon in *Glengarry Glenn Ross*. I didn't have the good leads anymore. I couldn't vouch for what I was writing. I mistakenly described the then-buzzy LA hard rock band The Icarus Line as emo in my

column. If I didn't completely get a record, my brain simply filed it as "emo."
For the next six months, every couple of days, the guitar player from The
Icarus Line, who'd tracked down my private handle, would instant message
me. The box only ever contained one word: "emo." If I could still have written
well about such things and stayed open-minded, I think I would have been
able to check my vanity about the physical aging, but everything was tied up
in the character I'd invented after five years at *Spin*, the public me: the byline
. . . was me. I came home to nothing else. No plants, no fish, no cat, no dog, no
woman; just cigarettes, coke, whiskey, and what Woody Allen calls showbiz
tranquilizers (I'm paraphrasing, of course). There's that famous Chris Rock
line from his iconic *Bring the Pain* special: "Nobody wants to be the old guy
in the club." Once I got my Strokes cover, their first in America, where was
there to go? The Vines? The Hives? Well, I did those too. My lack of a need
for accountability and emotional retardation made me feel special and young.
My sister was engaged to be married. The people I went to high school and
college with had families. I had the new White Stripes album before anybody
else.

I was in the office one day when a coworker, Jason Roth, one of the few
people who would talk to me when I was first hired, came into the online pod
where I was catching up.

"You guys have to hear this." He pulled up his e-mail on a free monitor
and downloaded a song.

"It's called 'Losing My Edge,'" he said. There was a huge smile on his face
as we listened, but the lyrics didn't make me smile. The song, about a thirty-
something guy who senses *"the kids . . . coming up from behind,"* smarter, sexier,
and with a *"borrowed nostalgia for the unremembered eighties,"* was the first single by LCD Soundsystem. Feeling defensive and vulnerable, the singer brags
about his Zelig-like appearances at all the great cult moments in modern rock
history—*"I was there in 1974 at the first Suicide practices in a loft in New York
City. I was working on the organ sounds with much patience"*—about his record
collection and the fantasy band he will never start. He sings about what he
knows and how what he knows is all he is. And how it's now being sucked
away. In just under eight minutes, my raison d'être of thirty-three years had
been reduced to a punch line. There was no being a rock snob anymore after
that song.

CHAPTER 18

I never let on that I had any regrets about some of the choices I'd made in the effort to become what I thought was a real writer and the kind of character people can't ignore. Regret wasn't rock. It was so not punk rock that they made punk rock T-shirts with "I regret nothing" printed on them in French, sometimes over a silk-screened image of the young Keith Richards. I was rock, but in private, it was hard to ignore the loneliness and impossible to deny the daylong hangovers my lifestyle was now producing as I entered my thirties. I had a gut feeling that the only thing that might ground me was a relationship with a good woman. I didn't believe in God, so women were the only undeniably superior power source I revered, the only magic I knew. And yet, I suspected that in order to enjoy an actual relationship, the kind that weathered the ups and down without a trip to the divorce lawyer, that sense of magic had to be neutralized as well. People had problems. Sometimes, like Julie, they came to me with them. A coward runs away. A real man stays.

Frustrated that at thirty I still knew almost nothing about women, despite having one in my bed nearly every night (and, more often than not, being too drunk to fuck), I decided to do what I always did when things vexed me: write a play about it. The working title of *Shyness Is Nice*, my first play of the new millennium, which I'd begun shortly after closing *Bomb with Carrie*, was *Two Emo Boys Die Violently*. The story concerned Rodney and Stew, who are pushing thirty and are still virgins. They've never had sex because they are afraid it would offend the famously celibate Morrissey. Their friend Fitzgerald, named after my new agent, is a former emo nerd who has made himself over as a hipster (this was around the time the theater press was referring to me as the "hipster playwright" . . . the word was not yet gag inducing but well on its way). Fitzgerald hires an Australian hooker, Kylie, to deflower his buddies, but pays her with fake drugs. When Kylie's Nick Cave–obsessed, female pimp, Blixa, shows up for revenge, all hell breaks loose in a bloody, funny, dirty fashion. *Shyness* took the anti-gentrification anger of my 1999 play "*. . . Worry Baby*" and made it sweeter. Also sexual ineptitude is always, always funny. None of us really have the hang of it, even though we pretend to. For my generation, having the hang of it, being good in bed, was almost tacky. Intimacy was gross. Still, I was growing frustrated with my ignorance. I was hanging out with Patricia Ann one night, and she was chopping out lines and listening to "Drops of Jupiter" by Train, which for some reason, she was prone to playing on repeat at the time. "Drops of Jupiter," over and over, when I happened to ask her if I was good or bad in bed. We'd slept together about a dozen times at that point.

"It's not that you're bad. It's more like you're not really there. Sleeping with you is like being in the room while you're jerking off," she said. "You don't know what you're doing with us down there."

"Show me," I pleaded, and after a few more spins of Train, she obliged.

This began a sort of centerpiece scene in the new play, where Kylie instructs Stew on how to eat pussy and lights up a cigarette while he goes to work.

Shyness was easily my best play and clearly destined to be our biggest hit yet. The cast knew it. Jack knew it. Kirsten knew it and even convinced the Westbeth's in-house producer Arnold Engelmen to get behind us. Every line killed; every scenario milked the tension and awkwardness and sweetness until it was dry. It's like when a band (like, say, Train) stumbles upon a hit song, then goes for years trying to figure out how to repeat the formula.

We were ready to open when Zoe returned to my life, as my therapist Petunia always warned she would when my life got good. I'd seen her for a drink at the Standard on Sunset the previous year when I was in LA to interview the recently reunited Cult for a small *Spin* feature. She was in bad shape then, depressed and a little lost.

"When I swallow, I can taste blood. That's not normal is it? Do you taste blood?"

"No blood." Maybe I wasn't so badly off after all as far as my interior went.

I still loved her though. Take away all the mess and bad, youthful decisions, and our connection was as strong as it had been nearly a decade earlier. After watching *Titanic*, and in a fit of romantic fervor, I wrote her a long letter telling her that she was the love of my life and wishing her well. I'm not sure how much of that had to do with Leo and Kate and how much actually had to do with Zoe, or perhaps it was just the high-grade oxygen I seemed to be breathing after getting hired by *Spin*.

When I was in LA writing *Bomb* with Brendan, we spoke on the phone a lot and caught up, laying the tracks for a possible New York visit. She'd decided somewhere along the way that she wanted to be an actress, and given her looks and connections, she was fairly quickly cast in an indie production called *Down and Out with the Dolls*. She had a small part playing a debauched Portland rock star in an all-girl band (the titular Dolls). Her character was named Fauna. Fauna. I've certainly given some of my characters some ridiculous names, but still.

Zoe stayed in my apartment while in the city, and as we'd done nearly a decade earlier, we pretended the outside world was not there for as long as we could. We locked the doors and had sex for hours—in the kitchen, in the windowsill. In quieter moments, eating, watching TV, I got the sense of what could have been if we'd been a little less wild and a bit more faithful in our youth. I knew I was setting myself up for heartbreak again. There was no way that this was going to last, but I didn't care. It was like saying a long good-bye, and when she went back to LA or whatever planet she'd taken residence on, I would be more capable of weathering it. I had a job now. I was published. I'd written a hit play, like Max Fischer. She couldn't hurt me anymore. I didn't need her. The last thing I remember was having sex with her, drunk, while for some reason wearing one of her dresses. In the morning she was gone. I haven't seen or spoken to her since. She left behind a pair of big, stomping Goth boots, the kind Gene Simmons of Kiss would take on a space expedition. I put them in the closet, and when I moved out, they stayed behind, a house-warming gift for the new tenants. I wasn't heartbroken so much as hard tasked to replace her with someone better, someone who got the new me. A fellow writer seemed ideal.

Emma Forrest was, to my eye, perfect. Beautiful, British, talented, all the right albums, all the right movie references. It'd be easy. I'd simply settle down with her. I'd hang up my leather, archive my toilet-stall notepad, flush my drugs, and we'd be a power writing couple. The minor technicality that we were both, at the time, seriously crazy didn't seem to cloud this romantic daydream one bit. My editor, Carrie Thornton, wanted me to meet her. Emma was working on a book with Carrie as well, and so I put on my good shark-skin suit and walked over to the dark, Soviet-themed Lit Fuck bar KGB on Sunday afternoon for a reading. In person Emma was even more beautiful than she was in her author's photo, which I'd studied while concocting this arranged writer marriage over cigarettes and chocolate milk . . . and blow. She was petite but curvy, with thick, curly brown hair, dark eyes, smooth, pale skin, a handsome nose, and a wry smile. As with Alex, I found her carefully pronounced British vowels exotic. She looked like a dark-haired Carole King, very Jewish, very sexy. She was ten years younger than I was and about a foot shorter, but she had a big enough personality and had been a music journalist since her teens, so she didn't seem so green. She'd actually been at it as long as I had.

That afternoon, Emma was reading from her first book, *Namedropper*, and before she started, she asked the crowd whether they could identify the source of the following lyric: *"You try to scream, but terror takes the sound before you make it."* I knew it was from *Thriller*. Someone called it out, and I felt a little less special.

I liked Emma's writing as much as I could like any other writer's work. Helping each other work and get better didn't factor into my vision for us. I didn't think it through to that point. As long as I could sense some talent, but not so much that thought I couldn't box with it, I was okay.

If Emma and I were formally involved, it was in a relative sense. There were so many demons in both our lives at the time that wrangling them was more or less a full-time gig with little room for another, but for a while, we helped each other through. I'd call her and ask if I could come over because I had the fear and literally needed someone to hold me down and vice versa. Emma lived right up the street on Bleecker. She'd buzz me without warning, always with some kind of adventure to lead me on. Someone had spray-painted a swastika on a bare wall on a wheat-pasted poster on Seventh Avenue, and would I come with her to cover it up? Where and how could she donate a bunch of coats, and would I help her carry them? Could I come hang her framed one-sheet for *Straight No Chaser*? Sometimes she would grab me and kiss me, then say, "I don't know why I just did that." We'd e-mail each other constantly, and she'd sometimes say, "I'm going to save these so they can be published one day." We were going to be the Jewish Simone De Beauvoir and Jean-Paul Sartre. When Emma's novel came out, I took her to the Jane Street Tavern and "interviewed" her for a feature in the *New York Post*.

Sometimes when we'd kiss, I'd try to take it further, but she'd push me away and say, "I can't sleep with you because I like you too much."

She said it often. I didn't get it. If you like someone, don't you want to act on it? Emma wasn't the first girl to occupy my thoughts and confound and charm me, but she was the first equally ambitious writer. She was the first one with writer's rules—in other words, really fucked-up ones. She only slept with people she disliked? I guess this is why there aren't more power literary couples besides ol' Simone and J.-P. When I challenged her on these weird codes, perhaps a bit hypocritically, as I lived by a dozen of them myself, she finally explained, "The problem with this is that you want to be Iggy Pop. But I'm already the Iggy Pop in my life."

"We can't both be Iggy Pop? I mean, why can't we be Iggy Pop together, Emmylou?" It was my nickname for her, an overt reference to the singer Emmylou Harris.

"There can't be two Iggys in one relationship. It's better this way. You can be Iggy Pop whenever you like. And I can be Iggy Pop whenever I like."

"But I don't want to be Iggy Pop anymore. I'm sick of being Iggy Pop at all. You can be Iggy Pop. I won't mind."

"You say that now, but I don't believe you. You're not ready to not be Iggy Pop."

She was right. Emma had written novels. She was on a smoother path than I was, as far as having an uncloudy venue for her personal expression. The plays I did were collective experiences, but I had nothing that approached Emma's books as far as truly consequential and risky writing went. *Neutron Bomb* was Brendan's baby, which I happened to rear with Carrie. We'd pieced it together in my disgusting kitchen with me in the chair and her on an upended milk crate I used to store records. I'm still very proud of the book, but as far as I'm concerned, its only real success was that it got Carrie and Jim wondering what I would do next. It sold well enough that there could be a second book. I'd spent the first ten years since graduating from Bennington just trying not to give up, laboring to get anything published. Now, a major book editor was asking me, "What else do you have?"

Back in 1999, Victoria De Silverio, Michael Hirschorn's assistant when I met her, now a contributor to the mag, and forever my unrequited office crush, and I had an idea for a front-of-the-book feature on reuniting The Smiths. Morrissey, Johnny Marr, Mike Joyce, and Andy Rourke had split in 1987, and now the latter two were suing the other two (who were songwriting partners) for back royalties. In that time, a new generation had come on to their music and aesthetic, and like The Velvet Underground and Joy Division before them, The Smiths were now bigger than they ever had been while a living, functioning rock band. In late August of that year, Vic and I sent an e-mail to Dave Moodie:

"A pitch we desperately need your support for: Repairing the Severed Alliance for the Betterment of the New Millennium."

We were both about to turn thirty. The nineties were about to end. And we were feeling older, vulnerable, and in need of inspiration.

"Two intrepid reporters and lifelong fans take it upon themselves to reunite The Smiths. The piece should have the feel of a documentary, a step-by-step chronicle via a series of diary-like reporting, photos, and interviews."

We broke the execution of the proposed assignment down into phases:

PHASE ONE

Intro and statement of intent

1. Make a timeline listing the band's great successes and events that precipitated the breakup.
2. Interview Mike Joyce and Andy Rourke. Object: to get them to say that they're game for a Smiths reunion if Morrissey and Marr are. Maybe they'll even give back the money they won in court.
3. Send around a petition; get as many signatures as possible from fans. Also, interview obsessed fans.
4. Go to flower shop. Send Moz gladioli from Marr and vice versa, with phony cards attached.
5. Make a donation to a pro-vegetarian organization in Johnny Marr's name and send the receipt to Morrissey.
6. Interview a relationship therapist on repairing severed alliances.

The Irish journalist Johnny Rogan had recently published an iconic book on the band's history and premature split titled *Morrissey and Marr: The Severed Alliance*.

7. Interview a United Nations expert/spokesperson on diplomacy.
8. Interview bands from the eighties that did reunite to great success: Bauhaus, The Cult, New Order.
9. Interview concert promoters and industry people about just how much $$$$ a Smiths reunion would gross.
10. Interview bands from the nineties that worship The Smiths: Courtney, Deftones, Gallagher brothers.
11. Interview Manchester politicians to see if they would declare a Smiths holiday.
12. Talk to Rock and Roll Hall of Fame about possible special premature induction.

The Smiths were not eligible until 2008, and at the time of this writing, almost five years after that date, those idiots still haven't even nominated them.

13. Talk to Alan [Light] about a possible cover feature if they reunite.
14. Get pleas for a reunion signed by Morrissey's icons, like Bowie and David Johansen.
15. Find sick children who promise to get better should they reunite.

The first Coachella music festival, out in Palm Springs, had been announced, and Morrissey was one of the headliners. There were rumors that Johnny Marr would join him onstage (rumors that have preceded every Coachella fest ever since).

PHASE TWO

1. As the Coachella festival approaches, the reporters hit LA and document the fact that Morrissey and Marr both live in Southern California. See if they have any mutual friends and interview these people. See if they've ever crossed paths.
2. Interview Morrissey's and Marr's current retinue of musicians, flacks, and friends, people like Joe Brooks, who runs the Make Up monthly club at the El Rey, as well as members of Beck's band, and El Vez, the Mexican Elvis who is opening Morrissey's tour.
3. Interview organizers of Coachella to see what we can do to help encourage an onstage reunion: put the two in the same dressing area, etc.
4. Interview Johnny Marr.
5. Interview artists at fest: Rage, Chemicals, Pavement, JSBX, etc.
6. On-site interview with Morrissey.

Note: If they do reunite at Coachella, we can take credit and close the piece on a triumphant note. If they don't reunite, we can end the piece with either an open letter or an address to which fans can send their ideas about what else we can do . . . or where we can go.

As daffy as all this sounds, we managed to get it assigned. We flew to Coachella. We appeared on Richard Blade's show (reciting a Richard Gere–style Buddhist prayer, sending out dedications, and receiving, for our troubles, tent-sized KROQ T-shirts from the very game Mr. Blade). We befriended El Vez, buying him a falafel at the Bereket Middle Eastern joint on Houston Street after his show at the Mercury Lounge. We'd interviewed Mike Joyce (in the back room of the Library bar of all places), Andy Rourke, and Johnny Marr and were chasing Morrissey all over the East and later West Coast on his current tour.

Part of our plan was sincere. We believed in this cause and were willing to travel and try. Turning thirty does make you a little nutty, and Victoria and I were doing so about a week and a half apart. Part of it was *Spin* staffers' typical pop-cultural clairvoyance. This was a few years before the reunion culture that would dominate the summer rock festivals later in the decade. And part of it was that Vic and I just wanted to hang out and relive our Smiths super-fan youth, when things seemed much simpler. We were far enough from it that we'd forgotten all the pain of actually being teenage. And I, of course, wanted to be close to Vic for entirely different reasons—perfectly unrequited in The Smiths–ian sense. The piece never ran in *Spin*, and by the time *Neutron Bomb*'s follow-up was being discussed, Victoria had left for *Blender*, a new magazine founded by the publishers of *Maxim*. While many other writers I admired ended up finding work there (and I freelanced for them and *Maxim* briefly in the late 2000s), I found *Blender* vulgar from the start. Every issue had a bikini babe on the cover. They'd boiled *Spin*'s lengthy and thoughtful stand-alone reviews down to hundreds of capsules.

Carrie Thornton was also a huge Smiths fan and quickly acquired the follow-up to *Neutron Bomb*. It would be based on the abortive *Spin* feature but novelized. And unlike with *Bomb*, I had the title going in: *How Soon Is Never?* It referenced the Smith's most famous single, "How Soon Is Now?" and seemed to capture the frustration and humor of the faithful but impatient Smiths fan. You didn't have to read the book to know what it was about, and before I even wrote a word, the title was my beacon. Jim was right. Titles are crucial.

I could tell that Jim and Carrie were worried about me. I was flattered and mildly annoyed that they kibbitzed on the phone about my drugging and carrying on. *Neutron Bomb* had been a difficult close, with my adding material up until they literally took the project away from me and shipped it off to the printer, but hadn't the end result been worth it? I was getting a bad reputation among the music publicists as well.

"If I seem jaded, it's because I am," I warned a very young Interpol after meeting them and their publicist, Nils Bernstein from Matador Records, at the Tribeca Grand Hotel.

Usually it was my policy to tell the publicists to fuck off while I did the interviews, and I resented those who sat in. The worst were those who listened in to phoners. You sometimes thought it was just you and the artist, and then you'd hear another voice on the line: "I don't think you should answer that one . . . Sorry." But Nils and I were pals, and this was Interpol's first American interview. I didn't hold it against him, but he was about to wish he'd never gotten out of bed. Once, I did my homework. I read up on Pee Shy back in 1997 and kept that practice for the first part of my career, but I'd been phoning it in since The Strokes. I knew nothing about Interpol except that they had a stupid name and had been compared to Joy Division by some of the British music press, sometimes positively and sometimes negatively. Joy

Division were still the revived cult heroes they'd been when I wrote *I Wanna Be Adored*, and when new bands weren't ripping them off, they seemed to be pillaging Gang of Four or The Pop Group, both bands I grew up listening to. Being the third or fourth band out of The Strokes–frenzied New York rock scene wasn't helping Interpol's confidence either. They were already on the defensive.

"I try not to be a lazy journalist, and don't want to knee-jerk compare you to Joy Division, but if it's there on record singing in a fake British accent . . . ," I baited the lead singer, Paul Banks.

"I actually *am* British," Banks responded with a well-placed and very cool thrust.

I immediately got flustered and defensive. I'd figured he was from Williamsburg. The vibe was toxic.

"I don't feel compelled to point that out," he told me.

"I don't think postpunk has been explored or expanded on in a way that's . . . that's interesting . . . ," I trailed off. I meant to say in a way that was interesting to me. I worried I was getting out of touch.

"Okay. Let's get this over with. This is a pull quote. I want all of you to give me a pull quote."

When I got to Banks, he said into my tape recorder, "Can I get some more sushi."

Nils nearly crawled under the table. The tiers of summer rolls, that awful hotel with its acid jazz piped in, something about it marked the beginning of the end for me.

Even my fellow *Spin* writers and editors were losing patience with me. I'd used the occasion of an edit meeting to shoot my mouth off and even mock other people's ideas.

"I have an idea, but I think I'm gonna save it for a book," I said and adjusted my shades to block out the death glare Charles Aaron was shooting me.

"That's not cool," he told me afterwards. I admired Charles beyond words. He'd written the best stuff I'd ever read in *Spin*, and easily the best stuff *I'd* ever written was with him. But for some reason I had it in my head that he was the enemy . . . simply because everybody was. Coke makes you paranoid. I liked to pick fights.

"You're just mad cause I know more about hip-hop than you do," I razzed him in edit meetings. I only attended them to mouth off anyway. "I'm from Long Island. You know who else is from Long Island? Rakim. Chuck D. I was born in Queens. Queens is in the house."

My ego was out of control, and I was suffering for it, and even though I didn't believe a single word coming out of my mouth or going into my writing, I had to stand by it all or simply disappear. I flirted with Sia when we'd have our annual contract-renegotiation dinners in expensive steak places like the Old Homestead.

"Maybe I won't sign. I mean, if I didn't work for you, I'd be able to hit on you."

This of course, like most things that came out of my mouth at that time, made almost no sense. I already did work for her. And I *was* hitting on her.

"If I said, 'Okay, let's go find a hotel room,' you'd completely back down," Sia correctly pointed out. I was just puffed up, bored, lost, and spun around with coke and valium and liquor. I couldn't understand why getting everything I wanted wasn't making me feel happy or complete. The only way to kill this poseur Batman asshole I'd invented for myself and now couldn't shake was to kill myself or get fired. Killing myself seemed more practical. I couldn't quit *Spin*. It was my dream job. But if I got so obnoxious that it became impossible to put out the magazine with me on the masthead, then maybe they'd suicide-by-cop me. Nothing worked though. I got into bar fights. I got arrested. I smoked in the office. I didn't even try to hide my coke use, sniffing loudly as I staggered from cubicle to cubicle, peaking in and glaring at my fellow music journos. Sia only found this more and more amusing.

"Marc, can you get your mug shot from the time you were arrested?" she'd ask. "We should use it for your next contribs photo."

And Ultragrrrl, now an in-demand DJ after I taught her how easy it was to spin (in the same fashion that Bonnie Thornton had instructed me), was even crazier than I was. She'd started a blog in order to remember what she did the night before because she'd fallen into the habit of being routinely overserved. It was called "Sarah's So Boring Ever Since She Stopped Drinking." In her "Free Winona" T-shirt, she sported a hairstyle that seemed to grow more severe and absurd with each passing week. We held the academic and serious staffers in a monkey grip of rock-and-roll folly. It was fun in the way speeding down the highway before the wall or the tree comes up at you is fun.

In the spring of 2002, I flew to London to do a feature on Coldplay's second album, *A Rush of Blood to the Head*. I took the job just to keep moving, even though I was in hock and had no travel money. I landed at Heathrow with no dollars to exchange for pounds and took the train into the city, then checked into the Hilton in Kensington, which was being paid for with the *Spin* credit card. I called one of my London friends, Leslie, and said, "Come over to the hotel. Drinks are on me. But bring cash." A pretty, brunette American, she was in London working for Manolo Blahnik and making a good living. She arrived in high heels, looking beautiful.

"Here's the deal. I have no cash, but I have this card. If we can get around on your dime, we can eat and drink on mine for as long as I'm here." We'd get drunk at the hotel bar, and I'd charge it all to *Spin*. After she went home, I'd find myself back up in my room, in the fetal position, on my floor, headphones over my ears, blasting *Sgt. Pepper's Lonely Hearts Club Band* into my brain in some electric-shock-therapy-style effort to remind me that "Rock is good. Rock is good. Rock is good."

Coldplay was good.

I got along with Chris Martin. I shouldn't have because Coldplay wasn't really my kind of band. They were a little too bookish and wimpy, but I found Chris smart and funny and charmingly self-deprecating. He knew what people thought about his band, and he didn't care. He was ambitious. They'd already been booked to headline Glastonbury. Everyone knew the new album was going to take them to a very high level of fame. I'd take a Leslie-funded taxi over to their office by Hyde Park, and the cab driver would know exactly where I was headed.

"Have you heard the new album?"

"It's not bad," I said.

I had it in my coat pocket, and for a moment I thought about selling it to him, but they'd started hanging people for such offenses in the wake of Napster. Here was a guy counting the days to the release of this record, driving his black cab all over London, and I could have just handed it to him—leaked it. It'd be my job. And it'd be a lawsuit. I'd be more of a pariah than Sean Fanning, the Napster dude. But I'd be free to write. In prison. I decided it would be doing dirty to the band, and I liked Coldplay, even though I was obliged to be cynical about them.

I walked in, and Chris was playing air guitar to the new song "Politik," which opens the record. He was jumping around, slashing the imaginary strings. "This is what we're going to open Glasto with," he smiled. For a second, I felt lucky, like this was our line of work. We got paid to fantasize about rock and roll. He played it, I wrote about him playing it, but both of us were well-compensated air guitarists.

"You're looking poorly, Marc," the band's assistant said. I could feel my liver creeping up into my chest, looking for an escape route.

"Thank you." Whenever anyone British says anything, even with alarm and disgust, it sounds like a compliment.

Leslie and I had been too drunk to fuck for two days, draining bottles of expensive wine on *Spin*'s dime. When I finally checked out, took the tube to

Heathrow (with money I'd borrowed from Chris Martin), and flown home, I was convinced that I'd snuffed my career at *Spin*. It was suicide by Coldplay. I showed up at *Spin* the following Monday to go over proofs with Jon Dolan, my editor. While in his office, Sia came out of her own office and calmly approached me.

"Hi, Marc," she said.

"Hey, Sia. What's up?"

"John told you we're going to have to cut the Coldplay story for space?"

"Yeah."

"It's too bad. It was good."

"Thank you."

"I'm not sure if it was three-thousand-pounds-in-expenses good."

It wasn't her money. And it was all in the name of rock and roll, such bad behavior. We weren't a gardening magazine. This wasn't *Golf Digest*, not that you'd know it from a cursory glance around the office. Take away the stacks of promo CDs and posters on the wall, and it could have been *US Weekly*. Most of the staff simply kept their heads down and worked hard. I could have learned from them. Instead, I learned how to smoke crack.

Archie Freed, the legendary rock figure who signed MC5 and The Stooges, was struggling with a book on Joey Ramone, who'd just died. Jim asked me if I was interested in coming on and helping him close it while I figured out what to do next. Starstruck about the prospect of working with a genuine pioneer, I said yes, and one evening Jim walked me over to Archie's apartment. The first thing you see on entering Archie's place is his wall of fame: sort of like a diner or dry cleaner's ornamentation, except instead of B-listers and soap stars, it displayed photos of every pop-cultural figure who'd ever meant anything to me, all of them posing with Archie like he was Leonard Zelig: photos from Max's and parties, famous people like David Johansen, Cyrinda Fox, Nico, Divine, Jagger, Townsend, McCartney, Warhol, Stiv Bators, and, of course, Iggy. Archie was short and handsome in that middle-aged way that sometimes made men look a little toady (like Don Johnson as *Nash Bridges* versus Sonny Crockett). He spoke in a lethargic, fey, drawl, and energy-wise seemed dazed and not really into the book, like he'd rather I just relieved him of it all and salvaged the deal so he wouldn't have to return the advance. I sat at his coffee table while he chatted on the phone with Debbie Harry (perhaps for my benefit), asking her what she remembered of Joey. I poured through what he'd already written, and it wasn't much, but I was way too moon-eyed to back out. This was Archie Freed! Archie Freed of "Archie Says," one of punk's great, sad ballads. I walked home listening to *Rocket to Russia* and *End of the Century* on my headphones. The next time I went over to Archie's to work, I realized what was really keeping him from getting any work done.

Archie was badly strung out. He was disappearing into his bedroom every five minutes to pack the crack pipe and take a hit.

"Why *crack*? Don't you have any coke?" I asked after declining to take a hit.

"You've never done crack? It's better than coke."

"Actually, I think it's the only drug that I've never done," I said. There were still countries I'd never seen, and sexual positions I'd never tried, but I treated drugs like Beatles albums. Had to have them all. There's no trophy for doing every drug ever invented, but when would I ever get the chance to smoke crack again—with one of my heroes to boot? This guy knew Jonathan Richman!

"Doesn't it make you an addict as soon as you smoke it? Like that's all you think about afterwards?"

"Oh, bullshit," Archie said. "I went to the Chinese place for soup this afternoon."

Soup. It was always drugs or soup.

Sometimes I'd come over, and a young street hustler, probably pulled off Sheridan Square, would just be leaving. The place was becoming a real crack den. There were rumors about him answering the door naked and incoherent when business associates came calling. I was afraid of what I'd find each time I arrived, but I didn't want to let him down. I liked that I was becoming his friend. We'd go up the street to the local bar and drink vodka, and he'd dish about his life in rock and roll. It was the next best thing to befriending Warhol. That was impossible, but Archie, a living, breathing rock landmark, was alive and right in front of me. I felt like maybe if I could get into his head, I could figure out how to salvage this Joey book.

"Okay, I want some," I said one afternoon. "I want some crack. Who's got the crack?"

Archie didn't even care. He was king hell blasé. He packed the pipe and handed it to me, then shrugged. I lit the glass, and my head filled with white light for a second. My bones surged with electricity, and I giggled and fell backwards on the bed and lost my vision for a moment.

I'm blind! I thought, then worried that my soul was leaving my body. Before I could panic, the feeling was gone, and a flood of jabbering voices and idiot ideas, all my own, washed over my brain. I got up and smoked a cigarette. I felt my eyeballs bulging against the bones of their sockets as I inhaled and exhaled, trying to remember how to breathe.

I handed the stem back to him.

"Okay, I get it. Thank you. I am never doing that again."

Crack was terrifying. Maybe the brain gets used to it if you keep carpet bombing it with base, but I just wanted to be able to say, and of course write, that I'd "smoked crack," and with the great Archie Freed.

The snow was coming down in heavy clumps as I trudged back to my apartment. I couldn't sleep, so I called Patricia Ann and begged her to come over, which she did, then listened to me rant and rave incoherently for hours. She'd later tell me, "I'd never seen anyone so insane." And yet, some people did that shit every ten minutes.

I quit the Joey book shortly thereafter. Legs McNeil eventually released one with Joey's brother, Mickey Leigh, called *I Slept with Joey Ramone*. We were scrambling to beat them to the marketplace, hence all the speedy powder. Once again, Legs got there first.

You'd think hitting the pipe would be a good place to curtail my hard drug depravity, but I wasn't quite finished yet. Ryan Adams, the singer-songwriter, was recording a new album down in New Orleans, and I would have full, unfettered access, and was I interested? I pitched it to Sia and Charles and was flown down there, not realizing that Ryan was in worse shape than I was. Only two years earlier, he'd been the boyish kid playing his acoustic guitar in front of the Twin Towers four days before they were hit. But he'd gotten strung out on heroin and cocaine and gone semi-mad after the release of his first two solo albums, *Heartbreaker* and *Gold*. They were both excellent, and still I think his best work, but if The Strokes hadn't come along, Ryan, despite his self-promoted love of death metal and hardcore punk, would just be another Tonic or Wallflowers—easy-going-down, vaguely "modern" rock. He just had a gift for the adult-oriented, unthreatening ballad. Still, in the ensuing months, he'd East Villaged up, recorded a version of *Is This It* on a Casio-type keyboard, picked fights with more successful and still-mainstream artists like John Mayer, and run wild all over Manhattan by night. Like all of us, Ryan had Strokes envy, and now he was sharing their manager—and I guess some of their drug habits. I'd see a bit of my younger self in him when we crossed paths either at a rock show or in the back of a bar like Niagara. He was barely in control of his considerable talent, pretty, and flirting with death as a way to figure out who he truly was, but not interested in the answer at the expense of the drama. Watching Ryan hit the ATM, the dope man, and the bag was like watching myself do the same eight years earlier. We were more or less of the same generation. When he sang, I didn't hear myself. Like my ex Andie, he had a beautiful and true voice when he let himself go there, but he got caught up in imitating either his heroes or those more firmly and comfortably entrenched in the zeitgeist.

"I just want to walk down the street and feel this thing like I'm in a movie," he confessed to me one night on a bar stool at 7B.

"Yeah, I know. I know."

Down in New Orleans, putting up track orders and then changing them, taking lunch orders and then changing them, poor Ryan was a dervish of rock-and-roll ADHD. The guy could not sit still and was unable to unload his head fast enough. He'd sit in front of the computer and type words into the search engine.

"Is there an I-eat-worms-dot-com?" He'd talk in his own voice, then lapse into a sub-Beavis, adenoidal metal head parody. He'd look up ex-girlfriends like Winona Ryder on chain-of-love websites, then say, "True, true, true, not true." I wasn't sure if he was showing off for me or not. He didn't seem fully aware that I was writing a piece on him. I was just there in the studio for some reason. Was I a dealer? Did I play the triangle? Who was I again? And then he'd act like my oldest friend. I didn't need do my usual routine of ducking into the bathroom to jot down notes so I wouldn't forget them. I could just watch him and write out what he was doing and saying, right in front of him, and he was either oblivious or encouraging. When I ducked into the toilet, it was because Ryan had just handed me a baggie.

We were all staying in an old hotel that used to be a slave quarters. It was Gothic and creepy, with hanging gardens and a murky fishpond in the back. This was a different New Orleans from the touristy one in the French Quarter. It was very run-down and poor and funky, and as with Jeff Buckley in Memphis, something there was calling him either to his doom or to a masterpiece. In the studio, it seemed like the former. He couldn't seem to make the sound in his head synch up with the musicians. He played back a track called "The House Is Not for Sale," a very Smiths-sounding number. John Porter, who produced that band, was at the board. The Smiths were Ryan's all-time favorite. Mine too. We bonded over them. It's nearly impossible for one Smiths superfan to dislike another.

As the sessions ground on, they sent out for crates of beer because the band was sounding too good to Ryan's ears. He wanted them a little ragged, but these were thirty-year veterans. I've never understand why studios line their walls with gold and platinum records. It puts so much pressure on the artist, and Ryan was literally busting his brains trying to create a masterpiece, when he should have just been fucking around. He was young, starting to make money, and attracting interested journos like me. Where was the joy? I might as well have asked myself that. "Swing baby, you're platinum," Phil Hartman's Frank Sinatra scolds Jan Hooks's Sinead O'Connor in a great old

Saturday Night Live sketch, *The Sinatra Group*. Both of us sorely needed a little more of that ring a ding ding in our lives.

Ryan scribbled and rescribbled track orders on the wet-erase board on the studio wall. This is, again, how the music we romanticize is made. It's drudgery, often a hair-pulling, hurry-up-and-wait, crazy-making grind. I am sure if you sat in the studio during the making of *Blue* or *Songs in the Key of Life* or *Nevermind the Bollocks* or *The Queen is Dead*, *Parklife*, or *Grace*, you'd be bored out of your skull. Just as you would be waiting for Godard or Tarantino or any other legendary director to set up the lights on one of his sets. There's no glamour in making the art. It's just work, and watching it being made is like watching people carry bags of concrete up a building side over and over again. You don't say, "Ahhhh," until you see the glass-and-steel skyscraper shimmering in the pink sunset.

"I don't do coke!" Ryan said as he handed me a foil wrapper of coke and swatted the drape of long, brown hair away from his darting eyes. It was four in the morning, and we were in the fourth of four consecutive bars.

"Me neither."

I took the foil into the toilet stall. Wired now, he and I hit the street, and Ryan immediately ran ahead of us at top speed, seemingly with his eyes closed, singing "Frere Jacques" at the top of his voice like it was a Reagan Youth song. I was certain that I would never see the kid alive again. Ryan had the romance.

"Everybody wants to go on forever, I just wanna burn up hard and bright," he sang in *Gold*'s "Firecracker." But that's a good trick. Not everyone can pull it off. Some of us are stuck here, repeating ourselves. He was a low-life, as desired, but his brain was so teeming, he never slept or felt at peace and kept not dying. He was a mess. He confessed as much to me. Each woman he fixated on then was supposed to help him get to sleep and slow his brain, but they never did. I'd already done all the stupid things he was doing and lived, when some of my friends and fellow downtown hipsters had been those firecrackers. Pop. Game over. And I'd slept with all the women I'd thought would soothe me and survived that heartbreak too. Why was I still doing these things with the next wave? The new young women. The new Jeff Buckleys. And after Ryan overdosed or drowned, would I still be there, like some vampire in a too-tight leather jacket, eyeing the bag of drugs in his painted denim jackets, some half-remembered ode to Slayer or Danzig?

Back in New York, I'd meet Ryan Adams at 7B or Niagara, and he'd duck into the bathroom to do some heroin, and I'd follow him and do a bump as well.

"You shouldn't do this. You have a lot of good going on. You're too talented, man" I'd say to him, but I was really talking to myself—again. I was even looking at myself in the mirror as I said this, while Ryan was peeing.

Professionally speaking, I was doing follow-up work on the New Orleans piece. The album, titled *Love Is Hell*, had been postponed, and he'd formed a new band already and had a whole batch of new, short, poppy new wave songs. One night, we found ourselves in the tiny studio under the HiFi Bar on Avenue A, Jesse on drums, Ryan on guitar and vocals, me on drugs . . . all of us on drugs, but I had nothing to play. At one point I grabbed the mic and tried to sing, and Ryan quickly took it back after hearing my voice.

Sometimes I'd watch him scrawl lyrics in his little notepad, the same kind I used to jot down notes for my features. One time he ripped a page off and handed it to me. It read, "Junkie Journalist." He scribbled and handed me another one: "Sometimes the cliché is better than the truth because the truth is just a boring cliché. P.S. you eat worms." I still have them in case the Rock and Roll Hall of Fame wants 'em.

I'd hang out in Ryan's apartment in the landmark Roosevelt Medical Building on the East Side and do lines of heroin and lines of cocaine at the same time, sitting under his American flag tapestry and just letting the tape roll as we did the junkie rambles. I'd pass out on his couch with a cigarette in my hand, the tape still rolling, recording unintelligible mumblings. I'd get up to pee and look in the mirror and ask, How are you still doing this? I'd come back, and he'd rise and grab a shrink-wrapped vinyl edition of *Heartbreaker* and press it into my hands.

"I don't want this, man," I'd laugh. He'd stare dolefully at the album as if wondering how he'd come up with it. Ryan's windows had a bird's-eye view of the intensive care unit of Roosevelt Hospital. At one point he walked over to the window, placed his forehead on the glass, and stared down at the beds.

"People are dying in there," he said.

"People are dying in here," I replied.

What the fuck am I doing down here? I thought. I have a novel to finish. I'm on a deadline. I've written fuck all. This fucking guy is going to die soon. And he can! He's allowed. He's already written *Heartbreaker* and *Gold*. I had no business messing with speedballs, not at my age, and not without a real, true, good book with my name on it. Speedballs are ridiculous anyway, like putting "applesauce all over a good pork chop," as Jim Carroll once observed.

It didn't occur to me that the extreme escalation of my behavior might have something to do with some kind of post-9/11 stress and depression. When at home, I'd line up sedatives on my desk and eat one after another after another. I'd keep a big pile of cocaine in an Egyptian mosaic box and snort a bump when I felt myself fading. I'd play "Love Burns" by Black Rebel Motorcycle Club on repeat and get staggered, then leave the house, walk down to the Library, and stay there until last call with my painter friend Damien, who was the bouncer and a visual artist. Then he'd pull the grate down and kick everyone out, and we'd do more blow until midday, gathered around a cute little pile of white powder talking about God and listening to Oasis. Some of my friends had seizures; visiting them in the emergency room didn't stop me. They were simply pussies who couldn't handle their drugs. Others got busted. That didn't stop me either. I was too slick for the cops. I also got into survivalism and ordered a big knife with a compass buried in the handle and a "go bag" that I could run with if the city was ever hit again. The only things in it, besides the knife, were a flask of whiskey, a little transistor radio, a vial of coke, and a carton of cigarettes.

I should have been working on my novel. Instead, I formed a band.

Marc Spitz and the Spurts, with David Greenberg and Chrissie from my old Chelsea Hotel caper, even though David was the only one of us with any musical talent. I should have checked myself into some kind of institution right there. If you ever hear me talk about my new band, please, just stop me. It's a true indicator that I've lost the plot. In the basement of The Slipper Room we rehearsed songs like "They're Way Sluttier in LA." David was living in the Chelsea, strumming his guitar and playing Hank Williams, and tried to get me to get serious about songwriting, but I wasn't serious about anything except wanting to die. I'd go to sleep every night praying, "Please don't let me wake up. Please don't let me wake up. Please don't let me wake up."

If there was one thing that revived me, possibly even saved me, it was that old Bennington College Lit Fuck sense of competition. It's why people make comebacks after all isn't it? Why the Stones tour every few years even though they don't need the money. They can't abide by someone else, younger, maybe even better, the Coldplays and U2s, taking over that alpha spot.

Spin circa 2002 and 2003 was quickly becoming a Murderer's Row: look at the masthead from around then, and you will see writers who would become major voices in media and culture a decade later: Jon Dolan, Dave Itzkoff, William Van Meter, Jon Caramanica, Andy Greenwald, Phoebe Reilly, Will Hermes, Caryn Ganz. Meanwhile Sia had used her new clout to bring some name writers into the fold who didn't have the same level of chemical and emotional damage that I had. Dave Eggers was doing a column, and Chuck Klosterman was shaping up to be a major contributor. While I was digging my ditch in the West Village and only occasionally taking the train across town to terrorize various edit gatherings, Chuck was becoming a star. One afternoon I stalked over to St. Mark's Bookshop and found a copy of his first book, *Fargo Rock City*, which had much better placement than *We Got the Neutron Bomb*. I was in the music books ghetto. He was in new nonfiction.

I walked up to the Hollywood Diner on Sixth Avenue, ordered a cheeseburger and vanilla milkshake, and read nearly half. I finished it the next day sitting at the Waverly Diner on Sixth Avenue. I had no stomach by the second go-around. Chuck was good. It would have been so much easier if he were a fraud. I decided the thing to do was to kill him.

At a *Spin* staffer's birthday party at The Slipper Room, I cornered Chuck on the staircase and asked him if he wanted to get high. He said he'd never done it before, and like an after-school-special pusher, I said, "Come on!" hoping he'd do some coke and stroke out.

When Chuck was not around, I'd tell people his aw-shucks Midwestern thing, with his casual clothes, yellow hair, and spectacles, was just a pose. He was really a schemer.

"He's really like Ed Norton in *Primal Fear*," I'd swear. "You know, stammering, calling people 'sir' and 'ma'am,' pretending he doesn't know his own suit size, but he knows, man. He killed the bishop. Guy is the fucking devil once you pull off the mask."

Chuck had the same title as I did, but unlike me, he chose to work in the office. Where else was he going to go? He'd just moved to the city. The office was his only social circle. I had options. They were dangerous options, but at least they were there.

Eventually something very unusual happened between the two of us. I started to like the guy. I didn't want to admit it, but as he had much of the *Spin* staff, he'd charmed me too. It happened after some prick at the *New York Press* wrote a hatchet piece about him, which made me feel ashamed that I was ever resentful and jealous too (as this writer clearly was). Timed to Chuck's new book *Sex, Drugs and Cocoa Puffs*, which was even better and more popular than his first, this dude called Chuck a "living WMD" and observed, "He looks like a sex offender." The piece made me see the ugliness in my own jealousy and spite. Also, you know how Keith Richards will constantly slag Mick Jagger, but if anyone else says a word out of school about the guy, they get the skull-ring knuckle sandwich? I was *Spin* stuff. I could hate on a fellow colleague, but if someone outside the family did, I'd circle the fucking wagons. I'd bring down the fist on 'em.

I sent Chuck an e-mail telling him to shine it on, that he had my support and just to let me know if there was anything I could do for him. And I meant it. I realized that I was lucky to have peer like him at the magazine. It raised the bar. With every piece I wrote from that point on, I brought more to the mix than I might have if Chuck Klosterman had never come to town.

"It's like The Beatles and The Beach Boys," I told him once, explaining my theory at a party at Pianos, the bar they built after evicting Aaron Beall.

"Who gets to be The Beatles?" Chuck asked.

"Well, me."

"I think *I'm* The Beatles, Marc."

"Fine, then I'm the Stones."

"Wait. What happened to The Beach Boys?"

I soon got another sorely needed jolt of inspiration to remind me that the rocker is always the problem, not the rock, a realization that slowly guided me back on course not only to finish my novel but to turn in a series of solid *Spin* features, on time and with a minimum of drama. One night Emma Forrest called and said she was down at Toad Hall, a bar in SoHo, and I should come join her and some friends for a drink. As was typical of Emma, she didn't mention who her friends were, but as soon as I walked into the bar, I heard a chant coming from the back room. It was "White Riot" by the Clash, but just the chorus: *"White riot, I wanna riot, white riot, a riot of my own."* Over and over again, like a football chant. The leader of this chant was sitting at the woodblock table rolling a hash joint. Emma didn't drink or do drugs, but her mates were clearly running on a different circuit. Their leader looked familiar. His hairline had receded, and he'd thickened, but his face and voice and clothes were unmistakable: Joe fucking Strummer. I recognized Alex James, the bass player for Blur, as well, beautiful with those angular new wave cheek bones, but clearly shit-faced. The other guy, bearded and gnomish, was Damien Hirst, the artist. Joe looked me over and whispered to Emma, "Who's that? He alright?" Emma vouched for me, and Joe nodded and extended a wet paw for me to shake. "Alright, Marc, sit down and join us." He licked up the joint, lit it, and then handed it to me. Nobody was going to tell Joe Strummer to put out his joint. The drugs went around, and the pints were refilled, and Joe and I huddled in the corner and talked about good rock and roll and how the best rock and roll makes you dance and forget yourself and feel truly alive, and the lightness I felt was justified. I was a true believer again, and one of the ultimate true believers was confirming it.

"Let's go fucking dance, man. I know just the place," I said.

"Oh yeah?"

"Shout."

"Shout."

David Greenberg showed up and joined the party. Emma vouched for him, and he talked to Joe like he'd known him forever. Like he'd been on the

Anarchy Tour back in 1977. Emma vouched for David, and I vouched for Shout, and Joe, who didn't have to vouch for shit, said he'd have to go back to the hotel and get some stuff, but he'd meet us there. I never thought he'd show, and I suppose I could have just gone home, but I was a true believer. The music was good, and the good will out, so I walked over to Bar 13 and met Patricia Ann and Chrissie, who were already there. They didn't dance. They were too cool.

Bar 13 was packed. While I was waiting at the bar, I could feel a rippling change in the energy of the room and knew Joe had arrived. His hairline was receding, his face a little puffier, but he was still instantly recognizable to any self-respecting hipster kid, and every one of them seemed to hit the "Shout" retro dance party on Sundays. Joe cut through the crowd and found me. I bought him a drink and introduced him to my friends, who smiled shyly, star struck. Joe asked Chrissie to dance, but she said she didn't dance. Undaunted, Joe began dancing, the twist of all things, to "Glad" by Traffic, "Me and Baby Brother" by War, then "Funk No. 49" by The James Gang, great, loud vintage rock and roll. Embarrassed that my pretty, female friends had spurned him, I joined in, twisting with Joe Strummer.

"Aright, Marc," he said. "Aright!"

Less than a year later, Joe was dead at age fifty. I called up Chrissie and scolded her. "You should have danced with Joe Strummer."

Life was good. I knew it. Tomatoes tasted good. A cold Coke in a glass bottle was good. There were movie theaters and taco stands and parks where people had planted flowers. There were violent rainstorms. Stopping everything to watch *The Godfather* and *The Godfather Part II* (if not *III*) back-to-back was good. Great white sharks were good. The water buffalos in the Museum of Natural History were good—perfect specimens and, if you are feeling spiritual, evidence of God. Yes, a second war was about to begin; yes, the Yankees had started to suck again; yes, the new mayor, Michael Bloomberg, was talking about banning cigarette smoking in bars. But was that really a reason to fall asleep every night praying not to wake up? I knew I was lucky. I knew I had built a good life for myself. I'd escaped Long Island. I'd made it to the city. I'd become an artist. My only real problem—the one that superseded all others, including the drugs and the temper and the punk rock attitude—was that this was all I was.

CHAPTER 19

I finished *How Soon Is Never?* in some kind of fever while playing Bessie Smith and Elliott Smith at top volume. It wasn't The Smiths, but it was a Smith, and another Smith. Once I started writing about myself, my father, my childhood, Long Island, W-LIR, and The Smiths, it all seemed to come out in a great flush, like the enemas I'd administer in a panic after yet another bender. I'd buy them at the Rite Aid on Hudson Street and shove them up my ass while reading *Page Six*. I wrote about hating my job, lusting after Victoria, and being terrified of getting old. It was like forty therapy sessions in forty days, but it didn't read that way. It read, for once, like the truth.

I call my narrator Joe Green in the book (after the famous athlete) but it was all me. They say your first novel should be autobiographical. Technically, this was my third. I'd written a novel called *Joyriders* about me and Julie Bowen when I was banging tar out in LA. I have no memory of writing this novel, but it exists. I own the only printed copy and am afraid to open it— four hundred pages that I do not remember typing. Maybe the cat wrote it. Drugs. Cats.

Good writing is almost harder to process than bad writing. Bad writing just makes you hate yourself and want to eat a full Domino's pizza with a side of chicken wings or watch hateful porn. Good writing makes you fucking superstitious. As *How Soon?* wound down, I would be afraid to cross the street in case I got hit by the M8 bus, and nobody ever got to read the finished version. But good writing focuses you like nothing else. You could go to the gallows. You could die and not mind, like the Jesus and Mary Chain (and later Pixies) once sang.

I had an assault rap hanging over me from some stupid bar fight and was facing maybe a year in jail if the charges weren't dropped. I didn't know if I had AIDS, hepatitis, cancer . . . I'd stopped getting tested after Julie Bowen dragged me into her clinic to hear her results after we slept together unsafely. I'd returned to LA on assignment for *Spin* and met her for what I thought was lunch but was actually lunch and a visit to the doctor. The result was negative. I'd dodged the bullet that time, felt like Jim Morrison for two minutes, then continued to act a fool. There'd been carelessness since. I hadn't even been to the doctor since starting my career in rock and roll. Or the dentist. I was sure I would not see thirty-five, but it didn't matter. I was finally writing something that at least I finally believed was good. And it wasn't just that. It was a matter of what was good about it. Bullshit can be good too. It's harder to make the truth sing, and I was improbably doing it at what was easily the lowest point I'd ever sunk to physically and spiritually. I had no choice but to go back to the source, to Long Island, to hearing The Smiths, to being an innocent. I'd spent decades denying my Long Island roots, terrified that I'd be outed as just another suburban jackoff. *How Soon?* didn't deny my Long Island roots. It explored and sometimes celebrated them simply because they were immovable. They were honest. I'd owned a Bennetton jersey (blue and white) and a Robbie Nevil album. I'd eaten gummy bears. We all did out there. I didn't come into the world a skinny punk. When people asked me where I was from, I could finally say, "Long Island," instead of the intentionally vague "New York," or "I was born in Queens," which was technically true, but it was Far Rockaway Queens, only about five minutes by car from Lawrence where I grew up. Lawrence . . . Long Island. It was time to own it, and once I started confessing, I couldn't stop. Aren't all first novels confessions anyway?

I'd done a few cover stories with an editor at *Spin* named Doug Brod. He was slightly older but hailed from the very same area. Five years earlier, when I first arrived at *Spin,* I would never have bonded over the Island with someone from the South Shore who'd also managed to sneak into this romantic, urban rock-and-roll realm. But *How Soon Is Never?* freed me to reminisce about the malls and the Malibu Night Club and Sunrise Highway with the guy.

The book's publicist, Jason Gordon, who blogged under the handle Product Shop NYC, was one of the first to read it after Carrie and Jim. Like me, he was reared on W-LIR (although he knew it as DRE and his "Screamers of the Week" were "Shrieks of the Week"). When W-LIR would do holiday countdowns when I was in high school, "Blister in the Sun" and "A Question of Lust" were tops, whereas Jason's "Stairway" equivalents were Fugazi's "Waiting Room" and Jane's Addiction's "Jane Says." We met during a happy hour at Lit, a dark bar on Second Avenue, and he told me honestly what he liked and disliked about the book, its strengths and weaknesses. And among the strengths, he agreed, was that Long Island was there on the page. Ironically, it would soon cease to be there as a refuge or an option in real life.

My mother called one afternoon shortly before I finished the book.

"I just got off the phone with your sister and told her the same thing," she said.

"What's wrong?"

"We put the house up for sale. We're moving to the city. If you want anything, furniture, books, tell me, and I'll put it aside for you."

"No way. Why?"

"I'm tired of cooking and driving."

My mother was pushing sixty. She didn't want to do housework or grocery shop anymore. She wanted to order in. She was tired of gas stations and parking meters; she wanted to walk to the movie theater. I'd always counted on being able to go back to the safety of the Island if things got too hairy. Who knows how much more I would have walked the line in the city and in Hollywood if that option weren't available to me? Now, I would have to find that sanctum on my own. In Manhattan. In my room. In my heart, or improbable as it seemed, in someone else's heart. There'd be no easy ties to the suburbs anymore. I'd have to concoct a sort of portable Long Island of the Mind.

"So do you want anything?"

"Yes, Mom," I said. "I want everything."

One night, shortly before the galleys of *How Soon Is Never?* went out to the printer, I was hanging out with Albert Hammond Jr. and his beautiful blonde girlfriend at the time, Catherine of the talented country-rock duo The Pierces. She looked like a young Gena Rowlands but sang like Maria McKee of Lone Justice. Like every straight hipster boy who drank below Fourteenth Street, I had a crush on her. We got a cab to the West Village and ended up in Sean Lennon's townhouse. It was late, nearly last-call late, and there was no liquor. We were listening to music, and Sean said he was going to the bodega for beer. I offered to walk with him. I don't know if I felt protective of him, or what. He was a grown man, nearly thirty, but I just didn't think he should be out there alone. While waiting in line, I pulled out the galley and showed it to him, as if to say, "I'm okay. I'm not some crazy person, obsessed with your dad or anything." It was unnecessary. Showing up with Albert vouched for me. Sean took the galley, blue with white printing, like ever other galley that Random House, the biggest publishing house in the world, mass-produces.

"That's a great cover!" he said as we paid for the beer and grabbed the paper bag.

"It's the galley cover, Sean," I said. "They all have this cover. Random House books."

"Oh, no, you have to use it," he said. "It's perfect."

And I guess it was.

Book parties are strange, like birthday parties for people who need to be the center of attention on every other day of the year, or in the case of book production, every two years. On the one day that you are actually the center of attention, you end up hiding and counting the minutes until it's over. The book party in the Tiki Lounge basement area of Niagara on Avenue A (formerly King Tut's Wah Wah Hut, where I once saw a cat overdose on junk back when heroin was something we drove around looking for like preteens look for fireworks) was packed.

I spent most of the time in the alley, smoking cigarettes. Chloë Sevigny showed up with her friend Tara Subkoff. Chloë loved the book; she was in it, after all, at the end as the girl Joe Green (a very thinly veiled version of me) meets in Don Hill's after giving up on Miki (aka Victoria). Yes, it really happened. Most everything in the book did. It's weird meeting people you've written about after they realize what you've really thought of them all this time. I'd sent the book to my father, and he promptly stopped answering my calls. I guess he objected to the way he was portrayed.

My mother was angry that I wrote out some of her Lawng Island speech phonetically, but she was, again, happy I wasn't dead or in jail. She came to the party beaming. Chris Wilson was there; he seemed impressed that Chloë and Tara were there and did me the favor of putting it in *Page Six*. George Gurley, the sweet but perverse *Observer* writer, cornered me and managed to extract a drunken quote about vagina size and why it's not deemed as important as penis size by society. That was the moment I stopped talking in sound bites. I came across like an ass. No more.

Vicki was hovering around the party like she wanted to come in, but I was afraid she would ruin it for me by making me miss her. After it wound down, I walked down to the Library. Julian met me there, and we drank till last call with a couple of hipster girls. Vicki came in, and I felt, as I always felt in the company of Strokes, that it was cool for her to see me with one of them. Julian, these two strange hipster girls, and I picked up some beer and ended up back at my apartment doing coke until the sun came up.

The Strokes' second album, *Room on Fire*, was about to come out, and Julian had a copy of it. He asked for my stereo, and I pointed to the little red Sony boom box.

"This is what you listen to music on?"

He played the album, then my *Talking Heads '77* CD. He seemed like he wished his record sounded like the Talking Heads. We all still wanted to be more like our heroes, no matter how much we accomplished. It never ends. Maybe it's the only reality there is—our frustrated selves. This was my second book. Julian's second album. Both our teenage dreams had come true. And here we were, in the middle of the night, druggy, drunk, and miserable. Everybody wants to be someone else, I thought. Nobody knows how to be themselves. The thing was, some people did. I just had no clue. And the rock-and-roll people I surrounded myself with, some of them would never have to figure it out. That's why they got into rock and roll in the first place.

"You shouldn't do blow through a dollar bill anymore," one of the girls warned me. "You'll get hepatitis."

I probably already have it, I thought, and snorted away. It didn't matter. The book was out now. I'd said my piece. I was ready to die. I always was at a certain hour of the night, but never in the morning as I took my penitent shower and bargained with God.

If I was going to be even a minor literary celebrity, my model at the time was JT LeRoy. He seemed the perfect press darling to emulate: talented, flamboyant, fearless, a survivor. That guy was real. If you look at old copies of *How Soon?*, you may notice only one blurb has ever been on the cover of any of the print editions. It's from JT. Who does not exist. Not that I or most anybody else knew that in the fall of 2003.

> "*How Soon Is Never?* gorgeously captures the ache of waking up one day old enough to realize you ain't Peter Pan, not even God, but still young enough to believe in the inscrutable potential of music." —JT LeRoy, author of *Sarah*

In the fall of 2003, JT had the kind of career that every reasonably young Lit Fuck envied. Shirley Manson, Winona Ryder, Lou Reed, Gus Van Zandt, Marianne Faithful, and even my LA pal Genesis P-Orridge were among his fans. Hot crazy person Asia Argento decided to make a John Waters movie out of JT's book *The Heart Is Deceitful Above All Things* (but forgot to add irony). And for some reason, he'd latched onto me. JT let me know that he'd read my work in *Spin* (to which he'd contributed some pieces as well) and wondered if I, being of like mind, would possibly help promote the band he was associated with, Thistle. He sent me a blank CD of their music, as well as gifts like a long, white, curved, raccoon-penis-bone pendant. I got birthday cards and a Christmas card with a drawing of a man in a Santa hat and garter belts on the cover. Santa has a party of four tied up. He's holding a chainsaw, about to dismember them all, and says, "First of all, I'd like to wish you a merry Christmas."

JT and I finally "met" at a *Spin* party, yet another one held in the bar at the Tribeca Grand. We found ourselves backed into the same corner as hired promotional photographers hit us with their flashes. He kept whispering to me about how strange it was to be attacked like that.

"I know," I said.

This was the first time anything like that had happened to me, and I didn't find it strange at all. I liked it. I knew they were only shooting me because we were the two freaks in the room. I liked that too. We were both wearing sunglasses indoors. He wore a hat; I wore a knotted scarf. We posed in solidarity. I had no idea, like many who'd done the same, that I was not bonding with the HIV-positive, former truck stop boy-whore from West Virginia with the abusive mother and perfect writer's voice, rescued by a concerned doctor and championed by Dennis Cooper, among other Lit Fuck heroes. It was actually a girl named Savannah Knoop with taped-down boobs. I saw pictures of her once the scandal broke in *New York* and the *New York Times*, and I am quite certain that if I'd known, I would have come on to her.

I met JT again at a reading a few months later, where various celebrities were gathered to read his work. Courtney Love was there, and I found myself at a table between her and the actor Norman Reedus, who would later appear on the zombie drama *The Walking Dead*. Courtney was in rare form, chain-smoking and babbling about how someone had stolen all of the Nirvana money she'd told me five years earlier she didn't want to live on. It had been five years since I wrote that review of *Celebrity Skin*, five years since she'd straddled the worlds of Hollywood and indie rock, and I feared that the former had gotten to her wholly. She'd been involved with James Barber, a former record company executive turned producer, and I'd become friendly with him (again, I instantly called "Jim," even though he preferred James). Barber was producing Ryan Adams's reactionary rock-and-roll album, which he hastily made after his label rejected the *Love Is Hell* album he'd struggled with down in New Orleans. While even Ryan eventually disowned that album, at the time it probably kept him from derailing. Barber seemed to have a calming influence. I'd sent him an early copy of *How Soon Is Never?*, and he'd responded with a long, glowing review via phone, which was and is always enough to put me in your corner. He seemed like the ultimate record-collecting indie rock autodidact, and I could easily imagine him with the old Courtney, but not this one.

"I don't care if you're related to Marlon Brando," I told her as she tried to explain a recent news item. "Seriously, I don't. Where's the new album?"

Courtney was right in telling me to avoid eyeliner and junk in our e-mail exchanges. I was hoping to do the same for her, and get her back on the path somehow towards making another *Live Through This*. She was certainly talented enough to write more than one. She could have had her Dylan '65–'66 or Stones '69–'72-style trilogies of time-stopping, all-powerful records, but I could see myself losing her even then as she turned the subject again and again to the missing money.

"If you make a great record, you'll make a lot of new money," I told her perhaps naively. I had no idea what it was like to be a "millionaire culture icon." It was easy for me to dispense facile advice. I'd done it to Ryan too.

"Just stop doing drugs," I'd tell him, usually while waiting for him to share his drugs. I never had any money. It didn't seem to matter since there was always someone to pay the bills, and I idolized artists with money or tax problems anyway: Dorothy Parker, Marvin Gaye.

I could see Genesis shouting abusively at the crowd, "Shut up!!!!! Shut!!!! Up!!!! Shut up!!!!" The eternal performance artist, anything for a jolt. The crowd didn't seem impressed or rattled. It was a long way from the early seventies. This was New York, not London. Arms were folded; lips were pursed.

"Let's go smoke a cigarette," I said to Courtney. "I have something for you."

We found a narrow hallway in the club and lit up. It was so narrow that when we sat down, we had to put our feet against the opposite wall like a four-legged human bridge. I reached into my coat pocket and handed Courtney a copy of *How Soon Is Never?* She looked over the chapter titles.

"You're About as Easy as a Nuclear War," she read aloud and smiled. "Some Girls Are Smaller Than Others." She giggled. It was a sweet moment, two indie rock nerds, briefly sheltered from their debilitating poses, sharing a laugh over an inside joke. I heard the noise from the event, and suddenly JT appeared like Bela Lugosi from the mist. And walked up to the bridge we'd made with our legs.

"Do you want to pass?" I asked. He nodded shyly, and I pulled down my legs. Courtney did the same.

"Won't you come back in?" he asked. Courtney was the most famous person in the room, and JT had noticed the void she left when we walked out.

"Let's get out of here," I said, hoping I could somehow lead her away from this gross scene. "Let's just go to a bar or something. Play the jukebox."

"I don't know where my car is."

"We can just walk. It's New York." The notion hadn't occurred to her, but then, it didn't occur to me that it might not be so easy for someone like Courtney just to barhop on foot. Or to grocery shop or buy a pack of cigarettes without it making the *Page*.

"There's a driver outside." She got up and walked toward the street, determined to find some chauffeured vehicle. We hopped in, and the driver immediately told us the car belonged to Damon Dash.

"I know Damon Dash," she said. The driver wasn't having it and sent us back to the front entrance of the club. As we hit the pavement in front of the venue, a wave of blinding flashbulbs soaked us like napalm. Their heat actually burned my eyes shut. When I opened my eyes, all I saw was hot white. Courtney didn't seem to blink. I lost her as she got into the back of another black SUV.

The next time I saw her, a total stranger was sucking on her bare breast in a Midtown Wendy's. I never saw her again, but she was good enough to grant me interviews for various book projects in later years and to send me some music that was better than anything she'd put out as a solo artist or with her new version of Hole. Maybe she'll reunite the original members of Hole and tour in 2014 to mark the twentieth anniversary of *Live Through This*. It'd be the smart thing to do. We're all in our forties now, us nineties kids. It's time for smart moves.

CHAPTER 20

It was Paris. Monmarte to be specific, and I had Rogaine in my hair. I was jet-lagged after flying out of JFK and checking in. I was ready to jerk off and go to bed, when there was a knock on the door of my tiny room at the Hotel de Flore. I'd checked into the hotel late, had a quick meal of bread, cheese, and soup, and figured I'd meet the band in the morning. But now I was staring at Kim Deal—shorter hair, a little heavier, but most definitely Kim Deal. She wore a long, baggy football jersey and jeans. She was on the phone with her twin sister, Kelly, and narrated into the phone.

"Yeah, he just opened the door."

"Hi, Kim."

"You're Mark?"

"That's right."

"Mark Blackwell, right?"

"No, Marc Spitz."

Mark Blackwell was another *Spin* contributor from Kim's nineties heyday.

I realized my hair was sticky with Rogaine. I was not as cool as Kim Deal.

"Can you hold on one second?"

I went into the bathroom and started drying my hair, but the medicine had soaked into the follicles, so I gave up and just spiked it

"I can't sleep," she said as I returned. "I'm still jet-lagged. Do you wanna do the interview now? We can go for a walk."

"Um . . ."

"Come on. Let's just try it. We can always do it again tomorrow."

I grabbed my recorder and cigarettes and put on my shoes, and we went down to the lobby. Kim took my Radio Shack recorder as we strolled along the rue Lamarck in the middle of the Parisian night. As I watched her walk downhill, I thought of Herve and Ron and Jack. What would they do if they were here with me? Play it cool, for sure. Why was I the one out of our little group to end up meeting all these people? And how long would my cool hold out? I'd gotten good at keeping it, but this was a big one.

We found an open café across from a closed oyster bar. Candles burned in old wine bottles. A gypsy played guitar as a few tourists lingered at the bar, smoking and singing. One couple outside was splitting an onion soup. Kim asked the waitress if they served nonalcoholic beer. She'd been sober about a year and change.

"Do you mind if I get some wine?" I asked. She shook her head. I ordered a red table wine and lit another cigarette.

The Pixies were back together after twenty years. Like The Smiths, they'd become legends after splitting; unlike The Smiths, they'd put their differences aside to make millions of dollars playing their old hits to kids who hadn't been born when *Come on Pilgrim* first came out (and to Gen Xers like me, who were starting to have their *Big Chill* moments). I was flown out by Sia to do the official oral history of the band, which Charles would edit. "Life to the Pixies," we called the cover story. It was the one plum gig that Chuck didn't snipe. Kim held my tape recorder up to her lips and began whispering into it. I couldn't hear what she was saying.

"What are you doing?"

"The interview. Duh."

"I'm supposed to ask you questions, Kim."

"I know what you need. Don't worry. You need my life story, right? I'm telling you my life story."

"Can I hear it?"

"You will."

I didn't argue. It actually wasn't the first time this had happened to me. Gene Simmons of KISS once actually told me over the phone, "Shut up and listen, and I will give you exactly what you need."

She talked, and I sat across from her, staring at the questions I'd carefully prepared. I wouldn't be asking them tonight, but something told me I'd need them the next day.

"How's it going?" I inquired.

"It's a really good interview. Trust me. You're gonna love it."

"I don't know."

"Do you have a problem trusting people?"

"Yes."

When she was finished, I paid the tab and gathered my recorder and lighter.

"Don't listen to it yet."

It was nearly four in the morning.

"What do you want to do now?" she asked.

"Still can't sleep?"

She shook her head. I got the sense that it was strange to her, playing with Black Francis, Joey Santiago, and Dave Lovering again after so many years, to massive crowds . . . arena crowds. And doing it straight. She'd brought Kelly on the tour with her for moral support.

"Do you want to go find Jim Morrison's grave?" Kim asked. "We can spit on it. I heard it's right by the hotel."

I thought about standing over Robert Frost's grave, all those years ago at Bennington. What Pixies cassette was in my car tape deck then? *Doolittle*, I bet.

"I don't think Jim is buried near here."

"Yeah. There's a graveyard right by the hotel. I saw it when we came in."

"That's Père Lachaise?"

"Yeah. Père Lachaise."

We walked uphill back toward the hotel and the nearby boneyard. The main gate was locked, so we tried to see if we could rappel down into the place from a high wall.

"This is it," she said, as we stood before a concrete wall. In the dark, neither of us could gauge the distance from the top of the wall to the graves and grass below.

"Should we just hop it?" I asked. Kim shrugged. I sensed danger, and for once, I went the other way. Something was telling me, "Don't do it. Do not do this. Bad."

"I don't know, Kim."

Just then, a skinny, handsome, but shaking French boy in a too-tight leather jacket (Strokes, like) came up to us. He didn't recognize Kim. He was looking at me. Maybe he knew I was American. He held out his hand and said something in French.

"Are you okay?" I asked, a little tipsy from the wine and the adrenaline of our near leap over the cement and possible grave pissing.

I reached into my pants and handed him a few francs. He snatched them up quickly and ran off.

"No. No. No. Why did you do that, Marc?" she asked.

"What? He was hungry, no?"

"He was a junkie."

"He was?"

"You can't tell?"

"I used to be able to." I hadn't made the French connection.

"He's not going to spend that on food."

I watched as the kid sprinted off down the street, thinking, well, if it takes one to know one, then maybe I'm not one anymore.

We ended up back in her hotel room, smoking and watching a Basil Rathbone movie on her little TV. In the morning, I went out to get coffee and pastries and more cigarettes. I decided to revisit the wall over the graveyard and see how far a drop it was. I quickly determined not only that this was not Père Lachaise (but rather Monmarte Cemetery) but that if we'd hopped the wall, we surely would have joined some of its most famous residents, like Zola, Berlioz, and Truffaut (as well as Mr. Mojo Risin' interred some miles to the east of us), in the endless sleep. I thought about how easy it would have been just to drunkenly say, "Fuck it," and jump. Dying rebelliously and romantically was simple. Living, that was the real trick.

I spent the day with the Pixies, eating noodles with Charles Thompson (aka Black Francis) and Joey Santiago in some sushi bar that had been recommended to them, interviewing Charles in a launderette while he folded his socks and roomy drawers, and riding with them to the show at Le Zenith that night. I watched them sound-check to Neil Young's "Winterlong," and a few hours later, I watched the show from the side of the stage.

When they played the opening chords to "Where Is My Mind," something happened to me. I started crying. The nineties were over. I had to let them go. This was me letting them go . . . with my tears. A new generation was in the spotlight, and in the crowd that night, one that had barely been born when the Pixies released *Surfer Rosa* and *Doolittle*. I thought of the show at the Ritz in November 1991. Of Zoe and me hopping up and down in the pit, then speeding back up to school to nest in the mountains. How many years ago was that? Fifteen, almost. I thought of the last time I'd cried: in the bathroom in London after Alex and I got rid of our baby. How many years ago had that been? Almost ten. Had I not cried in ten years? I counted and tried to pinpoint another instance when the waterworks had come real-style and couldn't. I cried for that too, for not being able to cry. I was in the dark, behind the amps among the road cases. Nobody could see me. Nobody cared, but I could feel the rock-and-roll spirit leaving me as the band played "Into the White."

CHAPTER 21

In the film *Three Days of the Condor*, Faye Dunaway says to Robert Redford's on-the-run spy, "When things calm down, you're going to be a very sweet man to be with." I felt things slowly calming down. Chloë Sevigny had been leaving me messages, but I was always traveling. I'd gone to Stockholm to interview The Hives, Paris to interview Franz Ferdinand, Sydney and Melbourne to interview to The Vines. For weeks, we played phone tag, as you tend to do with your more famous pals.

"So, are you single?" she asked when we finally connected in New York.

"Yeah, why?"

For a minute I thought she'd woken up in the middle of the night and realized I was the one. Our handful of dates back in the late nineties were somehow . . . very belatedly magical?

"Good. I want you to meet my friend Natasha," she said.

Her friend Natasha was also a famous indie actress. Natasha Lyonne, who was in *The Slums of Beverly Hills* and played Woody Allen's daughter in *Everyone Says I Love You*. She was about to become a notorious *Page Six* fixture thanks to a drug-induced meltdown—not exactly a catch. She was stopped for drunk driving and told the arresting officer, "I'm a movie star. Can I talk to my entertainment lawyer?"

"Why?"

"You both love drugs."

"Actually, I'm kind of seeing someone."

If you'd told me that the woman who would finally sit me down, smack me around, get me straight, and basically save my life would come out of the rock-and-roll realm presided over by Ultragrrrl, in her "Free Winona" T-shirt and her squinty, zooted eyes, and her Libertines posters, I'd never have believed it. I'd first noticed Ultragrrrl's roommate, Elizabeth Goodman, or Lizzy, at Kelly Osbourne's party at the Sunset Marquis in West Hollywood. It was the night before the annual Coachella festival in 2002, the year The

Strokes first played. I had run into her a few times after that: at a secret Cold-play show at the Bowery Ballroom and while starting work on The Vines cover story in the dressing room at the Ed Sullivan Theater shortly before The Vines smashed their set during a live taping (prompting Dave to wonder aloud if they were "troubled teens"). She fascinated me because she always looked perpetually displeased and suspicious. It had taken me nearly five full years to begin to question anything about this glamorous gravy train I was on, and here was this recent college grad, perpetually clad in a Black Rebel Mo-torcycle Club T-shirt, jean shorts, and flip flops, who saw through the whole scene immediately. How did she do that? One dark eyebrow arched when I talked as if she doubted every word that came out of my mouth. At the time, I was wearing expensive, black, Lou Reed–style Gucci sunglasses everywhere I went, indoors and out. I hated flip-flops. I still do. Never owned a pair; never trusted anyone who did. They are not shoes.

But Lizzy was different. I couldn't stop thinking about that raised eye-brow. Nobody had treated me skeptically to my face, certainly not anybody that young and new to the city. Ultra was friendly with every band, and Eliz-abeth, one of her two roommates, was clearly flirting with that lifestyle, but it didn't fully suit her either. Her father was a philosophy professor at the Uni-versity of New Mexico. He taught her Emerson, which means he taught her self-reliance, which also means he taught her not to be pushed around by overgrown rock boys like me. Her mother was a successful lawyer. She was raised in a one-story adobe ranch-style house in Albuquerque, New Mexico. There were toads and other critters in the garden, a goat on a chain, and a nearby corral with horses, which she learned how to ride as a very young child. She later competed as a jumper and took the discipline with her when she attended the University of Pennsylvania and then hit Manhattan. Lizzy was tough and dark. She told me as much, as we clinched one night on the roof of Ultra's building, watching the Fourth of July fireworks burst over the East River.

"Yeah, right," I said. Nobody was as dark as I was, or as tough, especially not this snooty Ivy Leaguer slumming on the modern age scene that I'd helped mythologize with my work at Spin. Ultra and I were hardcore. She was a weekend hipster. But I was absolutely wrong. Of all the women I'd messed around with, and there were dozens if not a hundred, she was the darkest and the toughest—and also the most honest and no-nonsense. What on earth was she doing in 3A? Ultragrrrl's place on Rivington Street, known all over the New York rock scene and even as far away as London and Paris as simply "3A," had become a semi-legendary two-bedroom Lower East Side hub where bands of varying degrees of post–new rock success (and talent), like The Cooper Temple Clause and The Music, flopped after playing the Bowery Ballroom or the Mercury Lounge. Ultra was already famous for picking the bands that would click. She dragged me to see Muse when they were still playing tiny bars like Brownies in the East Village. We saw The Killers at Pianos nearly a year before I would be flown to Vegas to write about them for their first major American cover story in *Spin*, and she'd brought members of My Chemical Romance to my latest play, *Gravity Always Wins*, at the HERE Arts Center in SoHo (about a disturbed man who post-9/11 surgically alters his face to resembles Michael Jackson's, in case you were one of the 7,000,850 New Yorkers who missed it).

I would sometimes pass through 3A to smoke pot with Ultra. One afternoon when Elizabeth wasn't there, I let myself into her room and checked out her bookshelf. It was the size of a full wall and filled with all the right titles (including my first book, *We Got the Neutron Bomb*). I guess this was some kind of privacy violation, but I wasn't sure I could take her seriously as a potential girlfriend if it wasn't up to snuff. I looked over her folders of CDs, stacked under various discarded towels and papers and clothes (she had recently graduated from Penn and still lived like she was in the dorms, a bit of a scattered student).

Hmmm G. Love? What's that about? Boards of Canada? I don't know them, but I've heard of them. Are they Canadian? Serge. The Vaselines. That's a plus. Which Beatles? Not just best-ofs. Good. Good. *Revolver* too. Elliott Smith. Nice. What hip-hop? Not just Lauryn Hill. Does she really listen to the second Wu-Tang Clan album? Does anyone?

I knew that she was friends with Rob Sheffield, my favorite rock writer. She also knew *Rolling Stone*'s Jenny Eliscu. And before The Strokes were famous, she'd been involved with Nick Valensi, my bête noire subject, the one who was, to his credit I now think, the most truculent with the music press. He was a tough mother too, and I shudder to think what their arguments must have sounded like back then. But if she'd managed to love him, maybe she could love me too. Could that happen? Was I too damaged? I knew she liked me. We'd already slept together. And it meant nothing, just like always. But the conversations we had afterwards, the way she treated me, or refused to be treated by me, that was new. But a girlfriend? I'd never had one. Zoe had been an accessory, a Nancy to my Sid; our relationship was absolutely tied up in our careers and desire to be famous. Julie was an object of desire who lost all her power over me once we finally consummated our attraction to each other. Alex and I never had a chance. That was fate. Andie was a benefactor. A girlfriend, who sleeps next to you, whose toothbrush hangs next to yours, whom you try to make better and who tries to make you better? I'd never had one. Where does one even start? Dinner and a movie? Do you fill out a form? Where do you go? Who do you need to know? And can you trust them? It was like *Donnie Brasco* and Rob and Jenny were Al Pacinos, the veteran Mob soldiers. I was Michael Madsen, the suspicious boss. And Lizzy was Johnny Depp, the new guy who needed vouching for. They endorsed her in one way or another, so I asked her out on a proper date.

She accepted. Maybe she had her own Al Pacino, someone vouching for me and insisting that despite my cigarette smoke, bloodshot eyes, and sour puss, there was something to me.

On the night of our scheduled date, I wasn't sure I was even going to show up. I got drunk early at a party in Bob Gruen's studio and had visions of going home, making some Kraft Macaroni & Cheese, and passing out. I visualized emptying the Kraft box into a pot, cooking the pasta, and stirring the cheese in. Kraft macaroni and cheese was Kurt Cobain's favorite food. He ate it even after he'd made $1 million. I'd sometimes add a can of Red Devil chicken spread and always a lot of hot sauce. I don't know what Kurt used to add. Heroin probably. There was something about it that said, "Fuck you. I'm still punk. I'm still street," especially when you'd gone a little upwardly mobile and off the pavement. I didn't tell Elizabeth that I almost blew her off for a meal that cost about $3 and change, with little or no real nutritional value. And I didn't confess (although it's perfectly clear to me now) that I got drunk in the first place because I was terrified about having to be "real" for more than twenty minutes with someone who clearly was not a Ricki Lee or Andie to my Tom and Duckie. She was a real person, and she might as well have been wearing a black hood and holding a large axe.

"I'm sick," I lied into the phone as I reclined on Gruen's couch deep in the core of the Gothic Westbeth Building where Diane Arbus committed suicide—another genius-freak artist dead too soon by her own hand.

It was another of his holiday parties. I would later work with Bob, using many of his great rock-and-roll photos in some of my books, but at the time, my agent James Fitzgerald was the real guest, and he just brought me to these things for the free booze and food and to gawk at people like Tina and Chris from the Talking Heads (and Tom Tom Club) or Roberta Bayley, who shot the cover sleeve for the Ramones debut.

Lizzy knew I was lying immediately. I believed I was a really good liar. Writers have to be good liars. But she could see through me.

"That's okay," she said when I told her I didn't think I could make it.

"Can we do it some other time?"

"No."

"What do you mean?"

"I don't want to reschedule. You can come over now, or that's okay. I hope you feel better."

Someone had opened the window to let out the cigarette smoke. Bob's living room was off the Hudson River, and a cold breeze blew in. Maybe it had traveled all the way down from Troy, taking two or three hours to reach Greenwich Village, gathering speed and strength along the way. It was a determined little gust of air, and it invigorated me, erasing my drunk and the seductive allure of Kraft Macaroni & Cheese, whose real appeal, I think, is that it's easy.

"Wait. What's okay? You won't see me unless I come over right now?"

"That's right."

"Fine," I said. "Meet me at The Slipper Room. I'm leaving now. But I'm walking."

"Take your time, Marc," she said. "Take your time."

I made big, symbolic moves. It was all I knew how to do, privately and publicly. I let some blood bleed through and sent it away via FedEx to be tested for HIV, then went and gave a drunken reading at CBGBs Gallery and alienated the entire room. The writer Jonathan Ames, whose work I admired, tried to introduce himself to me, and I gave him attitude. When I called to get my results, I insisted on playing Nick Cave's "The Mercy Seat" at top volume. Upon learning it was negative, I couldn't help but feel a little disappointed. I didn't know how to be un-damaged. It would have almost been easier to just reckon with a disease then deal with being nearly thirty-five and normal, going to dinner and a movie with a girl who loved me. Loving her back too.

Lizzy and I would go out to parties or rock shows. She'd usually be my "plus one." There were some generation-gap issues. She didn't know who Howard Jones was, but was that any reason to break up? I warned myself about my snobbery. I girded myself against things that seemed to fly in the face of my rock and roll. She didn't wear makeup, for example. Again, not a deal breaker, even though I still loved my black eyeliner.

"Let it go," I said. "Let it be." I did, over and over again, until one day I realized that I was in love. I just felt it, on the street, like bird shit on my head. A plop of love.

"I want to punch myself in the face," I'd tell her after that, with little or no sense of shame. "I'm so in love with you."

"I know," she'd say. "I love you too. What is that?"

It changed a little bit once she moved in. I could present my best poses to her on dates and at parties, but what about the boring downtime, the chores, the grooming, the snoring? Would we become boring and normal? We did do dinner and a movie, art films or madcap experiments like Bob Dylan's *Masked and Anonymous*, but still a provincial routine. I was still so insecure about being just another schnook, about not being an across-the-board rock journalist, always on. I didn't want anyone to know I secretly liked Hall & Oates and *Sex and the City* and usually got to places on time. When she'd sleep over, before officially moving out of 3A and into my apartment, I'd get up early and walk downstairs to Manatus, the twenty-four-hour diner on Bleecker Street. I'd order two coffees, then go to the men's room, fix my hair, and brush my teeth. Sometimes I'd even sneak an outfit into a plastic bag and change there. How much longer could I keep that up? And what would be the big deal if she saw me in sweatpants anyway? She liked me. She was there. I liked her. We'd give each other a lot of passes. By Christmas 2003, her records and books were my records and books. We got a little live, potted tree, and I cut Tom Petty's picture from the inner sleeve of Tom Petty and the Heartbreakers' *Greatest Hits* into a star and placed it on top. She went home to New Mexico, and I ached for her. I found a piece of paper she'd scribbled on. All it said was, "Always," over and over again, one word covering the whole sheet. What did it mean? "Always." I asked her about it. She seemed to blush, like she was now sharing one of her quirks with me too.

"It's just something I do."

"That's cool."

Soon we developed shared quirks. We'd eat dinner (and study the wine list) at the Jane Street Tavern and make sure to steal one of the crayons they leave for customers to doodle on the wax paper placemats; but only the black ones. When either of us had to travel, we'd always carry a black Crayola as a talisman to ensure that we'd make it back to each other again . . . back home. I learned about her because I was curious, not just so I could write about it. This is the first and only time, actually, that I've ever written anything about her. I wasn't collecting people anymore. I was just . . . doing shit with them. Living. Being real. And I liked it.

In March of 2004, I was invited to read from *How Soon Is Never?* at the North Star, an indie-flavored tavern in Philadelphia, and Elizabeth and I took the train there. Jason Gordon, the book's publicist, came out too. Nobody told me that I'd essentially be opening for the Goth cabaret act The Dresden Dolls, who had a rabid and impatient fan base. The place was packed with about two hundred people, three or four of whom were carrying copies of my book. I read quickly and got very drunk. The next morning, we walked from the hotel down to the square where Lizzy used to work when she was a Penn student. She pointed to places that had personal significance, and I noticed that I wasn't writing in my head or tuning her out. I was simply listening. It was a relief.

Lizzy talked in her sleep. I listened to that too.

"Get on the bus! Form a line!" she'd say, instructing the unruly little students that she saw in her dreams. It always woke me up. I'd turn over and say, "What?" then slowly realize she was not having a conversation with me. I would have gotten irked, but I realized that this was basically the same as every conversation I'd ever had before she came into my life. One-sided. I'd been sleepwalking. Sleep talking. And now . . . that was over. I was doing things like eating brunch. What was "brunch"? She got me into *The West Wing*, which I'd never seen and became obsessed with. Tennis too. I quickly saw the sport as romantic. We went to the Italian Market on that Philly trip and bought vegetables and cheese, and before catching the train back to the city, we stopped by the famous Mütter Museum of medical research. The Mütter appeals to more mainstream tourists, but there's also a steady stream of macabre punk rockers queuing up to see the syphilitic tongues, horned arms, and hydrocephalic fetuses, the famous Siamese Twins Chang and Eng, and the lady who turned into soap. Freaks, I thought to myself as I stared at them. Freaks like me.

Only I was feeling less and less freaky every day. It took these exhibits to put it into perspective. As hard as I had tried to deny it, a part of me belonged among the "normal." The following Christmas, I went out to New Mexico with her. When her parents gathered on Christmas Eve and drank tea and whiskey and listened to "Chimes of Freedom" by Bob Dylan without any irony, just in total appreciation for the song and the spirit, I didn't roll my eyes. And I didn't need to be the center of attention. On Christmas morning, Lizzy's mother rang an heirloom "Christmas bell" at sunrise, and everyone gathered to exchange presents by the tree. And it was corny. And it wasn't corny too. That was what made it perfect: it was both. You can be both. Lizzy's mom made a dynamite ham, which sat on the table all afternoon, everyone picking at it as they lazily passed.

In the spring of 2004, we also got a dog, a basset hound named Joni Mitchell, ironically after the author of the greatest breakup album of all time. Lizzy had a case of biophilia, given her nature-full upbringing. She'd not been on horseback since moving in with Ultra and felt like a part of her was missing. For her birthday, I rented her an hour with a horse from the old Claremont stables, which are now closed. His name was Gillespie, and as I huffed through Central Park, Lizzy sauntered on his back. But it wasn't enough. She'd download dog porn, clips of puppies bounding across lawns. Her relationship to nature was . . . unnatural to me. I had to get used to it. I bought her a massage because she was complaining about stress, and after returning to the apartment all floaty, she happened to put on the Sigourney Weaver film *Gorillas in the Mist.* There's a scene in which the apes are attacked by poachers. Elizabeth just lost her mind. She began screaming, her face flushed bright red. I'd never wanted to stop anyone from crying before. Usually tears were my cue to exit.

"It's only a movie. Those are dudes in gorilla suits. Those are not real gorillas! They're In SAG." I suddenly had to be mindful of what was on TV, our TV. I was desensitized. She was one with the planet. So now I had to get one with it as well. Only I didn't like nature. I lived in New York City so I didn't have to deal with nature. And every pet I'd ever owned had met with a sorry end.

It had been almost a decade since Alex and I adopted Odessa. Longer than that since the cat ran away. There'd been a lot of drugs and a lot of rock and roll and a big, thick fog in my brain since then and absolutely no effort to make amends for being a shitty pet owner. I embraced the idea with little resistance. After all, nobody ever bothered to remind me, "Oh, by the way, dogs get up at 7. Rock writers who work out of their kitchen, noon. You will never be able to sleep late again. Have a nice day."

Nothing got me out of rock and roll more completely than this goddamned cow-eyed, black, brown, and white, floppy-eared, snowshoe-pawed basset hound puppy. It was the final break with the old me. In interviews with *Spin* subjects, I'd talk about my dog. I complained to Trent Reznor when I went down to New Orleans just before Katrina to interview him.

"You know, you have to be a person. You can't be a persona," I told him. "A persona can't walk the dog. The dog needs a person." Once I painted my nails black to feel more like this man. Now, sitting across from him in his home studio, I kvetched about picking up poop.

Trent politely nodded. I told Bob Pollard of Guided by Voices how early I had to get up and how it was twice as hard if I'd been drinking the night before.

"Yeah, I bet," he shrugged, then went to fix himself a drink.

I thought record collector Howlin' Pelle Almqvist of The Hives would be fascinated to know that of all the vinyl piles in our apartment, Joni would always pull Steve Miller Band's *Book of Dreams* from the stack and chew the edge. He was not.

The girlfriend, the dog, it all came at a time when I thought I was going to become very rich and famous. Kirsten Ames, my manager at the time, had gotten me a meeting with HBO in LA, and I'd flown out there three or four times pitching a TV version of my first play, *Retail Sluts*, which they seemed very interested in. We'd even staged it at their workspace on Melrose Avenue. I'd signed with CAA and then ICM, two huge and powerful agencies. I took meetings with Carolyn Strauss, who was president of the network. With

Chris Albrecht, she'd brought *The Wire* and *The Sopranos* to TV. *Entourage* had just premiered, and maybe the next buzzy show was going to come out of something born on the Ludlow scene. But I was scared, overwhelmed; I was just figuring out how to be a person, and that was more important to me. I felt threatened by all this business, and Kirsten didn't seem to want or be able to protect me from it. I just wanted to write. I was a raw nerve. But I had to pitch. And smile. And shake hands. And without the pose, I was just too shy. I'd actually vomit. Arnold Engelmen, who'd produced *Shyness Is Nice* at the Westbeth after our step-up production with Bob Rake, saw potential for hits in me. There was talk of reviving my third play, ". . . *Worry Baby,*" another violent, anarchic Ludlow play, with name actors and a big budget. There was a reading at the Westbeth with Josh Hamilton as Dexter, the hero, Justin Vivian Bond as the homicidal chemistry teacher Mrs. Normandie, and Armando Riesco (who plays the inventor of "silent Velcro" in *Garden State*) as the wigga drug dealer Larippo. Then there was the even bigger reading at a crisp theater space called Ars Nova, with Swoosie fucking Kurtz as Normandie and Paul Rudd as Dexter. Paul was a sweetheart and a huge rock geek, so we got along, discussing Smiths album tracks. But again, the pressure of processing all this without my crutch was impossible. I was convinced now that I had cancer, or would get it if HBO picked up my show or if my play made the jump from Off-Off to Off-Broadway (a jump that costs at least a hundred grand). I needn't have worried. HBO passed, and God spared me, I guess, from backsliding into drugs and ego tripping by replacing Swoosie Kurtz with Lorraine Bracco during the most recent backers' audition of ". . . *Worry Baby.*" With all the potential investors there, and Paul and Lizzy and Kirsten, Bracco showed up late, hadn't read any of the play, and during her scenes with Paul kept commenting on the script.

"Oh, God, is this really what happens? No. Do I really say this?" instantly taking the audience out of the scene and killing all the chemistry and energy dead. It's still hard for me to watch her be so great as Melfi in reruns of *The Sopranos.*

Arnold lost interest in my violent plays. "There's a new war coming," he told me. "People aren't going to want to see all that blood on a stage."

Maybe he was right. I hoped he was wrong about the war escalating.

I'm weirdly grateful the TV thing didn't happen. And while it would be nice to have a real playbill instead of a Xeroxed piece of 8-by-11 printer paper as a program, I am sure that success would have taken me away from her. I was a fragile and corruptible motherfucker without my pose, and I'm 99 percent sure I would have found a way to finally do myself in, with all that money and tension. I was still learning every day, how to be a good boyfriend, and a protector. We'd take Joni to Chumley's, the old writer's pub on Bedford Street. They had a dog friendly policy and Joni adored their cheeseburgers. I wouldn't even look longingly at the rows and rows of mounted book jackets overhead, or marvel that I was sitting in the same booth that Faulkner or Eugene O'Neill may have occupied. I didn't wonder what they ordered, and whether I would be more legit if I had what they were having. My eyes were on my girl and our dog.

And yet, even a routine puppy accident was enough to send me right off the path.

Early one afternoon, Joni Mitchell peed on the kitchen floor. I'd gotten used to cleaning these puddles up, but I was on deadline and trying in vain to balance my new life with my old rock life, while slowly grabbing the roll of mounted paper towel, sopping up the yellow with one hand, and spritzing some cleanser and mopping up the whole thing with the other. Usually that was it and back to work, but I had just deposited the papers in the trash and sat back down at my desk when I smelled poop and looked to see Joni squatting in the bedroom.

"I can't do this," I said. "I can't. Too hard."

I left the dog, left the poop, grabbed the oversized Time Warner Cable remote control like I was Chauncey Gardner, put on my bathrobe, and walked outside. I lit a cigarette, got a seat at a little bar on Grove Street, ordered an Irish whiskey, and calmly phoned Lizzy at work. The bartender told me that it was illegal to smoke in there. I put out my cigarette, grabbed my cell phone, and called Lizzy.

"Hi. Can you come home?"

"What's wrong?"

"I'm holding the remote."

"Seriously?"

"Yeah. The dog. The Bloomberg . . ."

"Where are you?"

"Bar. Grove."

"Okay, okay . . . Hang in there. I'm on my way."

EPILOGUE

The best song about hanging up the hipster stance is not "Watching the Wheels" by John Lennon or "Tower of Song" by Leonard Cohen. I believe it's Bongwater's "Folk Song," which closes their 1991 album *The Power of Pussy*. In it, Ann Magnuson encounters a rich, hip, angry anarchist punk in Tompkins Square Park. She is sexually and spiritually drawn to him, but at this point she's damaged goods. He is young and on fire. She is starting to feel her age, having been stomping around those streets since the days of the Mudd Club. *"You think you can live forever . . . or do you have this adorable and misguided notion that death is something really radical and cool?"* she sings. *"I'd like to help you sing your tune . . . but I've been making friends with this here death and it seems a might too soon . . . and I said . . . Hello death, goodbye Avenue A."*

I'm now the age my father was when I first played him "Don't Let's Start" by They Might Be Giants and so broke his mind. And while I'm not in sweatshirts, I have bent a bit toward the casual, fallen from grace with Mod.

In addition to "Don't Let's Start," with its *No one in the world ever gets what they want and that is beautiful* lyric, which so shattered my father and set me on my path, They Might Be Giants' debut album also contains a song called "I Hope That I Get Old Before I Die." Eleven tracks separate the two. It took me almost twenty years to work my way from one to the other, and that sequence-expanse was the difference between being a bullshit artist and a real artist. A real writer wants to live to be a hundred so that he or she can just keep writing truthfully about life at ninety-seven and ninety-eight.

I stayed at *Spin* another year and a half, but really, where do you go after interviewing Morrissey (which I did for the May 2004 cover story). This would have been a mind fuck for me if I hadn't written a book about how much I adored The Smiths and was forever ruined by their breakup. But not only had I done that, I knew that Morrissey knew that I had. A friend of my sister's found my e-mail address and wrote, "I thought you might like to know, I just sold Morrissey a copy of *How Soon Is Never?*" He worked at Book Soup, the great book mart on Sunset in West Hollywood (where I would soon do a promotional reading from the book). It took a lot to rattle me. Remember, I slept through earthquakes and regarded most rock stars the way a plumber regards a clog—just something to deal with and collect my fee. But I'd revealed a lot in *How Soon?* I'd shown the unprotected side of myself. Somehow it was okay to share this with the book-buying public but not with the two people it concerned the most, Victoria and Morrissey. As I drove to the Beverly Hills Hotel, the pink palace where Moz insisted on doing the interview after some negotiation (*Spin*'s cover-story budget doubled overnight), and waited in the storied wood-paneled Polo Lounge for Morrissey to arrive, I got the fear. I went to the bathroom to check my hair and suit. My squinting tick, which I'd tried hard to keep down, had returned. I tried to enter the movie and turn on my pose, but I couldn't get in anymore. I'd rendered myself too sincere. Instead, I haplessly stuck paper towels to my forehead to blot the sweat. When Morrissey finally arrived, perfumed and perfectly attired, he didn't seem to own sweat glands.

Morrissey was the one interview that required the most intellectual endurance. There were no crutches beyond a cup of tea. I didn't smoke. I didn't wear sunglasses. I felt as if I'd be okay so long as I kept him interested. I don't remember breathing. He still didn't cop to reading or even buying the book, but he knew there was a book and that other people, his fans, his "Scottish aunt" (as he claimed), were telling him about it. Mostly, Morrissey wanted to know if there was any movie interest in it (there was) and just what percentage of the book was true and what was imagined. I'd already been asked that a dozen times and still had no answer. All of it? None of it?

"Do you know, I feel like someone else wrote the book," I told him. I wasn't used to being so honest. It was the part of me that I wanted to become that put it out there. "Like, I don't remember writing it. I have a distance from it so maybe it is sort of a literary thing, and you kind of inhabit it. I mean, it's deeply personal in places. Maybe I'm just a little bit frightened because I'm talking to you about it."

I reminded Morrissey that I was a fan, and he softened to me.

"So was it thumbs up or thumbs down?"

"I'm not telling you," he said and sipped his tea.

"Well, you agreed to the interview, so it can't be that bad?"

"A detail," he laughed. I'd made Morrissey laugh. I thought of slow dancing to "How Soon Is Now" with Chloë Sevigny at Don Hill's. Or sitting in my car in the rain, contemplating suicide upon finding out that he and Johnny Marr would play together no more. He made me feel a million different real emotions. And I'd just made him chuckle. It was not a fair exchange, but at least I'd started repaying.

"I don't want to make any big hint," Morrissey said when I pressed him for his review of my book. "It won't be good for you. You'll suffer in the long run."

"Thank you," I said, "Maybe some day I'll come to understand why."

I get it now. It's the same as the HBO thing, the Off-Broadway thing. My head was already twice its normal size and would have exploded. I wasn't ready. It was too much. After we shook hands, and Moz asked me what I was listening to (Franz Ferdinand at the time), I went back and stole the teacup he'd drunk from. I stashed it in my suitcase and brought it back to New York for Ultragrrrl. It was my thank-you to her for abetting me and being my sidekick. It was also her pink slip. I didn't need her anymore. I still loved her, but there'd be no more carousing with me. Take thy DJ skills and go, my child.

As a rock writer, I thought Morrissey seemed like the perfect place to jump off with grace. I knew that it was over at *Spin*, not just for me but for *Spin*, the way it was. It would have to adapt to stay alive. The whole business would, as Ron Richardson predicted. We all needed to find our feet.

Balance was a bitch. I went, as is my way, full stop in the other direction, to the point that I'd wash a dish immediately after eating off it, and became a fat and happy househusband. I wrote a bit for *Uncut* in England, but my heart wasn't in it. A few biographies, but my heart wasn't in them either. Lizzy and I got a second basset hound, Jerry Orbach (*Law and Order* was another of her TV favorites), but soon even we drifted apart. Lizzy wasn't going to be the one to save me. Another person can't save you. She got me on the right path, and now it was up to me to finally be myself. Partnering was a bit of a cheat. I still adore her and our dogs and am proud of how successful she's become as a rock writer herself. Maybe I taught her a few tricks about my side of the moon, just as she reminded me that going to Target and getting a slushy doesn't make you any less of an artist.

Even now, as I can see fifty in the distance, I am still trying to find a balance. I left *Spin* in 2006 after nine years and fourteen cover stories. It was time. As with some of my less successful biographies, people can tell when you do it for the money. You always get sent a big box of your books when they're published. It's written into most contracts. Once I took one of those boxes to the Strand, the famous bookstore on Lower Broadway, to sell. "These aren't worth much," the buyer shrugged. And he was probably right.

I'm still not going to be Gordon Lish any time soon, but I think I may finally be ready to teach. I've even devised a practical class for writers, one that would tell them how it really is out there and maybe spare them some of the mistakes I made on my own the first few times around. I'll call it "Paying Your Quarterly Estimates."

I don't really know anyone anymore. Brendan Mullen died on his sixtieth birthday, which broke my heart. I miss that guy a lot, especially when I'm working on something big like this book. Like Lizzy and Jim, he was a second pair of eyes that I trusted. Brendan died too young but probably lived longer than he ever thought he would at one point, back in the seventies when he was a real punk. That's how it goes. I gave the *New York Times* a quote for his obituary, and they used it. It mentioned how he hated The Strokes. He would have hated that they appeared in his *Times* obit even more.

The city is big enough, and people tend to walk in their own circles enough, that you really can never see someone again if you want. Even downtown. I never see Victoria, for example, the inspiration for Miki in *How Soon Is Never?* Like Morrissey, she's never admitted to reading it, but Chuck Klosterman once told he'd had a conversation with her about it. I see Chuck about once a year for a catch-up drink.

I still do theater every year or two. Some shows are better than others. Few are as good as "*. . . Worry Baby*" or *Shyness*. Our type of theater had that coltish anarchy and violence to it, that snotty thing that was hard to conjure after thirty-five and after 9/11.

When Adrienne was found hanging in the bathroom of her old apartment on Abingdon Square in November of 2006, the *New York Post* ran a cover story saying it looked like a suicide. I was in a bodega across town across from the old Grace Church, getting my then girlfriend some oatmeal, when I noticed her face on the front page and grabbed the paper.

No way, I thought before I even had time to be sad or shaken. Not possible. I thought of Magnolia Bakery and banana pudding and how we joked about it being adult baby food. I thought of being good to yourself as a lifestyle. I'd not seen her in years, but there was no way that anything could have happened to her in that short time that would have altered her philosophy so drastically. She was too strong. The police didn't believe it either and eventually arrested an illegal immigrant named Diego Pillco, who'd murdered her after being caught trying to rob her and made it appear like a suicide. He knocked her out, tied a sheet around her neck, dragged her into the bathroom, and hanged her from the shower bar while she was still alive. He was nineteen years old.

Magnolia Bakery has since become a fetish object, with clean-cut tourists lined up around the block daily to fill dainty, white paper gift boxes with cupcakes. Each day, after taking a snapshot in front of the townhouse on Perry Street where Carrie Bradshaw supposedly lived (as if a weekly columnist could afford one), a few hundred *Sex and the City* fans from all over the country and as far away as Russia and Japan, hit it for a sugar fix. I live up the street now, having moved to the far West Village myself, and I see the tour buses come and park, I watch the passengers file out with their digital cameras and their big smiles and their bad pants, and I think of Adrienne. She was on to something back in 1995. There's now a whole "be good to yourself" industry.

Adrienne has a memorial plaque set in the dirt and surrounded by pale green and purple flowers in the garden at Abingdon Square Park across from the building where she was murdered. Sometimes I take my dogs there and sit next to it.

"I don't know, Adrienne," I say out loud. "How do people do it?"

When I feel sorry for myself, I think about what happened to her and remember how she told me, "Be good to yourself." I think of how she would have loved to have the chance to get old, keep writing, and learn new things. And this works fast.

The Holiday is gone now. Max Fish will supposedly be gone soon. St. Vincent's, where we dropped Jack off to die, is gone. When I heard it was closing, I supposedly said, "Where am I going to die now?" I was totally serious, but it sounded like a quip. Now, it's just a quip. I don't care where I die. Only how I live and not how I think I'm supposed to live. How I just . . . live.

I mostly stay in the West Village. A sign outside my apartment reminds me that the whole neighborhood is a fucking landmark, but I tend to forget. Sometimes I see people on TV or hear a song on my computer and wonder what that guy or gal is really like; then I remember that I interviewed him or her for *Spin*. I met most of the people I ever wanted to meet. And they told me what they were like. But then, it wasn't really me then was it? And most of the time it wasn't really them either.

I drink at my local, go to the movies in Chelsea, and walk my dogs along the river or sometimes in the park (I once saw Sam Shepard there and felt pretty cool since he had a poodle and I had a hound, which seemed a much more Shepard-like dog). I often stand on the boardwalk and stare at the river, the Empire State Building to one side, the Statue of Liberty in the harbor to the other, the *Queen of Hearts* docked and bobbing, and sometimes I marvel, I made it. I live in New York. This is New York. The new World Trade Center building is nearly done. It's part of the skyline now. I ride my green Raleigh down to Murray Street and stare at the scaffolding gliding up its surface, rebuilding, renewing . . . going forward. The river is choppy some days, black and mirrored on others; sometimes it smells salty; other days it smells like muck. I think about Flight 1549 landing on the surface expertly in the dead of January. It's possible—a safe landing after a perilous flight.

I don't recognize the Lower East Side when I go down there. It's like a bad *Blade Runner* version of the amazing place it was, and I say that knowing that *Blade Runner* was set in LA. I wonder what the kids do now when they want to collect material for a book or put up a play in a little black box. Where do they go, because they surely aren't welcome on the Lower East Side any more. Brooklyn? Astoria? Maybe Long Island is next. All the hipsters will move in and ruin it like they ruined Williamsburg. Or saved it, depending on whom you ask. If you ask old people like me, you know what we're gonna say. It's almost our duty to say it.

"New York has closed itself off to the young and the struggling," Patti Smith told the writer Jonathan Lethem at a recent lecture at Cooper Union. "But there are other cities. Detroit. Poughkeepsie. New York City has been taken away from you. So my advice is: Find a new city."

Lou Reed and Laurie Anderson live on my street now. I sometimes see him walking his little dog and laugh to myself, This is what happens to Long Island boys, no matter how badass they think they are. When I'm out with the dogs, I frequently get asked for directions. People seem to assume that if you are walking two hounds, you probably live nearby. I still get a rush of pride when I tell people how they can get to the Hi Line or Magnolia Bakery or the Spotted Pig or even Ground Zero. I feel like a New Yorker. One day, in the late winter of 2011, I decided to take the train out to the Island again. There was nobody to see, but I downloaded a PDF of that brown-and-white Far Rockaway schedule, printed it out, and took a cab up to Penn Station from my neighborhood. It was strange seeing ads for things like flip phones or checking accounts where you could take a picture of a paper check and e-mail a deposit. At sixteen, I couldn't imagine any of that. I had no idea what the future was going to be like. Only what I wanted. I got out at Lawrence station and walked down Lawrence Avenue . . . that endless road, the road out and the road in. The one I'm on in my dreams. I picked up a pinecone and stuck it in the pocket of my overcoat, hoping it would exorcise me, as some talisman or fetish, but I'm not sure I need it anymore. When I arrived at the house that used to belong to my mother, I stood on streets so much wider and emptier than Manhattan streets, with such clean, black tar rolled over the asphalt, and I stared at it. They'd taken the white picket fence away and installed a basketball net at the end of the drive where I used to wreck ant hills and watch the ants rebuild, slowly, carefully . . . confidently.

I don't live here anymore, I said to myself. I live in Manhattan. I felt the pinecone in my pocket. I would take it home with me.

On the way back up Lawrence Avenue toward the train station, I heard the Far Rockaway–bound train arriving. I remembered how exciting it was to see the lights of the train approaching when the inbound train was on its way. The bells would clang, and the gate would come down, stopping all traffic. Coming back on the outbound train was not nearly the same rush.

By the time I arrived at the station, most of the passengers had gotten off and were making their way to their cars and cabs and homes. I spotted a teenage girl, maybe fifteen or sixteen, walking fast toward Central Avenue. She wore a flannel shirt. Most of her hair was blue at the tips, but the roots were growing in brown. There was silver in her ear, and it glinted in the sun. Maybe she'd cut class. It was about four in the afternoon, about the time you'd want to get home from "school," if you were going to devise a ruse that would enable you to stay in Manhattan during the best of a weekday morning and afternoon. I wondered if this was the case. What movies she had seen. Maybe she'd stocked up on hair dye. I'd figured all that stuff was easy now. Anything you wanted, you'd be able to find on the Internet. And every suburban town was now a cosmopolitan locale, even if all the neighbors still recognized each other by their cars on the road, like they did in the mid-eighties. Maybe I was wrong about that. Maybe it was still a thing to be weird in the Five Towns. Still a thing to escape to Manhattan to figure out who you were and how you were going to get through this life without bending to them and letting them change everything you loved about yourself. I watched her go, then took a seat on the cement bench, where I sat once as a junior high school kid, and a high school kid, and a junkie, and an unready father with Alex, and, now, as a forty-two-year-old man. I lit a cigarette and waited for my train to come. A computerized announcement now tells you exactly how far away it is. But I didn't need the update. I could feel it coming for me.

ACKNOWLEDGMENTS

I'm very grateful to James Fitzgerald for reading a very early version of this book and encouraging me to continue. For nearly two years, he remained there 24/7 to help me find and improve my story. Ben Schafer at Da Capo took a chance on *Poseur* and saw immediately what it could be, because he was there too, back in the old days. I won't forget the leap of faith and wish to thank him for his skill and guidance as an editor. Thanks to Elizabeth Goodman for the emotional rescues and vanilla milkshakes. Joni Mitchell and Jerry Orbach helped get me out of my head by requiring a pee every three hours. Thanks to Maureen Callahan for the very necessary movies and martinis. Certain people from my past were kind and patient enough to return there with me, via memory-jogging interviews or conversation, including my parents, Ricki Josephberg and Sid Spitz, Ron Richardson, Tracey Pepper, Richard Sherman, Adam David, Ron Shavers, Bonnie Thornton, Alan Light, Justin Dixon, Marti Zimlin, Damien O, Alan Light, and Alexandra Dewez. Thanks to Connor Raus for his vision and patience. At Da Capo Press: Annie Lenth, Jennifer Kelland, Jeffrey Miller, Kate Burke, Justin Lovell, and Sean Maher. Thanks to Carrie Thornton, Rob Gelardi, "British Alex" Griessmann, "Jesus Christina" Godfrey, Tom "Birdy Bacon" Vaught, Bryan Smith and everyone at the Radio Bar, Richard Allen, Omar, Johnny, Jesse and everyone at Black and White. Thank you everyone at Café Minerva. Thanks to Chuck Klosterman and Rob Sheffield for reading early versions. Finally, thank you Mariano Rivera, Derek Jeter, Jorge Posada, and Andy Pettitte.

I know or have interviewed a few of these writers; I haven't met most of them, but I came to feel as if I knew them all well through their life stories, which I read for inspiration and sometimes instruction: Rupert Everett, Malcolm X, Nick Kent, James Wolcott, Joyce Johnson, Belinda Carlisle, Edmund White, Rob Lowe, Dean Wareham, Robert Evans, David Carr, Jancee Dunn, Klaus Kinski, Patti Smith, Anthony Bourdain, Nile Rodgers, Rob Sheffield, Chuck Barris, Mary Karr, Steve Martin, Bob Dylan, Kris Needs, John Waters,

Jeanette Walls, Keith Richards, Julia Phillips, Anatol Broyard, Andrew Mc-Carthy, Richard Pryor, Ernest Hemingway, Sebastian Horsley, Christopher Plummer, Juliana Hatfield, Nelson George, Alex James, and Frank Langella.

For more *Poseur* text, photos, audio, archival material, and events go to www.marcspitz.com. Please visit the Marc Spitz page on Facebook, and follow him on Twitter (@marcspitz) and Instagram (MARCSPITZNYC).